VIRTUAL
ARCHAEOLOGY

VIRTUAL ARCHAEOLOGY

Great Discoveries Brought to Life Through Virtual Reality

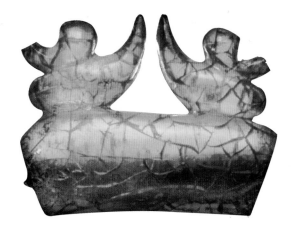

Foreword
Colin Renfrew

*with over 700 illustrations,
660 in colour*

THAMES AND HUDSON

Contents

Translated from the Italian *Archeologia: Percorsi virtuali nelle civiltà scomparse* by Judith Toms (pp. 7–149 and Glossary) and Robin Skeates (pp. 150–283)

This edition © 1997 Thames and Hudson Ltd, London and Harry N. Abrams, Inc., New York

Foreword © 1997 Colin Renfrew

© 1996 Arnoldo Mondadori editore, Milan

ISBN 0-500-05085-6

Printed and bound in Spain

The Publishers are grateful to the Taisei Corporation, Tokyo, for making available the illustrations on the following pages: 4 above right; 5 above left; 12 above; 13; 68 above and below; 88 below; 89 above and below; 90 centre and below; 93 below; 152 centre; 175 above; 176 below; 177 above; 179 below; 231 centre; 232 above and centre; 233; 263 above and below; and 266 below.

General Editors

Maurizio Forte
CINECA/Project CEE Icarus
Alberto Siliotti
Centre for Archaeological Documentation, Verona

Contributors

Patrizia Anconetani University of Ferrara
Maria Carmela Betrò University of Pisa
Edda Bresciani University of Pisa
Maurizio Cattani IsMEO, Rome
Annie Caubet Louvre, Paris
Serge Cleuziou CNRS, Paris
Mauro Cremaschi University of Milan
Roberto De Nicola Consiglio Nazionale delle Ricerche-IRSIP, Naples
Jacobus van Dijk Dutch Institute, Cairo; University of Groningen
Furio Durando Liceo Federico Delphino, Chiavari
Walter Ferri University of Pisa
Maurizio Forte CINECA; Project CEE Icarus
Joaquin Galarza CNRS, Paris
Louis Godart University 'Federico II', Naples
Riccardo Guglielmino Scuola Normale Superiore, Pisa
Audran Labrousse CNRS, Paris
Sabatino Laurenza Consiglio Nazionale delle Ricerche-IRSIP, Naples
Daniel Lévine Musée de l'Homme, Paris
Laura Longo University of Milan
Francesco Mallegni University of Pisa
Ivana Marra Consiglio Nazionale delle Ricerche-IRSIP, Naples
Paolo Matthiae University 'La Sapienza', Rome
Giuseppe Nenci Scuola Normale Superiore, Pisa
Lorenzo Nigro University 'La Sapienza', Rome
Maria Cecilia Parra Scuola Normale Superiore, Pisa
Annaluisa Pedrotti University of Trento
Carlo Peretto University of Ferrara
Emiliana Petrioli University of Florence
Isabelle Pierre CNRS, Paris
Filippo Salviati University 'La Sapienza', Rome
Alberto Siliotti Centre for Archaeological Documentation
Rainer Stadelmann German Archaeological Institute, Cairo
Simonetta Storti Scuola Normale Superiore, Pisa
Isabelle Tisserand-Gadan University of Paris XIII
Maria Adelaide Vaggioli Scuola Normale Superiore, Pisa
Massimo Vidale Istituto Centrale del Restauro, Rome

For their help with the English edition, the publishers would like to thank:

Warwick Bray University College London; **Michael D. Coe** Yale University; **Dominique Collon** British Museum; **Aidan Dodson** University of Bristol; **Jessica Harrison-Hall** British Museum; **George Hart** British Museum; **Simon James** British Museum; **Ian Jenkins** British Museum; **Robert Knox** British Museum; **James Mallory** University of Belfast; **Simon Martin** University College London; **Colin McEwan** Museum of Mankind; **Mary Ellen Miller** Yale University; **Chris Scarre** University of Cambridge; **Susan Woodford** British Museum

For Roberta

Foreword

Archaeology as a discipline is always on the move. New discoveries every year bring with them fresh glimpses of the past. New techniques bring entirely novel insights into the material that we have, and into the processes of research. And above all, new interpretations reveal to us a deeper understanding of the human past, and offer a keener awareness of the preconceptions that we ourselves bring to its reconstruction.

In this refreshing book the brisk pace of contemporary discovery is admirably brought out. Maurizio Forte, the General Editor, is himself a specialist in computer applications, and he understands well the prodigious power of the computer in helping us to recreate and to visualize anew the sites that archaeologists have excavated and studied. As he puts it, the aim is 'to make archaeological information ... visually real': the great quantities of data now available must actually be made to *inform* us, not just sit in a data bank. He goes on to show how the power of the computer to store and display data allows the production of 'an atlas of archaeological models' that can actually offer the archaeologist alternative solutions to the problem of reconstruction.

In every case it is the archaeologist who has to supply the data. If the aim is to reconstruct a ruined site to show how it originally looked, then ultimately the archaeologist is responsible for providing the missing elements. If there is guesswork involved, the archaeologist does the guessing. But now he has to do it in a logical and structured and ultimately more fruitful way. The very task of setting up a computer reconstruction obliges the archaeologist to pose the right questions, and then to answer them. This whole procedure makes the computer reconstruction a valuable research tool.

Computer-aided reconstructions – 'virtual archaeology' – have been used in numerous parts of this wide-ranging volume. Roman Pompeii offers an excellent example of a sophisticated project: the entire city was buried in AD 79 under a thick mantle of ash, and the greater part has now been uncovered. The computer program requires the archaeologist to make decisions about the original texture and colour of all the surfaces of the buildings. Decisions have to be taken, or alternative possibilities formulated, about the destroyed upper parts of buildings. The computer reconstruction also brings to the surface interesting questions about the original lighting of each room and house. The resulting 3-D experience has to be seen to be believed: that is what virtual reality is about. It is very well conveyed in the numerous graphic reconstructions seen here.

With so wide a selection of important recent discoveries across the globe I cannot comment here on all the projects covered in this ambitious survey. The time range takes us from Old Stone Age Isernia in Italy, 700,000 years ago, to China in the time of Kublai Khan, the Mongol ruler in the thirteenth century AD. Geographically we are taken from ancient Rome and classical Athens east to the early royal dynasties of Japan, and across the Pacific to the surprising figures in the Nazca desert of Peru. The ancient Near Eastern city of Ebla in Syria is the subject of an authoritative case study by its excavator Professor Paolo Matthiae. The discovery of the remarkable palace archive of clay tablets dating from c. 2300 BC is described, and the use which he is making of computer-aided analysis of their contents is explained. It is fascinating also to learn that mention of Ebla has been found 300 years later in the records in the great Hittite city of Hattusas, far to the north.

Another important study, not yet as well known as it deserves to be, is that of Joaquin Galarza of the CNRS in Paris. He gives an informative account of his investigations into the script of the Aztecs at the time of the Spanish conquest of Mexico.

There is a moral in the melancholy story reported by Giuseppe Nenci and his colleagues in Pisa of the important discovery of nine major inscriptions on bronze – civic decrees – found at the Sicilian city of Entella, and dating from the end of the fourth century BC. Only one of these is safe in a museum (in Palermo). The other eight are 'all now in foreign collections'. The looting of archaeological sites by robbers – *clandestini* and *tombaroli* are the Italian terms – is one of the greatest problems in archaeology today, and this is a timely reminder of the harm that private collectors do in purchasing such material. Archaeology in the third millennium will no doubt have its problems, and this may be the greatest of them.

On every page of this fascinating book the reader will find new discoveries or computer-aided reconstructions which aid the imagination of the viewer just as they raise questions which tax the ingenuity of the archaeologist. It gives an excellent view of the pace of archaeological research as the second millennium of our era nears its end.

Colin Renfrew
Disney Professor of Archaeology
University of Cambridge

Introduction

Tomorrow will be a working out, at increasing intensity and on a larger scale, of forces unleashed yesterday during the Upper Palaeolithic. Information is still piling up, and faster than ever. The task of processing and analyzing it is still crucial, still formidable, and so is the task of communication – creating new, more compact symbols, more sophisticated images on television-type screens, more sophisticated chunking methods. Survival still depends on using all our resources, art and ceremony as well as technology, to build stable societies out of increasing numbers of rugged and unpredictable individuals.

John Pfeiffer, *The Creative Explosion* (1982)

'Towards a virtual archaeology' is the evocative title of an article published by Paul Reilly in 1991. In it he describes some of the possible courses that might be taken by the archaeology of the future – an archaeology we can imagine as being essentially technological, multidisciplinary and virtual (in the scientific sense of the word), because it will be linked into the fields of computer processing, simulation, experimentation and computer reconstruction. But will the archaeology of the future be like that? What language will it be using in the third millennium? What will its fields of investigation be? Above all, how much of the ancient world will we be able to reconstruct from the remnants of its material culture, sites and buildings?

The possibilities that are increasingly being created by scientific and technological research have opened new horizons for archaeology and redrawn its boundaries. As progress marches on, we will be able to reconstruct ever larger segments of our most distant past, leading to a more accurate understanding of the macrocosm of the ancient world. The problem for archaeology is to retrieve the maximum possible amount of information from the material culture, so as to recapture its non-material aspects as well.

However, this process of amassing and interpreting information is a continuous one; what we cannot find out or understand now, we will be able to comprehend in the future – provided we do not destroy or lose the underlying data. It is important, therefore, not to waste information or lose access to it. In this process of acquisition, restoration and re-presentation the assistance of computers and other technology has become vital, and it is here that the term virtual archaeology becomes valid. The archaeology of the third millennium will very likely be a science with a strong technological element that will enhance out of all proportion our ability to explore, to interpret and to classify, bringing with it a greater and more penetrating ability to reconstruct the past. Loosely speaking, it will be a computerized archaeology, because it will involve the large-scale use of computer and archaeometric science in a major scientific endeavour to develop a truly virtual research laboratory. The 'quality' of archaeological information and classification will in future create the bases of a new cognitive science.

Excavation and fieldwork are sometimes rather embarrassing for the archaeologist, because (paradoxically) they involve partially destroying the site that is the object of research without ever being able to recapture the whole of the information it contains. In the course of exploration the archaeologist destroys stratigraphy and structures and removes large quantities of soil in order to be able to interpret the excavated remains 'Seeing what's underneath' is essential for interpretation, but it never provides a whole answer. In many cases – including the cities richest in history – ancient structures hide yet earlier structures. Troy, for instance, had at least nine main phases dating between

▽ *Computer reconstruction of the cranium of archaic* Homo Sapiens, *based on fragments from Salé and Thomas Quarries, both in Morocco. The three-dimensional visualization has assisted analytical study of the cranium.*

3000 BC and the Roman period (Troy IX), and other phases again dating to the Late Antique and subsequent periods. Each one of these phases describes and represents a different city, and each would become intelligible to archaeologists only after thorough investigation – and yet this would have to involve the removal of overlying structures from later phases. Stratigraphy represents an extremely varied and complex sequence of innumerable pieces of information that are often difficult to identify – but not one of them is insignificant, and (ideally) not one should be destroyed.

Archaeological excavation is therefore a complex process that, if carried out correctly, allows a reconstruction of past events – or of a small part of them. This is the constant problem of archaeological research. Only a small amount of intelligible information can be recovered from the ground – a minute percentage of classifiable 'events' at a site – and the very activity of excavation inevitably involves some degree of destruction of the information that is buried.

A banal example: How much information do changes in the architecture or furnishings of one's own house (or even the living-room or bedroom) contain about what has taken place in it? Only one's own memory can reliably record *all* that has happened there, for few of the actions and events will have left visible traces: the changed position of a piece of furniture, a mark on the wall or a chipped tile. If our house is destroyed, an archaeologist investigating its

◁ *Computer reconstruction of Cahokia, a tenth- to twelfth-century settlement on the Mississippi opposite present-day St Louis. In the background is a tumulus. This reconstruction is taken from the documentary* 500 Nations, *which dealt with the history of the ancient American civilizations.*

remains in the distant future will be able to reconstruct very little of what took place in it. If no related documents have been found, he or she will find it very hard even to work out which room was which (without the furnishings, how do you distinguish a living-room from a bedroom?).

Therefore, the ability to reproduce virtually the whole exploratory phase of archaeological research is the decision-maker's tool that enables us to answer the question 'How much do we reconstruct?' It is perhaps our only means of refining ever more accurate classifications and interpretations. It therefore also represents the last stage of research: the recreation of an ancient space, including even its most esoteric aspects – not arbitrarily and unchangeably, but virtually.

The methods at the disposal of archaeology – first put on a scientific basis when it enlisted the aid of information science and computers in the 1960s – can now justifiably be called multidisciplinary, because they span so many areas of the applied sciences. The interaction between research in archaeology, geology and the physical, natural and information sciences is now providing an ever firmer methodological foundation. However, one of the great goals of archaeology is to be a presenter (or re-presenter) of information – of what can be deduced and extrapolated from its data and finds. Alongside research, therefore, it has an equally important role of communication and dissemination to develop. Amongst the many fields of research, archaeology – synthesizing the most disparate hypotheses in an all-embracing scientific attempt to reconstruct the past – is one of those best able to capture the imagination of the public.

The object of this book, as its theme clearly shows, is to offer to the reader the most faithful re-presentation of the ancient world possible: highly realistic in information and with a high scientific content. The common thread of its chapters is the new directions being opened up by the conjunction of archaeological research and technology. Through the interaction between exact science, information technology and new research methods it embarks on a technological voyage into the past. It does not set out to be either a systematic overview of archaeology or an atlas of the ancient world, because it does not pretend to be chronologically exhaustive, nor yet a compendium of archaeological techniques. It aims to be a book of scientific visualization, of 'commentaries' and of

▷ *Computer reconstruction of Lascaux Cave; the detail (right) shows a painting of a horse. Lascaux, one of the great examples of prehistoric painting, forms an important part of our cultural heritage. The creation of a virtual reconstruction allows the public to 'visit' the cave, even though it is now closed.*

archaeological *actualités*, real places and virtual models of world archaeology. Perhaps a good definition might be an atlas of archaeological models. The details of recent archaeological discoveries are particularly vivid, and in many cases include hitherto unpublished details. The Alpine 'ice man' of Similaun and the Palaeolithic camp of Isernia; the megaliths of Europe and the rock art of the Sahara; the Faiyum and the Egypt of the pharaohs; the princes of the Italian Iron Age and the origins of Rome; the urban culture of ancient Ebla and the Phaistos disc and Minoan Crete; the Beijing of the Mongols and the urban civilization of central Asia; the cities and empires of the Americas and the deciphering of the Aztec script – these are only some of the subjects that are dealt with here.

To make the archaeological information contained in the text visually real we have sought to complement it with illustrations showing the most significant historical and technological reconstructions of the past, made possible by leading-edge developments in scientific research. These explorations will allow the reader to follow in the footsteps of the most recent scientific research, even as far as the latest finds and fieldwork results.

The ancient world to be explored through the images in the following pages is also, at last, an archaeological world in colour – very different from the monochrome world to which earlier reconstructions have accustomed us. The polychrome renderings of building materials – from Parian marble to wood, from stone to travertine, from limestone to terracotta, and so on – convey the colour and texture and vitality of the architectural finishes and the ancient buildings they adorn. Thus, these illustrations communicate one of the fundamental components of archaeological information. In sacred buildings, for example – in the temples, chapels and great public buildings of antiquity –

colour may have been the expression of symbolism, grandeur, energy. Above all, though, colour presents images anew, in all their theatricality, harmony and architectural coherence.

The computer-aided reconstructions come from laboratories across the world – from Japan to the United States, from Europe to Africa – and some have been created especially for this book.

△▽ Virtual reconstruction of the underground hall in the tomb of prince Wadji at Khelua, in the Faiyum. An access shaft leads from the hall to the subterranean funerary chambers; the detail shows a computer graphic restoration of the first pillar.

Since we are dealing with virtual images, it will be possible in the future to update them in the light of further research and new fieldwork results; we are happy to think that such a possibility could make this book a 'work in progress', with future editions taking account of new findings and thematic developments. Moreover, in future it will be possible to export most of the virtual archaeological models to computers across the world, thus allowing systematic and authentic interactive exploration in three-dimensions.

Experts from all over the world have collaborated on this book, which is subdivided into five sections: the archaeology of Africa, the archaeology of the Near East, the archaeology of Europe, the archaeology of Asia, and the archaeology of the Americas. In each section the reader will find some of the most important results of recent

archaeological fieldwork, analysis and interpretation – particularly of those cases where technology and computer-assistance have been fundamental to the research and interpretation of the data. The main sites in each section are located geographically on satellite images, and the accompanying maps, plans and tables contain the latest information. The illustrations then complement the text by simulating an interactive virtual-reality guide to a world of computer graphics, travelling through computer-processed scientific images that bring three-dimensional information to the two-dimensional space of the printed page. Each section of the book may be seen as a 'multi-dimensional' environment, in which text, boxes, images, maps and thematic plans complement each other in providing multidisciplinary information on the different aspects of a theme.

Why is the virtual reconstruction of an archaeological site so important? Because, over and above its strong popular impact, computer reconstruction allows the presentation of complex information in a visual way that enables it to be used to test and refine the image or model that has been created. It is very much more than a graphic reproduction; it is a simulation. And, because it is a simulation, it

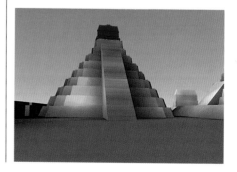

△ Computer reconstruction of a Mongol camp. Note the very regular arrangement of the yurts, the typical Mongol tents.

△ Architectural reconstruction of a pyramid-temple at the Maya city of Tikal, one of the greatest urban sites of pre-Columbian Central America.

provides a non-intrusive and non-destructive means of exploring a model in three dimensions and from an infinite number of viewpoints. Furthermore, it allows objective verification to be made of possible interpretations of architecture, material culture, topography, palaeo-environmental data, restoration, museum display, and any number of other factors. This makes virtual reality a highly useful tool for enlarging our knowledge of a field that has hitherto been under-explored, perhaps because it is concerned with the past.

In April 1995, at 'Technology, Instruments and Applications', the third International Conference on the World Wide Web (now the major element of the Internet, the world's largest digital network), a new graphics language was presented. Virtual Reality Mark-up Language (VRML) is a language that describes three-dimensional objects and allows the user to move from texts into three-dimensional spaces and *vice versa*. It is a completely new way of visualizing information in three-dimensional space via hypermedia links, allowing the information/objects to be rotated, moved and observed from any angle. This powerful graphic language opens up new and extraordinary possibilities for handling multimedia data in three-dimensional form. It is not impossible that, in the near future, the information that is in this book will be available in VRML format, offering the opportunity of exploring virtual archaeological parks furnished with physical and conceptual models, with finite territories and multidimensional ideas.

To you who are starting on your virtual journey to the places and cultures covered in this book, *bon voyage*!

Maurizio Forte

We are evidently unique among species in our symbolic ability, and we are certainly unique in our modest ability to control the conditions of our existence using these symbols. Our ability to represent and simulate reality implies that we can approximate the order of existence and bring it to serve human purposes. A good simulation, be it a religious myth or a scientific theory, gives us a sense of mastery over our experience.

Heinz Pagels, *The Dreams of Reason* (1988)

▽ *Computer reconstruction of the ceremonial centre of Tenochtitlan, the Venice of Mexico. The Aztec capital's ancient splendour has been restored by means of computer processing, which has recreated the original in all its clarity and colour.*

Saharan Rock Art

Sahara

*T*he rock art on mountainous massifs in the middle of the Sahara documents humanity's transition from a life based on hunting wild animals to one based on exploiting domesticated animals. In the Sahara this was accompanied by climatic and environmental changes that transformed vast areas of savanna, populated by the animals depicted in the rock art, into the inhospitable, hyper-arid desert of today. It has proved difficult to assess the date of these mysterious pictures, and so of this epoch-making change in human cultural history, but we now have a new archaeological tool that may make this possible. The patination that covers exposed rock in the desert is a product of past climatic conditions. Hence, if it can be analysed and dated by reference to the climatic changes, the patina can give a benchmark for dating the works that underlie it or the rock engravings that are cut through it. This may supplement relative dating based on the subject matter – extinct wild animals, or surviving domesticated species, for example.

▵ *Acacus (Wadi Sennadar). Rock varnish developed homogeneously across the almost sheer rock face in this photograph. On the jutting wall at the right, by contrast, it has only formed along the rain-water runnels.*

Stylistic analyses of rock art have established a relative chronology for its development, although there are still doubts and arguments about how this relative sequence should be expressed in the absolute terms of calendar years. Another technique for relative dating is to compare the amount of patination on rock engravings with that on the rock face into which they have been cut. The oldest carvings have the same desert 'rock varnish' (a black mineral film, consisting mostly of iron and manganese salts) as the surrounding rock surface, but the more recent the carvings, the more their patination differs. Recent studies have shown, however, that this rock varnish may be more than just an instrument for relative dating. The factors which determine its development are mainly controlled by climate, so it is capable of providing palaeo-environmental information, which may be correlated with what is known of the geological history of the area from other sources.

It used to be thought that rock varnish was produced by an exudation of iron and manganese salts contained in the rock, released by changes in the small amount of water in the atmosphere. However, modern instruments – such as the scanning electron microscope and the electron microprobe –

▵ *In the Messak Settafet (Wadi In Elobu) desert rock varnish covers the plateau and the river pebbles of the wadis. The varnish is a black mineral film, mostly composed of iron and manganese salts, which is useful for dating rock art and for an improved understanding of the palaeo-environmental context.*

◁ *Location map:
The mountain
chains of the
Messak Settafet
and the Acacus in
the Libyan
central Sahara.*

have shown that it consists of fine dust (especially clayey particles) blown onto the rock surface by the wind. Its characteristic chemical trait is a high manganese content, which is responsible for the peculiar black colouring. In the form of hydroxide, this is found in an anomalous concentration that may sometimes reach sixty times the amount in the rocks that produced the blowing dust. This is the result of changes occurring on the rock surface: not only physical and chemical processes (greater mobility of manganese than of iron), but also biological processes, caused by bacteria that concentrate manganese. Such bacteria can only flourish in quite specific ecological conditions. In humid conditions, competitive species (such as lichens and fungi, or higher plants) are favoured, while over-arid conditions create an alkalinity that inhibits the development of bacteria; manganese-rich rock varnish can therefore only develop under moderately arid conditions. Thus, while rock varnish is still forming in some deserts, it has ceased in others.

This is the case on the Messak plateau and the mountains of the Tadrart Acacus, where rock varnish uniformly covers the surfaces of the massif, the walls of the wadis, the pebbles on the wadi beds and any other object lying there (from hunting implements to megalithic monuments). However, in the Tadrart Acacus rock varnish is absent from the faces of shelters and from projecting surfaces, where it has generally formed only along water run-offs. The walls of both these massifs, including the surfaces on which the varnish is preserved, are

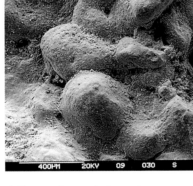

△ *Seen under an electron microscope,
the rock varnish sample from the
Acacus (Wadi Teshuinat) seems to be
made of fine, particularly clayey,
materials which accumulated on the
sandstone grains.*

scored with grooves (caused by landslides or wind erosion) which expose the original rock – and this is bright yellow or covered with a thin, reddish iron patina. The varnish is therefore a relic of climatic conditions from an earlier era.

To understand in greater detail the processes by which rock varnish is formed, field observations have been combined with analyses of a large number of samples by electron microscopy and EDAX (energy-dispersive analysis of X-rays). In all the samples examined by electron microscope, the varnish was found to have a lenticular form, filling the gaps between the grains of which the sandstone is composed and reaching a thickness of 20 to 100 microns. It was divided into three layers, each with different physical and chemical characteristics. The upper layer consisted of argillaceous and silicaceous particles formed from

quartz and aluminium, sometimes with the presence of alkali. The middle layer was formed from undulating sheets (typical of organic sedimentation) of iron and manganese. These sheets were black and corresponded to the classic descriptions of rock varnish. The lowest layer consisted of clay that was rich in non-laminar iron, distributed irregularly and of very varied chemical composition; in particular, the presence of phosphates of calcium of organic origin was noted. In contrast to the upper two layers, the third layer was sometimes eroded and discontinuous.

Each of these layers reflects a different palaeoclimatic situation. The lowest provides evidence of an alteration of the rock surface under quite humid conditions; the high level of phosphates and the large quantity of clay suggests that this may have been caused by mosses and lichens. The second layer, characterized by the high level of manganese, was the work of manganese-concentrating bacteria and therefore indicates moderately arid

▷ *This feline was found in Messak Settafet
(In Habeter), incised into a homogeneous
surface now pitted with deep cavities
caused by thermoplastic detachment.*

◁▷ *Computer-enhanced representation of the rock wall at Tan Zoumaitak (above). The use of the computer helps the precise reproduction of the painted figures (right) – which in this instance range from humans wearing elaborate ornaments to creatures such as rams and jellyfish.*

conditions. The top layer, made of clay that had undergone no alteration *in situ* and sometimes contained alkali, is an indication of marked aridity.

The humid environment, typical of the first millennium of the Holocene (after 8000 BC), gradually changed to the present extremely arid conditions from about 1000 BC. Some archaeological indicators imply that the manganese-rich varnish was formed between the end of the sixth millennium BC and the beginning of the fifth in a moderately arid steppe environment.

The relationship between the varnish and the rock carvings is clearly exemplified by the carvings of Ti-n-Ascigh (Wadi Sennadar, Acacus). The four styles of Saharan rock art are superimposed or juxtaposed, each in a different relationship with the rock varnish.

The grooves of the engravings of extinct buffalo (*Bubalus antiquus*) and rhinoceros, which belong to the Large Wild Fauna (or *Bubalus*) Period, are corroded and uniformly covered by manganese-rich varnish. The giraffe from the Round-headed Figures Period

is also covered with varnish, but the incisions are perfectly preserved. Giraffes of the Pastoralist Period are cut through the rock varnish, and the incisions themselves lack varnish, having instead a red-brown patina. Finally, the grooves of the late carvings of camels expose the unaltered rock.

The same sequence was found in the Messak Settafet, at In Habeter and In Elobu: the carvings of figures belonging to the Large Wild Fauna Period, which are stylistically the earliest, were covered by the same amount of black varnish as the rock, and the grooves had been distinctly worn before being covered by the varnish. There are pictures of bovids, and then of domestic animals and anthropomorphic figures that are also covered by the same intensity of rock varnish present on the rock, but whose incisions are fresh and unworn, with the carving marks still intact. Then come figures belonging to the Pastoralist Period; the grooves, which are cut into the black varnish of the rock, are brown or reddish and lack the manganese-rich deposit, or have it only in an attenuated form. Finally, there are the recent figures of the Camel Period which completely lack rock varnish.

From all this, it is clear that the manganese-rich varnish is a useful (albeit low-resolution) indicator for dating rock art and for understanding the palaeo-environmental context of Saharan rock art. The varnish, which formed there between the sixth and fifth millennia BC, marks a watershed that divides the petroglyphs carved before it formed from those that were carved after it was formed, or when it had declined.

To the first group belong the carvings of the Large Wild Fauna Period and the earliest of the Pastoralist Period. However, there is a physical distinction between them: only the grooves of the carvings of the Large Wild Fauna Period corroded before the manganese-rich patina formed over them. The nature of this corrosion is still uncertain. It is possible that it results from wind erosion, but it is perhaps more probable that it was caused by the action of lichens or mosses in the humid conditions of the beginning of the Holocene (these could also have caused the layer found at the base of the rock varnish in some samples). These carvings date to almost as far back as the Early Holocene. The earliest pictures of the Pastoralist Period, which succeed this group, are separated from them by a period in which erosion of the walls took place in a climate still too humid for manganese-concentrating bacteria to survive.

	Periods of Saharan Rock Art	
10000 BC		
	Large Wild Fauna (or *Bubalus*) Period (mainly engravings)	
		early
	Round-headed Figures Period (mainly paintings)	
		late
5000 BC		early
	Pastoralist (or Bovidian) Period (engravings and paintings)	middle
2880 BC		late
1500 BC	**Horse (or Equid) Period** (engravings and paintings)	
AD		
	Camel Period (carvings and paintings)	

➤ *Ti-n-Ascigh (Wadi Sennadar, Acacus). Four styles of Saharan art are superimposed in these rock carvings: (1)* Bubalus *and rhinoceros belonging to the Large Wild Fauna Period; (2) giraffe of the Round-headed Figures Period; (3) giraffes of the Pastoralist Period; (4) camels from a later period.*

In the massifs of the Acacus and the Messak the ecological conditions in which the desert varnish could form seem to date to the end of the sixth millennium BC and appear to have accompanied the decline of the humid period in the Saharan area. The deposits in shelters and caves of this period indicate that the Saharan landscape, especially in the Messak Settafet, was then an arid steppe, and no longer a wooded savanna.

After the fifth millennium BC, the manganese-rich rock varnish no longer formed in the centre of the Saharan massifs. The aridity was now more marked, and the deposit that accumulated on the surface of the rock consists of clay and alkali blown off the surfaces of the many lakes (which were gradually drying up) surrounding the mountainous massifs. Also the large number of pictures with red incisions – including the famous Hellcats of In Habeter, Wadi Mathendush – show that in this period, too, the valleys of the Acacus and the Messak were densely populated. This agrees with the fact that the upper layers of many pastoral deposits in the shelters and caves of the area have produced radiocarbon dates between the end of fifth and the beginning of the third millennium. It is difficult, in the area studied, to identify carvings attributable to the Horse Period, but the more recent examples of the Camel Period have no patina and reflect the extremely arid conditions of the massifs in recent millennia.

➤ *The Hellcats of In Habeter (Wadi Mathendush). Their red patina contrasts with the surface of the rock, which is covered with a manganese-rich patina.*

Bibliography

R.I. Dorn, 'Case and Implications of Rock Varnish Microchemical Laminations', in *Nature*, 310 (1984), pp. 767–770.

P. Graziosi, *L'arte rupestre della Libia* (Naples 1942).

F. Mori, *Tadrart Acacus. Arte rupestre e culture del sahara preistorico* (Turin, 1965).

T.M. Oberlander, 'Rock varnish in Deserts', in A. Abrahams and A. Parsons *Geomorphology of Desert Environments* (London, 1994), pp.106–119.

N. Petit Maire, *Paleoenvironments du Sahara, lacs holocenes à Taoudenni* (Paris, 1991).

P. Rognon, *Biographie d'un desert* (Paris, 1989).

U. Sansoni, *Le più antiche pitture del Sahara* (Milan, 1994).

A.M. and A. Van Albada, 'Art Rupestre du Sahara', in *Dossiers d'Archéologie*, 197, October 1994.

F. Willett, *African Art*, rev. ed. (London and New York, 1993).

Giza: The Last Wonder of the Ancient World

Egypt

*T*he pyramids of Giza stand on a rocky plateau some 40m (130 ft) high – a north-eastern outlier of the Libyan escarpment – with a distant view of the Nile Delta. This dominating position must have been an important element in the choice of location for the oldest monument at the site – the Fourth-Dynasty Great Pyramid of Khufu (Cheops), who ruled Egypt from about 2551 BC to about 2528 BC. So, too, must the availability of limestone for building: stone from the site itself was used for the core of the Great Pyramid, and fine-grained, almost marble-like limestone from nearby Tura for the external casing.

Below the plateau, the landscape slopes gently eastwards towards the Nile, where a small bay was usable as a harbour, and between the pyramids and the river there was sufficient space for a town of the pyramids to be built; this contained a royal residence, the villas of the court and the senior officials and, a little to the south, quarters for the labourers and the workshops of the great pharaonic construction sites.

Before the Great Pyramid was built, the irregular surface of the plateau was partly levelled, with outcrops being removed and natural cavities closed off, leaving only one natural rock outcrop at the centre of the planned structure.

This was surrounded by an accurately levelled area on which the base of the pyramid was marked out, and paving was laid around the base. The work was done with a precision admirable even by present-day standards, the maximum difference in level between the central point of the north face and the south-east corner being no more than 2.1 cm (0.8 in.). The only instrument that would have been used to create the flat surface was the basic level (theories involving the making of a small artificial lake with mud-brick walls and flooding it to provide a datum-line have been disproved). To avoid displacement due to the weight of the finished structure, the corners were built on a lower layer of foundation blocks laid at an inclination of 2–5° towards the centre.

Orientation towards astronomical north, which had already played such an important role in the construction of the Third-Dynasty pyramids, reached a remarkable degree of precision in Khufu's Great Pyramid, which deviates by only 3' 6" from true north. The most recent measurements of its sides and corners, using modern instruments, show a precision that is impressive even today. The maximum disparity in the length of the sides is about 4.4 cm (1.75 in.) – a margin of error inevitable over distances of more than 200 m (650 ft) with the methods of measuring then available (cords

▷ *This small ivory statuette is the only sculpture of Khufu (Cheops) to survive. Khufu, here wearing the red crown of Lower Egypt, was the second pharaoh of the Fourth Dynasty and reigned between 2551 and 2528 BC.*

and rods) – and the difference between the orientation of the corners averages only 2' 48". The natural rock outcrop left at the centre of the pyramid site is known to have prevented the builders from measuring the diagonals directly, and that the only other way to measure them would have been by means of wooden set squares, with the required bisecting line determined by the repeated laying out of circles of various radii. The precision achieved in building this pyramid with the tools and methods then available can only be explained by an almost superhuman striving to achieve the highest possible accuracy.

Each side of the Great Pyramid was 440 ancient Egyptian cubits (about 230 m, or 755 ft) long, and its faces

△ *The three pyramids, built on the plateau of Giza by the Fourth-Dynasty pharaohs, are the only one of the seven wonders of the ancient world to have survived into our own time. These monuments (today situated at the southern edge of Cairo) show that even in very ancient times the Egyptians had sophisticated technology.*

◁ *Location map:
Giza lies towards the
northern end of the
Nile valley, which is
over 1,000 km
(620 mi.) long.*

▷ *The pyramid of
Menkaure still
retains some of the
facing of red granite
that covered its base
and lower courses.*

sloped at 51° 50' 40" – a *seket* (angle of slope) of 5.5 hand-widths per cubit of height – so the pyramid must originally have reached a height of 280 cubits (146.60 m, or 481 ft). It is still 138.75 m (455 ft) high today. The facing of fine Tura limestone, from a quarry just across the Nile, is now preserved only on the lowest course, and most of what can be seen today is the stonework of the core. This was made of blocks of local nummulitic limestone, accurately laid in horizontal courses that diminish in size from the base of the pyramid to the top, though not constantly. The

largest blocks are three cubits (about 1.5 m, or nearly 5 ft) high, and the average height is one cubit (about 0.52 m, or 1 ft 8½ in.). Today 201 courses remain, but there must originally have been 210.

Contemporary sources give practically no information about how the pyramids were built. Since each is unique, and there are no surviving illustrations or textual descriptions, we can only draw conclusions from the pyramids themselves and the archaeological traces left around them. Near several pyramids there are recognizable traces of ramps. A single ramp set at right angles to the flank of a pyramid is unlikely to have been used, because of the enormous length, height and width that would have been involved. Nor does the use of a spiral ramp seem probable, because this would have covered the corners and faces of the pyramid – which would have had to be visible in order to control the angle of slope. Most likely, the labourers worked up to a height of 25–30 m

(80–100 ft) using several small ramps, the material from which could subsequently be amalgamated to form a single ramp that would enable a height of 100–120 m (300–400 ft) to be reached. At this height 97% of the mass of the structure would have been in place, and the remainder could have been built using small ramps and stairways and, if necessary, a variety of wooden levers.

The entrance to the Great Pyramid is 17 m (55 ft) up, near the centre of the north face. It leads to a system of funerary chambers inside – the most imposing architectural expression of the Old-Kingdom royal beliefs about the life beyond death –

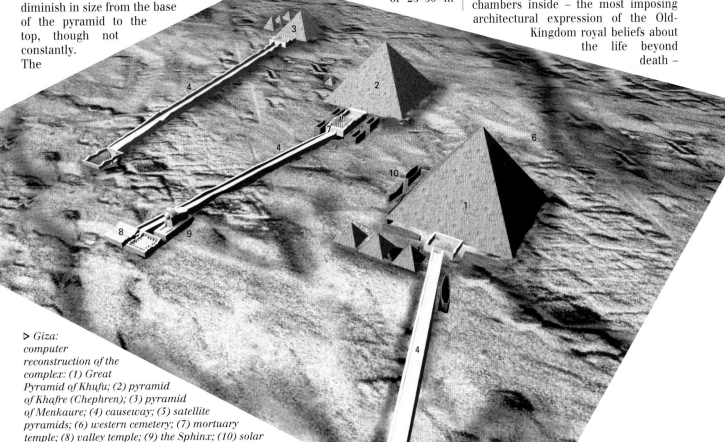

▷ *Giza:
computer
reconstruction of the
complex: (1) Great
Pyramid of Khufu; (2) pyramid
of Khafre (Chephren); (3) pyramid
of Menkaure; (4) causeway; (5) satellite
pyramids; (6) western cemetery; (7) mortuary
temple; (8) valley temple; (9) the Sphinx; (10) solar
boat pits.*

that constitutes a ritual setting for the dead pharaoh's celestial voyage into the afterlife. A passage (1), only 1.20 × 1.09 m (4 ft × 3 ft 7 in.), leads down through masonry and bedrock at an angle of 26° 34' 23" for 200 cubits (about 105 m, or 345 ft) before proceeding horizontally for a short way and opening into a rock chamber (2) that lies 30 m (98 ft) below ground level. This chamber was never finished, maybe because the depth and stale air prevented further work, or perhaps it was deliberately left unfinished to represent the inhospitable domain of Sokar, god of the world of the dead. In the centre of the eastern part of the chamber was a deep well, deepened further in the nineteenth century AD by excavators searching vainly for hidden treasure. A passage 16 m (52 ft) long leads southwards from the chamber; this, too, was left incomplete. This was probably intended to lead to a subterranean cult tomb that was never built.

Some 28 m (92 ft) from the entrance, an ascending passage (3) branches off upwards from the descending passage. The lower part of the ascending passage is still blocked by three slabs of granite – an obstacle that can be circumvented via the passage made in antiquity (perhaps around 2000 BC, after the end of the Old Kingdom) by tomb robbers who plundered the royal burial. After a further 39 m (129 ft), a horizontal passage 38.70 m (127 ft) long (4) branches off to the intermediate chamber (5), otherwise known as the 'Queen's Chamber', and a shaft (known as 'the Well') leads steeply down to the entrance to the subterranean rock chamber.

The ascending passage meanwhile leads on into the Grand Gallery (6): one of the most impressive creations of ancient Egyptian funerary architecture, 47.85 m (157 ft) long and with a corbelled vault 8.48 m (28 ft) high. (New excavations and measurements by the German Archaeological Institute have confirmed earlier suggestions of a precedent for the Grand Gallery in the three great funerary chambers of the Red Pyramid at Dahshur, where the corbelled vaults are up to 15 m, or 49 ft, high.) From here a small passage and a room containing granite portcullises lead into the mortuary chamber (7), otherwise known as the 'King's Chamber'. This room is entirely faced with black granite, and at its western end is the simple granite sarcophagus of Khufu – the lid of which, broken in ancient times, has been lost. The mortuary chamber measures 10 × 20 cubits (5.24 × 10.49 m, or 17 × 34 ft) and 11 cubits (5.48 m, or 18 ft) high. Its roof consists of nine enormous granite slabs.

Above the roof of the mortuary chamber are five so-called 'relieving chambers' (8), with granite slabs just as large and a gabled roof of gigantic limestone slabs. From an engineering point of view, all these 'relieving chambers' make no sense, in terms of spreading the weight of the pyramid above and protecting the mortuary chamber, because the gabled roof of the topmost one – which is incorporated into the centre of the pyramid – does the job by itself. However, one should not forget that the formulation and

▷ *The Great Pyramid of Khufu:*
(1) descending passage; (2) burial chamber (as first planned); (3) ascending passage; (4) horizontal passage; (5) the 'Queen's Chamber'; (6) Grand Gallery; (7) actual burial chamber: the 'King's Chamber'; (8) 'relieving' chambers; (9) so-called 'air-shafts'.

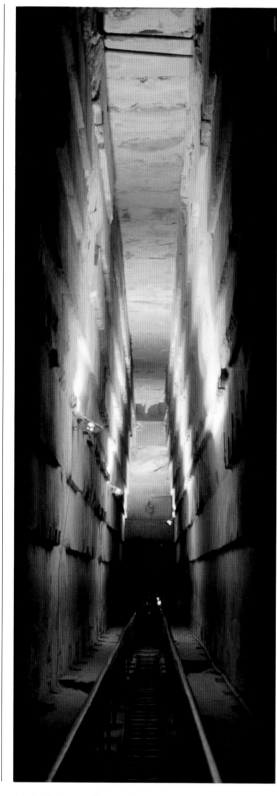

△ *The Grand Gallery, which leads to the 'King's Chamber' in the centre of the Great Pyramid, is one of the architectural masterpieces of ancient Egypt.*

application of such engineering principles is an architectural achievement of the eighteenth century AD, and earlier builders had to proceed purely empirically. Be that as it may, the roof of the mortuary chamber has successfully withstood small thread-like cracks, formed during construction, and the slight shifting that has taken place as a result of earth movements. In any case, manhandling the ceiling slabs (weighing up to 40 tons), and setting them in position at a height of 60 m (197 ft) so precisely that the joins between them are barely visible, constitutes a pioneering accomplishment on the part of the ancient architects, and one still unrepeatable today.

From both the King's Chamber and the Queen's Chamber, very narrow, square shafts (9) angle obliquely upwards towards the outside of the pyramid on the north and south sides.

Pyramids of the Fourth Dynasty (2575–2465 BC)

Seneferu (*c.* 2575–2551 BC) at Dahshur
Pyramid name: 'Seneferu Gleams'
This king built two pyramids at Dahshur (the 'Bent' and the 'Red') and another at Seila. He may also have at least finished the pyramid at Meidum.

Khufu (*c.* 2551–2528 BC) at Giza
Pyramid name: 'The horizon of Khufu'.
The most complex and imposing pyramid at the site.

Djedefre (*c.* 2528–2520 BC) at Abu Roash.
Pyramid name: 'The starred vault of Djedefre'.
Unfinished.

Khafre (*c.* 2520–2494 BC) at Giza.
Pyramid name: 'Khafre is great'.
The second-largest pyramid.

Baka (*c.* 2494–2490 BC) at Zawiyet el-Aryan.
Only the preliminary excavation for the pyramid was completed.

Menkaure (*c.* 2490–2472 BC) at Giza.
Pyramid name: 'Menkaure is divine'.

Shepseskaf (*c.* 2472–2467 BC) at South Saqqara
Pyramid name: 'Shepseskaf is pure'.
A giant *mastaba*, now known as the 'Mastabat Faraun'.

Only 20 cm (8 in.) square in section, these have been interpreted as shafts for ventilation or illumination, or as guide-passages pointing towards the star Orion. Recent research by the German Archaeological Institute at Cairo, however, has shown that they were probably shafts to enable the soul of the dead king to rise directly into the sky. The openings at either end were certainly all closed at one time (some still are), to be opened only by the dead king by means of a ritual formula.

Up to now the three chambers of Khufu's Great Pyramid have been interpreted as reflecting three successive phases of construction. But this may well be mistaken, since there are no signs of any structural modifications in the external masses of this imposing monument. The system of funerary chambers embodies the meaning and spiritual substance of a pyramid, and it is hard to accept that the ancient architects, who conceived and built a cult monument with such perfect measurements, should fail to arrange for the essential element of religious belief to be expressed in its construction.

All royal tombs of the Old Kingdom, from the Predynastic Period to the end of the Sixth Dynasty, contained a succession of three rooms. During the Fourth Dynasty (2575–2465 BC), under the influence of solar religion, this succession – which had originally been a horizontal one – had become vertical, and the culmination of this change is represented by the pyramid of Khufu.

A mortuary temple once stood in front of the centre of the east face of the Great Pyramid, but only parts of the foundations have been preserved. This temple consisted of a vast open court with basalt paving and a pillared colonnade. At the feet of the granite pillars stood statues of the pharaoh carved in various types of stone. The walls of the colonnade were of fine white limestone decorated with coloured reliefs, and in the middle of the court was an altar, on which daily offerings were presented.

At the west side of the temple, directly in front of the pyramid, lay the key cult room: the inner sanctuary, Where the funerary offerings were made, and which had a 'false door' through which the dead king could enter and accept the gifts. A covered causeway 1,800 m (1.1 miles) long, its walls decorated with finely incised inscriptions, ascended to the mortuary temple from the plain, where the valley

△ *In 1954 a dismantled boat was found, a few metres below the surface, in a pit by the south face of the pyramid of Khufu. It has been reassembled (top) and is 43.4 m (142 ft) long and more than 5.9 m (19 ft) wide: it is now displayed close to the find-spot. Another boat (below), here photographed* in situ *via a special probe, lies in a pit adjacent to the first.*

temple and the residence of Khufu were located.

Sporadic excavation of the valley temple (which lies beneath a present-day settlement) has shown that this, too, had a basalt pavement, and recent excavations 2 km (1¼ miles) east of the pyramid plateau have uncovered the foundations of an imposing basalt wall, probably the east wall of the town associated with the pyramid.

Close to the east side of the Great Pyramid, are three small pyramids; each has at some time been attributed to Hetep-heres, the mother of Khufu, and the two queens Merityotes and Henutsen, although this is not certain. In addition, a cult (subsidiary) pyramid of Khufu has been discovered only recently. Alongside the east and south faces of the pyramid lay deep, wide rock-cut pits, designed to hold the heavenly boats of Khufu (the pits by the south face were found with their contents intact).

The easternmost pit on the south face contained a river boat 43.4 m (142 ft) long and consisting of 1,224 separate pieces, which had been dismantled into 651 parts to fit into the pit. The other pit on the south face contained a similar dismantled boat, which, however, has suffered much from modern environmental conditions; this was photographed in October 1987 by a *National Geographic*-sponsored team, which inserted into the sealed pit a special camera on the end of a probe.

Khufu's successor, his son Djedefre (2528–2520 BC), began a pyramid on a high spur of the desert plateau near Abu Roash, north of Giza. However, in the eight years of his reign, only the great excavation

for the foundations and around 20 m (65 ft) of the structure were completed. After his premature death his brother, Khafre, came to the throne.

Khafre (2520–2494 BC) built his funerary monument at Giza, to the south of that of his father Khufu. The pyramid has sides that measure 410 cubits (215.25 m, or 706 ft) long, shorter than those of Khufu's, but its steeper angle of slope (53° 10') enabled it to reach the impressive height of 143.50 m (417 ft), only 3 m (10 ft) less than that of Khufu's pyramid. The two lower courses were cased with dark red granite, the rest with limestone; this casing is still well preserved on the upper courses, and only the capstone (*pyramidion*), probably made of pink granite, is missing. In 1880–82 Flinders Petrie discovered that the inclinations of the four sides differed slightly towards the top of the pyramid – something that it was not then possible to explain. New research at Dahshur has now shown that the ancient architects were unable to balance out irregularity in the construction, which increased over the last 20 metres. The pyramid's axis is only 5' 26" off true north; one assumes that the architects (and those of Menkaure's pyramid) used Khufu's Great Pyramid as the basis for their measurements.

In comparison to those of earlier pyramids, the system of chambers in Khafre's pyramid seems so strikingly simple that some have sought to

explain it by assuming changes in the construction plan, or even the existence of hidden chambers. The latter can be excluded as a result of Luis Alvarez's work in 1970, which involved taking an 'X-ray' picture of the pyramid using extremely precise measurements of cosmic radiation. However, the purpose of having two entrances and two passages to the mortuary chamber is still unexplained and will only be clarified by means of new and up-to-date investigations. The reason for this arrangement may have been Khafre's advanced age when he came to the throne. This would have made the completion of the mortuary chamber seem urgent, especially since it had taken eight years for his predecessor's to rise to a height of only 20 m (65 ft).

The original plans envisaged a subterranean rock chamber, an intermediate chamber (built above bedrock) and a mortuary chamber higher up in the structure, just as in the pyramid of Khufu. The last was never finished, and the intermediate chamber was extended westwards instead. The extension was built with a step and the floor was paved with granite. The chamber must have been entirely cased with granite, and its measurements – 4.99 m (16 ft 4½ in.) wide, 14.15 m (46 ft 5¼ in.) long east-west, and 6.86 m (22 ft 6 in.) high – are not in whole-cubit units. The change in the rock floor level and the traces on the side walls show clearly that it was intended that the

◄ *Khafre, ruled from 2520 to 2494 BC. He came to the throne after the short reign of his brother Djedefre (2528–2520 BC), Khufu's immediate successor.*

△ *This stele, between the front paws of the Sphinx, tells how, many centuries after it was made, Thutmose IV unearthed the monument from the sand that partially covered it.*

chamber should be divided, most probably by means of a wooden partition. Against the west wall, sunk into the pavement, was a simple, dark granite sarcophagus similar to that of Khufu. Because of its size, it must have been put in position from above before the mortuary chamber was roofed over.

The mortuary temple close to the east face of Khafre's pyramid, and the valley temple at the edge of the desert, are better preserved than those of Khufu, being made of cyclopean blocks weighing up to 200 tons. Internally, though, both had been stripped of the statues and the granite casing they once contained. The compact architecture of both temples gives the impression that they have been cut out of the rock or somehow detached from the mass of the pyramid.

Again, the mortuary temple was centred on an open court for offerings with a pillared colonnade, in front of which stood statues of the pharaoh. Facing the colonnade lay a transverse and longitudinal pillared room. To the west, the offerings room was bounded by a complex of five long, narrow rooms for statues and another complex of storerooms; beyond these was the transverse hall, which contained the 'false door' through which the dead king entered from his tomb. Externally, the surfaces of the façade and sides of the temple are smooth and austere.

The large number of rooms and corridors, laid out in closed blocks, is in contrast to the plan of Khufu's temple – and even more so with the simple arrangement of corridors and chambers in the Khafre pyramid. It is possible to see this as evidence of a relationship between the design of the pyramids and

the ritual and funerary functions associated with them. A rich and complex set of chambers in the pyramid seems somehow to correspond inversely to a simpler and more open plan for its mortuary temple – and *vice versa*: if the pyramid's system of funerary chambers is not complicated, then there are more rooms in the temple. There was, therefore, a very precise set of requirements governing the spaces that formed the cult setting for burial rituals, and it had to be met overall, whether in the pyramid or in the temple.

Khafre's valley temple, too, relates to the mortuary temple in its internal architecture and type of decoration, pillars or columns. It is as massive and cubic as the vestibule of the mortuary temple and has the same smooth, polished pillars made of red granite from Aswan. Its hall, lit by openings in the top of the walls, once contained

△ *The pyramid of Khafre was 143.5 m (471 ft) high – only 3 m (10 ft) less than that of Khufu. However, because it is built on slightly higher ground and has more steeply sloping sides, it looks the most imposing of the Giza pyramids. Some external facing of limestone from Tura is preserved on the upper part.*

◁ *Mark Lehner's computer reconstruction of the Sphinx, the colossal statue sculpted from the rock at the foot of the causeway to Khafre's pyramid.*

twenty-three seated stone statues, including the famous statue of Khafre with Horus in the form of a falcon, which was found ritually buried in a shaft at the temple.

To the west of Khafre's valley temple is the colossal Sphinx, almost 55 m (150 ft) long and 20 m (65 ft) high, sculpted from a rocky mass – the remains of the stone quarry of Khufu. In the Old Kingdom this was the image of the pharaoh that united the potency of the animal kingdom with the intelligence of humanity. Scholars variously date the work to the time of Khufu or of Khafre. The grandiose conception, representing the pharaoh on a superhuman scale as lord of the cemetery, and its unique execution clearly point to Khufu, who instituted the cemetery of Giza and whose pyramid was destined to surpass all others in its monumentality.

Khafre's son, Menkaure (2490–2472 BC), placed his own funerary monument in the last space left on the southern part of the plateau at Giza. His much smaller pyramid marks a conscious departure from the colossal structures of the Fourth Dynasty. This was not a rejection of his predecessors (whose cult Menkaure confirmed by decree) but rather a change in the understanding and significance of pyramids and cult temples for the king and his times – a changed image of the manifestation of royal divinity. The pharaoh did not aspire to a greater similarity with the sun god, but to be the son of

the sun. To this was added a growing symbolism of colour, reflected in the use of coloured stone.

The base and the sixteen lowest courses of Menkaure's pyramid were faced with blocks of dark red granite, and the upper part with fine, light yellow limestone. Its measurements – 200 cubits (some 104.60 m, or 330 ft) square and 65 m (205 ft) high – are less than half those of Khufu's and Khafre's pyramids, but its system of chambers is as magnificent as that in the former. In contrast to the Great Pyramid, however, the design of Menkaure's concentrated on subterranean excavation, and, in a pioneering achievement, its architects introduced the granite slabs that roofed the mortuary chamber through a second passage, in order to create the impression of a false vault. The mortuary chamber contained a granite sarcophagus with 'palace façade' decoration, which Howard Vyse removed for shipment to England in 1838 (but the ship sank off the Spanish coast *en route*). The temples of Menkaure's pyramid also have a very simple plan, with a stronger emphasis on the open court. A wealth of statuary, sculpted in a variety of materials, was found in them.

The pyramids of Khafre and Menkaure have always been overshadowed by the Great Pyramid of Khufu, both physically and in the minds

of visitors – though all the pyramids jointly were considered by the ancient Greeks as one of the Seven Wonders of the World. However, Khufu's pyramid – with the almost inconceivable accuracy of its measurements, its precise orientation towards the north, the exactness of the levelling and the individual measurements and the apparent approximation of its angle of inclination to the value of π – has throughout history prompted some people to dwell on the mystique of numbers and the cosmos. No other ancient architectural work has been so much written about and speculated upon. In its passages and funerary chambers, above all, some people have thought that the whole history of the world and of salvation can be read. Since the discovery of the treasure of the tomb of Tutankhamun in 1922, the ranks of such mystics have been augmented by modern pyramidologists, who proclaimed fantastic finds of hidden chambers, rich in treasure and mystery.

In the face of all this, one can only re-emphasize that the pyramids of Giza are the tombs of Fourth-Dynasty pharaohs. Just like the medieval cathedrals of Europe, they are expressions of a profound religiosity and of the desire to vanquish death and achieve eternal life by creating monumental buildings.

▷ *The Sphinx, as it was around 1860, before the removal of the sand that partly covered it.*

Bibliography

J. Baines and J. Málek, *Atlas of Ancient
Egypt* (Oxford and New York, 1980).
I.E.S. Edwards, *The Pyramids of Egypt*
(Harmondsworth and New York,
1991).
A. Fakhry, *The Pyramids*, 2nd ed.
(Chicago, 1964).
L. Grinsell, *Egyptian Pyramids*
(Gloucester, 1947).
N. Jenkins, *The Boat beneath the
Pyramid* (London and New York,
1980).
J.-P. Lauer, *Le mystère des pyramides*
(Paris, 1988).
M. Lehner, *The Complete Pyramids*
(London and New York, 1997).
R. Stadelmann, *Die Ägyptische
Pyramiden* (Mainz, 1991).

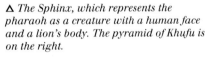

△ *The Sphinx, which represents the
pharaoh as a creature with a human face
and a lion's body. The pyramid of Khufu is
on the right.*

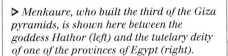

▷ *Menkaure, who built the third of the Giza
pyramids, is shown here between the
goddess Hathor (left) and the tutelary deity
of one of the provinces of Egypt (right).*

25

Saqqara: From the Past to the Future

Egypt

*T*he ancient burial ground of Saqqara, which lies some 30 km (18 miles) from Cairo on the desert plateau, is one of the best-known and most-visited sites of ancient Egypt. It is part of the massive cemetery – extending over more than 30 km – of the ancient city of Memphis. The rise of Memphis coincides with the beginning of Egyptian history, the time around 3100 BC, when it was decided to build a capital for the then new union of Upper and Lower Egypt into a single kingdom. The site chosen was a point where the narrow valley of the Nile begins to broaden out, just above the head of the Nile Delta. Herodotus attributed the foundation of Memphis to the mythical initiator of the Egyptian dynasties, Menes – whom recent studies tend to identify with Aha, a king buried in the cemetery of Abydos, in Upper Egypt.

occupation dating to the thirtieth century BC have been found. There is no archaeological data from these early stages of Memphite history, and little from the Old Kingdom (2575–2134 BC), the period when the city is said to have reached the height of its magnificence. Yet, the city's rise seems to be confirmed by the appearance, at the beginning of the third millennium, of monumental tombs made of mud brick in the cemeteries of Saqqara, a little way to the north, and there is evidence that seems to link the early king Aha with the Memphis area.

Ever since their discovery, there has been debate about whether these tombs constituted the royal cemetery of Egypt's first two dynasties. They are partially interred structures, often of considerable size, with a superstructure in mud brick. In the First Dynasty (2920–2770 BC) their exteriors were decorated in the typical 'palace façade' style, consisting of elaborate alternating inset panels and projections, which implies royal use. Further confirmation

The palm groves of present-day Mit Rahina hide the secrets of earliest Memphis: the nucleus of the original capital must have been to the north and north-west of the so-called 'Palace of Apries' on Kom Tuman, where traces of

△ *The plateau of Saqqara and its main monuments: (1) pyramid complex of Djoser; (2) pyramid of Unas; (3) tombs of Horemheb and Maya; (4) pyramid of Sekhemkhet; (5) underground tomb of Bakenrenef; (6) pyramid of Teti; (7) Serapeum; (8) cemetery of the First Dynasty; (9) gallery with sacred animals.*

△ *Djoser's pyramid complex, seen from the south-east, with the Step Pyramid behind and, in the foreground, the remains of the buildings designed for the celebration of royal jubilees.*

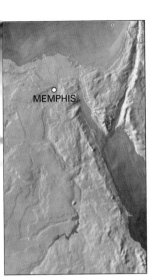

◁ *Location map:
Memphis lies near the
junction of the
narrow valley of the
River Nile and its
Delta. In antiquity the
city stood on the left
bank of the river,
which now flows
further to the east.
Saqqara and Giza
formed two parts of
the vast Memphite
cemetery.*

seemed to come from stelae and other artifacts from tombs inscribed with names of Proto-dynastic kings. However, in the cemetery of Umm el-Qa`ab at Abydos in Upper Egypt there were many other burials, also of royal appearance and datable to the reigns of the first kings of Egypt. Recent archaeological research seems to show that, at least up to the First Dynasty, only the cemetery of Abydos, far to the south, may bear the label 'royal'; the sumptuous tombs of Saqqara most

probably contained the burials of Memphite nobles or high officials. Yet, by the dawn of the Third Dynasty (2649–2575 BC) the centre of attention had clearly moved from Upper Egypt to the Memphis area, and its 'city of the dead' testifies to the lost splendour of the living city.

On the plateau of Saqqara, around the middle of the third millennium BC, the brilliant architect Imhotep built the extraordinary complex of the Step Pyramid of Djoser, immortalizing the name of this Third-Dynasty king. (Another architect, Jean-Philippe Lauer, has worked patiently since 1927 to reconstruct the buildings of the complex and restore their appearance and their architectural and conceptual unity.) The royal tombs of the Old

▽ *A recreated bird's-eye view of the central
area of Saqqara, showing virtual-reality
reconstructions of the pyramids of Djoser
(centre, with associated buildings), Unas
(lower left) and Userkaf (upper right).*

Kingdom – which, from the Third Dynasty, took the form of a pyramid with associated temples for the obsequies and subsequent cult of the pharaoh – are spread across the Memphite desert plateau in a strip from Abu Roash and Giza in the north (Fourth-Dynasty pyramids) to the extreme southern part of the Saqqara cemetery (Sixth-Dynasty pyramid of the last pharaoh of the Old Kingdom, Pepy II). Saqqara – itself covering an area more than 6 km. (3¾ miles) long and up to 1.5 km (1 mile) wide – was not used for royal burials after Djoser's time until the Fifth Dynasty (2465–2323 BC). The other kings preferred a site slightly to the north, at present-day Abusir, and a little further on at Abu Ghurab they erected temples for the solar cult, which were a characteristic of the Fifth Dynasty. Some Fifth-Dynasty pharaohs built their pyramids at Saqqara, however – among them Userkaf, the first of the dynasty, and Unas, the last. The pyramid of Unas was the earliest to contain, carved on the

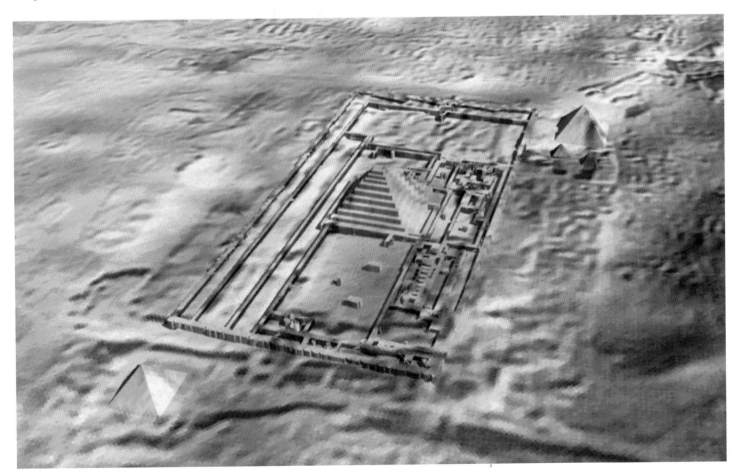

The Tomb of Horemheb

At the end of the Eighteenth Dynasty, around 1330 BC, Memphis became the capital of Egypt once more. Some twelve years earlier the 'heretic' pharaoh Akhenaten had moved the seat of government from Thebes to the newly founded city of Akhetaten (el-Amarna), in order to devote himself to the worship of his sole god, the Aten (sun disc), in a location far from the traditional centres of Egypt's polytheistic religion. After his death, however, the status quo was restored, and the ancient centres, Thebes in the south and Memphis in the north, regained their importance.

Between 1975 and 1995 a joint expedition of the Egypt Exploration Society, London, and the National Museum of Antiquities in Leiden uncovered ten tombs varying in date from the end of the Eighteenth Dynasty to the Ramessid Period. The largest and most important were those of Horemheb and Maya: two men who played key roles in the government of Egypt during the reign of Tutankhamun.

Because Tutankhamun came to the throne at the age of only nine, the government was carried out by Horemheb, Maya and another general, Ay. Of the three, Horemheb was perhaps the most influential; not only was he commander-in-chief of the army – and as such largely responsible for Egypt's foreign policy – he was also Tutankhamun's regent. After Tutankhamun's premature death, Ay became king, and Horemheb succeeded him. The other great official of the period, Maya, was overseer of the Treasury and was responsible for the restoration of the traditional religion and for re-opening the temples closed by Akhenaten. The tombs of Horemheb and Maya were built side by side at Saqqara and closely resemble each other in architectural layout.

The tombs consist of two basic elements: a superstructure in the form of a temple, intended for the funerary cult of the tomb-owner and his wife, and an underground complex destined to receive their

△▷ Parts of a virtual-reality visit to the tomb of Horemheb. *Above:* simulation of an aerial view of the building as it is today. *Right:* the first colonnaded court as it must have appeared when built.

mummified bodies and their extensive funerary equipment. The entrance to the buildings consists of a great pylon with a central gateway giving access to a series of courts and chapels. Beyond the pylon lies an open court that, in the case of Horemheb's tomb, contains a peristyle of twenty-four columns. A doorway in the west side of the peristyle leads into a large vaulted room, originally decorated with painted mud plaster, where, on the left-hand side, there were two niches for statues of the tomb-owner and his wife. This 'statue room' is flanked by two narrow vaulted storerooms, again with painted decoration, each with its own doorway facing east. Beyond the statue room lies a second peristyle

court, smaller than the first; three doorways in its west wall give access to three chapels, the central one of which is the cult chapel, the focal point of the tomb-owner's mortuary cult.

The decoration on the limestone facing of the courts

The underground complex of the tomb of Horemheb was originally designed for his own burial and that of his first wife Amenia, who died when the building project had only just begun. It contains two burial chambers, one of which

△▷▽ Other images from the animation. *Above left:* the first court seen from the east peristyle. *Above right:* the second colonnaded court, showing the entrance to the main chapel; on its roof was a small mud-brick pyramid surmounted by a stone *pyramidion* (capstone), of which some fragments were found to the west of the tomb. *Below:* the east wall of the second courtyard with one of the blocks that was placed there (detail, *right*).

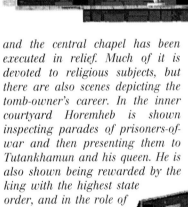

and the central chapel has been executed in relief. Much of it is devoted to religious subjects, but there are also scenes depicting the tomb-owner's career. In the inner courtyard Horemheb is shown inspecting parades of prisoners-of-war and then presenting them to Tutankhamun and his queen. He is also shown being rewarded by the king with the highest state order, and in the role of intermediary between the king and a group of foreign rulers.

actually received Amenia's mummy and funerary equipment. Although these chambers have some interesting architectural features, their walls are undecorated.

The complex was later extended with a staircase, a vaulted passageway, a pillared hall, and a new underground burial chamber (the dating of which is uncertain, although there is evidence to suggest that it dates from the time when Horemheb had finally become king himself). However, this chamber

was never used for his burial because, around his seventh regnal year, Horemheb started work on a tomb for himself in the Valley of the Kings at Thebes. It was there that he was eventually buried, and the Memphite tomb was used for the burial of his second wife, Mutnodjmet.

29

walls of its chambers, the accumulation of religious texts, spells and magical formulae known as the 'Pyramid Texts', which transmit the often enigmatic essence of the oldest Egyptian religion. After the Sixth Dynasty (2323–2150 BC), it was not until some centuries later that the Theban kings of the Twelfth Dynasty (1991–1783 BC) returned to the area and built their pyramids a little further south, at Dahshur. Family members and court nobles followed their king in this choice of location, and the cemeteries of the private citizens with their splendid *mastaba* tombs, rich in polychrome decoration, crowd around the pyramids.

△ *The burial chamber of the pyramid of Merenre (2255–2246 BC). The king's sarcophagus is carved with his names and titles. Next to it lies the uncovered receptacle for the canopic jars that contained the viscera.*

Incredible as it may seem, the archaeology of the pyramids has not yet revealed all Saqqara's secrets. As an example, aerial photography points to the existence of a large walled area to the west of the unfinished Third-Dynasty step pyramid of Sekhemkhet – archaeological investigation here has recently been started by the National Museum of Scotland. Also, the Fifth-Dynasty pyramid of Menkauhor lies buried somewhere awaiting its discoverer (some believe it to be a ruined monument east of the Sixth-Dynasty pyramid of Teti). It was only in 1988 that the French Archaeological Mission at Saqqara, under Jean Leclant, found the three pyramids belonging to the queens of Pepy I (first half of the twenty-third century BC).

The pyramid of Pepy I (2289–2255 BC) lies in the southern zone of Saqqara, together with the pyramids of the other Sixth-Dynasty kings (except for that of Teti, the dynasty's founder, which stands at Saqqara's northernmost point). It has produced examples of the 'Pyramid Texts' that are the finest so far known – admirable for the fineness of the carving and the marvellous turquoise green (the colour of eternal renewal) of their hieroglyphics. The fame of Pepy's pyramid was such that many scholars have claimed that, from the Middle Kingdom, the name of his pyramid (*Mennufer*: 'stable and perfect') was adopted for the city (Memphis), replacing the more ancient name of *Ineb-hedj* ('white wall'), which came from the facing material of its walls – either the luminous limestone of Tura or white plaster. Late in the Old Kingdom, in the Eighth Dynasty, the little-known pharaoh Ibi built a small brick pyramid close to the Sixth-Dynasty pyramids.

◁ *Detail of the texts carved on the walls of the pyramid of Unas (2356-2323 BC), the last king of the Fifth Dynasty. As far as is known, Unas was the first king to have carved in his burial chamber and on his sarcophagus the formulae relating to the destiny of the dead pharaoh in the beyond – perhaps part of a ritual read during funerary ceremonies from ancient times: 'O Unas, you do not go there dead, you go there alive...'.*

The history of Saqqara as a royal cemetery did not end with the Old Kingdom: its ancient cemeteries were remembered by the mostly unknown kings of the First Intermediate Period (2134–2040 BC; Ninth to Eleventh Dynasties) – Merykare being buried there in a long-lost pyramid. Two kings of the Thirteenth Dynasty (1782–1650 BC) built substantial but unfinished pyramids of mud brick here, and there is also evidence from the private tombs that there was uninterrupted use of the site at least up to the beginning of the second millennium BC. However, there is a gap from late in the Middle Kingdom (2040–1640 BC) until the New Kingdom, when the first tombs of the Eighteenth Dynasty (1550–1307 BC) were built at Saqqara. The fate of Memphis and its cemeteries in the turbulent period after the break-up of the Middle Kingdom and under the domination of the Hyksos is unclear.

It is only in the last twenty years that the renewed splendour of the ancient capital under the New Kingdom (1550–1070 BC), between the Eighteenth and the Twentieth Dynasties, has been fully revealed. Memphis was then a cosmopolitan and refined city, the political capital, whereas Thebes was the religious centre.

The cemeteries have produced the most striking remains, although the information emerging from recent excavations on the site of the city itself is just as important. The Anglo-Dutch Mission,

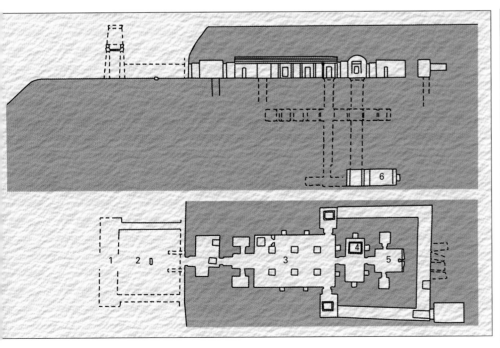

△ *Longitudinal section and plan of the tomb of Bakenrenef, vizier of Psammetichus I
(664–610 BC), including the substructure dating to the Twenty-sixth and Thirtieth
Dynasties: (1) pylon; (2) court; (3) pillared hall; (4) offering room with main shaft;
(5) mortuary chapel; (6) sarcophagus chamber.*

△ *The outer court of the tomb of Horemheb
(1319–1307 BC) as it is today, with the
columns of the western peristyle in part
reconstructed. On the walls of the courtyard
Horemheb was shown receiving 'the gold of
the reward', the highest pharaonic honour.*

led by Geoffrey Martin, has discovered a
series of noble tombs, dating from the
reigns of Tutankhamun to that of
Ramesses II, which have at last illuminated the art, life and history of the
Memphite court in that period. The most
important of these is that of the general
Horemheb (see box on p. 32), later to
become a pharaoh, and thus the occu-
pant of an underground tomb (KV57) in
the Valley of the Kings at Thebes. Like
other tombs found by the Anglo-Dutch
team, and by a Cairo University expedition to a nearby area, Horemheb's
Memphite tomb is of a type that is
typical of the New Kingdom in this area.

The Pyramid of Pepy I

Before the advent of virtual reality, only archaeologists could have mentally reconstructed the architecture of Pepy I's pyramid complex, which was robbed and burnt millennia ago. Thanks to computer restoration, it is now possible for anyone to explore the monument in three dimensions, inside and out.

The pyramids of Egypt were built primarily as transpositions into stone of a theological and political ideal. Being at the head of a well-structured, hierarchic society, the pharaoh was believed to stand between men and gods, and the pyramid functioned as a type of gigantic stairway raised between earth and heaven. The builders of these pyramids hoped that they would be indestructible, but unfortunately they now lie in ruins. That of Pepy I, built in about 2300 BC at Saqqara, contained an

▲ Part of the ruined funerary complex of Pepy I (2289–2255 BC).

inestimable treasure: a version of the famous 'Pyramid Texts', which are the earliest known group of religious funerary precepts.

The funerary complex of Pepy I was sacked, burnt, dismantled and then covered for centuries by the desert sand. Even after thirty years of excavation by the French Archaeological Mission to Saqqara,

only vestigial remains of the buildings have been found. However, the patronage of the electricity company Electricité de France and the power of the computer have made it possible not only to travel through a forgotten architecture, but also to attempt a rediscovery of the essential quality of Egypt and its magical universe.

Computer restoration reduces the complex architecture of the tomb to simple volumetric forms and then rebuilds it virtually. Its main technological contribution is that it recreates and reveals spaces that no longer physically exist. This may appear magical, but nothing has been invented: it is all based upon well-documented information.

A building defines two volumes or spaces: one external, which may be seen as a sculptural form, and one internal. This is the essence of architecture: with the other plastic arts the viewer remains physically outside the work, but architecture may be entered – and the spectator is surrounded by three-dimensional space.

Until now, though, all the systems of representation used for architecture have taken into consideration only the three traditional dimensions, ignoring a fourth element that relates to the sequential movement of the viewer's angle of vision over time. In order to experience and interpret the interior of a building, we need to be present within it and also to move within it. It is only by moving within the building, observing it from all points of view, that we ourselves create the fourth dimension, that of time.

Computer restoration reverses the hitherto normal representations. For the first time the volumes of the internal spaces are restored and lost architecture can be experienced as an environment. The life of a monument, experienced as an art object partly created by time (with ourselves as the moving centre) is now translated by the computer into a stream of images. It simply reverses our perception: no longer do we move within the architecture – the architecture now moves around us.

In studying Egyptian architecture, we have always in the past relied upon drawings or literature to help us understand and recreate the structures, but now architecture can be recreated as it should be: as a temporal environment. The techniques of computer restoration are constantly evolving, and today one can dream of moving through the monument of Pepy I in relation to the daily movement of the sun, and studying the texts and the restored bas-reliefs by its changing light. Thanks to the computer, it will now be possible not only to move through a building that has been rediscovered after millennia, but also to do so at a precise time, one hour in the eternity of the pharaoh.

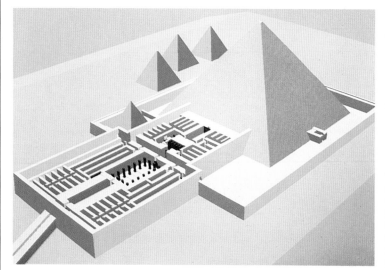

◁▽ Three virtual images showing reconstructions of the funerary complex of Pepy I. *Left*: the main pyramid, funerary temple and satellite pyramids. *Below left*: the temple courtyard. *Below right*: the room in which the royal statues were venerated.

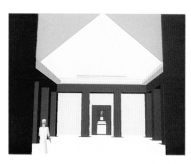

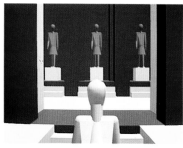

▷ *A facing block from
the tomb of Bakenrenef.
The carvings include an
image of the vizier with
his scribal equipment
held against his
shoulder. This is an
example of the refined
bas-relief produced by
Memphite artists in the
mid-seventh century BC, at
the beginning of the Saite
Period.*

This takes the form of a miniature temple incorporating a large open court, often with columns on one or more sides, and a shaft leading down from the court to the underground burial chambers.

Perhaps still more exciting was the rediscovery of the tomb of Maya, Tutankhamun's Treasurer and the man responsible for restoring the traditional religion and reopening the temples after the reign of the 'heretic' pharaoh Akhenaten. This tomb was first discovered, and in part cleared, by the German Egyptologist Richard Lepsius in the last century, but all trace of it was subsequently lost, and its rediscovery came, quite unexpectedly, eleven years into the Anglo-Dutch expedition's investigations. The beauty of its delicate reliefs, painted in an unusual manner and worthy of Maya's prestige and importance in the events of the period, were more than adequate compensation for the long wait.

After Ramesses II (1290–1224 BC) founded a new capital, Piramesse, in the eastern Delta, fewer officials seem to have been buried at Memphis and its cemeteries. However, embalmed bulls continued to be buried in the Serapeum, the gigantic funerary complex devoted to the sacred bulls of Apis founded under Amenhotep III (1391–1353 BC).

Relatively few tombs of the Third Intermediate Period (1070–712 BC) are known at Saqqara. Major tombs appear once more in the Late Period, under the Twenty-sixth Dynasty (664–525 BC), and the work produced there at that time is remarkable for its creativity and its vitality. Most nobles chose to build their tombs in the area around the Step Pyramid, though others have been found over an area spreading northwards to Abusir and even Giza. The senior officials excavated their tombs in the high rocky ridge that dominates the alluvial plain and the road to Memphis. In an attempt to exclude tomb-robbers, they adopted a new type of burial in wide, deep shafts with the underground burial chamber at the bottom. The stone sarcophagus was ingeniously lowered into the chamber, and after the funeral the shaft was filled with sand. The tomb of Bakenrenef, vizier of Pharaoh Psammetichus I, which is the only remaining example of these rock-cut tombs, reveals their noble conception and grandeur. Since 1974 archaeological investigation of this tomb by the University of Pisa, under the direction of Edda Bresciani, has recreated its history (see below) and carried out detailed consolidation of the tomb, and is about to restore the damage caused by tomb-robbers and the geological instability of the area.

The Late Period also saw the enlargement of the cemetery for sacred animals, and since 1964 the excavations of the Egypt Exploration Society have thrown new light on a cult that must have been one of the most characteristic aspects of Greco-Roman Saqqara. Next to the Serapeum, whose labyrinth was initiated in the time of Ramesses II and enlarged and embellished from the Twenty-sixth Dynasty onwards, galleries were excavated for innumerable ibises, falcons and sacred baboons, for cats (*Bubasteion*), for dogs (*Anubeion*), for sacred cows (Mothers of Apis), and (cited in papyri but still not located) for the lionesses of the goddess Sekhmet.

This cult of sacred animals, which so profoundly affected late Egyptian religious belief, was not confined to the catacombs. Terraced white funerary temples were built along the rocky escarpment, and crowded together in their enclosures were incubation chapels, oracular temples and housing for the many employees of the cult, priestly and secular. Papyri and *ostraca* (pieces of limestone or pottery bearing writing or drawings) in demotic Egyptian and Greek give a vivid picture of this teeming, busy world.

The tomb of the vizier Bakenrenef, who served under the Twenty-sixth-Dynasty pharaoh Psammetichus I (664–610 BC),

△ *The façade of the tomb of Bakenrenef
with the refacing which dates to the Roman
Period. In the seventh century BC the façade
extended further into the court.*

architectural and decorative schemes of its separate chambers is, as always in the best examples of Egyptian art, the expression of a perfectly coherent system of philosophical and religious thought. Its architect was inspired by a variety of models, from the subterranean royal tombs of the New Kingdom in the Valley of the Kings to the earliest *mastaba* tombs of the Old Kingdom. The plan, complex and harmonious, has an external court (doubtless preceded by pylons); a first chamber influenced by the themes and the style of the Old Kingdom but with astronomical motifs decorating the ceiling; and a great pillared hall, its vaulted ceiling decorated with dark-blue and gold images of Bakenrenef adoring the hours of the day and night, and its walls decorated with historical and legendary texts and vignettes drawn from the *Book of the Dead*. Lying transversely to the pillared hall is the offering room (from which a shaft descends to the sarcophagus chamber), and, finally, there is the main cult chamber – the mortuary chapel – with two small lateral rooms.

is cut into the steep cliffs of the desert plateau a few hundred metres from the Step Pyramid of Djoser and closely resembles contemporary tombs on the Asasif at Thebes. Penetrating more than 40 m (130 ft) into the rock, it is arranged on two underground levels, made up of networks of galleries and funerary shafts. The conception of the tomb and the perfect correspondence between the

△ *The ceiling of the mortuary chapel in the tomb of Bakenrenef is decorated with paintings of stars and ten great vultures with open wings (images of the goddess Nekheb, protectress of royalty) and the royal symbols of a shen-ring and a feather fan in their talons. Cleaning carried out between 1985 and 1987 has restored the splendour of the ancient colours.*

△▷ *Two details of the great funerary painting (second century AD) found in 1975 in the south shaft of the tomb of Bakenrenef. This masterpiece of Roman funerary painting illustrates unusual religious themes. Since 1995 it has been on display in Cairo Museum.*

The 'Pyramid Texts' and the Computer

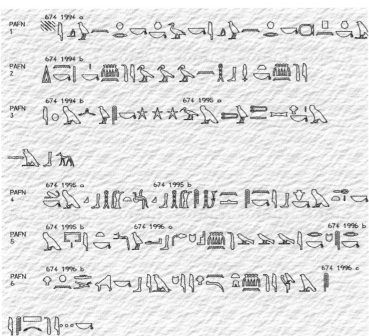

The 'Pyramid Texts' were edited, published, indexed and completed by various researchers. G. Maspero completed the first survey; K. Sethe produced a synoptic overview; G. Jéquier contributed supplements after the work done in the pyramid of Pepy II and those of the queens of Pepy II and of Ibi; and R.O. Faulkner reinvestigated the new texts with reference to Sethe's publication. After more than twenty years, the French Archaeological Mission at Saqqara (MAFS), under Jean Leclant, felt that it was necessary to recommence the study of the texts in relation to their location. He also proposed a new numbering system that embraces a codified cataloguing of the walls and allows one immediately to find the location of a particular text in each pyramid. Since, over time, each researcher has added to or corrected the numbering of the texts and columns, it has become increasingly difficult to use all these various references without accumulating errors.

A computer expert, Alain Croisiau, has written a program that has enabled all the references to be integrated into an organic structure that uses the new numbering system. The new structure also includes all the texts so far published, and incorporates the different versions found in the pyramids of Teti, Pepy I and Merenre. The linked drawing program creates the hieroglyphics exactly as they were found in the originals and adds, if required, the phonetic values of the signs and the text's reference code in categorical classification systems, such as those of A.H. Gardiner. Storage of all the vocabulary documented in the course of research on these texts allows the automatic creation of a lexicon that includes the graphic variants of any word and its appearances in the various texts, treated both semantically and syntactically. This programme is open-ended: other connections may be established, for example, with the 'Sarcophagus Texts', and translations and comments may be added.

'I have come to you, (for) I am your son;
I have come to you, O Pepy, (for) I am Horus.
I give you your staff, (for you are) at the head of the souls;
   (I give you) your sceptre (*nhbt*), (for you are) at the head of
      the imperishable stars.
I find you knit together;
your face is that of a jackal;
your body that of Qebehout.
   She refreshes (*kbh*) and gives strength to you in your heart
      in your body,
in the house of your father Anubis.
Be purified and sit (to be) at the head of those who are greater
      than you;
sit on your throne of bronze, on the seat of the foremost of the
      westerners.'

(Translation by Jean Leclant and R. O. Faulkner)

△ Print-out of some of the lines of hieroglyphic text on the north wall of the passage from the antechamber to the mortuary chamber of Pepy I's pyramid, with their translation alongside.

▽ The east wall of the mortuary chamber in the pyramid of Pepy I after reconstruction and restoration by the French Archaeological Mission at Saqqara.

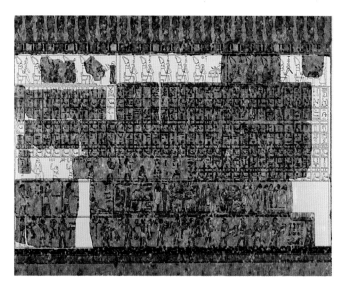 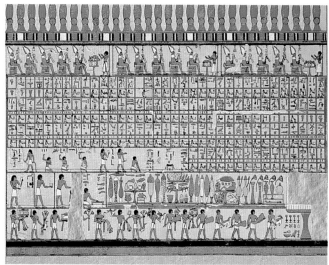

△ *Virtual-reality images of the east wall of the offering room in the tomb of Bakenrenef: (left) showing the surviving fragments restored to their original positions; (right) with interpolation of the missing sections.*

By the time the University of Pisa's expedition began exploration of the tomb in 1974, it had deteriorated seriously. Centuries of ground movement (the area is geologically unstable) and the activities of tomb-robbers, most active in the nineteenth and twentieth centuries, had caused the collapse of sections of the structure and the loss of a great deal of the finely carved and painted limestone facing that had covered the rock walls. Whole sections of the walls, and even some larger pieces detached from the vault of the pillared hall, had been sold to museums or private collectors in Europe and America. The ceiling of the underground funerary chamber was cracked, and erosion of the exterior over time had caused the rock to crumble and collapse, completely destroying the façade.

From the outset, one of the main priorities of the expedition was to restore and protect the tomb, and to return it as far as possible to its original state. Consolidation and rebuilding began at the end of 1985, drawing on the knowledge, built up by previous archaeological campaigns, of the monument, of the important family that had used it for around a millennium (from the seventh century BC to the second century AD), and also of the history of Saqqara in the Late Period.

Research conducted in collaboration with the architect Salah El-Naggar of the Egyptian Antiquities Organization (now Supreme Council for Antiquities) revealed the alterations in plan made during the building of the tomb, as well as later additions and modifications. It also brought to light hitherto unseen sections of decoration that had been hidden by sand or later alterations to the tomb, or even reused in later walls. The system of subterranean shafts and galleries – some dating to the Twenty-sixth Dynasty, and some built by Bakenrenef's Thirtieth-Dynasty descendants – was explored and studied for the first time, and some 8,000 blocks and fragments of wall-decoration that had fallen to the floor, or lay ruined in the shafts, were recovered. Thousands of exquisitely made objects, datable to various periods of the tomb's occupation, were found during excavation of its various sectors and will be important in reconstructing the history and culture of Egypt in the Late Period.

Finally, the expedition explored other underground chambers close to Bakenrenef's tomb. These included the notable tomb of a prophet of the goddess Sekhmet, never before examined, which dates to the fourth century BC.

The tomb of Bakenrenef needed many forms of repair: rebuilding work, the reattachment of surviving blocks to the walls, conservation and consolidation of the stonework and paintings (not only the painted ceilings, but also the colours of the hieroglyphic texts and their accompanying scenes) and restoration of the decorative scheme. The restoration programme and the identification of the appropriate techniques provided an excellent opportunity for

△ *The tomb of Bakenrenef: virtual-reality image of supporting walls in the vestibule 'stripped' to reveal the underlying decoration, partly still in situ.*

archaeologists and other specialists to experiment with a broad range of procedures and address some of the controversial questions in the modern debate about restoration. From 1985 to 1987 – as the site became a sort of training workshop for Egyptian archaeologists, architects and restorers, under a technical training programme financed by the Italian Foreign Ministry – consolidation of the tomb was completed.

In 1992 a simulated reconstruction of the tomb appeared: one of the last products of these years of study and experiment. Computer science had played an important role in the restoration of the tomb, and the simulated reconstruction was achieved with the help of virtual-reality techniques. In the first phase, computer techniques were applied to the restoration of the various sections of decoration, with the ultimate aim of enabling the surviving fallen pieces to be reattached in the right places and, possibly, of interpolating the missing portions.

◄ The tomb of Bakenrenef has undergone more than one modification during its thousand-year life: from afterthoughts in the course of the original project to loving restorations by the vizier's descendants in the Thirtieth Dynasty (380–343 BC) and emergency work in the Roman Period. In a journey backwards from the real image of the tomb today, the animation restores the appearance of the vestibule to what it was, first, in the Roman Period, and then in the seventh century BC. One of the four original columns and the bas-reliefs on the walls are shown.

This was a very complex problem. Its scale was enormous (some 8,000 detached fragments of decoration were found during the excavation of the site, and further substantial portions of the wall-facing are in museums elsewhere). The original appearance of the decoration was unknown – although, fortunately, much of the tomb had been described and drawn by Lepsius around 1843, when the decorated facing was still in quite good condition (though, even then, there were sections missing). The task resembled a gigantic and formidably difficult jigsaw puzzle – with no help to be gained from the shape of the pieces, because many sections of the decoration had been lost and others damaged when parts of the tomb collapsed.

Analysis of the material remaining revealed how the whole decorative programme of the tomb had been conceived and executed as an integrated whole, consisting of a complex group of related texts, images and motifs distributed throughout the tomb according to a carefully thought-out overall scheme. Within this scheme there were many variations, as the artists adjusted the combinations of motifs, measurements and colours for each different composition, and even for each wall. However, the overall system and rigour of the decorative scheme provided the key that enabled computer algorithms to be designed to assist in the repositioning of the blocks, and rules for automatic research procedures to be deduced where there was no precise model to follow.

Details of the surviving blocks were recorded on a database in the form of a formalized description of each block and a digitized image of each of its decorated faces. The digitized images were carefully captured in the most consistent lighting conditions possible and in such a way as to avoid distortion.

It is far easier to build up small units into a larger whole by the use of images than even the most precise of verbal descriptions. Attempting to discover the

◄ Three-dimensional model of Bakenrenef's tomb 'extracted' from the rock into which it is cut. The virtual reconstruction is based on this model.

37

original placing of elements of wall decoration involves trying to identify connections between individual surviving fragments and manipulating them in various arrangements to create proposed reconstructions whose plausibility can then be assessed. In such procedures the computer can be of considerable help. However, some information – such as form, colour and style – is hard to codify verbally and is better entered into a database and analysed on a computer if it is recorded in the form of an image.

The computer technology available for such an analysis was still at a relatively early stage of development in 1985, especially where personal computers were concerned. The quality

△ *The magnificent painted vault of the offering room of Bakenref's tomb. The painted ceilings, which were hard to remove, were the only parts to escape the attentions of tomb-robbers in antiquity.*

and definition of digitized images was rather limited, and so too was the power of the microprocessors then available. However, a certain amount was achieved in spite of these difficulties, and a series of interesting experiments took place using techniques of image-manipulation and image-processing that had been pioneered in the archae-

ological restoration field. The legibility of digitized images was improved by increasing the contrast or emphasizing certain characteristics (the outlines of figures and carved symbols, for instance), and automatic selection of an image outline and the automatic reading of measurements and morphological data were developed. Some forms of virtual reality could also be applied to the images of the decorated fragments: copying a given colour from the image of a well-preserved piece and applying it to the image of a less well-preserved piece. The same method could be used to complete hieroglyphs and pictures on those sections in poor condition by reference to other, better-preserved sections. During these trials

the computer screen became the 'virtual wall' on which possible arrangements of the fragments could be tested by moving their virtual *alter egos* around to find the best positions for them.

Producing hypotheses for the various ways in which the scanty remains of artifacts or ancient buildings may be completed or reconstructed, and being prepared to try many alternative solutions in the process, is an almost daily exercise for the archaeologist. Today visualization techniques are a tool of fundamental importance in this complex process of analysis and imagination. In the particular case of the tomb of Bakenrenef, they not only served as a flexible and powerful instrument for testing reconstruction hypotheses, they also provided a means effectively to 'virtually restore' the monument. The hundreds of splendid fragments of the tomb's decoration that are kept in museums – not to mention those in private collections or scattered around the antiques market – are unlikely ever to be reinstated *in situ*. Moreover, although the number of surviving fragments is considerable, it is so small in relation to what is lost that in many cases – even if all the decoration of one wall could be reconstructed *in situ* – what survives would only form islands in a sea of bare rock. This would then throw up the problem of how much of the missing sections to fill in.

▷ *A virtual-reality image of the offering room into which the funerary shaft of Bakenref's tomb opens. None of the facing visible in this image is now in situ.*

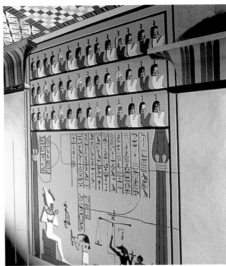

◁ *The virtual-reality visitor
to the tomb of Bakenrenef is
taken from the vestibule into
the pillared hall, whose walls
were decorated with scenes
and texts drawn from the*
Book of the Dead. *On the
vault of the central nave were
twenty-four images of
Bakenrenef adoring the hours
of the day and night, which
are now partly destroyed or
kept in various museums.*
Right: *the judgment of the
dead before the god Osiris,
reconstructed on the basis of
surviving fragments.*

This is a typical case in which virtual restoration can usefully act as a substitute for actual restoration. In actuality, only a few blocks could be replaced on the walls, while others would remain in their display cases or on the walls of museums – and the picture of what the wall must originally have looked like would only exist on paper or in the mind of the Egyptologist. In virtual reality, the whole wall can be recreated with a more-or-less accurate simulation of the colours, materials and techniques used to decorate the real wall – and then it can be 'rebuilt' as required, to illustrate other suggested reconstructions or a later phase in the history of the monument.

Up to the 1990s the visualization methods used in the preparatory phases of the restoration of Bakenrenef's tomb were two-dimensional only. Work concentrated on the restoration of the decorative scheme, and this led to a concentration on the surfaces of the monument at the expense of its architectonic volumes. As the initial phase was completed, however, it gradually became clear that the visualization should be expanded into three dimensions, so as to 'see' the tomb with all its wall and ceiling decoration restored and its structure and architectural elements in their original condition. This work was largely carried out by the Department of Scientific Visualization of CNUCE of Pisa.

As a first step, a three-dimensional geometrical model of the tomb was created, based on surveys. All the significant information on materials, colours and bas-relief techniques, all the graphic and photographic documentation of the tomb and the fragments, and the drawings illustrating suggested restorations of the decoration were then used in the construction of a 'visual model', which, with the geometric model, makes up the complete virtual model. Photographic documentation of the decoration fragments was abandoned because of

△ *Another view of the pillared hall in the tomb of Bakenrenef taken from the animation. In the background, below the starred vault with the representations of the hours, is a passage leading to the offering room (part of the lunette above the passage is preserved in the Field Museum, Chicago); on the left is the entrance to the gallery that surrounds the offering room and the mortuary chapel.*

➤ Left: *painted wooden statue of the goddess Neith found in 1975 in the tomb of the priest-sem Pashentaisut, son of Ankhhap, north of Bakenrenef's tomb.* Right: *statuette of a nude woman, in coloured gesso, found in 1975 outside the tomb of Pashentaisut. The large black wig, protruding stomach and long pubic hair associate the find with images used in the Greco-Roman Period as a talisman of fecundity.*

The animation of Bakenrenef's tomb allows the viewer to 'move' through parts of the monument not only spatially but also in time, showing decoration that (for the most part) is no longer *in situ* and structures that belong to different phases of the tomb's history. However, the aim of this virtual reconstruction is to demonstrate the techniques of this type of restoration, offer a selection of images that illustrate the problems encountered and propose possible solutions. It does not therefore include all that has been learned about the original appearance of the tomb. For example, it does not incorporate the hypotheses that have been developed about the appearance of the tomb's façade during the Saite Period, when the vizier was buried, nor those about the appearance of the sanctuary, since both of these structures belong to a period that is still under study.

problems over visual consistency (due to differences in camera angles and colour rendering – especially with fragments in museums and private collections), as was the idea of using digitized photographs for surviving material, to distinguish it from infillings rendered by means of drawings created by visualization techniques. The simulated reconstruction of the tomb is now entirely based on drawings.

The next step was to build up an animation drawing based on the various 'views' of the tomb that had been created. From the point of view of archaeological restoration, the most significant advantage of this is the ability to suggest the evolution of a site or structure over time, including any modifications made to the monument – something that is of obvious interest in the case of Bakenrenef's tomb, which underwent more than one trans-formation during its thousand years of use. Once again, virtual reality elegantly avoids some of the problems that would be posed by permanent *in situ* restoration. For example, 'intrusive' structures of later date that hide some of the decoration in the vestibule of the actual tomb may be 'removed' in the animation – to reveal the processions of bearers of offerings, and the deceased ready to receive them – all without a

chisel touching the stone. What could be more effective and yet respectful of the existing structure?

△ *Simulating the types of relief used by Egyptian artists three-dimensionally was one of the most challenging tasks faced in the virtual reconstruction of the tomb of Bakenrenef. Various algorithms were tried in order to obtain the different effects of depth and of the play of light and shade demanded by the different techniques used by the sculptors.*

Besides the question of 'intrusive' structures, the animation has also addressed the problem (important for correct restoration, even by virtual means) of distinguishing existing elements of a structure from those that have been interpolated or inferred. Two different procedures were offered: a static approach was applied to the pillared hall and a dynamic approach to the neighbouring offering room.

In the static method it was decided, for convenience, to show the parts for which the reconstruction is not yet secure as white surfaces with the architectonic outlines indicated; to visualize in colour those areas subject to restoration hypotheses of a high degree of reliability (while suggesting the outlines of the fragments, so as to distinguish surviving from interpolated sections); and, finally, to simulate bare rock in the areas for which no reconstruction has yet been suggested. In the dynamic method the various elements of a decorated wall (sections *in situ*, fragments found in the tomb, fragments in museums and parts interpolated in the suggested reconstruction) are shown in an animated sequence.

Finally, the funerary shaft of the tomb has been used for an experiment in the use of visualization. Here Bakenrenef's stone sarcophagus (acquired by Ippolito Rosellini in Alexandria in 1828 and now kept in the Archaeological Museum, Florence) is replaced in its original context.

The results so far achieved by this animation seem promising. The illusion that it creates of entering the monument, looking around and examining the smallest corners and details, and of following the tomb's transformations over time, is spectacular. But that is not all. Animation can also be a powerful scientific instrument, provided it is solidly based on reliable data. Because it functions both as a virtual restoration and as an archaeological tool, it must be able to guarantee precision and realism. This combination of roles requires high levels of accuracy, quality and clarity in images and the rendering of details and colours. At the moment, unfortunately, these are still relatively expensive to obtain and generally beyond the slender means of university researchers. However, the swift development and continual improvement of visualization techniques are beginning to make virtual travel through the monuments of the past a reality.

Now that funding has ceased for the project of restoring Bakenrenef's actual tomb, this 'virtual tomb' is the only one that can give an idea of the original splendour of the monument. The hope (and the aim of the research) is that the virtual reconstruction of the tomb may soon be accompanied by its actual restoration, using interactive and virtual-reality animation techniques as a sort of 'living' museum of the history of the tomb and of modern archaeological restoration.

Bibliography

J. Baines and J. Málek, *Atlas of Ancient Egypt* (Oxford and New York, 1980).

J.-P. Lauer, *Saqqara. The Royal Cemetery of Memphis. Excavations and discoveries since 1850* (London, 1976).

J. Leclant, 'A la quête des pyramides des reines de Pepi I', in *Bulletin de la Société Française d'Egyptologie*, 113, 1988, pp. 20–31.

A. Labrousse (in collaboration with P.Cornon), *Regards sur une pyramide* (Paris, Fondation Electricité de France, 1991).

Various authors, *Tomba di Bakenrenef (L.24). Attività del Cantiere Scuola 1985–1987, Saqqara IV* (Pisa, 1988).

Various authors, 'Visualization and restoration in the tomb of Bakenrenef at Saqqara (L.24)', in *Informatique et Egyptologie*, 9 (Utrecht and Paris, 1994).

G.T. Martin, *The Hidden Tombs of Memphis* (London and New York, 1991).

△ *The limestone sarcophagus of Bakenrenef. (Above left: the digitized image. Above right: a detail.) In the virtual reconstruction the sarcophagus is restored to its original place at the bottom of the funerary shaft, more than 16 m (44 ft) underground. It had already been removed from the tomb before 1828, when Ippolito Rosellini acquired it in Alexandria.*

Faiyum: Restoration and Virtual Archaeology

Egypt

*T*he Faiyum – the 'Land of the Lake' of the ancient Egyptians – is surrounded by desert, bordered by the beach of a prehistoric inland sea derived from the Mediterranean, and watered by a thousand watercourses. It is not a proper oasis, because it is linked to the Nile valley by the Bahr Yusuf ('river of Joseph'; the ancient 'canal of Lake Moeris'). This enters the fertile depression at el-Lahun, where a Pharaonic-Period earthwork was linked to a port, and runs northwards for about 600 km (370 miles), parallel with the Nile, providing valuable water for irrigation.

The Faiyum was initially a home of Palaeolithic hunters and fishermen who exploited the natural resources of Lake Moeris, and the marshes and swamps around it. Later it supported Neolithic agricultural populations (the so-called 'cultures A and B').

There are few archaeological remains dating to the period of the Old Kingdom (2575–2134 BC), but more survives from the second millennium BC, when the rulers of the Twelfth Dynasty (1991–1783 BC), of Theban origin, made their new administrative capital at Itjtawy (present-day el-Lisht) on the edge of the Faiyum. From Senusret II (1971–1926 BC) onwards the pharaohs (with their pyramids) and the courtiers (with their cemeteries) favoured the 'Land of the Lake'. They

carried out land-reclamation and water-control and created a new province that underwent rapid agricultural and urban development. Nor did the rulers' interest in the Faiyum cease under the New Kingdom (1550–1070 BC). At Ghurab the British Egyptologist Flinders Petrie unearthed an important settlement with temples and palaces that produced splendid finds. One of the palaces had been the residence of Queen Tiye, mother of the pharaoh Akhenaten (1353–1335 BC).

Exploitation of the Faiyum was intensively renewed by the rulers of the Ptolemaic Period (304–30 BC), and the province was called 'Arsinoite' after Queen Arsinoe the deified wife of

◁ *A fisherman, standing in a papyrus boat, spears two fish with a double-pronged harpoon (shown in detail in the upper part of the picture). Wall-painting in the Middle-Kingdom tomb of Khnumhotep at Beni Hasan. (Illustration from I. Rosellini,* Monumenti dell'Egitto e della Nubia, *II,* Monumenti civili, *plate XXV)*

Ptolemy II. There is a considerable amount of historical, economic, social and literary information on the Greco-Roman Period. The many villages and estates (Karanis, Theadelphia, Dionysias, Narmouthis, Magdola, Philadelphia, Bakchias, Tebtunis, Kerke-osiris, Soknopaiou Nesos) have yielded an enormous quantity of papyri written in Greek and Demotic Egyptian. Some of these were excavated clandestinely and sold in Europe and America, and some were unearthed by official excavations (from those of Bernard Grenfell and Arthur Hunt to those conducted during the twentieth century by institutions such as the University of Michigan and the University of Cairo). Italian excavations took place in the village of Tebtunis, which preserves the remains of an important pre-

△ *Dawn over Lake Qarun, which Classical authors called Lake Moeris. This large salt lake – the remnant of a sea of the Oligocene and Miocene periods – is rich in fish, and its marshes attract millions of birds of many different species during the migration seasons.*

▽ *Satellite image of
the Faiyum; red
denotes the fertile
zone, while grey
indicates the desert.
The photograph
shows clearly the link
with the Nile, Lake
Qarun and, in the
lower left, the two
lakes of Wadi Rayan.
Today, as it was in
antiquity, the Faiyum
is a fertile and
productive
agricultural area.*

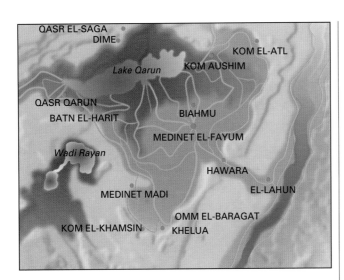

◁ *Map showing the
sites of greatest
archaeological
interest in the
Faiyum.*

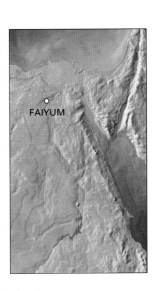

▷ *Location map: The
Faiyum depression is
in the western desert,
almost 100 km (62
miles) south-west of
Cairo, and is linked
to the Nile by a
branch of the Bahr
Yusuf river.*

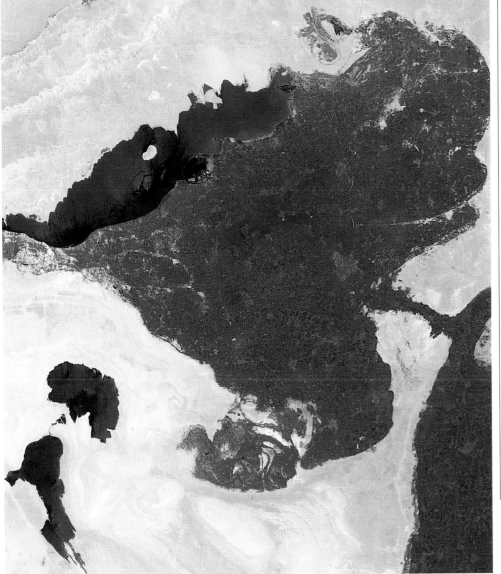

Ptolemaic temple and of a large area of settlement. In the 1980s these excavations were restarted by an Italian–French mission.

The Faiyum offers modern visitors unforgettable landscapes, but there are few well-preserved monumental archaeological remains. The majority of the temples, cities and ancient cemeteries have suffered irreparable decay or have been covered with sand by the wind that blows constantly from the Sahara. Among the most important surviving monuments are the Roman temple of Qasr Qarun (Dionysias), near the west end of Lake Qarun, and the austere Middle-Kingdom temple of Qasr el-Sagha, in the desert to the north of the lake. This was found in 1884 by Schweinfurt, and the recent studies of Dieter Arnold have dated it to the Twelfth Dynasty, rather than to the Old Kingdom, as was once thought.

The capital of the 'Land of the Lake' was Shedet, which, according to the Greek historian Diodorus, was founded by Menes (Aha), the first historical pharaoh. In the Greek Period it was called Crocodilopolis, or 'city of the crocodile', the city god (and protector of the whole region) being the crocodile god Sobek – with whom was associated the Falcon 'Horus of Shedet', an aspect of the god of pharaonic royalty. These creatures were reared at the different temples of the Faiyum dedicated to them, and when they died the sacred crocodiles were embalmed and buried with full honours. The remains of Shedet were recognizable up to thirty years ago in the dusty heaps known as 'Kiman Fares' but have now disappeared. The cartouches of the pharaohs Amenemhet III (1844–1797 BC) and Ramesses II (1290–1224 BC) are faintly detectable on the few leaning column fragments that are the only visible evidence that remains of the imposing temple that was once dedicated to Sobek.

At Biahmu are the ruins of Kursit Faraun (the 'thrones of the pharaoh'): two massive stone statue bases, standing in the middle of a rich and fertile countryside. Almost four thousand years ago these supported colossal statues of the pharaoh Amenemhet III, which were described by Herodotus and other ancient historians, but which had disappeared by the end of the eighteenth century AD.

The pyramid of the great pharaoh Senusret II was built at el-Lahun

around a knoll of natural rock, with stone walls supporting a mass of mud bricks. Now badly damaged, it is no more than a disappointing undulating hill riven with fissures. To the south of the pyramid lay the shaft tomb of princess Sithathoriunet, where in 1914 Guy Brunton found a treasure of splendid jewellery (parts of which are

△ *The temple of Medinet Madi. In the foreground is a sunk relief of the Ptolemaic Period sculpted beside the portal. In the background is the entrance to the Twelfth-Dynasty temple dedicated by Amenemhet III (1844–1797 BC) to the cobra goddess Renenutet and the crocodile god Sobek. The temple was excavated by Achille Vogliano in 1935.*

now in the Egyptian Museum, Cairo, and the Metropolitan Museum, New York). Not far away, Flinders Petrie unearthed a walled town, generally known as Kahun, that housed officials and priests concerned with the pyramid.

At Hawara the pyramid that marks the burial of Amenemhet III retains its dignity, even in its decay into a mass of mud bricks. Here, too, was the destroyed pyramid of Princess Neferuptah, where, in the intact burial chamber, tomb-offerings of precious bracelets, necklaces, sceptres and belts were found. The scanty ruins of the funerary temple connected with the Hawara pyramid are generally identified with one of the most typical of

pharaonic monuments in the Western imagination: the mysterious and symbolic Labyrinth. Herodotus, who claimed to have visited the complex in person, marvelled at its twelve covered courts and three thousand rooms.

In the south-west Faiyum Amenemhet III (under the Grecianized name of Promarres, or Lamarres, he was the subject of a cult that lasted until the Roman Period in the Faiyum) founded the small city of Gia, later named Narmouthis, and now called Medinet Madi. Here there is a temple, begun by Amenemhet III and finished by Amenemhet IV (1799–1787 BC), which is still well preserved, encased within Ptolemaic enlargements. It was dedicated to the cobra goddess of the harvest, Renenutet, and the crocodile god, Sobek, and is so far the only temple of the cult to survive from the Middle Kingdom. Excavated by

Achille Vogliano, it has been convincingly dated on the basis of scenes, texts and royal cartouches.

The Faiyum occupies an important place in the history of monasticism and of Egyptian Christianity. In recent years the Polish Centre for Archaeology has been working at Deir el-Naqlun, which is rich in important wall-paintings of the twelfth century AD. In 1978 an expedition from the Universities of Milan and Pisa, working at Kom Madi, not far from Medinet Madi, found a cult chapel with original and evocative wall-paintings on religious, historical and commemorative themes in the Greco-Egyptian style. Ten churches, decorated with sculpture and pictures dating to the early Christian period, have been discovered at Kom Madi and Medinet Madi, in the area of the ancient settlement of Narmouthis. The

◁ *Cartonnage mummy-casing from
Hawara (second century AD); the face of the
deceased is painted on a panel in typical
Faiyum style. (London, British Museum)*

△ *Two pictures (first century BC) from a
chapel at Kom Madi found by E. Bresciani.*
Top: *the sacrifice of the red bull.* Above: *a
symbolic hunt in the desert.*

Medinet Madi: Aerial Photographs and Photo-interpretation

The combination of scale drawings and photographs can provide a rich and metrically correct description of the layout of settlements. To produce cartographic reliefs, it is necessary for the buildings, or their remains, to be distinguishable on the ground and measurable with sufficient accuracy. Archaeological remains of a number of significant buildings are known from the ancient city of Gia, or Medinet Madi, including the temple of Renenutet (with its courts, dromos and kiosk) and some public buildings and churches. The majority of the buildings are still buried by sand, however.

One method used to create a topographical map of an ancient town is stereoscopic aerial photogrammetry. This requires that some characteristics of the photographs be known: such as the type and focal length of the camera used, and the altitude and exact position of the aircraft over the ground at the moment of each exposure. Unfortunately, in the case of Medinet Madi, the single aerial photograph available had been taken in 1934, was not stereoscopic and did not depict clear points of reference in the landscape.

However, by exploiting archaeological traces, it was possible to produce an interpretation of this photograph. It lacked the key element of topographical aerial photography – the

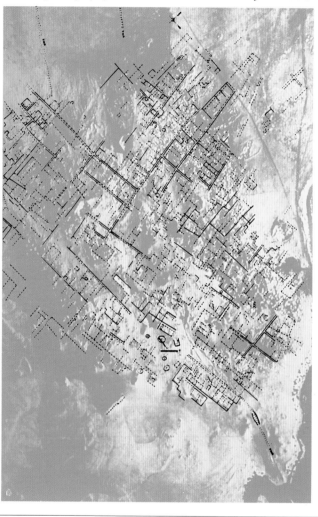

stereoscopic effect. All the same, some of the information that this would have provided was obtainable; the photograph had been taken early in the morning, when the sun was barely above the

horizon, so that even quite low ground features were casting long and pronounced shadows. Photo-interpretation by Alessandro Ercoli succeeded in distinguishing, with a greater or lesser degree of certainty, all the alignments of buildings consistent with the geometry of a city; the few elements with a different orientation that could be attributed to geological factors were omitted from the interpretation. It was then possible to draw almost the entire plan of the settlement from the shadows of the ruins as they appeared fifty years ago.

This plan was verified at the site, by comparing it with natural features which could be identified with certainty, and with those architectural details visible on the ground that could be matched to the lines on the photo-interpretation. Within the limits imposed by the small scale of the original photograph, there was a perfect correspondence between the map 'extracted' from it and that obtained by topographical survey.

◁ The reworking of a 1934 aerial photograph of Medinet Madi that resulted from the photo-interpretative work of A. Ercoli and W. Ferri in 1989.

excavation of church MM84A provided information that enabled computer techniques to be applied to Coptic archaeology. Synthesizing data from the excavation with other data from the same period, and using a system called 'Ashade 386', C. Marchini has experimented with making simple three-dimensional representations, or virtual maquettes, of the church.

One of the objectives of the University of Pisa expedition at Medinet

Madi has been to increase our understanding of the urban fabric of the ancient town from the Middle Kingdom to the late Byzantine Period, based on a systematic topographical survey and using methods drawn from other technologies, including photo-interpretation (see box).

In 1981 the Pisa team was engaged in a survey of the ancient sites of the south-west Faiyum within a radius of about 15

△ *Restorer Gianluigi Nicola working on a salt-encrusted offering table found in the tomb of Wadji (beginning of the second millennium BC) at Khelua.*

km (9 miles) of Medinet Madi: an area including Tebtunis, Talit and Kom el-Khamsin, Medinet el-Nahas (threatened by high, mobile sand dunes), and taking in Wadi Rayan, one of the most evocative areas of the western desert. The most important and unexpected find occurred at Kom Ruqaiya, or Khelua (an Arab toponym meaning 'cave', and also 'hermitage'). The ruined tomb complex here had already been identified and described by Dieter Arnold during a survey of the Faiyum in the 1960s. However, he was unable to name the owner of the tomb, since the chambers had been reduced to a huge pile of debris, and wind and sand had smoothed all the exposed surfaces, erasing the texts and parts of the

▽▷ *Renewed excavations by the Archaeological Mission of the University of Pisa have uncovered ten churches at Medinet Madi.*

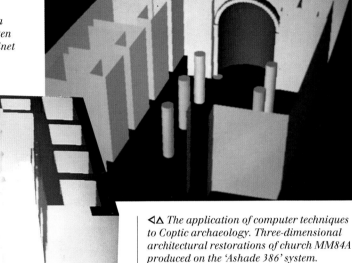

◁△ *The application of computer techniques to Coptic archaeology. Three-dimensional architectural restorations of church MM84A produced on the 'Ashade 386' system.*

sculpted scenes, even on the two pillars that were still standing.

The Pisa expedition discovered the lower part of a large male statue, now in the Museum of the Faiyum, at Karanis. Hieroglyphic inscriptions gave the name of the tomb-owner – Wadji (which may be translated as 'I prosper') – and his many important titles, including 'prince', 'governor', and 'head priest of the meadow', which refers to

the marshy area of the Faiyum favoured by the Middle-Kingdom pharaohs for hunting and fishing expeditions.

After a survey and three years of intense archaeological activity at Khelua (1992–4), two contiguous monumental tombs cut into the limestone cliffs have been excavated (T.Kh. A, the tomb of Wadji, and T.Kh. B). Shaft tombs of a little-explored Middle-Kingdom cemetery on the plateau have also been identified.

In both tombs the rock ceilings had collapsed due to weakness in the sedimentary limestone, and perhaps also because of an earthquake that may have occurred around the ninth or tenth centuries. The ceilings had broken into heavy blocks of between ten and thirty tons each, pulling down with them the facing blocks, pillars and everything else in the chamber. However, the fall had also protected what lay underneath

△ *The vestibule, or chapel, of the tomb of Wadji at the end of 1994, showing the twelve square pillars built from blocks of limestone. The main chamber – with sculpted walls and pillars, niches and the shaft to the subterranean funerary rooms – was built underground (see pictures on p. 49).*

it and prevented its destruction by wind, sand or tomb-robbers.

The vestibule and underground chamber of tomb Kh. B were cleared by the use (unusual in Egyptian archaeology) of very powerful cranes, weighing from twenty-five to fifty tons, to remove the fallen rock and extract the enormous blocks without damage. The underground chamber was found to be supported by pillars with broadly chamfered corners: a style that could have marked the transition phase towards the octagonal columns seen at Beni Hasan. This tomb – whose owner has not yet been identified (it may, perhaps, have been Wadji's mother Nebetmut) – seems to have been usable at least until the seventh to ninth centuries AD, when it was occupied by eremitic Christians who left a great deal of evidence of their presence.

In the vestibule of T.Kh. A (from which an access shaft leads to the sub-terranean funerary rooms found in 1992) were twelve square sculpted pillars. They were in varying states of preservation but, surprisingly, their colours had been preserved. The pillars were slightly chamfered at the corners and narrowed towards the top, and the figure of prince Wadji, accompanied by five columns of carved hieroglyphic text, was carved on each face. The hieroglyphic inscriptions document his striking variety of responsibilities, roles and honorific titles, and also record the name of his mother, Nebetmut. His name and titles were also found on the architraves of the underground chamber in large, elegant sculpted

◁ *In 1981 a statue bearing carved hieroglyphic texts relating to Wadji was discovered among the fallen ceiling blocks of the hypostyle hall in his tomb at Khelua. The statue is now in the Museum of the Faiyum at Karanis.*

hieroglyphs. Unfortunately, the reliefs that decorated the walls of the underground chamber are only partly preserved; they repeatedly show the prince sitting before a table holding a funerary meal, while rows of people bring him further offerings.

The vestibule, or chapel, of the tomb was built of stone blocks, and not cut into the rock like the underground chamber. It contained twelve square pillars and was reached via a ramp from the base of the cliffs. Against the back wall were the bases and feet (the legs were broken off at the ankles) of six large monolithic statues depicting Wadji standing with one hand on his chest and the other holding the border of his cloak. The headless bodies – reckoned to have been between 1.6 m and 1.8 m (5 ft 3 in. and 5 ft 11 in.) high – lay on the floor. In front of the base of the first statue on the left of the door was a fine offering table encrusted with salt (as were the bases and statues). It has now been restored.

It is the first time that private statues of this period, style and size have been found, and found *in situ* as part of the funerary architecture. But what is most extraordinary, and unknown elsewhere in pharaonic civilization, is that the statues decrease in size towards the corners of the room, which gives the effect of a wide perspective view.

Some of the problems that these tombs have raised remain unanswered. For example, under what pharaoh did Wadji live? The insistence of this dignitary – perhaps a man who originally came from the Faiyum – on his court titles and his relations with the (unnamed) ruler may indicate the

Δ *Virtual reconstruction of the vestibule of the tomb of Wadji. In the foreground are the statues of the prince and governor of the 'Land of the Lake', restored and replaced on their bases. Beyond the portal, with its hieroglyphic inscriptions, is the hypostyle hall, which has twelve pillars carved with sunk reliefs showing the deceased and accompanied by hieroglyphic texts. (Studio Giammazusti La Tozze, SOBECA, Rome)*

*Faiyum: Restoration and
Virtual Archaeology*

second part of the Twelfth Dynasty (Amenemhet III or IV). And what was the city for which Khelua served as the cemetery? Was it Gia/ Medinet Madi, whose Twelfth-Dynasty cemetery has not yet been found, or perhaps some other, still unidentified city in the Garaq basin? Could it have been the city that preceded the Greco-Roman Tebtunis?

Meanwhile, thanks to the work of the physical anthro-pologist Francesco Mallegni, something is known about Wadji from his skeleton, found in the burial chamber (see box on p. 50). He died at the age of fifty-six (quite an advanced age for the pharaonic period), suffered from osteoporosis and arthritis, had a healed fracture of a rib, and (as deduced from an examination of the bones of his right arm) practised archery. Procedures developed in the last few years to reconstruct the features of Egyptian mummies (plastic reconstruction and the use of computerized tomography to produce three-dimensional images) have made it possible to recreate the features that Wadji probably had in youth. Comparing the results of this exercise with the statues and reliefs from his tomb shows that his sculptors sought to present a realistic portrait of their subject.

Much work has been done at Khelua to identify the architectural structures and to assess the condition of the stonework and sculptures and the stability of parts of the monumental complex – all this with a view to restoring and rebuilding

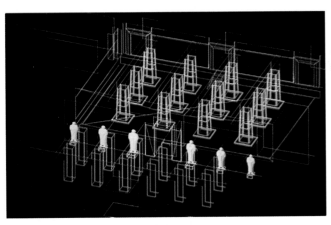

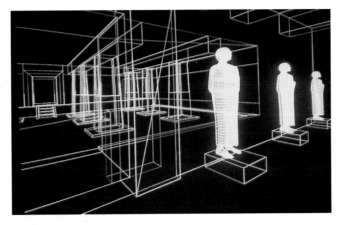

△ Top: *Sunk relief of prince Wadji on one of the twelve pillars of the great underground chamber in his tomb. The figure of Wadji, surmounted by five columns of hieroglyphic text, was carved on each side of each pillar.* Centre: *Two examples of preparatory studies for the virtual reconstruction of the reliefs of the vestibule and underground chamber.* Bottom: *Two completed virtual reconstructions of the underground chamber.*

the structures (pillars, statues) and roofs of the tombs in such a way as to respect the desert environment that gives this monument its charm. Computer-generated three-dimensional models of ruined monuments can now be produced in order to assess the environmental and aesthetic effectiveness of restoration proposals before work begins on the monuments themselves, and the Department of Egyptology at Pisa University has worked with such techniques for years (see the section of the preceding chapter that discusses the tomb of vizier Bakenrenef at Saqqara).

It was decided to apply these techniques to the tomb of prince Wadji (then only recently excavated), so as to provide an integrated architectural picture of a monument from the second millennium BC. Despite the damage to the tomb – the collapsed pillars, the statues knocked from their bases, and the wall-decoration mostly erased by the wind – enough reliable information and enough reconstructible elements

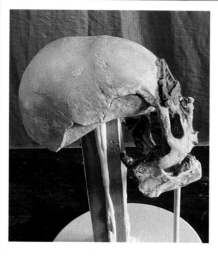
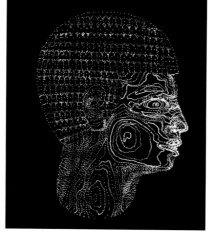
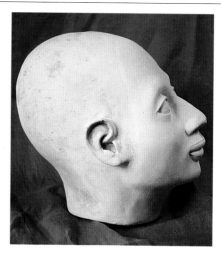

A Youthful Face for Prince Wadji

△▽ The transition from the incomplete cranium found in the mortuary chamber of Wadji's tomb to the proposed three-dimensional reconstruction of his face.

The methods, already used in the medico-legal world and in physical anthropology, to reconstruct a three-dimensional image of an individual face from the bones of the cranium are being developed to do the same for Egyptian mummies. Researchers have used both computerized tomography and physical methods.

*The method chosen to reconstruct the face of prince Wadji from the partially preserved cranium found by Edda Bresciani in his tomb at Khelua in 1993 is that described by Douglas H. Ubelhaker (*Human Skeletal Remains*). This uses calculations of facial-tissue thickness at the various points on the cranium (ten unequal points and eleven equal) proposed in the Rhine and Campbell tables (1980) and by Rhine, Mooer and Westen (1982); these indicate the measurements to be applied to the bone with the help of cylindrical markers. When the markers have been fixed in place, they are joined up using thin strips of plasticine, and the remaining uncovered areas are then filled in.*

The process ends with the refinement of the features. Reconstruction of the most characteristic facial elements – the form and size of the nose, the shape of the ears and the thickness of the lips – needs to be based on the general shape the cranium, but it is not possible to recreate them with the same degree of objective probability as can be done for other parts of the face.

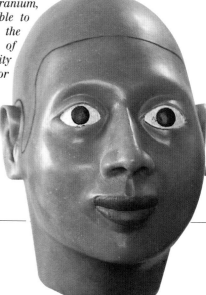

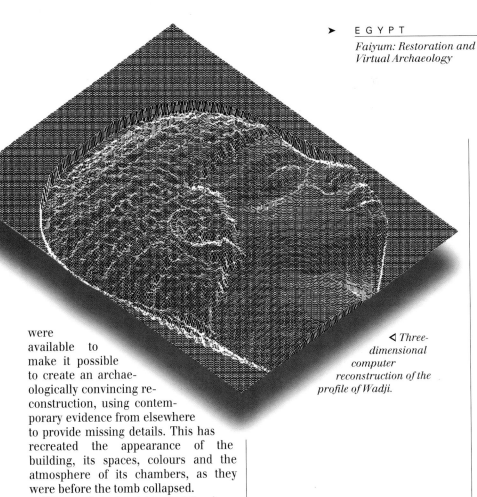

◁ *Three-
dimensional
computer
reconstruction of the
profile of Wadji.*

were
available to
make it possible
to create an archae-
ologically convincing re-
construction, using contemporary evidence from elsewhere
to provide missing details. This has
recreated the appearance of the
building, its spaces, colours and the
atmosphere of its chambers, as they
were before the tomb collapsed.

The result is that 'virtual visitors' can
move around inside the tomb. They can
admire the perspective of the statues in
the vestibule and pass through the great
door into the gloom of the underground
chamber. They can be guided by a simulated light that moves between the
pillars, revealing glimpses of the scenes
sculpted and painted on the walls –
before gradually illuminating them – and
they can move around a pillar to admire
the well-modelled profile of the prince.

This project has brought together
topographers, architects, experts in
computer graphics and photogrammetry and Egyptologists to create
a graphic record of the texts and the
scenes found in Wadji's tomb. Besides
generating suggestions for restoring
both the architectural features and the
decoration, the process has helped to
develop the use of virtual reality in
archaeology. Methods for rendering
sunk reliefs and shadows have been
refined, and new solutions sought for
the problems of the spatial representation of statues carved in the round, of
locating sources of illumination in
space, and of using filmed images in
conjunction with three-dimensional
animations.

▽ *Alongside a reconstruction of the prince's
face is his image beautifully sculpted in
stone; the sculpture was found in the tomb
during the excavations, on top of a pillar in
the underground chamber.*

Bibliography

N. Abbott, *The Monasteries of Fayum*
(Chicago, 1937).
E. Bresciani, 'Informatica ed egittologia
a Pisa', in *Geoarcheologia*, 1, 1990,
pp.61–78.
G. Caton Thompson and E.W. Gardner,
The Desert Fayum (London, 1934).
E. Doxiades, *The Mysterious Fayum
Portraits* (London and New York,
1995).
B.P. Grenfell, A.S. Hunt and D.G.
Hogarth, *The Fayum Towns and
Their Papyri* (London, 1900).
A. Vogliano, *Un'impresa archeologica
milanese ai margini orientali del
deserto libico* (Milan, 1942).

Karnak: A Temple in a Computer

Egypt

*T*he history of the temple to the god Amun at Karnak, the glory of the great capital of Thebes, is one of continuous metamorphosis over more than twenty centuries. Just like a gigantic body, this architectural expression of Egyptian theological concepts never stopped growing, evolving and transforming itself from 1900 BC to the fourth century AD, when the rise of Christianity brought the world of the ancient pagans to an end. All that remains today of the largest and most complex of all the temples of ancient Egypt are ruins and thousands of blocks of stone, scattered over a wide area.

The Great Temple of Amun is the most impressive temple complex of ancient Egypt, and is situated some 2 km (1¼ miles) north of the present-day town of Luxor in Upper Egypt. Between the two once lay the great capital of the New Kingdom – which the Egyptians called Waset and the Greeks Thebai, and which we know as Thebes. The temple complex was begun during the Middle Kingdom, under Senusret I (1971–1926 BC), and was developed and modified over more than two thousand years, although its structure remained the same during the whole of the New Kingdom (1550–1070 BC). Each pharaoh sought to make his own mark on this transcription in stone of the religious beliefs of the period, erecting new buildings or destroying others built by his predecessors.

Its plan reflected the ancient Egyptians' conception that the world was governed by the daily passage of the sun from east to west along the divine or celestial axis, and by the Nile, whose course from south to north marked the terrestrial axis, linked with the concept of territory and of the role and power of the pharaoh. The complicated, T-shaped structure of the temple is laid out along these two axes, in two ranges of buildings, punctuated by ten pylons (from the Greek *pylon*, 'gate'): great monumental gateways that lead between its courts and other structures. The first to sixth pylons are on the east–west (celestial) axis, and the seventh to tenth are located along the north–south (terrestrial) axis.

The first and westernmost pylon – the largest and most recent – was built by the pharaoh Nectanebo I (380–362 BC) during the Thirtieth Dynasty. Through this imposing entrance, which was never completed, one enters the first courtyard. On the far side of this the second pylon leads into the great hypostyle hall, which has the third pylon, built by Amenhotep III (1391–1353 BC), on its eastern side. The hypostyle hall, its ceiling held up by 134 gigantic columns, was a symbol of the primordial marsh; its northern part was built in the period of Seti I (1306–1290 BC) and its southern part in that of Ramesses II (1290–1224 BC). Beyond the third pylon is the point at which the terrestrial and celestial axes meet, marked by four obelisks erected by Thutmose I (1504–1492 BC) and Thutmose III (1470–1425 BC). Another two obelisks were added by Queen

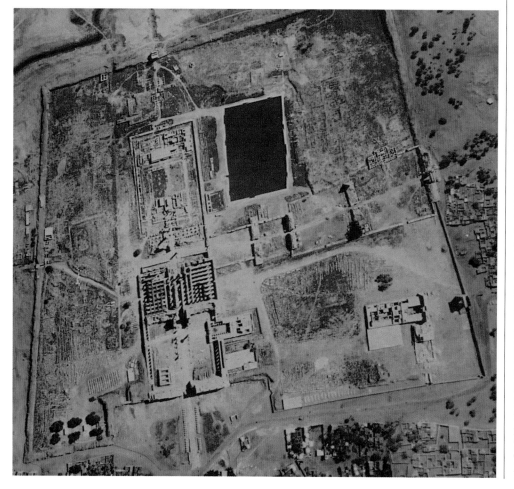

△ ▷ *The temple precinct of Amun in an aerial view and in a detailed plan: (1) avenue of ram-headed sphinxes; (2) first pylon; (3) temple of Ramesses III; (4) second pylon; (5) hypostyle hall; (6) obelisks; (7) third pylon; (8) fourth pylon; (9) fifth pylon; (10) sixth pylon; (11) Middle-Kingdom court; (12) Akhmenu of Thutmose III; (13) temple of Amun-who-hears-the-prayers; (14) Sacred Lake; (15) kiosk of Taharqa; (16) seventh pylon; (17) the 'Cachette Court'; (18) eighth pylon; (19) ninth pylon; (20) tenth pylon; (21) temple of Khons; (22) temple of Opet.*

one first enters the famous 'Cachette Court' – so called because at the beginning of the twentieth century a hidden space was discovered here in which around 17,000 bronze and 900 stone statues were concealed. This court is bounded on the southern side by the seventh pylon, to the east of which is the Sacred Lake: a great artificial basin symbolizing Nun, the primordial ocean. The eighth pylon was built by Hatshepsut and altered by Amenhotep II (1427–1401 BC).

The next two pylons (the ninth and tenth) were erected by Horemheb (1319–1307 BC) who, having restored the cult of Amun, demolished the temples dedicated to the solar god Aten (built by the 'heretic' pharaoh Akhenaten) and used the blocks (*talatat*) in building these pylons. To the west of the ninth pylon is a temple dedicated to Khons (a lunar god – in Theban theology the son of Amun and the goddess Mut, with whom he formed the 'Theban triad' – usually represented as a youth with the child's side-lock of hair, and often with a lunar disc on his head). Beyond the

Hatshepsut (1473–1458 BC) in the area between the fourth and fifth pylons.

To the east of the sixth pylon lies the oldest part of the temple, dating to the Middle Kingdom (2040–1640 BC), which is represented today only by a great courtyard bounded to the east by an imposing architectural complex (the Akhmenu).

Following the north-south axis, which starts between the third and fourth pylons and which was the route followed by the great royal processions,

tenth and southernmost pylon is an avenue flanked by a double row of ram-headed sphinxes (one of the many animals sacred to Amun). This avenue runs to the nearby precinct of Mut. There it joins the route linking the temple of Karnak with Luxor 3 km (1.9 miles) to the south, to which the god Amun travelled annually at the festival of Opet.

The temple of Karnak has long presented great problems for archaeologists seeking to comprehend the evolution of its build-ings, visualize all the stages of its develop-ment and under-stand the techniques used by its ancient

Middle Kingdom

Amenhotep I

Thutmose I and
Thutmose II

Hatshepsut

Thutmose III, Amenhotep II
and Thutmose IV

Amenhotep III

Horemheb and
Ramesses I

Seti I, Ramesses II, Seti II
and Ramesses III-XI

Bubastids

Kushites

Nectanebo I

Hakoris

Ptolemaic and
Roman Periods

53

◁ *Computer reconstruction of the canal that once linked the temple of Karnak to the Nile, showing the basin which opened out in front of the avenue of ram-headed sphinxes that precedes the first pylon. It was from here that the great procession of the festival of Opet departed and the sacred boat of Amun, together with those of Mut and Khons and that of the pharaoh, went up the Nile to the temple at Luxor.*

These researches have allowed Egyptologists to distinguish several stages in the development of this extraordinary monument. In the Middle Kingdom (2040–1640 BC) there was a first sanctuary, now entirely lost, that matched the court in front of the Akhmenu of Thutmose III. Under the first pharaohs of

architects. French Egyptologists of the CNRS (Centre Nationale de la Recherche Scientifique), working with their Egyptian colleagues at the Centre Franco-Egyptien at Karnak, decided to take the computer techniques developed by Electricité de France to study and monitor nuclear power stations and apply them to a detailed analysis of this long evolutionary process.

In 1986 they began to subject thousands of items of information and thousands of architectural and topo-graphical measurements to computer analysis, dividing and subdividing the complex structures of the temple into progressively simpler and more elementary forms so as to reduce them to easily definable geometric elements. This enabled them to obtain a series of virtual images of the spaces, structures and volumes of the Karnak complex that have helped to improve our knowledge both of the technologies used in antiquity and of the evolution of the site over a period of two thousand years.

△ *Thutmose III (1479–1425 BC) contributed notably to the enlargement and embellishment of the Karnak temple; he erected a third pair of obelisks and the majestic sanctuary called Akhmenu.*

◁ *The first pylon (from the Greek pylon, 'gate') of the temple was begun by the pharaoh Nectanebo I (380–362 BC) in the Thirtieth Dynasty (or perhaps by one of the early Ptolemies) and was never completed. This monument was intended to be the largest of all the pylons in the temples of ancient Egypt.*

*Karnak: A Temple
in a Computer*

◁ *Virtual reconstruction of the hypostyle hall, which lies between the second and third pylons. In this vast space, built under Seti I (1306–1290 BC) and Ramesses II (1290–1224 BC), rise 134 gigantic columns. The bas-reliefs on the perimeter walls, once vividly painted, illustrate episodes in the great liturgical festivals.*

the Eighteenth Dynasty (1550–1307 BC) the temple expanded westwards, and new pylons and structures were erected, including obelisks, the Sacred Lake and the processional way linking the temple of Karnak with that of Luxor. During the Nineteenth Dynasty (1307–1196 BC) work was begun on the building of the great hypostyle hall. At the end of the New Kingdom (1550–1070 BC) the temple of Khons was erected; and in the reign of the Thirtieth-Dynasty pharaoh Nectanebo I (380–362 BC) or later the first pylon, which forms the present entrance to the temple, was begun.

But what was the function of this magnificent temple that each pharaoh

Δ *The first courtyard lies between the first pylon and the second pylon (which leads to the great hypostyle hall). Its central area was occupied by a colonnade erected by Taharqa' (a pharaoh of Nubian origin, 690–664 BC) from which only a few of the columns have survived. The sacred boat of Amun paused here, before leaving the temple.*

wished to enlarge (or at least embellish) and where, according to information derived from the Harris papyrus, there were no fewer than twenty thousand priests of the cult of Amun? The ancient Egyptians called the temple of Karnak *Ipet isut* ('most select of places'), and it was the great harem of the god Amun, the 'unknowable', the king of the gods. From here – once a year, at the great festival of Opet at the end of the summer – a procession departed for the temple of Luxor, or *Ipet resyt* ('southern harem') as it was called in antiquity.

The sacred image of Amun was taken from its tabernacle in the most secret part of the

◁ *One of two 'heraldic pillars' (so called because they were carved with the emblems of Upper and Lower Egypt: the lotus, seen here, and the papyrus) that supported the roof of a vestibule.*

temple and placed on a simulacrum of a boat made of gilded wood, which was carried on the shoulders of the priests to the central part of the temple where the great obelisks stood. Here, the boats of Mut (the divine wife of Amun) and

their son Khons also arrived, brought from their own temples. The divine procession paused in the great court of the temple to await the royal boat, which arrived from the north; then, after the pharaoh had completed the sacred ablutions, the procession left the temple and headed for the landing-stage at the basin just beyond the first pylon. There each of the ritual boats was placed on its ceremonial boat which was then towed by another craft up the Nile as far as Luxor.

△ *Computer science provides a visual impression of the likely appearance of the polychrome bas-reliefs that decorated the temple walls.*

At Luxor the procession reformed among joyfully applauding crowds, and Amun of Karnak entered his 'southern harem'. In the most sacred part of the temple complex rites were celebrated that commemorated the divine birth of the ruler. In the half-light of the most secret rooms the mother of the king was magically impregnated by Amun, who assumed the appearance of her earthly spouse, and produced a new being, a divine son: the pharaoh.

As the earthly dwelling place of Amun, the temple of Karnak thus expressed in architecture a theological and political idea that saw in the king a fusion of the divine and the human, of heaven and earth, that would ensure eternal prosperity for his country. It was because of this that the pharaohs devoted particular attention to the sanctuary at Karnak, which, as a result, became the greatest temple complex of ancient Egypt.

△ *During the great liturgical festivals a procession of priests, dressed in long, white linen tunics and with shaven heads, carried on their shoulders the sacred boat of Amun contained in its* naos *(a Greek term referring to a simulacrum of a temple), from which protruded the prow and the stern decorated with a ram, the emblem of the god.*

The Puzzle of the Talatat

In the first years of his reign, Akhenaten (Amenhotep IV, 1353–1335 BC), who imposed the cult of the single solar divinity – the sun disc, or Aten – built a new temple to the Aten to the east of Karnak. Its walls were carefully built of small blocks of sandstone of regular size (56 × 26 × 22 cm, or 22 × 10 × 8¾ in.) decorated with polychrome bas-reliefs. Under Tutankhamun the ancient cult of Amun was restored, and Akhenaten's buildings were dismantled under Horemheb – with the material (over 400,000 blocks) reused for the foundation and the fill of new pylons (the second, ninth and tenth) erected to reaffirm the eternal glory of Amun. Dismantling the dangerous remains of one of Horemheb's pylons (the ninth), French archaeologists found around 12,000 decorated blocks (called talatat in Arabic) from Akhenaten's temple in the rubble fill.

Reconstructing Akhenaten's temple from these talatat is like a gigantic stone puzzle with an enormous number of variables. It would have taken a long time to solve because a large amount of the material was missing: many of the blocks had been reused by the Arabs for new buildings, and others had crumbled or been irremediably ruined by water seepage. A first group of talatat was manually reconstructed at the beginning of the 1970s, and the result is on show in the Museum of Ancient Egyptian Art at Luxor, but the complexity of the task made the reconstruction very partial.

In 1984, following on from slightly earlier US/Canadian work, French archaeologists of the Centre Nationale de la Recherche Scientifique decided to apply computer techniques to the problem. First, they created a database of digitized information about the blocks, stored on optical disc, to allow the creation of complex images from the data relating to each small element. They then incorporated an 'expert system': thus the Talatat Project was born.

The system proved capable of creating new assemblages of talatat, and so of proposing groupings and subgroupings. Images of the relevant blocks could be moved around, according to the system's suggestions, on a 'virtual wall' on the computer screen. The results so far obtained have provided new information, not only about the architecture of the complex of Karnak but also about the development of iconography, which is closely related to the establishment and evolution of the cult of the Aten.

△ Akhenaten (Amenhotep IV, 1353–1335 BC), the 'heretic' pharaoh who imposed the cult of a single solar divinity (the sun disc, or Aten), carved on a talatat.

◁ A virtual animation of the chapel that held the sacred boat of Amun, with priests carrying it out of the temple.

Bibliography

J. Baines and J. Málek, *Atlas of Ancient Egypt* (Oxford and New York, 1980).
J.C. Golvin and J.C. Goyan, *Les bâtisseurs de Karnak* (Paris, 1984).
J. Lauffray, *Karnak d'Egypte, domaine du divin* (Paris, 1979).
Various authors, *Karnak, le temple d'Amon restitué par l'ordinateur* (Paris, 1989).

The Royal Cemeteries of Thebes

Egypt

*O*n the east bank of the Nile, around 500 km (310 miles) south of Cairo, at the site of the present-day town of Luxor, lay the ancient city of Waset, better known under its Greek-derived name of Thebes. It was the capital of Egypt during the New Kingdom (1550–1070 BC) and one of the great cities of the ancient world. Today, only the imposing ruins of its temples remain as evidence of the size and glory of this site.

The cemeteries of Thebes, where Osiris (lord of the other world) and Anubis (the 'embalmer') reigned, lay to the west on the opposite bank of the Nile, spread over the slopes of the mountains, which at this point border the river. It was in the west that the sun-god Re, in his divine boat, was believed to end his daily journey across the sky and begin his voyage into the depths of the nocturnal world. Here were buried kings and princes, wives of the pharaohs and high officials of the empire, artists, workmen and also people of modest social status who, not having the means to build a real tomb, used a simple trench cut in the rocky ground.

The royal tombs of Thebes are grouped mainly in two particular sites at the northern and southern limits of the whole necropolis: the Valley of the Kings and the Valley of the Queens. Between the two lie the civil cemeteries (erroneously called the 'tombs of the nobles'), which are distinguished from the royal tombs by their architecture and, above all by their decoration. These cemeteries contain over five hundred tombs spread over a number of locations known by their modern names: Asasif, Dra Abu el-Naga, el-Khokha, Sheikh Abd el-Qurna, Qurnet Murai, Deir el-Medina and Deir el-Bahri.

The Valley of the Kings

The Valley of the Kings, a deep cleft in the limestone mountains, is called *Biban el-Moluk* ('the doors of the kings') in Arabic, evidently referring to the entrances of the many tombs, which were visible here even in antiquity. Branching out from the western side is a secondary valley, the West Valley. The tombs of only two pharaohs: Amenhotep III (1391–1353 BC) and Ay (1323–1319 BC), Tutankhamun's successor, have been found here.

The Valley of the Kings is overlooked by the mountain called el-Qurn, also known as the 'Theban horn', whose triangular form evokes that of a pyramid, the typical monument for royal burials of the Old Kingdom. It was probably the presence of this feature, considered sacred to the cobra goddess Meretseger, and the fact that access to the valley was difficult (which offered a certain degree of security) that encouraged the first pharaohs of the Eighteenth Dynasty (1550–1307 BC) to build their eternal resting-places here.

It is not known who was the first ruler to be buried in the valley. It may have been Ahmose (1550–1525 BC), the first pharaoh of the Eighteenth Dynasty, or his son Amenhotep I (1525–1504 BC), whose tombs have never been located with certainty; or perhaps Thutmose I (1504–1492 BC) or Thutmose II (1492–1479 BC), to whom tombs KV20/KV38 and KV42 respectively have been attributed.

KV20 is certainly one of the oldest tombs in the Valley of the Kings. Unique

◄ *A few kilometres north of Luxor the Nile makes a wide curve round the outlying spurs of the Theban mountains, where the royal tombs are located.*

VALLEY OF THE KINGS

◁ *Location map: The
Theban necropolis
lies in the valleys of
the mountains that
line the western bank
of the Nile, at Luxor.
In the cosmology of
the ancient Egyptians
the West was
associated with the
other world and the
world of the dead.*

planned for Thutmose I, founder of the Thutmosid dynasty, and later enlarged to hold the remains of his daughter Hatshepsut.

The building of a personal tomb, in which the transformation and the regeneration of the dead king would take place, was one of the principal preoccupations of the pharaohs in life. In general, the site was chosen early in the pharaoh's reign, and a plan was prepared for the monument, specifying not only the architectural character-istics but also the decoration and the passages from various ritual texts that would be illustrated on the walls to enable the dead king to overcome the numerous obstacles he would en-counter in the other world and to rise again assimilated to the sun.

Once the project was fully worked out and had obtained royal approval, the team of workmen, who lived in the neighbouring village of Deir el-Medina, was divided into two squads, each of which worked on one side of the tomb. They were allowed one rest day every

ten days, plus various festival days. The time it took to build a tomb varied (from a few months to some years, according to the size of the underground chamber) and the work was linked, at least within certain limits, with the duration of the pharaoh's reign.

The plans of the royal tombs are complex, but in general include a stairway, a long,

▷ *The gold mask
of Tutankhamun,
discovered by
Carter in 1922,
is the most
beautiful and
precious object
found in the
Valley of the
Kings.*

inclined rock-cut passage link-ing one or more halls and terminating in the burial chamber (called the 'gold room', gold being the metal that symbolized the incorruptible flesh of the gods) built to contain the sarcophagus of the pharaoh. This was also the place where, according to the religious doctrines of ancient Egypt, the king was transformed into a divine entity. From the funerary chamber his soul ascended to rejoin the sun god Re in heaven, and later in the New Kingdom this was symbolically repres-ented by the curved ceiling of the room with its illustration of the goddess Nut (personification of the sky). An architectural peculiarity distinguishes the tombs of the Eighteenth Dynasty from those of the Nineteenth. In the earlier tombs the descending passage turned to the left or right, usually at 90°, but in the later tombs the passage is straight and takes a shallower line.

In their fully developed form the tombs were decorated with polychrome bas-reliefs on the walls, representing scenes of the other world and of the voyage that the pharaoh had to undertake, overcoming many tests, to

in design, with its great curving and descending passages, it is the longest tomb in the Royal Valley (over 200 m, or 655 ft, long). Its burial chamber contained two quartzite sarcophagi, one of Thutmose I, the other of Hatshepsut, one of only three female pharaohs in Egyptian history. It is reasonable to assume that the tomb was initially

▷ *The Valley of the Kings contains
over eighty tombs.*
*Eighteenth Dynasty: Thutmose I
(KV38); Thutmose II (42);
Hatshepsut (20); Thutmose III
(34); Amenhotep II (35);
Thutmose IV (43); Amenhotep
III (33); Tutankhamun (62);
Horemheb (57). Nineteenth
Dynasty: Ramesses I (16);
Seti I (17); Ramesses II
(7); Merneptah (8); Seti
II (15); Siptah (47);
tomb of the sons of
Ramesses II (5).
Twentieth Dynasty:
Ramesses III (11);
Ramesses IV (2);
Ramesses VI (9);
Ramesses VII (1);
Ramesses IX (6);
Ramesses X
(18);
Ramesses XI
(4).*

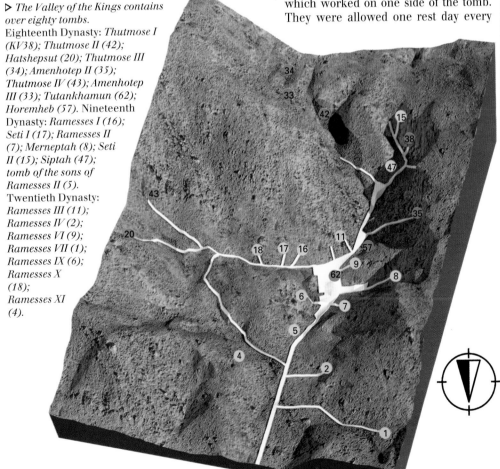

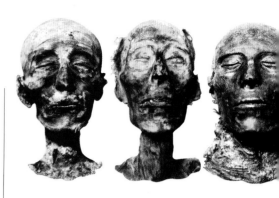

reach the kingdom of Osiris. The texts painted on the walls were taken from the great religious compositions of the period (such as the Book of Amduat, the Book of the Dead, the Book of the Gates, the Book of the Caverns, the Book of the Earth, the Litany of Re) and from commentaries, usually with related pictures. The presence of these texts in the tomb provided the deceased with knowledge of the magical formulae necessary to overcome the difficulties to be faced on the journey to heaven.

The Valley of the Kings continued to function as a royal cemetery during the whole of the Eighteenth, Nineteenth and Twentieth Dynasties up to the period of Ramesses XI (1100–1070 BC), who was the last pharaoh to be buried there. The ancient Egyptians called this site *ta sekhet aat* ('the great meadow'), and the road which now winds along the valley bottom follows the route that in ancient times was used to transport the royal sarcophagi to their eternal homes. Having buried the pharaoh,

▽ *The Valley of the Kings is called Biban el-Moluk ('the doors of the kings') in Arabic, referring to the tomb entrances clearly visible on the valley sides.*

▷ *In 1881 and 1898 two caches of royal and noble mummies (hidden c. 1000 BC for protection from tomb robbers) were discovered. They included the pharaohs whose heads are shown (left to right): Merneptah (found in the Valley of the Kings, tomb KV35, in 1898), Ramesses II and Seti I (both found at Deir el-Bahri, tomb DB320, in 1881).*

there was no need to return to the tomb, since the veneration of the pharaoh was practised in the cult temples, called 'houses of a million years', on the plain between the Theban mountains and the Nile.

Contrary to popular belief, the entrances to the royal tombs were only hidden during the Eighteenth Dynasty. From the time of Ramesses II (1290–1224 BC) they were visible, and the ancient police of the necropolis not only guarded the access road to the valley but also inspected the tomb entrances regularly to check that the seals affixed at the moment of burial remained intact. These precautions must have been ineffective, however, because archaeology and papyri of the period show that as early as the Eighteenth Dynasty tombs were being

desecrated and plundered. Ultimately, when nearly all the tombs had been violated, the priests had to remove the bodies of many of the pharaohs – including that of Ramesses II – away to at least two secret hiding places (one of which was the famous cache at Deir el-Bahri, located in a valley to the south).

Of more than eighty tombs so far found in the Valley of the Kings only around twenty belong to actual pharaohs. Others were used for princes, princesses, members of the royal family and senior officials, and a few were abandoned when the workmen ran into areas of unsuitable rock.

The first tourists to visit the Valley of the Kings were Greek and Roman. The historian Diodorus Siculus, who travelled to Egypt in 57 BC wrote: 'It is said that these are the tombs of the

ancient kings: they are splendid and have not left posterity the chance to make anything more beautiful.'

Thereafter the site was forgotten for centuries until it was 'rediscovered' by the Jesuit Claude Sicard, who travelled in Egypt between 1707 and 1712 and identified the sites of ancient Thebes and the Valley of the Kings. Many other travellers followed, some of whom made important studies and finds: in 1734 the Englishman Richard Pococke visited the valley and drew the first map of it – which included eighteen tombs, of which only half were accessible. Later, in 1769, the Scotsman James Bruce explored the tomb of Ramesses III (1194–1163 BC), and after the Napoleonic expedition of 1798 scholars discovered the tomb of Amenhotep III (1391–1353 BC) in the West Valley and made the first scientific survey of the necropolis. Some years later, in 1817, the Italian-born adventurer Giovanni Battista Belzoni identified the tombs of Ramesses I (1307–1306 BC), Seti I (1306–1290 BC) and Ay (1323–1319 BC), the last-named in the West Valley. Some time after these sensational discoveries the Englishman James Burton found two tombs without inscriptions, as well as a third (KV5) that has more recently been explored by Kent Weeks (see below). Between 1824 and 1830, in the years following the decipherment of the hieroglyphic script,

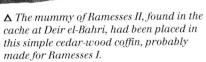

△ *The mummy of Ramesses II, found in the cache at Deir el-Bahri, had been placed in this simple cedar-wood coffin, probably made for Ramesses I.*

△ *The Theban mountains seen from the east, showing the civil cemeteries and the temple of Hatshepsut at Deir el-Bahri. Beyond the ridge lies the Valley of the Kings.*

John Gardner Wilkinson worked tenaciously in the Valley of the Kings, identifying tombs and allocating to them, for the first time, a numbering system still used today.

During the period 1828 to 1850 the valley was the destination of scholars, travellers and artists of great renown, including Jean François Champollion, Ippolito Rosellini, Robert Hay and Richard Lepsius. Only in 1898 did the Frenchman Victor Loret find the tombs of two great pharaohs in the valley – Thutmose III (KV34) and Amenhotep II (KV35) – and in the next year the smaller and more modest tomb of Thutmose I (KV38).

At the beginning of the twentieth century, in 1903, Howard Carter located the tomb of Thutmose IV (KV43) and, between 1903 and 1908, the Englishman Edward Ayrton found the virtually intact tomb of Yuya and Tjuyu (KV46) – the parents of queen Tiye, wife of Amenhotep III – and those of the pharaohs Siptah (KV47) and Horemheb (KV57). Some years later, in 1922, in collaboration with Lord Carnarvon, Carter found the most spectacularly preserved tomb of all: KV62, the famous burial of the boy-king Tutankhamun, pharaoh from 1333 to 1323 BC. The tomb contained an enormous wealth of funerary offerings and furniture. In recent years only the remarkable dis-

▷ *Anubis is one of the gods who appears most frequently in the iconography of the royal tombs. He was the lord of the cemetery and presided over the embalming ritual.*

coveries made in the valley by the American Egyptologist Kent Weeks have generated comparable international publicity.

In 1995 Weeks was cleaning inside tomb KV5 (found before 1835 by Burton

Nefertari and her Tomb

The Valley of the Queens contains the underground tomb of Nefertari, considered by many specialists to be the most beautiful tomb in the whole of Egypt. Because of severe problems affecting its splendid wall-paintings the tomb was closed to the public in the 1950s, and it was not until 1986, on the initiative of the Egyptian Antiquities Organization and the Getty Conservation Institute, that a first emergency intervention to stabilize the paintings was undertaken. After detailed multidisciplinary studies by an international team of scientists, conservation and restoration began in 1988. The plaster was first consolidated, and then the fragments of painting that had been detached from the walls were reattached. Finally the paintings were cleaned, with various types of dirt being removed, and the old destructive and unsightly filling was replaced with a mortar of exactly the same composition as that used in the Pharaonic Period.

Nefertari Meryetmut (a name meaning 'the most beautiful of all, beloved of Mut') very probably married the great pharaoh Ramesses II before he came to the throne. Her importance, over and above the many other wives of the pharaoh, is confirmed by the fact that she always accompanied Ramesses, even on important journeys – such as the one he made to Nubia in the twenty-fourth year of his reign (towards 1255 BC) for the inauguration of the small temple of Abu Simbel dedicated to the goddess Hathor. On the façade of this temple Nefertari's figure is sculpted at the same size as that of the pharaoh himself. This is most unusual, since sculptures of queens were normally so much smaller than those of the king: barely higher than his knees. Nefertari's origins remain a mystery, though there are some indications that her family came from the Thebes area and that she had a family link with the pharaoh Ay, who was possibly her father or grandfather. Although Nefertari had five or six children, none of them came to the throne. Ramesses II's son and successor Merneptah was born to another 'great royal wife', the queen Isenofret whose tomb has not yet been found.

The tomb of Nefertari suffered severe damage during the period of torrential rain that occurred in post-Ramessid times, but deterioration accelerated after its discovery by Schiaparelli, which evidently caused a change in the microclimate of the tomb. After the publication of scientific reports between 1970 and 1983, a first stage of emergency conservation took place in September 1986. Organized by the Egyptian Antiquities Organization and the Getty Conservation Institute, this dealt with about 20% of the wall surface and was aimed at stabilizing the paintings; more than 10,000 pieces of cotton gauze and Japanese paper were applied to the most endangered areas of the wall-paintings as a stop-gap measure. In 1987 agreement was reached between the two bodies on the full-scale implementation of conservation treatments defined and tested during the emergency conservation.

△▽ *Above:* axonometric view of the burial chamber and the rooms that contained some of the grave goods. *Below:* computer reconstruction of the descending passage that leads to the chamber.

In detail, the project set out to consolidate the paintings that were flaking and cracking, to remove dust and salt crystals, to consolidate loosened plaster, and to re-attach the fragments of detached plaster and pieces of rock whose loss had caused gaps to appear in the wall surfaces. It was also decided that repainting and the reconstruction of missing areas should be kept to an unavoidable minimum.

◁ The cartouche of Nefertari Meryetmut, whose name means 'the most beautiful of all, beloved of Mut'. Nefertari probably married the future Ramesses II before he came to the throne.

The conservation and restoration were preceded by in-depth biological, geological and mineral-crystallographic analyses using the most sophisticated scientific methods. Researchers also carried out non-destructive colorimetric analyses, computer-enhancement of the images, and multi-spectrum photographic analyses. The environmental conditions in the tomb were constantly subjected to microclimatic monitoring. Geological and hydrological studies were made of the entire area, so as to assess the geology of the rock out of which the tomb had been cut, and, consequently, the influence of the surrounding environment on its deterioration.

A multidisciplinary team of Egyptian and foreign specialists, including scientists, conservators and restorers, archaeologists, historians and engineers carried out tests to monitor the environmental conditions in the tomb, in order to identify the cause of the salt crystals

△ This restored painting in the burial chamber shows the three main divinities of the world of the dead: Anubis, Hathor-Imentyt and Osiris.

∇ Carvings on the south-east pillar of the burial chamber: the god Osiris; a *Djed*-pillar, symbolizing resurrection; Nefertari in the presence of the goddess Isis; and an aspect of Horus (*Hornedjhirotef*) linked with a priestly function.

that threatened to detach more of the already fragile plaster and propose an appropriate treatment. In February 1988 the final phase of conservation began under the direction of Paolo Mora. This involved reattaching the detached fragments and then cleaning the paintings by removing various types of dirt, such as atmospheric dust, black smoke and soot deposits from oil lamps (removed with a very soft rubber) and the fingerprints of tourists. Finally, the old, badly

applied filling was removed and replaced with a mortar similar to that used in the Pharaonic Period.

Restoration of the tomb was completed in April 1992, but the Egyptian authorities decided that it should remain closed to the public. The presence of too many visitors inside such a delicate monument would create the risk of altering the microclimate and, above all, increasing the humidity of the air, which could compromise all that the restoration had achieved.

To avoid depriving the tourists of the pleasure of such an artistic inheritance, the tomb of *Nefertari* was reopened in 1995. Meanwhile, alternative solutions for the preservation of these wonderful paintings are being sought. The idea that seems to command the greatest following is that of constructing an exact copy of the tomb somewhere in the Valley of the Queens; a project similar to what has already been done at the Lascaux cave in France.

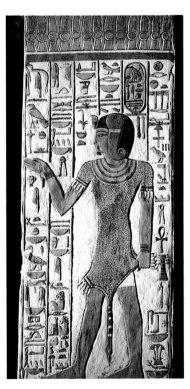

and sited at the beginning of the valley, about 30 m, or 100 ft, from the tomb of Ramesses II) when he unexpectedly penetrated into an entirely unknown part of the tomb and discovered an exceptional series of funerary chapels. With ninety-five chambers so far discovered, the tomb has a completely original architectural layout and is one of the largest in the valley. The initial investigation has indicated that many of Ramesses II's fifty-two sons must have been buried here; four of their names have so far been identified on the tomb walls. Two long corridors join at right angles to make a T-shaped tomb, and, most unusually, there was a giant figure of Osiris, carved out of the rock, in a niche at the point where the corridors meet. This tomb, although it was robbed in antiquity, will certainly continue to provide new information about the period and the family of Ramesses II.

The Valley of the Queens

The Valley of the Queens – so named by Champollion – is a wadi located in the most southern part of the Theban necropolis containing more than a seventy-five burials, the earliest dating

△ *The stopper of one of the compartments of the canopic chest in Tutankhamun's tomb depicts the young pharaoh wearing the classic* nemes *headdress.*

from early in the Eighteenth Dynasty (around the sixteenth century BC). Of the decorated tombs, the earliest dates to the time of Seti I and, under him and Ramesses II, was used for the interment of royal wives. Later, during the Twentieth Dynasty, Ramesses III also prepared tombs for his sons there.

The site was chosen because it was considered sacred, and therefore suitable for a royal cemetery. Its sacred qualities were its closeness to the so-called 'Theban horn', and the presence of a cave-waterfall whose form and setting suggested religious and funerary significance; the cave could have represented the abdomen or uterus of the celestial cow (one of the manifestations of the goddess Hathor), from which gushed forth waters that prefigured the imminent rebirth of those buried in this privileged place. The burials in the Valley of the Queens can be divided into two stylistic groups: the first includes the funerary shafts, which date to the Eighteenth Dynasty (1550–1307 BC); the second consists of the great Ramessid tombs of the Nineteenth and Twentieth Dynasties (1307–1070 BC). The latter are complex in structure and represent true funerary apartments: simplified versions of those in the Valley of the Kings. Burials of the remains of the wives of the pharaohs began only in the early Nineteenth

▽ *An historical photograph of the room dubbed by Carter the 'Treasury', adjoining the burial chamber, with a* naos *in gilded wood supporting a figure of Anubis wrapped in a shawl.*

△ *The burial chamber in Tutankhamun's tomb, found by Howard Carter in 1922. This is the only part of the tomb decorated with wall-paintings. At the centre is a great quartzite sarcophagus that contains the first of the three coffins holding the mummy; only these objects have been left in situ.*

◁ *This unguent holder in the form of the god Bes was part of Tutankhamun's rich funerary treasure. (Egyptian Museum, Cairo)*

Dynasty with the inhumation of Sitre, wife of Ramesses I and mother of Seti I. After the end of the Ramessid period the site was methodically plundered by thieves, as judicial papyri and other evidence attests. During the Third Intermediate Period (1070–712 BC), from the Twenty-first Dynasty, the tombs in the valley were systematically reused for the burial of persons of non-royal blood connected with working the land of the immense priestly estates. Transformed into a cemetery for the people at the beginning of the Roman Empire, the Valley of the Queens retained its mystique until the middle of the fourth century AD.

From antiquity onwards many of the tombs in the valley suffered severe problems associated with the hydrological and petrological characteristics of the site. The problem of areas of poor rock must have faced the workmen who built the tombs in the Valley of the Queens 3,500 years ago, forcing them to employ such techniques as the use of *muna*, a special plaster often used to face all the walls and ceilings of the underground chambers. Sometimes the rock was of such inferior quality that the architects preferred to stop work and begin again elsewhere – which explains the number of tombs left unfinished. In addition, there is much evidence of a period of torrential rain in post-Ramessid times, which had a devastating effect on the tombs.

The first person to conduct systematic excavations in the Valley of the Queens

was the Italian Ernesto Schiaparelli, director of the Egyptian Museum, Turin, who worked on the site between 1903 and 1906 with Francesco Ballerini. It was his excavations that uncovered all the most important tombs in the valley (for example those of the children of Ramesses III: Sethhirkhopshef, Amenhirkhopshef, and Khaemwaset), but his most extraordinary achievement was the identification of the tomb of Nefertari, the 'great royal wife' of Ramesses II. At the end of 1906, when Schiaparelli stopped work in the Valley of the Queens, at least thirteen tombs had been discovered in addition to those already explored between 1826 and 1854.

It was only in 1970 that a series of annual expeditions was begun by the Centre Nationale de la Recherche Scientifique (CNRS) of Paris and by the Centre for Study and Documentation of Ancient Egypt (CSDAE) of the Egyptian Antiquities Organization (EAO). The work involved cleaning and completely resurveying the site, as well as a systematic study of all the burials in the valley. The valley was restored to its earlier state by the removal of debris and spoil heaps which had altered the landscape, including those from Schiaparelli's excavations.

Bibliography

A. Dodson, *After the Pyramids: The Valley of the Kings and Beyond* (London, 1997)

E. Hornung, *The Valley of the Kings, Horizon of Eternity* (New York, 1990).

J. McDonald, *House of Eternity: The Tomb of Nefertari* (London and Malibu, 1996).

N. Reeves, *The Complete Tutankhamun* (London and New York, 1990).

N. Reeves and R. Wilkinson, *The Complete Valley of the Kings* (London and New York, 1996).

J. Romer, *The Valley of the Kings* (London, 1984).

E. Schiaparelli, *Esplorazione della 'Valle delle Regine'* (Turin, 1923).

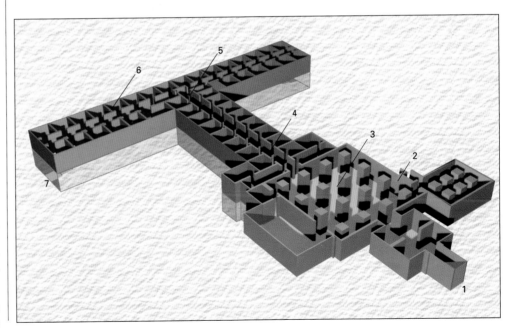

△ *In Tomb KV5, originally investigated before 1835 by the English traveller James Burton, unsuspected passages and chambers have been found as a result of excavations being conducted by Kent Weeks: (1) entrance; (2) area examined by Burton; (3) atrium with columns; (4) corridor; (5) statue of Osiris; (6) funerary chapels; (7) descending stairway.*

The Adventure of Abu Simbel

Egypt

The temples of Abu Simbel are on the left bank of the Nile in the region called Nubia, downstream of the second cataract and close to the Egyptian border with Sudan. The architectural complex at Abu Simbel is the most notable of this whole vast area, in which the pharaohs constructed many important temples. These were the subject of a spectacular salvage operation in the 1960s under the aegis of UNESCO, during the building of the Aswan High Dam.

The site of Abu Simbel was rediscovered in March 1813 by the Swiss traveller and orientalist J.L. Burckhardt, who also discovered the city of Petra, in Jordan. It consists of two rock-cut temples, both built by Ramesses II: the larger was dedicated to the sun-god Re-Horakhty, and the smaller to the goddess Hathor. Burckhardt, who travelled disguised as an Arab under the name of Ibrahim Ibn Abdullah, found the entrances blocked by sand, and – unable to enter the temples – had to be content with glimpses of the monumental façades.

Only in October 1815 was the English traveller and antiquarian William John Bankes, accompanied by the Italian Giovanni Finati, able to enter the small temple. In August 1817, after a month of work, Giovanni Battista Belzoni (an Italian-born explorer in the service of

△ *Computer restoration of the façade of the Great Temple of Abu Simbel. This is how the monument must have looked at the time of construction, with the four colossal statues of Ramesses II carved into the rock and brightly painted. It is thought that the head of the first colossus to the south, which today lies at its feet, collapsed shortly after the temple was built.*

◁ *Location map: Abu Simbel lies on the west bank of Lake Nasser, below the second cataract of the Nile and near the border with Sudan, around 850 km (530 miles) south of Cairo.*

the English consul Henry Salt) had removed the great mass of sand that blocked the entrance and was able to reach the interior of the Great Temple for the first time.

The Great Temple of Abu Simbel has a rock-cut façade about 30 m (100 ft) high and 35 m (115 ft) wide, decorated with four colossal seated statues of Ramesses II each almost 21 m (70 ft); next to the

vast legs of these colossi are smaller statues of the main members of the royal family. Above the entrance of the temple, in a central position, there is the image of the god Re-Horakhty with a falcon's head, while the upper cornice of the façade is decorated with a row of twenty-two statues of baboons. Beyond the vestibule is an immense hypostyle hall, its roof supported by eight pillars, followed by a second hypostyle hall. Beyond this is a second vestibule that opens onto the sanctuary – the small cult room at the western end of the temple.

This introduction is essential to understanding the religious sense of a building in which the architectural and decorative details carry both theological significance and a precise message: that

of the celebration of the living pharaoh, not only as king and victorious ruler but also as god.

The four statues of the façade depict Ramesses seated on his throne, wearing the double crown of Upper and Lower Egypt. Beside the legs of each were many smaller statues, no higher than the knee of the pharaoh. These represent his wife Nefertari (three statues) and other relatives, including his mother Mut-Tuy, daughters Meryetamun, Bintanat and Nebettawy, and two sons, the princes Ramesse and Amenhirkhopshef. Carved on the thrones in sunk relief were the countries and the peoples defeated during Ramesses' military campaigns. Above the entrance is a great statue of the god Re-Horakhty. This forms part of a rebus on Ramesses II's throne-name II (*Usermaatre*), since the hieroglyph *user* (the head and neck of an animal), and an image of the goddess Maat, the personification of cosmic order, are carved one on either side of the central figure of the god Re.

Inside the hypostyle hall, sunk reliefs portray the military campaigns the king fought in Syria and Libya and the

◁ *Cartouche carved on the base of one of the statues of the façade of the Great Temple. It denotes the name assumed by Ramesses II when he came to the throne as king of Upper and Lower Egypt: Usermaatre setepenre ('the god Re is great in truth and justice; the chosen of Re').*

famous battle of Qadesh against the Hittites: one of the most significant military episodes of Ramesses II's reign. The Osirid colossi of the hall, which show the pharaoh assimilated to Osiris, the principal god of the dead, are evidence of the eternal continuation of his royal role in the next world. Alongside the bas-reliefs on military themes, however, there is no lack of explicit references to the deification of the pharaoh. For example, there is a representation of Ramesses making an

◁ *Detail of polychrome sunk relief on the pronaos of the Great Temple, showing Ramesses II wearing the Blue Crown headdress. It is part of a scene depicting the battle of Qadesh, which the king fought against the Hittites in Syria in the fifth year of his reign.*

▽ *The original façade of the Great Temple. A stereo-photograph made before the temple was dismantled in the 1960s and rebuilt some 200 m (650 ft) further from the river and 65 m (215 ft) higher up, to escape the rising waters of Lake Nasser.*

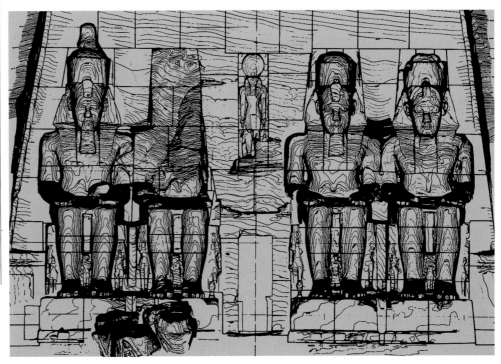

▷ *Detail of one of the eight pillars, fronted with colossal statues of the king around 10 m (33 ft) high, that support the ceiling of the* pronaos. *The king holds the attributes of Egyptian kingship: the heka (crook) and the* nekhakha *(flail). In the northern part of the* pronaos *the figures wear the double crown of Upper and Lower Egypt; in the southern part they wear only the white crown of Upper Egypt.*

offering in front of the sacred boat of his deified self. This stress on the pharaoh's divine nature reaches its apogee in the statues of the sanctuary, where, in front of a small altar where the *naos* with the sacred boat rested, there are four statues of the main gods of the period: Ptah of Memphis, Amon-Re of Thebes, Re-Horakhty of Heliopolis and the deified pharaoh himself.

The alignment of the Great Temple was calculated in such a way that on two occasions in the year the first rays of the morning sun, adored by the twenty-two baboons on the upper frieze of the façade, shine along the axis of the building, through the hypostyle halls and vestibules and into the sanctuary. There they illuminate, in pairs or singly, the statues of the deified pharaoh and of the solar gods Amon-Re and Re-Horakhty, while the statue of Ptah, is only touched by a strip of light and never completely illuminated.

Since the sun only reaches the statues of the sanctuary so directly on two days in the year (20 February and 20 October) it is logical to suppose that one of these dates corresponds to a significant date in Ramesses' reign. Although information about the chronology of events during his reign is fairly limited, it is known that both the temples at Abu Simbel were built in the first part of the reign. Astronomical calculations have shown that the heliacal rising of the star Sirius-Sothis (when, having been invisible while passing behind the sun, the star moves away from it and becomes visible again) occurred on 22 June in around 1260 BC, the year that the thirtieth anniversary of Ramesses' accession was celebrated. The Egyptians made the beginning of their civil year coincide with such phenomena, and it is known from

△ *The* pronaos *of the Great Temple is 18 m (59 ft) long, and its ceiling is supported by two rows of four colossi. This was the hall that Giovanni Battista Belzoni first entered in 1817, after removing the sand that blocked the entrance.*

epigraphic sources that the king's fifth and sixth jubilees were celebrated on the first day of the first month of the season of *peret* (sowing) – corresponding to 22 October. It is reasonable, therefore, to surmise that it was Ramesses' thirtieth jubilee that the architect of the Great Temple intended to celebrate in stone when the rays of the sun illuminated both the god Re-Horakhty and the deified pharaoh, identified with the solar god.

When the Egyptian government under President Nasser decided to build

△ *Twice a year, in October and in February, the sun's rays shine exactly along the axis of the temple and across the* pronaos *to the sanctuary –the small room at the western end of the temple – where they illuminate four statues of the gods (one of them the deified Ramesses II). This was probably engineered to celebrate Ramesses II's thirtieth jubilee.*

the Aswan High Dam, so creating an enormous lake (Lake Nasser), the temples of Abu Simbel – like many other lesser-known temples between Aswan and Abu Simbel – seemed to have been condemned to vanish beneath its waters. UNESCO launched an international campaign to rescue all the monuments in the area concerned. Between 1964 and 1968 both the temples at Abu Simbel were dismantled and rebuilt in the same alignment and layout about 200 m (650 ft) further from the river and 65 m (215 ft) higher up.

Bibliography

W. Emery, *Egypt in Nubia* (London, 1965).

W. MacQuitty, *Abu Simbel* (London, 1965).

T. Säve-Söderbergh (ed.), *Temples and Tombs of Ancient Nubia* (London and New York, 1987).

△ *Above the entrance to the Great Temple is a niche with a statue of the god Re-Horakhty placed between the hieroglyphic sign for the word user and an image of the goddess Maat. This group spells out the throne-name of the King, Usermaatre.*

▷ *At the back of the sanctuary are statues of the main divinities of the Ramessid period (Amon-Re, Re-Horakhty, Ptah) and the deified Ramesses.*

Çatal Hüyük:
The Origins of the City

*I*n the southern part of the Central Anatolian plateau rises a large mound dating to the seventh millennium BC: the site of Çatal Hüyük, one of the most remarkable settlements of early antiquity. In the small sector that has so far been studied over a hundred almost identical mud-brick houses were found crowded together. There were no entrances or streets, and the internal walls were decorated with extraordinary paintings showing scenes of hunting, bulls, mysterious geometric motifs and female divinities. Was this the 'oldest city in the world'?

Çatal Hüyük (a toponym meaning 'fork mound') lies some 40 km (25 miles) south of the city of Konya, and its Neolithic site is estimated to cover more than 12 hectares (30 acres). The original excavations by the British archaeologist James Mellaart in the 1960s, which covered only one-thirteenth of this area, unearthed a stratigraphic sequence of thirteen levels dating between 6800 and 5400 BC, according to the dating proposed by Mellaart. In the study the many houses excavated were made of local materials (sun-dried bricks and reeds) and were crowded together, with no gaps between them and no real defensive walls surrounding them in what has frequently been described as a 'beehive' type of layout.

There appeared to be no street network, and most of the perimeter walls were party walls. Access to the houses must therefore have been across the roofs, which were all flat. Each of the houses occupied an area of around 25 sq m (30 sq yd) and had an opening in the roof that acted as an entrance, skylight and chimney all at the same time. A single, roughly square room formed the main part of the house, and there was also an annexe, in the form of a small space that served

▷ *Many statuettes found at the site recall the Mother Goddess, who was linked to the concept of fertility.*

△ *Çatal Hüyük (a Turkish toponym meaning 'fork mound') as it is today. A small part of this Neolithic town, which has a total surface extent of over 12 hectares (30 acres), was excavated in the 1960s by the British archaeologist James Mellaart. Some thirty years later, in 1994, archaeological work was restarted by Ian Hodder of Cambridge University.*

Çatal Hüyük:
The Origins of the City

Pottery-making was quite well-developed at Çatal Hüyük and reached a high level of accomplishment, as shown by this burnished terracotta vessel from one of the houses of level IV.

as a storeroom. The walls, which contained many niches, were plastered and whitened with gesso, and were often decorated with paintings. Groups of houses, separated by small spaces, were each arranged around a larger internal space that functioned as a meeting place.

Alongside these small houses there were quite a number of other, larger structures that probably served as sanctuaries. Their walls were decorated with paintings of bulls, sometimes in relief, and with bulls' heads modelled in plaster, often incorporating the actual horn cores of aurochs (*Bos primigenius*). The frequency with which bovids were depicted was perhaps related to the cult of a bull god (not unlike that found in Crete during the Bronze Age, in Minoan and Mycenaean times) that may have grown up after the domestication of the first bovids – which in Anatolia may have occurred much later than elsewhere. Other pictorial themes were scenes of hunting, pictures of vultures, scenes relating to the cult of the dead and enigmatic geometric motifs surprisingly similar to those on modern Anatolian *kilim* carpets.

▷ *Location map: Çatal Hüyük lies in the centre of the Anatolian plateau, south of modern Konya, on one of the main trade routes.*

ÇATAL HÜYÜK

Interestingly, the chronological distribution of the sanctuaries and of the houses with wall-paintings is different, with the sanctuaries (numbering around forty) concentrated especially in levels VI and VII, while the paintings were found only in levels III to X.

The paintings connected with hunting are likely to have had a magic

▽ *The excavations at Çatal Hüyük show that it consisted of a conglomeration of virtually identical houses (1), interspersed with sanctuaries (2), all crowded together. Since there were no spaces between the houses, people must have moved around and entered the buildings via the roofs. There was no defensive wall around the settlement, but the outer houses had thicker perimeter walls.*

or ritual purpose: as in Palaeolithic cave art, it seems that people believed that success in hunting could be magically assisted by depictions of the prey. The pictures related to the cult of a bull-god may reflect the beliefs of a society based essentially on hunting and gathering. Their disappearance may be connected with the profound economic and spiritual evolution that accompanied the transition to an economy based on agriculture and stock-rearing. With the development of this economy came the rise of more truly Neolithic cults (also in evidence at Çatal Hüyük) of divinities connected with the concepts of fertility and fecundity – like that of the Mother Goddess, who is sometimes associated with such animals as the bull and the leopard, both associated with the idea of a vital reproductive force. Great importance was also attached to the cult of the dead, who were buried under the floors of the houses together with funerary goods. However, they were only buried after their bodies had been exposed outside the houses on special platforms, and defleshed by vultures (a custom documented by paintings found in the sanctuaries of level VII).

Examination of the many artifacts found in the excavations reveals a high frequency of very valuable objects made not only of flint but also of obsidian. The abundance of blades and daggers of obsidian – volcanic glass, which comes from the Hasan Dağ (a now extinct volcano visible from the site and depicted in a remarkable wall-painting) – makes it probable that Çatal Hüyük was one of the earliest centres to trade in this much-prized raw material. The finding of a block of copper-related slag also indicates a knowledge of metal ores, and the discovery of certain terracotta stamps, oval or circular, decorated with geometric motifs

△ *An enormous bull, painted in red ochre, decorates on of the walls in a sanctuary of level III. This painting ha often been misinterpreted as a hunting scene, but was probably related to a bull cult.*

▽ *A finely made necklace of hard stone and shell was found in a female burial of level VI (c. 6000 BC). (Konya Archaeological Museum)*

suggests they may have been seals – the oldest so far found – used to assert the ownership of objects. Agriculture was a vital means of sustenance for the population of Çatal Hüyük, as many finds of cereals (wheat, barley and spelt) show, but the rearing of animals (predominantly caprids) provided the greater part of the meat consumed (around 90%). This was supplemented by the meat of wild animals, which continued to be hunted (hunting was always important in the economy of the site).

The excavations have revealed the existence of an urban conglomeration of notable complexity and size in a Neolithic culture with a relatively highly developed religious life. All the

▷ *One of the most famous statuettes found in level II (c. 5750 BC). A female figure is giving birth, seated between two leopards. This is probably related to the Mother Goddess. (Ankara, Museum of Anatolian Civilizations)*

same, this does not mean that Çatal Hüyük should be seen as the 'first city'. Its houses of equal size, plus the absence of specialized zones, clearly show that it lacked the hierarchical organization characteristic of a city. Instead, Çatal Hüyük seems to have been a great proto-urban centre – the first so far discovered. Here we see the beginnings of urban life, trade and organized religion.

▽ *The walls of the houses were decorated with beautiful paintings, most now held at the Museum of Anatolian Civilizations in Ankara.*

△ *A wall-painting in a sanctuary of level VII (c. 6200 BC). It depicts funerary rites in which the bodies of the deceased were exposed on special platforms to be defleshed by vultures before they were buried inside the houses.*

▽ *Computer reconstruction by a German team from Karlsruhe of a sanctuary dedicated to the cult of a bull divinity, the expression of the male fertilizing principle and the complement of the Mother Goddess. The back wall is decorated with bulls' heads in plaster and the imprints of hands. Sets of actual bulls' horns (bucrania) were fixed to the benches.*

Bibliography

I. Hodder, *The Domestication of Europe* (Oxford and Cambridge, MA, 1990).

J. Mellaart, 'Excavations at Çatal Hüyük, 1963, Third Preliminary Report', in *Anatolian Studies*, XIV, 1964, pp. 39–119.

J. Mellaart, 'Çatal Hüyük West', in *Anatolian Studies*, XV, 1965, pp. 135–156.

J. Mellaart, *Çatal Hüyük: A Neolithic town in Anatolia* (London, 1967).

J. Mellaart, *The Neolithic of the Near East* (London, 1975).

Discovering the Ancient Land of Magan

Oman

*O*nly over the last two decades have the outlines of the recent prehistory of the Oman peninsula become clear. Careful investigations using modern archaeological techniques have revealed the evolution of an indigenous culture based largely on the local economy but also influenced by contact with the great urban civilizations of the third millennium BC: those of Mesopotamia and the Indus valley. The interaction of Arabian, Iranian, Indian and African elements that characterizes this region today has very ancient roots.

More than a hundred prehistoric sites have been identified along the coast of Oman, and from the sixth to the middle of the third millennium BC one can relate these centres, inhabited by fishermen and shell-gatherers, to the complex evolution of the coastline, as the sea (slightly higher in level than today) created large lagoons, which have now silted up. This environment provided small population groups with a variety of resources – aquatic birds, crustaceans and fish from the lagoons, complemented by hunting in the inland steppe area and by the fruits of the sea. The inhabitants of these coasts would doubtless have gained a certain mastery of seamanship, probably in boats that were rather frail.

Various developments occurred to disturb this equilibrium. At the end of the fourth millennium BC an agricultural economy developed in the inland centres, probably as a result of the development of copper mining in the mountains to meet the needs of the far-off urban centres of Mesopotamia (where this region was called the 'land of Magan'). The coastal communities were closely linked with those in the interior, to which they exported marine products (salted or dried fish and artifacts made of shell) in exchange for agricultural products and copper.

Then, towards the middle of the third millennium BC, there appeared a new culture – the Indus civilization, located in modern-day Pakistan and north-west India – which was also interested in the copper of the Omani mountains. Development of the coastal site of Ras al-Junayz and nearby Ras al-Hadd in eastern Oman, investigated by a Franco-Italian and a British expedition, was probably related to this. Ras al-Junayz was only occupied during the

▽ *Excavations at Hili, an oasis in the interior of Oman, have uncovered settlements based on a predominantly agricultural economy and dating to the end of the fourth millennium BC.*

RAS AL-JUNAYZ

◁ *Location map: Ras
al-Junayz lies at the
most easterly point of
Oman.*

winter (the summer monsoon winds prevented boats using the bay), but its inhabitants erected buildings of mud brick like those built in the oases of the interior. These buildings were used as places of work and storage by a community which, although living above all on fishing, was closely involved in a network of long-distance trade.

Molluscs furnished additional food, and some kinds, for example *Conus* or *Pinctada* (pearl oysters), were made into rings with the aid of tools made of worked flint from the enormous deposits of the nearby Jebel Saffan. A large number of date-stones confirm that foodstuffs were imported from the agricultural zones. Pottery was used at the site in this period, and this, too, came from the interior.

Evidence of trade with the Indus civilization is provided by many of the objects found at the site. In particular, there are shards of large jars made in the Indus valley; these are thought to have been used to transport foodstuffs (and so, in a sense, were the predecessors of amphorae). Some of the shards have brief inscriptions incised on them in the script of the Indus civilization (which has not yet been deciphered). A painted jar, an incised copper seal peculiar to the Indus and a comb made of elephant ivory are further evidence of the contacts between the two cultures.

The site occupied a shallow bay to the south of the promontory. During the winter, goods from boats sailing from the coast of Pakistan on the monsoon winds were transshipped here for onward transport to the oases of the interior. Ras al-Junayz was just one stage in the system of trade and navigation; there is nothing to suggest (though also nothing to disprove) that it was from this site that the copper mined in the interior was exported to the Indus valley.

The inhabitants of the village traded their own products – large mollusc-shells, as well as shell rings – with the crews of incoming vessels. Such mollusc-shells, worked to form drinking vessels, have been found in the Royal Tombs of Ur in Mesopotamia. Moreover, a manganese oxide of local origin, pyrolusite, was ground to make a black powder used as an unguent (kohl) and

kept in the shells of small molluscs of the genus *Anodara* – and *Anodara* shells containing a black powder have also been found in the Royal Tombs of Ur. For all that they have left no traces, there were probably other exports: for example, sea-turtle shells, which were prized by the Sumerians, or the operculi of molluscs, which, when ground up, were an essential ingredient in perfumes for incense.

During the excavations at Ras al-Junayz, in a building dated to around 2200 BC, evidence was unexpectedly found that underlined the importance of the relationships between different cultures. This took the form of two small seals of local manufacture, each with three marks identifiable as written symbols. None of the symbols has an equivalent in the writing system of

△▷ *Computer reconstructions of some of the
mud-brick buildings unearthed at Ras al-
Junayz. They appear to be similar to
buildings excavated in the interior of Oman.*

Mesopotamia (cuneiform) or in that of the Indus – systems that the inhabitants of Ras al-Junayz were probably aware of, but did not use. The symbols are, however, found in Iran, in Elamite linear writing of the second half of the third millennium BC. They are also comparable in form to those of the alphabet that was to appear, much later, in the western Semitic world (the few names of inhabitants of Magan that we know all belong to a western Semitic language group). Thus, a modest village of fishermen, forgotten by time, has given rise to new hypotheses about the fundamental problem of the evolution of writing.

Bibliography

V. Charpentier, *Un archéologue en Arabie* (Paris, 1992).
S. Cleuziou, 'Pays du Golfe (archéologie)', in *Encyclopedia Universalis*, III (Paris, 1990), pp. 560–70.
S. Méry, 'Origine et production des récipients de terre cuite dans la Peninsule d'Oman à l'Age du Bronze', in *Paléorient*, 17, II, 1991, pp. 63–89.
Various authors, 'Cachets inscrits de la fin du III millénaire a Ra's al-Junayz, Sultanat d'Oman', *Comptes Rendus de l'Académie des inscriptions et belles lettres* (Paris, 1995), pp. 453–68.

Ebla:
A Rediscovered City

Syria

Systematic exploration of Tell Mardikh, the ancient city of Ebla, in northern Syria about 60 km (37 miles) south-west of Aleppo, was begun in 1964 by the University of Rome 'La Sapienza'. Not only has this revealed the Proto-Syrian culture of the third quarter of the third millennium BC, it has also thrown light on a major centre of the Old Syrian culture of the first four centuries of the second millennium BC – particularly through the discovery of thousands of clay writing tablets from the royal archive. The result has been a fundamental re-evaluation of the history of the ancient Near East.

The first substantial revelation of the culture of the Old Syrian period came as a result of Leonard Woolley's exploration of Tell Atchanah-Alalakh between 1937 and 1949. The main aim of the excavations at Tell Mardikh in 1968 was to uncover more information about the historical roots of this culture in the decades after the reign of the great Babylonian king Hammurabi (c. 1792–1750 BC). The excavations produced the first evidence that allowed this site to be identified as ancient Ebla; this came in the form of an inscribed torso (part of a sculpture of a royal personage) dating to the beginning of the second millennium BC. The city of Ebla, which flourished between 2400 and 1600 BC, is repeatedly mentioned in ancient cuneiform and hieroglyphic sources from Mesopotamia, Anatolia and Egypt. It was traditionally assumed to have been located in southern Turkey, on the high plain at the foot of the Taurus mountains, until the excavations at Tell Mardikh showed it to be in the heart of northern Syria.

After its destruction by Sargon of Akkad towards 2300 BC, Ebla appears in the cuneiform sources as a region of renewed conquest by Naram-Sin of Akkad towards 2250 BC. It is also recorded as an area from which Gudea of Lagash, in the second half of the twenty-second century BC, obtained precious woods for his famous sacred

▽ *Aerial view of the lower city and the acropolis of Tell Mardikh/Ebla from the north-west. In the foreground is the gigantic cult terrace and courtyard used to house the lions sacred to the goddess Ishtar.*

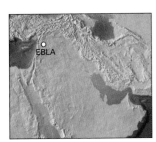

◁ *Location map: Tell Mardikh, ancient Ebla, is 60 km (37 miles) south-west of Aleppo in the heart of northern Syria.*

complexes built in honour of the god Ningir-su. Later, at the end of the eighteenth century or during the seventeenth century BC – when upper Syria was dominated by the powerful kingdom of Yamhad (with its capital at Aleppo) – Ebla is mentioned in the Alalakh texts in connection with a dynastic marriage linking its ruling family with the lords of Alalakh, a junior branch of the dynasty ruling at Aleppo.

Ebla was politically powerful in the centuries when Amorite dynasties were in control in Mesopotamia and Syria, and when the Middle Kingdom was flourishing in Egypt. Evidence of Ebla's political power has come from an epic narrative, the *Epic of the Liberation*, composed in Hittite and Hurrian, which was recently found in the imperial Hittite capital of . This epic celebrated the final destruction of Ebla (which it calls 'the city of the throne') by a great early Hittite ruler – probably Mursilis I, the conqueror of Aleppo and Babylon. Archaeological evidence has confirmed

that the destruction of Ebla took place around 1600 BC. Over a century later Thutmose III passed through northern Syria to consolidate the Egyptian empire in Asia founded by Thutmose I. He mentioned Ebla – now no more than a field of ruins, with a few houses perched on the central small hill of the acropolis – in his long list of conquered Syrio–Palestinian cities carved in the temple of Karnak.

Ebla was a great settlement of some 60 hectares (150 acres) and – with Carchemish, Aleppo, Urshu, Alalakh, and Qatna – was one of the largest urban centres of the Old Syrian period. After Ebla's final destruction its name was recorded sporadically, but only in economic documents – that perhaps referred to the region rather than the city – or in ritual texts from Hattusas or Assur that mention the religious traditions of the now almost abandoned city. However, even as late as the thirteenth century BC the name of Ebla was certainly recorded in a ritual of the great sanctuary of the god Assur at Assur. Amongst other divinities was Ishtar of Ebla (goddess of love, fertility and war), whose fame and cult had evidently spread beyond the area that the Old Syrian city had once dominated politically.

By about the end of the second millennium BC, the end of the Bronze Age and the first centuries of the Iron

Age, the name of Ebla had completely disappeared from written records.

Archaeological exploration has not yet provided adequate elucidation of Ebla's origins. However, much is now known about the city during the important Mature Proto-Syrian period (2400–2300 BC; the Mardikh IIB1 phase), which is documented by the surviving royal archive. It must then have been a vast urban centre of around 50 hectares (120 acres), its centre dominated by the architectural complex of the Royal Palace – over 10,000 sq m (2½ acres) in size (of which only a little less than

△ *Head of a Crowned figure made of ivory (1750–1650 BC) from the Northern Palace.*

2,500 sq m, or 0.6 acres, has been excavated). This complex is called 'Saza' in the texts of the archive. It consisted of a large 'audience court' (an open space with porticos and a podium for the royal throne on the north side); an administrative quarter (centred on an internal court containing the throne-room and the archive room); and the central sector. The last consisted of a complicated series of buildings and spaces for food-production, the storage of agricultural produce and workshops making cloth and metal utensils, as well as the residences of the ruler and (very likely) the most important dignitaries.

In the administrative quarter – in the great archive room, the small archive and the trapezoidal storeroom – over 17,000 tablets or fragments of tablets from the famous royal archives were found. This is considered the most remarkable epigraphic find in Near Eastern archaeology in the last fifty years. It constitutes an extraordinary

△ *Aerial view of the archaeological site from the south. The limestone ramparts of the ancient city can still dominate the surrounding countryside, reaching a height of 22 m (72 ft) on the eastern side. The summit of the acropolis and the structures that surround it are visible at the centre of the picture.*

▷ *Ivory statuette of a bare-headed figure holding a baby gazelle as an offering (c. 1750 BC).*

▽ *Computer reconstruction of Ebla in the period between 1800 and 1600 BC, seen from the south-west.*

collection of cuneiform documents (calculated to have amounted originally to some 5,000 tablets) datable between 2350 and 2300 BC and includes economic, administrative, judicial, literary and lexical texts. Among them are the oldest political treaty in history (agreed between Abarsal and Ebla), the first bilingual vocabulary in Eblaite and in Sumerian (over 1,500 words preserved) and the oldest Semitic literary text (a hymn in praise of the sun god Shamash). From these texts emerges a detailed picture of the institutions, economy and society of protohistoric Ebla.

Ebla was ruled by hereditary rulers, three of whom (Igrish-Khalam, Irkab-Damu and Ish'ar-Damu) are known in the years documented by the archive. The monarchy was supported institutionally by a second high-ranking office, that of vizier, and three bearers of this title are also known: Arrukum, Ibrium and Ibbi-Zikir. Particularly in the second half of Ish'ar-Damu's reign, the viziers seem to have set out to make Ebla into a leading power – it ultimately came to control not only all northern Syria but also part of Upper Mesopotamia – with solid diplomatic alliances, starting with Mari and Nagar (probably present-day Tell Brak).

Ebla's great success undoubtedly depended on its important strategic position, halfway between the valley of the Euphrates and the Mediterranean

coast, but it also had a sound economic base in agriculture and trade. On the one hand, the city's extensive agriculture (founded on cereals, vines and olive oil and on sheep- and cattle-rearing) made it largely self-sufficient in food. On the other, it prospered by exploiting distant sources of raw materials: wood in the Lebanese and Amanus mountains, and metals (especially copper, silver and gold) in the Amanus and Taurus mountains. It was very likely Ebla's control over the sources of raw materials, and its alliances with the major political centres of Upper Mesopotamia, that provoked a reaction from King Sargon of Akkad and led to the destruction of both Mari and Ebla around 2300 BC.

Probably enforcing a strict royal monopoly, the city seems to have become increasingly important as an entrepot for long-distance trade in the middle of the third millennium BC – in particular for the trade in much-prized lapis lazuli, brought from far-off Afghanistan and sent on to southern Mesopotamia and to Syria and Egypt. In this context it is interesting that over 22 kg (48 lb) of raw lapis lazuli and many fragments of Egyptian-produced alabaster and diorite cups were found in

△ *The monumental gate giving access to the great stairway, which leads to internal quarters of Royal Palace G (2400–2300 BC).*

the ruins of the administrative quarter of Ebla's Royal Palace. They included a diorite cup inscribed with two of the titles of the Fourth-Dynasty pharaoh Khafre (or Chephren, the builder of the second pyramid at Giza), and the alabaster lid of an unguent vase of Pepy I, the second pharaoh of the Sixth Dynasty. The latter provides the oldest archaeologically attested chronological link connecting Egypt, Mesopotamia and Syria around 2300 BC, and seems to show that Sargon of Akkad, Pepy I of Egypt and Ish'ar-Damu of Ebla were contemporaries.

The sacking of the Royal Palace of Ebla by Sargon's army left the archive rooms unlooted but completely ruined the valuable furnishings of the palace buildings. Despite all the damage, however, a series of important finds have been made, especially in the administrative quarter. These include the splendid steatite hairpieces that once adorned two life-size royal busts; fragments of high-relief sculptures (made of wood covered with sheet gold, or of limestone or lapis lazuli) showing processions of dignitaries; and inlaid panels celebrating military victories and marble plaques of victorious soldiers and images of divinities. Also found were many clay *bullae* (sealed clay dockets attached by string to goods) bearing imprints of the finely engraved cylinder seals of senior officials. The stately style of palace sculpture encapsulates a whole iconographic heritage strongly influenced by Mesopotamian seal-engraving of the final Proto-Dynastic period, but which includes such original Proto-Syrian creations as the great goddess who rules wild animals, the cow-woman (a female version of the bull-man) and an 'Atlas' holding a quadripartite cosmic symbol above his head.

Something is known of the post-palatial phase, Mardikh IIB2, which follows the sacking by Sargon. Recent excavations have uncovered a sector of the imposing archaic palace in the north-western part of the lower city. This must have been the royal palace of the twenty-second to twenty-first centuries BC: a period largely corresponding to the Neo-Sumerian period of southern Mesopotamia, when economic texts of the Third Dynasty of Ur mention messengers and merchants from Ebla visiting the metropolis of the Sumerian world.

This large building was constructed near an important sacred area of the lower city, dedicated to the goddess Ishtar, which could have been the major religious centre of Ebla. In the same area the archaeologists uncovered an impressive stratigraphic succession of great palaces superimposed one upon another. The intermediate palace, of which little is yet known, was built over the southern sector of the archaic palace, during Mardikh IIIA (probably between the twentieth and nineteenth centuries BC) and, in the final phase of the Old Syrian period, was covered by the great Northern Palace, which was one of the three palace buildings still in use at the end of Mardikh IIIB, towards 1600 BC. The urban centre of the Old Syrian period is better known than its predecessor in terms of both its layout and its major monuments, secular and religious.

As early as the twentieth century BC, the beginning of the new phase of

△ *The east side of the Western Palace. Note the monolithic jambs of the passages and the technique of building walls in mud brick on a stone base.*

◁ *Beakers of the classic plain 'caliciform ware', which was widely used in the third quarter of the third millennium* BC *(2400–2300* BC*). These examples were found in Royal Palace G.*

urbanization of Mardikh IIIA, the city was fortified with a great artificial rampart, over 20 m (66 ft) high, whose base was protected by stone facing some 5 m (16 ft) high. The citadel was probably enclosed by a stone and mud-brick wall, now only preserved alongside the tower that flanked the south-west gate. The outer fortified wall had four gates: the north-west gate facing towards Aleppo; the north-east gate (from which a road ran towards the Euphrates); the south-west gate facing towards Damascus; and the minor south-east gate facing the steppe. Only much later, perhaps at the end of Mardikh IIIA, was the citadel surrounded by a second fortified internal wall. This double structure of external and internal walls is recorded in the *Epic of the Liberation*, whose writers evidently knew the topography of the city at the end of the Mature Old Syrian period. By Mardikh IIIA, the citadel was the site of Royal Palace E, which extends over much of at least the northern half of the acropolis. The small sector so far excavated includes the area around a large court and the great Temple D. The sacred area of the temple (dedicated to the goddess Ishtar) occupied the western edge of the hill, with minor chapels arranged in front of the façade of the major sanctuary. Temple D had a typical Old Syrian plan of a tripartite longitudinal structure with a vestibule, an antechamber and a long *cella* with a niche to contain the cult image. This sanctuary at Ebla is the oldest antecedent of the type of building that includes Solomon's Temple in Jerusalem (tenth century BC).

In the lower city a circuit of monumental buildings surrounded the base of the citadel at least from the north-east round to the south-west. To the north-east was Temple N: dedicated to the solar god Shamash and oriented with its entrance facing the rising sun. To the north-west extended a large area sacred to the goddess Ishtar that included the great Temple P2 (the largest sacred building in the city) and the imposing Monument P3, a gigantic cult terrace with courtyard, used to house the lions sacred to the goddess. To the north of this area, which extended over not less than 10,000 sq m (2½ acres), was the Northern Palace, dating from the beginning of Mardikh IIIB, perhaps around 1800 BC. This notable ceremonial building covered more than 3,500 sq m (1 acre) and had an unusual trapezoidal plan,

△ *Basalt head (c. 2300* BC*) of a statue of a divinity, probably Ishtar, at the moment of its discovery in the area of Temple P2.*

determined by the pre-existing monumental palaces. Its main façade faced west and its central core consisted of a great audience hall.

Further south, in front of the west side of the citadel, was the Western Palace – 115 m (377 ft) long and covering an area of over 7,300 sq m (1.8 acres) – which was the major palace building of the urban centre and functioned as the ruler's residence. A large part of its southern front sector, which must have had a colonnaded façade, has been lost. The central area of the building had a hall, used as the reception area, in which the central space was subdivided by two columns and two irregular lateral aisles. In the better-preserved northern part of the palace were various service areas, including a food-preparation room with a long bench on which sixteen mortars were found, their pestles still in place.

South of the Western Palace were the small Temple B (a single-cell structure like all the others of the lower city) dedicated to Rashap, the god of the underworld, and Sanctuary B2: an irregularly shaped structure with a centralized plan, which was dedicated to the cult of the royal ancestors. This building had a large hall at its centre, with benches and a podium for the funerary symposium, around which were various sanctuaries with altars, where bronze statues of deified rulers must have been placed. The Western Palace, the Temple of Rashap and Sanctuary B2 form a complex that was built in a particularly important part of the city: the site of the tombs of the royal cemetery of Mardikh IIIB. The relationship between the cemetery area and the Western Palace is explained by the ruler's essential role of assuring the successful execution of the funerary rites of his dead predecessor and providing for regular cult ceremonies for the royal ancestors.

The royal cemetery must have been in use between the end of Mardikh IIIA, towards 1825 BC, and the later part of Mardikh IIIB, around 1650 BC, and perhaps beyond. About ten tombs have

The Monumental Architecture of Ebla Reborn on Computer

Computers have been used in Near Eastern archaeology not only for statistical analysis of various types of archaeological material and for settlement studies, but also to create three-dimensional reconstructions of ancient architecture. Pre-Classical buildings in the Near East are often preserved only at foundation level, since most of their elevations were made of sun-dried bricks of clay and straw, which only last for a short time once exposed to the elements. However, it has been possible to reconstruct how the forms and spaces of many of these buildings must have looked, thanks to evidence from rare survivals (such as Palace G at Ebla, where mud-brick walls were preserved up to 8 m, or 26 ft), or from clay models or representations in painting and sculpture, and also from calcu-lations of the strength of the foundations (generally preserved almost intact).

In the case of Ebla in the period of Hammurabi, three royal palaces, seven cult buildings, the tombs of the kings, the road and street system and the whole circuit of the forti-fications, with its four fortified gates, are known in detail. Solid modelling, by means of a computer-aided design (CAD) system, has allowed detailed reconstruction of each individual building and the study of its roofing system and arrangement of forms and spaces. Not only this, it has also made possible the generation of a com-puter model that can be used for 'virtual navigation' within the city. One can enter a gate, turn towards the acropolis and pass in front of the monumental porticoed entrance of the ruler's residence, the Western

△▷ Computer reconstructions of Ebla in the period 1800–1600 BC. *Top:* the lower city and the acropolis seen from the north, with the Northern Palace in the foreground. *Above:* Temple N, Temple P2 (in profile) and the terrace of the sacred area of Ishtar. *Right:* the ramparts and the eastern walls.

Palace – the city's largest palatial building, 115 m (377 ft) long and covering an area of over 7,300 sq m (1.8 acres). Or one can fly at a low level above the major sacred area of the lower city, dedicated to the goddess Ishtar. Over and above the undoubted fascination of the scenic effects of such reconstructions, the real benefits of the computer are revealed in the completely three-dimensional results; the digitization and drawing of the buildings makes them into 'real' constructions in a perfectly created virtual geometric space. Moving inside this space to regenerate particular buildings or archaeological strata, the archae-ologist is forced to deal with problems that would have remained hidden in a traditional two-dimensional reconstruction (a simple perspective drawing). The system allows one to reconstruct the

buildings progressively in three dimensions and to move freely inside them, and the instantly available images enable doubts to be resolved or different recon-structions to be proposed where evidence from the site, or com-parisons with other sites, suggest more than one possible solution. Different hypotheses can be tried out, and unconvincing solutions rejected. This is not simply playing with computer graphics. The reconstructions are based on accurate surveys of the site that take account of all the possible evidence, and the thicknesses, forms and colours of the buildings being reconstructed are strictly deter-mined by calculations of the strength and other characteristics of the materials and the various types of wall construction.

◁ Basalt stele of Ishtar (c. 1800 BC). The goddess appears in a winged shrine in the upper register.

been identified, most of which must have been robbed or disturbed in antiquity, and three have been completely excavated. The Tomb of the Princess, sealed between 1825 and 1800 BC or a little after, was found intact with important personal funerary equipment of gold jewellery and over sixty ceramic vases. The Tomb of the Lord of the Goats, which was robbed at the time of the Hittite destruction of the city, certainly belonged to a ruler; his burial (in around 1750 BC) included deposits of gold jewellery, bronze weapons, stone vases, ivory talismans and over seventy ceramic vases, as well as various Egyptian gifts. The Tomb of the Cistern, probably sealed towards 1650 BC, is the tomb that suffered most during the sacking and destruction of the city around 1600 BC. There is abundant evidence of monumental sculpture dating between 1900 and 1650 BC. Two lustral basins (each in two sections) can be dated to the first decades of the period. They have relief carvings showing ritual and mythic scenes on at least three of their four sides. The dominant scene is the banquet of the ruler, who is seated in front of an offering table heaped with unleavened bread. In some cases this must refer to the symposium for the feast of the New Year – a feast on which universal fertility was believed to depend – and, in others, to the benches for the cult of the deified royal ancestors.

To the same period also belong the oldest pieces of basalt votive statuary – amongst them the bust of the king Ibbit-

Lim, datable around 1900 BC. It carries the carved dedicatory inscription which in 1968 enabled Tell Mardikh to be identified as Ebla. Various other important remains of royal statuary – figures of enthroned rulers and standing queens – were found in the Temple of Ishtar in the lower city and are datable to the years between 1750 and 1625 BC. An iconologically important work is the Stele of Ishtar, made towards 1800 BC and found in a secondary temple in the area sacred to the goddess on the citadel. Its four sides were carved in relief with divine, ritual and mythic scenes, amongst which was the image of the great goddess, represented in a winged shrine on the back of a bull supported by two bull-men. This image symbolized not only the heavenly but also the chthonic nature of the divinity, who was assimilated to the planet

◁ Enthroned ruler, a detail of the ivory talisman (opposite page) found in the Tomb of the Lord of the Goats (1750–1700 BC). The talisman depicts the funerary banquet of the king, who appears on the left accompanied by two naked hereditary princes, seen frontally.

Venus – even then the goddess of universal fertility. Ebla has also produced important intaglio-carved ivories. The most notable are the open-work figures of the Egyptian deities (from Sobek to Horus, from Hathor to Osiris), which very probably decorated the back of a throne or ceremonial bed dating to around 1700 BC.

Although only a few fragments of tablets dating to the Old Syrian period have been found at Ebla, the names of some of its rulers during the Mardikh IIIA and IIIB phases may be reconstructed. Amongst the oldest, definitely dated to the twentieth century BC, are Igrish-Khep and his son Ibbit-

▷ The oldest treaty so far known: one between Ebla and Abarsal, a city still not identified. The cuneiform tablet was found in the state archives (c. 2350 BC).

Lim (who dedicated to Ishtar the statue that revealed to us the ancient name of Tell Mardikh). The ruler around 1750 BC was probably Immeya, who – on the evidence of a silver cup inscribed with his name found in the Tomb of the Lord of the Goats – may have been the person buried there. Indilimgur, in the seventeenth century BC, must have been one of the last kings of the city; he was the father of a prince who left the imprint of his splendid seal on the shoulder of some jars found in the Western Palace.

By the time the Hittites (under Mursilis I) conquered and sacked Ebla towards 1600 BC, putting a final end to the great Old Syrian centre, the high urban culture of Syria had already been diffused widely across the region. The cultural development that occurred at Ebla in the first part of the second millennium BC had drawn together the legacy of the remarkable florescence of Old Syrian urban society in the third quarter of the third millennium BC and laid the foundations of a great and truly Syrian tradition. This would last, maintaining its own distinctive characteristics despite interruptions and breaks, until the disintegration of urban life between the end of the eighth and the beginning of the seventh centuries BC, caused by the ascendancy of the Assyrian empire.

Philology and Computers in the Study of the Ebla Texts

The vast epigraphical treasure of tablets from the state archives of Ebla consists of a large quantity of texts – on accounting, economic, administrative, juridical, literary and lexical matters – written over some fifty years between 2350 and 2300 BC. Two of the fundamental problems are determining the chronology of the texts and cataloguing all the names they contain: dozens of names of gods, hundreds of city names and thousands of personal names – of dignitaries, officials, messengers and merchants present at the court of Ebla and registered in the (mainly monthly and annual) accounts in the archives.

Computerization of all these names is producing very important results. It is systematically establishing correlations between the divine, personal and geographic names that throw light on the cults in the cities mentioned, on which cities the persons mentioned belong to, and on the dating of Eblaite dignitaries of the three successive reigns in which the tablets were written. In particular, a detailed study of information about individuals at the court, based on assembling data on their 'careers', will allow many tablets of an administrative nature which are not datable from other information to be arranged in chronological order. Many such texts can thus be attributed to the reign of a particular king: Igrish-Khalam, Irkab-Damu or Ish'ar-Damu.

This study has produced information that is fundamental to reconstructing the history of the city immediately before Sargon's campaign in Upper Syria towards 2300 BC. For example, it has been discovered that there was a notable increase in Ebla's prosperity late in Irkab-Damu's reign and during the reign of Ish'ar-Damu. This was marked by the influx of growing quantities of silver and gold into the city as a result of the efforts of important dignitaries, called 'The Great' in the Eblaite texts. Reconstructing the chronology of the archive texts has also determined that it was only at the end of Mardikh IIB1 that Ebla made an alliance with the city of Nagar (probably present-day Tell Brak), drawn up in the cult centre of the god Dagan at Tuttul, and perhaps also with Mari in the Euphrates valley. One result of these alliances was to create a sort of monopoly over the sources of wood and metal in the Amanus and Taurus mountains. This undoubtedly provoked a reaction from the nascent political power of Akkad and prompted Sargon to undertake the famous expedition that led to the conquest and destruction of Mari, Yarmuti and Ebla, putting an end to the prosperity of Mardikh IIB1.

Bibliography

A. Kuhrt, *The Ancient Near East* c. *3000–330 BC*, vols 1 and 2 (London, 1995)

P. Matthiae, *Ebla. An Empire Rediscovered* (London, 1977).

M. Roaf, *Cultural Atlas of Mesopotamia and the Ancient Near East* (Oxford, 1990)

Various authors, *Ebla. Alle origini della civiltà urbana* (Milan, 1995).

H. Weiss (ed.), *From Ebla to Damascus: Art and Architecture of Ancient Syria* (Washington, DC, 1985)

Uruk: At the Heart of the Sumerian Empire

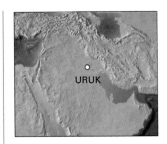

◁ *Location map: Uruk is on the Mesopotamian plain, a little more than 70 km (45 miles) north-west of Ur.*

Iraq

*O*n the plain of lower Mesopotamia the site of Warka, excavated since 1912 by German archaeologists, covers the ruins of the ancient Sumerian city of Uruk: biblical Erech. Uruk was one of the great centres of the Sumerian Empire, and the dynasties that succeeded each other here played a major role in the region's history throughout the third millennium BC. It is the land of Gilgamesh, Dumuzi and Enmerkar – the heroes of the Sumerian epics. Although the city lost its political role after the end of the third millennium, it remained a religious capital until the Parthian period (third century BC to third century AD), when some priests were still using cuneiform writing.

Archaeologically, the earliest periods are the most interesting, since Uruk is one of the few places where excavations have revealed a monumental complex dating to the second half of the fourth millennium BC. Moreover, Uruk provides the basis for much of our knowledge about the formation of cities and states: from here come the first known written documents (dating to around 3300 BC). The site is very large, extending over nearly 500 hectares (1,235 acres), but it is, above all, the sector called the Eanna – at the foot of the ziggurat dedicated in later periods to the goddess Inanna – which has claimed the attention of the German archaeologists. Due to erosion, the levels dating to the end of the fourth millennium BC appeared just below the surface at this point, and it was therefore possible to excavate them over a large area. Moreover, before putting up new structures, the ancient builders took care to raze the previous buildings to the ground, leaving only some brick foundations. This has allowed architects and archaeologists to reconstruct complete plans of the buildings without having to undertake the enormous excavations that would otherwise have been necessary.

Three levels from the second half of the fourth millennium BC were thus brought to light, levels which are fundamental to our knowledge of urbanization in Mesopotamia. The oldest levels are known only from one large trench that reached down to deposits dating to the end of the 'Ubaid period, in the fifth millennium. These 'Ubaid levels were followed by the Uruk period – notable for the disappearance of painted decoration on the pottery, which was now being produced 'industrially', perhaps already with the use of the potter's wheel. These levels cover the centuries of the so-called

△ *This copper figurine was found in the foundation deposit of a temple at Uruk. It represents king Ur-Nammu (2112–2095 BC) as a builder, carrying a basket.*

▷ *According to tradition, the site was enclosed by a rampart built by king Gilgamesh, but no trace of these defences has so far been found.*

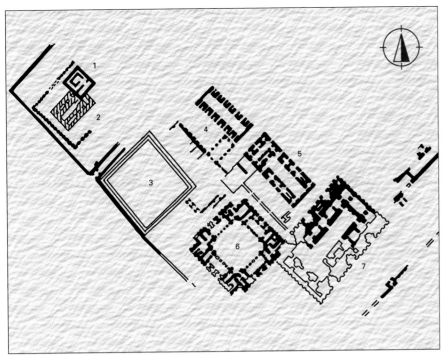

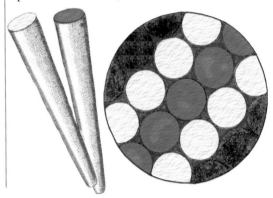

△ *The ceremonial centre of Uruk is the
part of the site that has been most fully
excavated: (1) Riemchengebaüde; (2) Stone
Cone Mosaic Temple; (3) Great Court;
(4) Pillared Hall; (5) Temple C; (6) Square
Building; (7) Temple D.*

'urban revolution', but only the most recent levels (V to III), which marked the completion of the process of urbanization, are well known. Monumental architecture appeared in the fifth level, datable around 3500 BC, but had precedents on the same site. The buildings with a tripartite plan and a central hall that characterize this level may be 'copies' on a much larger scale of the 'Ubaid-period houses known from other sites.

It is also in the fifth level that the first cylinder seals appear. These were pressed into wet clay, and were soon used to authenticate inscribed tablets. These seals also allowed the continuous repetition of scenes that were considered important, and on a much larger surface than the stamp seals used up to that time. Writing is present from the following level and very quickly becomes omnipresent: almost 5,000 archaic tablets were found at Uruk, abandoned in the rubbish or or used in fill when the information they contained was no longer useful. The same period saw an exceptional development of sculpture, used to represent the gods and the mighty.

The oldest monumental building on the site was the Stone Cone Mosaic Temple, dated to around 3500 BC (level VI). The building owes its name to its decoration, made from a mosaic of stone cones of various colours inserted into the clay of the unfired bricks – a technique that appears here for the first time. Around 30 m (98 ft) long, it is arranged on a T-shaped plan, with a central hall, flanked by two rows of rooms, opening to the north on to an oblong hall, itself flanked by lateral rooms. (This plan, involving a rectangular complex within which two largely identical buildings, one smaller than the other, meet at right angles, was to characterize all the monumental architecture of the succeeding levels.) A stairway in one of the lateral rooms of the main hall gave access to an upper floor or to the roof.

The so-called 'Limestone Temple', dated to level V but perhaps earlier, was an immense building, 78 m (256 ft) long and 30 m (98 ft) wide, on a tripartite plan. Its name derives from the fact that its surviving base (but perhaps the rest of the building as well) was made of quarried limestone, rather than the

△ *This type of mosaic, made of small cones of fired clay with painted heads, was found in
the Eanna Temple precinct and is typical of the Late Uruk period. The cones (enlarged plan
and section views in the diagram above) averaged 10 cm (4 in.) in length and were inserted
into the surface of the wall while it was still malleable.*

➤ *Ritual vase decorated with animal motifs in high relief, found in a level datable to the beginning of the third millennium* BC. *(Baghdad, Iraq Museum)*

mud brick traditional in Mesopotamia. It was long believed that the stone was imported from far away. However, it has been shown that the builders simply quarried the material from one of the outcrops of calcareous rock not far away in the plain.

The central hall of the temple is 11 m (36 ft) wide, and its roof doubtless needed large beams that must have been imported (perhaps Lebanese cedars were already being transported along the Euphrates). The hall was flanked on both sides by a row of rectangular rooms with access either to the outside or to the stairwells. The façades and the exterior walls were decorated with an uninterrupted series of rectangular buttresses and niches.

While the plan of the temple can be precisely reconstructed, thanks to its rigorous symmetry, the remains of the rest of the building are too poorly preserved to permit reconstruction of the elevation. Nor is it known whether the temple was isolated or flanked by other buildings. The first cylinder seal impressions are associated with this building, but they are already artistically fully developed.

The Limestone Temple was replaced by a vast architectural complex of sun-dried brick that included three structures of similar plan, but smaller, arranged on three sides of a rectangular court. This complex continued to evolve through various reconstructions.

One of the most spectacular of the other buildings in the area is the Mosaic Court or Pillar Temple. This was a raised colonnade supported by two rows of four enormous circular columns of mud brick, that linked two T-shaped buildings which flanked a rectangular court. The columns, and the four semi-columns that link the colonnade to the buildings at either end, were decorated with a mosaic of fired-clay cones; the heads of the cones, painted in red, black or pale yellow, formed a geometric pattern of double lozenges. Lozenges, chevrons and triangles are also found on the walls of the courtyard and the T-shaped buildings – where buttresses covered with decorative plasterwork alternate with niches with cone mosaics. This spectacular technique, characteristic of the Uruk period, is found at many Mesopotamian sites and even in Lower Egypt, but it subsequently disappeared.

In period IV, the buildings of the Eanna sector were arranged in a vast enclosed space almost 300 × 200 m (985 × 655 ft) containing *inter alia* Temple D, which was a large T-shaped structure measuring around 80 × 50 m (260 × 165 ft), and a building made up of four rooms with porticos opening on to a square court, the so-called 'Square Building'; inside the latter the first documents in pictographic writing were found.

The function of these buildings remains unclear. The traditional term 'temple', which has been retained here, came from the studies of the early German archaeologists, who saw them as temples where the 'priest-king' officiated – according to some theories, priest-kings were rulers of the archaic Mesopotamian cities. However, these buildings do not have any of the cult installations characteristic of a Mesopotamian temple, so they should more probably be interpreted as secular buildings (the residence of a temporal leader, who may or may not have had a priestly function), and the meetings that took place in them may not necessarily have been of a sacred nature.

On the nearby 'Anu Ziggurat', and contemporary to Eanna level III, stood the 'White Temple' – so called because of the thin coating of gypsum plaster on the walls – is more likely to have been a religious monument. It was built on a terrace or platform with a steep, sloping face decorated with buttresses, and it was reached by two stairways, and a ramp that was probably used by sacrificial animals. Inside are the various platforms and the altar that usually form part of the furnishings of Mesopotamian temples. This temple is quite small and its plan is very simple: a row of rooms, one of which is a stairwell, on either side of a central hall. The main access is through one of the lateral rooms in the centre of one of the long sides. Although it lacks both the T-shaped plan and the monumentality that distinguish the buildings of the Eanna Temple Complex, the White Temple continues a tradition that started much earlier: very probably dating from the end of the 'Ubaid period at Eridu. There was also an enigmatic building of the same period, the poorly

➤ *Alabaster statuette of a ruler, dated to the end of the fourth millennium* BC. *(Baghdad, Iraq Museum)*

recording administrative details about men and objects, as was to be the case throughout the whole of Mesopotamian history. Uruk has produced the best archaeological evidence for the early centuries of these three millennia of history.

Bibliography

R.M. Boehmer, 'Uruk 1980–1990: a
progress report', *Antiquity* 65, 248
(Sept. 1991) pp. 465–78.
A. Falkenstein, 'La cité-temple
sumérienne', in *Cahiers d'histoire
mondiale*, I, 4, 1954, pp. 784–814.
S. Lloyd, *The Archaeology of
Mesopotamia* 2nd ed.,
(London, 1984).
H.J. Nissen, P.
Damerov, R.K.
Englund, *Archaic
Bookkeeping*
(Chicago, 1993).
M. Roaf, *Cultural Atlas of
Mesopotamia and the
Ancient Near East*
(Oxford, 1990)
J. Schmidt, 'Zwei Tempel
der Obeid-Zeit in
Uruk', in *Baghdader
Mitteilungen*, 7, 1974,
pp. 173–87.
E. Strommenger and M.
Hirmer, *The Art of
Mesopotamia* (London,
1964).

preserved remains of which were found at the foot of the terrace.

According to Mesopotamian literary tradition, Uruk was enclosed by a rampart constructed by the legendary king Gilgamesh. Nothing of the rampart has been found, although it is reasonable to suppose that it would have been impressive.

▷ *The craftsmanship
of objects made at
Uruk is also seen in
the smaller finds,
such as this splendid
representation of a
bull (end of the fourth
millennium BC).*

It is interesting to note that *cire-perdue*, or lost-wax, casting appeared in this period. This technique – making a one-piece baked-clay mould around an object modelled in wax, and then pouring in molten metal to melt and replace the wax – allowed the creation of metal objects of complex shape: pinheads depicting animal figures being the earliest known examples.

The excavations provide evidence from the earliest periods of continual social change engendered by many and various technical experiments that led on to considerable innovations. Of these, potentially the most important were the use of cylinder seals and writing: techniques used in the administration and regulation of economic and social life. The script of Uruk is difficult to decipher, because it is still largely pictographic, but it reflects an advanced society willing to experiment (a dozen different numerical systems were used) and its own effect on society as a whole was long-lasting. It seems that, from the outset, this society was obsessed with

Most of the artifacts from this period were found in rubbish tips and pits, especially in the *Riemchengebaüde*, so called because of the type of bricks of which it was built. This monument seems to have been abandoned and used as a rubbish dump. Its contents provide evidence of the wealth and luxury of those in power. In the workshops of the Eanna complex, craftsmen carved cylinder seals, fashioned objects from imported copper, and sculpted vases and statues.

▷ *One of the most famous finds from Uruk is this alabaster cult vase, almost
1 m (39 in.) high, found in level III (c. 3000 BC). The decoration, of
extraordinary quality, shows a complex scene of the priest-king making an
offering to the goddess Inanna.*

Ur: The City of the Flood

Iraq

Between the two World Wars, excavations at Ur by the British archaeologist Leonard Woolley revealed the remains of what had once been the powerful capital of the Sumerian state. The site, still dominated by its now-restored ziggurat, has produced notable evidence of two of the stages of this Mesopotamian civilization. These date to the middle of the third millennium BC – the period of the spectacular 'Royal Tombs', whose luxurious contents have provided valuable information about Sumerian art, religion and society – and the period around 2000 BC, from which official and private buildings of this metropolis of southern Mesopotamia have been uncovered.

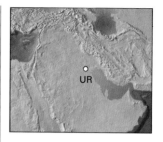

◁ *Location map: The Sumerian city of Ur lies near the Euphrates river in Iraq, whose territory includes a large part of ancient Mesopotamia.*

The origins of the city are much earlier: habitation levels and a cemetery dating to the 'Ubaid period (*c.* 5500–4000 BC) were found in a large, deep trench, often called the 'Flood Pit' – so named because Woolley believed a thick layer of sterile silt found in it was the deposit left by the Biblical Flood (an idea later abandoned). Also found at the site was a very interesting cemetery of the Jemdet Nasr period (towards 3000 BC), but it was the discovery of the Royal Tombs that really made Ur famous. The material found in these tombs (now distributed amongst museums in Baghdad, London and Philadelphia) forms one of the major attractions of these institutions' oriental collections, and it is generally these objects that one thinks of when Sumerian art is discussed.

The Royal Tombs were sixteen inhumation burials within a much larger cemetery, of almost 2,000 burials, that was used over a number of centuries. With such a mass of burials at different levels over a small area, it is difficult to determine a precise chronological sequence of the tombs – though they all date to between *c.* 2600 and 2000 BC, and the richest tombs are from the beginning of this period. The Royal Tombs are different from the simpler and more common tombs of the cemetery in consisting of an underground funerary chamber (sometimes

△ *A pendant made of lapis lazuli and gold in the form of an eagle with a lion's head. This was found at Mari but made in Ur, and may have been a gift from the king of Ur to the king of Mari.*

▷ *Virtual reconstruction of the centre of the ancient city of Ur. Leonard Woolley's excavations, carried out between the two World Wars, produced many finds and uncovered an important cemetery, the so-called 'Royal Cemetery of Ur', dating to the middle of the third millennium BC.*

more than one) of stone or fired brick, built at the bottom of a great pit and accessible via a ramp. The chamber was roofed with a corbelled vault (something that is characteristic of the tombs of dignitaries – such as those at Kish near Baghdad, or below the palace of Mari in Syria). Only one burial – that of Meskalamdug (from the name inscribed on a gold lamp in the shape of a shell) – was in the more usual form of a trench grave with the body lying in a wooden sarcophagus, and this one was distinguished by the wealth of tomb goods: fifty copper bowls, gold and copper daggers, hundreds of gold and lapis lazuli beads, a double axe and a helmet, both of electrum.

Some of the tombs at Ur had been robbed, but others were found intact. One of these was the tomb of Queen Puabi, whose name was engraved on a cylinder seal of lapis lazuli. The queen's body, wearing gold and lapis lazuli

△ *By the end of the third millennium BC Ur was an important city with a complex urban structure. It was dominated by a great ziggurat that rose up in a sacred quarter near the temple of the moon god Nannar. Ur was finally abandoned towards the fourth century BC, perhaps as a result of a change in the course of the Euphrates.*

jewellery, lay together with two others. Gold and silver vases, a richly decorated lyre, a games table and more than 250 other objects completed the tomb inventory. In another intact tomb that consisted of two chambers, one above the other, the upper chamber contained a single body in a wooden sarcophagus, while the lower contained five bodies, as well as vases and cylinder seals made of gold.

The most surprising finds, however, came from the access ramps. That in the tomb of Puabi contained the bodies of five soldiers and ten women (including a harpist), as well as a chariot drawn by two oxen; another

◁ Gold helmet from one of the Royal Tombs. It is finely worked in repoussé and belonged to Meskalamdug, a prince living around 2500 BC.

had not been sacrificed but had all committed suicide so as to follow the royal deceased into death. The animals, whose remains lay on top of the human bones, were sacrificed after the poison had done its work.

The 'Royal Tombs' of Ur still pose unanswered questions, one of which concerns the names of Meskalamdug and his successor Akalamdug. Their cylinder seals carry the title of king, but

did not have an optimistic vision of the other world, and the honour of sharing in a deceased dignitary's posthumous glory must have seemed a privilege.

The Royal Tombs found at Ur attest the wealth and power of the Sumerian dynasties. This warrior aristocracy was able to indulge in conspicuous consumption, showing off their gold and copper weapons, parading jewellery in which the blue of lapis lazuli and the red of carnelian set off the yellow of the gold, and wearing precious fabrics that one may imagine as richly embroidered with gold and silver. The metals were imported from Arabia, the Iranian plateau or Turkey, and lapis lazuli from the mountains of Afghanistan was greatly prized and actively traded in the third millennium BC.

Large carnelian beads etched with white designs were imported in their finished state from the Indus civilization – the only culture that knew how to make them. Lapis lazuli and other imported raw materials were worked in Sumer, however, and Sumerian jewellery and precious metalwork shows an extraordinary technical mastery. Gold and silver objects were abundant and very finely worked. Sumerian metalsmiths were skilled at such classic techniques as repoussé, which they used to created vases and complex objects (for example the electrum parade helmet from the tomb of Meskalamdug, or the bulls' heads that ornament most of the musicians' lyres). Above all, they developed two of the major techniques of gold-working – filigree work and granulation (making objects out of gold wire, or tiny gold globules) – which appear for the first time in this period. These techniques

contained fifty-nine courtiers and nineteen women (some with musical instruments), plus two chariots drawn by six oxen. In a third tomb (called 'the Great Death Pit' by Woolley), which had been robbed, were seventy-four bodies (sixty-eight women and six men). Each had a cup made of silver, stone or metal, and it seems probable that they

their names do not occur in the king lists known to us (nor do the names of any of the individuals found in the tombs). Funerary ceremonies like these have been found only at Ur, and they must have dated to those particularly dynamic and uncertain periods that saw the formation of aristocratic elites and dynastic systems. Mesopotamian society

△▷ Virtual reconstruction of the interior of one of the houses of Ur. It was built on two floors around an open central courtyard paved with fired bricks. The upper floor had a wooden balcony supported by columns which stood directly on the paving of the courtyard.

➤ In the course of his excavations, Leonard Woolley found two of these gold and lapis lazuli statuettes – which he related to the biblical ram caught in a thicket – which show goats standing on their back legs in front of a gold tree.

were undoubtedly invented in Sumer and were not used elsewhere until centuries later. One of the finest objects to be discovered is a gold dagger about 14 cm (5½ in.) long: its lapis lazuli hilt has been decorated in relief with gold nails and its scabbard has been adorned with filigree panels outlined with granulation.

Besides those of gold, silver and electrum (an alloy of the two), copper objects were common, and alloys of arsenic or, more rarely, tin (used in

➤ The exact function of this object, called the 'Standard of Ur', is not known. It may have been the sounding box of a musical instrument. The side illustrated shows peace after a battle shown on the other side. (London, British Museum)

perfectly controlled proportions) were occasionally used. Lost-wax casting, which appeared at the end of the fourth millennium, allowed more complex human and animal statuettes to be made than in a two-piece mould, and each casting was unique. Woodworking skills are evident from inlays of various materials, and it should not be forgotten that – although they have not survived – even the fabrics were very rich; textual sources record that the production of textiles was the main industry of Mesopotamia.

A great many objects were made of more than one material. Examples are two statues that Woolley found of a goat standing upright against a bush, made of gold, lapis lazuli and shell, or the wooden lyres decorated with bearded bull's heads whose decoration combines gold, mother of pearl, lapis lazuli and red stone. One exceptional object is what Woolley dubbed 'the Standard of Ur': a wooden double-sided panel, shaped like a lectern, which was overlooked by the robbers of the tomb where it was found. One side depicts warriors with battle wagons drawn by onagers which are trampling the defeated enemy, rows of soldiers dressed in long cloaks and wearing swords, and nude prisoners bowing before the king. On the other side rows of people carry agricultural produce and fish, or drive domestic animals, while the feasting king and his court are entertained by a musician with a lyre in the form of a bearded bull's head (of the same type as was found in the tombs). Together, the tombs, the rituals and such figurative representations give a vivid picture of the life of the Sumerian aristocracy.

Although the Royal Tombs give no clue to the names of the dynasties of rulers buried in them, the names of individual members of the Third Dynasty of Ur (which ruled throughout last century of the third millennium BC) have come down to us. The dynasty – the last real Sumerian dynasty to reign in the area – was founded by Ur-Nammu (2112–2095 BC), who re-established in southern Mesopotamia the state that had been disrupted by the end of the Akkadian empire. Its dominion extended over territory as vast as its predecessor's, and this period marked the city's economic and political apogee. Ur later fell (in about 2000 BC) under the combined assault of the Amorites from the north-west and the Elamites from the east.

△ *One of the objects found in the tomb of Queen Puabi was a wooden lyre decorated with a bull's head in gold and lapis lazuli.*

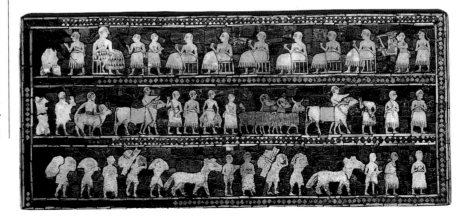

△ *This board, for a game of which a variation was still played recently in India, was made in a mosaic of different materials (wood, lapis lazuli, bone, fragments of limestone and shell). It was found in the Royal Tombs.*

The city was dominated by the great ziggurat built by Ur-Nammu. Of rectangular plan (62 × 43 m, or 203 × 142 ft), it still rises over 20 m (65 ft) high. The core was made of sun-dried bricks alternating with layers of rushes, whose purpose seems to have been to help to remove moisture. This was covered with a facing of fired bricks, held together with bitumen, whose sharp outlines give the structure a look of strength. The sides were decorated, rather than reinforced, with a series of regularly spaced buttresses. Three staircases – one at right angles to the façade, the other two parallel to the façade on either side of the central staircase – lead to the first level of the ziggurat. There seem to have been three levels, the last of which must have acted as the base of a small temple.

The function of ziggurats is still not clear, although they are, for us, emblematic of ancient Mesopotamia. They were a new type of monument at the end of the third millennium BC (not to be confused with temples built on terraces, a tradition going back to the fourth millennium), and generally only one was built for each city. That at Ur seems to have been the first to be built. Some texts mention gardens and trees on it, and a temple on the summit – although we do not know to whom or what it was consecrated.

At the foot of the ziggurat stretched a vast complex of sanctuaries. Among these were the monumental court of the moon god Nannar (flanked on all four sides with buildings and entered by a monumental gateway) and the 'Chapel of the Boat', so called because it would have sheltered the boat in which Nannar used to sail across the sky.

The monarchs of the Third Dynasty of Ur built subterranean mud-brick tombs in the complex near the earlier Royal Tombs but all have been robbed. The complex was used as a sacred place long after the decline of the city. The Kassite kings of the middle of the second millennium BC added new buildings, and in the sixth century BC Nebuchadnezzar II of Babylon (605–562 BC) completely rebuilt it as part of a huge programme to restore the country's past glory. He rebuilt the sanctuaries and enclosed the whole complex with a vast wall with a number of monumental gateways.

After the fall of the Third Dynasty, however, Ur's fortunes revived, and excavations have revealed a vivid picture of a settlement quarter of the nineteenth century BC, crossed by streets and lanes of beaten earth. The houses were laid out round a central space, and the ground-floor rooms were used as storerooms or working areas,

△▷ *The stairway leading to the great platform of the ziggurat at Ur, as it is today, after reconstruction. This extraordinary monument (see the page opposite for a virtual reconstruction) was built in the period of Ur-Nammu (2112–2095 BC) and of his son Shulgi (2095–2047 BC).*

▷ *Queen Puabi's headdress and
jewellery were amongst the
most precious finds from
the Royal Tombs.*

and also as latrines; a
staircase led to a gallery
running around the central
space, on to which the living
rooms opened. It is still not
clear whether the central
space was covered or not. It
seems that the upward ex-
tension of buildings was due to
the lack of space in the city
centre, where the great number of
small occupied areas, shops, workshops and hovels gives the impression
of severe overcrowding.

The numerous cuneiform archives of
this period give a detailed picture of a
city that was also a sea port linked to
the Persian Gulf (which lay much closer
to Ur then than it does now). An apparently elaborate and omnipresent
administrative system regulated economic relations
between the palace, with
its great state proper-
ties, the temples (which
also had substantial
land-holdings) and the
merchants, who were organized into associations.

The merchants of Ur
imported large quantities of
copper from the land of
Magan (present-day Oman),
and a variety of products from
the Arabian peninsula and from
the regions beyond the Straits of
Hormuz. They exported products
made in the city – especially cloth – and
agricultural produce. The often
dramatic rituals of its aristocracy and
the luxury of its palaces and temples,
were sustained by Ur's role as a
flourishing economic metropolis.

Bibliography

R.H. Dyson, 'Archival glimpses of the Ur
  expedition in the years 1920 to 1926',
  Expedition 20, 1977.
M.E.L. Mallowan and D.J. Wiseman
  (eds), 'Ur in retrospect', volume in
  memory of Sir Leonard Woolley, *Iraq*
  XXII, 1960.
P.R.S. Moorey, 'What do we really know
  about the people buried in the Royal
  cemetery?', *Expedition* 20, 1977.
L. Woolley, *Ur Excavations*, vols I and
  II, *The Royal Cemetery* (London and
  Philadelphia, 1934).
L. Woolley (rev. P.R.S. Moorey), *Ur of
  the Chaldees* (London and Ithaca NY),
  1982.

Babylon: The 'Gate of the Gods'

Babylon, whose Semitic name, Bab-ilu, means 'Gate of the Gods', was once the most majestic city in the world. It was not founded as early as other great centres of Mesopotamia, and is first mentioned around 2000 BC in a text which records that a king of Akkad built a temple to the goddess Ishtar there. Babylon developed rapidly into the main city of central Mesopotamia and became a 'royal city' in the nineteenth century BC, when a Semitic dynasty of Amorite origin was installed there. In the first half of the eighteenth century, during the reign of Hammurabi (1792–1750 BC), it dominated the region completely, and for over a millennium was the most important intellectual and religious centre in Mesopotamia.

After a brilliant period in the sixth century BC, under the Neo-Babylonian dynasty of Nebuchadnezzar II (Nabu-kudurri-usur II; 605–562 BC) and his successors, the city was conquered in 539 BC by the Persians, who made it their winter residence. Later Alexander the Great, who wanted it as the capital of his empire, died there in 323 BC. After that the site went into a slow decline, but, even though it was already deserted when Strabo visited it in the first century AD, the once great city was never forgotten. In the twelfth century AD the rabbi Benjamin of Tudela went to see the ruins of the palace of Nebuchadnezzar, and Pietro della Valle described its remains at length in 1616.

The first archaeological excavations at Babylon, between 1899 and 1914, were conducted by a German expedition, which unearthed the ruins of Nebuchadnezzar II's city. Twenty years later, excavations were restarted by the Antiquities Service of Iraq, which began reconstructing the principal monuments. Sadly, whether we think of the hanging gardens or the famous Tower of Babel, little remains of the marvels described by Classical writers – whose accounts have influenced our imagination far more than the excavations. National pride has been satisfied, nonetheless: an inscription in the hall of the Palace of Nebuchadnezzar celebrates the most recent rebuilding of this past glory of the Iraqi people under the rule of Saddam Hussein.

The broad outline of the city plan, as it is known today, had already been established by 1225 BC according to the evidence of a cuneiform text written during the reign of Nebuchadnezzar I (1124–1102) – or perhaps the layout

◁ *Alabaster, gold and bronze statuette (c. mid-third century BC) of the goddess Ishtar found at Babylon.*

▽ *Painted reconstruction of the famous Ishtar Gate at Babylon. The painting, by Maurice Bardin, is in the Oriental Institute Museum of the University of Chicago.*

BABYLON

◁ *Location map:
Babylon lies on the
east bank of the
Euphrates about 100
km (60 miles) south of
Baghdad.*

actually dates to the latter period, when the city was vying with the powerful Assyrian empire for pre-eminence in the region. The Neo-Babylonian king Nebuchadnezzar II (604-562 BC), who bore the name of his illustrious predecessor, certainly followed the existing plan in his restoration of the capital of his new and powerful empire to its former greatness. In this, however, he was following the common practice of Neo-Babylonian kings (626–539 BC) who, just like modern archaeologists, sought to distinguish the traces of the old buildings accurately before reconstructing them on the same lines.

Babylon lay on both banks of the Euphrates, which were linked by a bridge 115 m (377 ft) long and supported on two pillars made of fired bricks and blocks of stone. The city covered a roughly rectangular area of some 2,500 × 1,500 m (1.5 × 0.9 miles) and was surrounded by a double rampart with a large ditch in front of it. Nine monumental gates in the rampart opened on to the main streets, which were laid out largely in a gridiron

pattern. Most of the official buildings and the residences of the rulers and leading dignitaries were in the eastern part of the city, while the western part, across the Euphrates, contained housing for the general population.

In the heart of the city's eastern section, overlooking the Esagila Temple of Marduk and surrounded by a vast enclosure wall, lay the Tower of Babel. The name of this famous ziggurat (*Etemenanki* in Sumerian: the language still used for religious purposes in the first millennium BC) means 'the temple of the foundation of heaven and earth'. It was almost certainly built on top of an earlier structure that may also have been a ziggurat – another case of continuity of tradition, rather than innovation. It was square in plan, with sides 90 m (295 ft) long, and rose in seven steps to a height of about 90 m (295 ft) in the middle.

It would not have been possible to identify the city as Babylon simply from the archaeological remains. The clinching evidence came from two historical documents: a cuneiform text mentioning the arithmetical relationships on which a ziggurat similar to the Tower of Babel was based, and the description of the city by Herodotus, who saw it about

△ *Detail of the relief decoration in glazed brick that decorated the walls flanking the Processional Way. The moulded frieze represented 120 striding lions.*

▽ *This Babylonian tablet, dating to the seventh to sixth century BC, is one of the first maps of the world. The earth is shown as a circle and surrounded by an ocean, with the city of Babylon at the centre. (London, British Museum)*

△ *Plan of the central part of Babylon: (1) Ishtar Gate; (2) northern zone; (3) Temple of Ninmah; (4) bastion; (5) Euphrates; (6) Processional Way; (7) Tower of Babel; (8) Esagila Temple of Marduk; (9) Lugalgirra Gate; (10) Adad Gate; (11) Shamash Gate; (12) Urash Gate; (13) Enlil Gate; (14) Zababa Gate; (15) Marduk Gate; (16) Sin Gate; (17) Palace of Nebuchadnezzar II.*

△ *Stone tablet from the mid-ninth century BC found during the excavations at Sippar near Babylon. The sun-god Shamash, seated on a throne under a tent, is receiving King Nabu-apla-iddina (885–852 BC) accompanied by two gods. On an altar between the two groups is a symbolic representation of the sun. (London, British Museum)*

two centuries after its reconstruction by Nebuchadnezzar II. The city's most important axis was the Processional Way. This started at the monumental gate in the enclosure wall of the ziggurat, ran between the Royal Palace on the west and a series of temples on its eastern side, and passed through the city's double walls between imposing bastions at the Ishtar Gate. The main façade of this gate was 14.3 m (47 ft) high, and its walls were decorated with low-relief friezes of pacing animals, with alternating rows of bulls and dragons. On the section now reconstructed in the Museum of the Ancient Orient in Berlin, the decoration of glazed bricks depicted coloured figures on a blue ground. Beyond the gate, the Processional Way passed through a complex of fortified buildings, including

▷ *Reconstruction of the internal court of the Temple of Ishtar, which lies on the east side of the Processional Way, not far from the Temple of Marduk.*

the Northern Palace, and ran up-river to the Summer Palace about 3 km (2 miles) further on. This had a vast perimeter wall, as did the Temple of the New Year. According to the textual sources, that temple, which has not so far been discovered, played an im-

portant role in the annual festivals of the god Marduk.

Babylon contained some sixty temples, about ten of which have been uncovered. The most famous are the temples of Ishtar and Ninmah, but neither of these was as large as the Esagila Temple – the residence of the god Marduk – where the liturgies of the New Year, lasting for twelve full days, were performed. This temple, built much earlier than the first millennium BC, was destroyed in 479 BC by the Achaemenid ruler Xerxes I in reprisal for a revolt by the city.

The immense Palace of Nebuchadnezzar consisted of five successive courts, all but the first of which included an official hall along the south side. The hall of the third court, the largest, has been identified as the Throne Room, with its glazed-brick façade decoration representing 'trees of life' set above a frieze of lions. In the north-east corner was a series of fourteen vaulted rooms, arranged in two rows, with a pavement of stone slabs and a well. These have been interpreted, though without evidence, as the possible base of the famous hanging gardens. It was probably in the Palace of Nebuchadnezzar that Alexander the Great died.

◁ *Sandstone stele (mid-
seventh century BC)
showing Assurbanipal
(Ashur-bani-apli; 669–626
BC) – the king who rebuilt
the Temple of Marduk,
near which the stele was
found – carrying on his
head a basket of earth for
the ritual preparation of
the first brick.*

To the west, on the bank of the
Euphrates, an enormous bastion
protected the Treasure Room, where
the booty that accumulated during
conquests was kept; no trace of the
booty was found during the first
excavations.

Unfortunately, very few of the objects
found provide evidence of the art and
culture of the city that was for so long
the intellectual and religious capital of
Mesopotamia and one of the major
centres of the ancient world. It is as
though the desolation of Babylon,
foretold by the prophets as a punishment for Nebuchadnezzar II's treatment
of the Hebrew people, extends to its
archaeological remains.

Bibliography

R. Koldewey, *Das wiedererstehende
Babylon*, (Leipzig, 1925); new edition,
Bartel Hrouda (ed.) (Berlin 1990).

S. Lloyd, *The Archaeology of
Mesopotamia*, 2nd ed. (London and
New York, 1984).

J. Oates, *Babylon* (London and New
York, 1979).

M. Roaf, *Cultural Atlas of Mesopotamia
and the Ancient Near East* (Oxford,
1990).

H.W.F. Saggs, *The Greatness that was
Babylon* (London, 1962).

H.W.F. Saggs, *Babylonians* (London,
1995).

△ *The monumentality of the Ishtar gate can be recalled in the Museum of the Ancient Orient
in Berlin. Some 27 m (88 ft) high and decorated with glazed bricks on a blue ground, this
gate stood between the outer and inner walls of the city; from it the Processional Way ran to
the sacred area.*

Susa: From Site to Museum

Iran

*U*ntil recently, the ruins of Susa – the capital of Elam (1850–644 BC) and then of the Persian Achaemenid empire, until sacked by Alexander the Great in 329 BC – had been explored by French archaeological expeditions almost uninterruptedly for over a hundred years. The site has been made famous by the discovery of some highly important objects that appear in all the manuals of art history – among them the law code of Hammurabi, the stele of Naram of Sin (both taken as booty from Babylon in the twelfth century BC) and the reliefs of the archers of Darius. In contrast to the art works found there, we know less about the structures of the city, and its organization – probably because of the devastation wrought in its sackings by Alexander and by the Sassanian ruler Shapur II (AD 309–79). Systematic studies in the 1970s amassed a good deal of information, including royal inscriptions by rulers who wished to leave a record of their buildings for posterity, but there is still not enough to enable us to reconstruct the appearance of the city at the various stages of its history.*

The rediscovery of Susa begins with the Achaemenid dynasty (700–329 BC) The memory of the Persians was never lost from the Western imagination: their wars with the Medes and their rivalry with the Greeks provided the themes of such works of classical literature and art as the *Persians* of Aeschylus, or the mosaic at Pompeii depicting the battle between Alexander and Darius. The memory of ancient Susa, or 'Shushan, the palace, which is in the province of Elam', has been preserved in the Bible, which locates the story of Esther at this site. In more modern times Western travellers in the eighteenth and nineteenth centuries began to bring back copies of inscriptions, in three languages, left by Darius I (522–486 BC) and his suc-

cessors on the rock-face of Behistun and the walls of Naqsh-i-Rustam, the royal cemetery near Persepolis. Written in cuneiform script in Old Persian, Elamite and Babylonian, these inscriptions led to the decipherment of cuneiform in the 1840s.

History of the excavations

In the nineteenth century imposing accumulations of ancient deposits (tells) and fragments of Persian columns were still visible near the village of Shush, on the banks of the small river Shaur. Only a modest reminder of the site's former prosperity remained, in the form of a sanctuary built on the supposed site of the tomb of the prophet Daniel.

The first real scholar to take an interest in the

◄ *The law code of the Babylonian king Hammurabi (1796–1750 BC), found at Susa in 1901, is one of the earliest collections of laws in the world. (Paris, Louvre)*

ancient remains of Susa was the Englishman William Kennett Loftus, who went there between 1850 and 1853. He drew up the first known plan of the Persian palace on the Apadana mound, which he recognized on the main tell, and identified the city as the Shushan of the Book of Esther. A French engineer, Marcel Dieulafoy, travelled in Iran from 1884 to 1886 with his wife Jane, who left a lively and reliable record of their adventures illustrated with engravings (she provided a good description of Susa, as it appeared at the time). The pair undertook the first large-scale excavations of the ruins of the Apadana Palace, and found some spectacular objects which were sent to France – such as a stone capital with a double bull's head and some fragments of a coloured brick frieze. The lion frieze was then still almost in place, having fallen to the foot of the wall decorated with pennants on the north façade of the Court of Honour. The other decoration – friezes of archers carrying spears, mythological animals and tribute-bearers – had been reused in later buildings erected on the ruins of the Apadana Palace; it has since been reconstructed in the Louvre (on the basis of comparisons with the better-preserved Persepolis friezes, which are still *in situ*). When the decoration of Darius I's palace was exhibited in France it helped greatly to kindle the European public's interest in Iranian archaeology.

Like Dieulafoy, his successors Jacques de Morgan (from 1897 to 1908) and Roland de Mecquenem (from 1908 to 1946) were engineers. Their training led them to use methods more normal in mining than in archaeology – enormous excavations, tunnels and spoil-removal using trucks on rails – which, unfortunately, almost completely destroyed the main tell.

De Morgan's aim was to excavate the site completely, and in 1897 he secured the setting up of a French Delegation to Persia, which was given exclusive rights to carry out archaeological research in the country. A man of great intellectual curiosity and historical learning, he

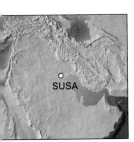

◁ *Location map:
Susa lies in south-
west Iran on the edge
of the Mesopotamian
plain, some 500 km
(300 miles) south-
west of Tehran*

realized that the Susa site concealed the accumulation of millennia of occupation, and that the acropolis was the heart of the city's religious life. During his excavations he unearthed various votive offerings deposited by the rulers in the sanctuaries of the principal gods particularly venerated at Susa Ninhursag and Inshushinak. Among the most important were the votive monuments of Puzur Inshushinak (*c.* 2100 BC) or the stele of Untash-Napirisha (*c.* 1340–1300 BC), found between 1898 and 1909. The so-called '*Vases à la Cachette*' ('vases of the hiding-place') found in 1907, contained a treasure buried on the acropolis towards 2500 BC; copper imported from Oman, alabaster from eastern Iran and cylinder seals of Sumerian origin provided evidence of the diversity of Susa's trade relationships in the middle of the third millennium BC.

South of the temple zone, 15 m (49 ft) below the surface, de Morgan ran into an enormous block of unbaked brickwork. The expedition headed by Jean Perrot in 1972–7 identified the structure as a high terrace built in the fourth millennium BC, probably the stepped platform of a sanctuary. This was one of

the first great official buildings of the city, comparable in its scale to the splendid monuments found at Uruk that were built at the beginning of the period of urbanization in Mesopotamia.

At the foot of this structure was one of the city's cemeteries, likewise dating to the fourth millennium BC, in which the earliest metal objects were found. Also buried beside the dead were painted pottery vases decorated with ibex, Afghan hounds and wading birds arranged in refined and complex compositions.

▽ *Detail of a brick relief frieze of the sixth
or fifth century BC from the Apadana
Palace, showing armed guards. (Paris,
Louvre)*

△ *The archaeological site of Susa, showing
the great trench cut by Jacques de Morgan
and, in the background, the 'castle' base of
the French excavators.*

Deciphering the texts

Near Eastern archaeology developed considerably after the First World War as a result of improved excavation methods, the use of pottery to date excavation layers, the identification of mud-brick structures – which led to the discovery of the great archaic Mesopotamian buildings at Uruk, Assur and Ur – and the systematic application of stratigraphic analysis. Despite this, Roland de Mecquenem continued to use the same methods as de Morgan, which makes it difficult to understand the layout and relationships of the architectural remains in mud brick. However, he did regularly publish the results of his excavations in the monumental collection of the *Mémoires de la Délégation en Perse* (MDP), begun in 1900. Above all, he had the good luck to benefit from the help of the great Assyriologist Father Vincent Scheil, whose work of decipherment is outstanding (as he himself announced, in his first volume of the MDP, 'here begins the history of Elam').

Father Scheil made texts available to other scholars almost as soon as they were found. He published the texts written in Akkadian – the Mesopotamian language of diplomacy of the

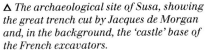

Modern exploration

Modern archaeological research at Susa began with Roman Ghirshman (from 1946 to 1967). He was principally interested in the private houses (to him we owe the excavations of the residential area in front of the acropolis), and his work at Dur-Untash, now Choga Zanbil – a royal city founded by Untash-Napirisha in the fourteenth century BC, has thrown new light on the most glorious period of Elam's history. Ghirshman was succeeded by Jean Perrot, trained as a prehistorian, who directed the excavations from 1967 until the time of the Islamic revolution in Iran. His refined methods of analysis enabled the structures found by his predecessors, in particular the terracing of the fourth millennium BC, to be better understood.

The new team dedicated itself above all to investigating Achaemenid Susa. The excavations of the so-called 'Palace of Shaur', built by Artaxerxes II (404–359 BC), were conducted in parallel with a new study of the Apadana Palace, built by Darius I and excavated by Dieulafoy. It seems that the latter combined in the same complex two completely different elements. The first was a palace of a Persian type well-known from Persepolis, largely open in character and centred on a hypostyle hall surrounded by porticoes in which the royal throne was located. The second was a Mesopotamian type of palace, more closed in character and with rooms grouped around a succession of courts. Two of these courts were linked by a double hall (probably a second throne room), wider than it was long, that was comparable to those of Assyrian palaces.

It is this 'Mesopotamian' part of the palace that was decorated with facings made of coloured glazed bricks representing friezes of archers, mythological monsters, and rows of tribute-bearers

time – and was one of the first to decipher the local language, Anzanite (a name taken from the royal title of the rulers of Susa, 'king of Anzan and of Susa') and translated the Achaemenid Persian texts. Thus it was that philology and not archaeology (which was reduced to simply providing the documents) enabled the history of Susa to be compiled. From this process the city emerged as one pole of a political and cultural spectrum, ranging from Anshan (located in the heart of Fars, the region of Persepolis) to Elam (the area around Susa, and therefore closer to the Mesopotamian world).

Among the Akkadian texts, the so-called 'Mesopotamian booty' group is particularly notable. These texts were carved on works of art brought to Susa from defeated city states in Mesopotamia. Found on the Susa acropolis, these include a unique collection of Mesopotamian royal sculptures, among them monuments (stelae and statues) of the Akkadian rulers Sargon I,

Manishtushu and Naram-Sin, the law code of Hammurabi from Babylon and statues of the king of the city of Eshnunna (Tell Asmar). Many of these still carry their original dedications, indicating their provenance and the name of the king who had them erected. Some also bear inscriptions of the Elamite ruler Shutruk-Nahhunte (1185–1155 BC), who had taken them to his capital to be consecrated to his gods. It is not yet known whether all the monuments of 'Mesopotamian booty' found at Susa were taken there by Shutruk, but the care these Elamite conquerors took to hand down to posterity the record of their victories over their powerful neighbours is clear.

△ *Proto-Elamite terracotta tablet (c.3000–2800 BC) inscribed with numbers and on which a cylinder seal has been rolled out. Its depiction of animals in human poses may have an allegorical meaning. (Paris, Louvre)*

◁ *Terracotta statuette of Middle Elamite date (c. 1300 BC) showing a woman with her arms and thighs emphasized, holding up her breasts. (Paris, Louvre)*

climbing the stairs. This recalls the decoration at Persepolis (where it was made of stone), with the same royal ideology being reflected in the choice of iconography.

It is possible to argue that the composite character of the palace built under Darius I during the first years of his reign, at the time of the reunification of the Achaemenid empire, stems from a particular striving for cohesion on the part of a ruler who wanted to appear as the unifier of his realm. The Achaemenid monuments of Susa were systematically sacked and razed to the ground by Alexander the Great and by Shapur II. However, they had been built on vast terraces, minute examination of which allowed Jean Perrot's team and his architect, Audran Labrousse, graphically to restore part of the palace complex, with its terraces, stairways decorated in brick and its monumental gates. The colossal statue of Darius, on a stand with a base decorated to depict subjugated peoples, in the Egyptian manner, was found in the eastern gate.

Persian palace decorations at the Louvre

Recent studies have inspired a new presentation of the Persian rooms at the Louvre in Paris. The transformation of the old Ministry of Finance into the Grand Louvre project will give more space for the Susa collections and for the stone decoration of the palace of Darius, with its protomes and square or bell-shaped column bases.

Since each piece's original position in the palace was not precisely known, it was decided to regroup the coloured-brick friezes by subject (archers, lions, mythological animals, tribute-bearers) and category (mural friezes, facings of

△ A small bronze model called 'sit-shamshi', which probably depicts a ceremony celebrated at sunrise. It dates to the twelfth century BC. (Paris, Louvre)

stairways, tiles on merlons, paving of gateways, tiles around windows and niches). The panels of the friezes of the archers, reconstructed by Dieulafoy, will be preserved in recognition of the role they played in the history of the museum and the rediscovery of the Persian monuments.

The removal, transportation and repositioning of the panels arranged at the beginning of the century will be overseen by the restorer, Michel Bourbon, who will profit from the experience gained when the Assyrian monuments were moved in 1992–3. Finally, the management of the Louvre has asked the architects B. Picard and I. Willerval to create some virtual images to show the spaces of the museum and the different elements of the decoration of the Persian palace.

Bibliography

P. Amiet, *L'Age des Échanges inter-iraniens, 3500–1700 a.C.* (Paris, 1984).

P. Amiet, *Suse, 6000 ans d'histoire* (Paris, 1988).

H.J. Nissen, *The Early History of the Ancient Near East, 9000–2000 B.C.* (Chicago, 1988).

Various authors, *La cité royale de Suse* (Paris, 1994).

◁ A computer model, made at the Louvre, that shows the decoration of the palaces of Susa and their arrangement in the museum.

Isernia: Europe's First Human Settlement

First occupied 700,000 years ago, Isernia La Pineta can claim to be one of the earliest human-inhabited sites in Europe – perhaps even the very earliest. The Palaeolithic site is a large one, and has yielded a considerable amount of archaeological material in a good state of preservation: plant and animal remains, as well as human artifacts. This has enabled a team of a dozen scholars from across the world to recreate in illuminating detail the environmental conditions and human activities at the site.

The site lay close to a river that flooded in wetter seasons, and the floods, together with volcanic eruptions, buried the objects left by humans under a thick layer of silt and dust, protecting them from the deterioration that exposure to the atmosphere would otherwise have caused. The habitation deposits were thus part of a deep and rich stratigraphic sequence.

The earliest layer in the sequence was formed during the last stage of sediment-formation in a lake that deposited clays and then the volcanic-related calc tufas known as travertines. The travertine layer was subsequently exposed and then eroded – and it was on the resulting surface that archaic humans first camped and left traces of their activities. These traces were then overlaid by riverine deposits in a phase that was accompanied by volcanic activity, which led to the deposition of tuffs (volcanic material). During this phase early people once again camped in the area, leaving another three distinct habitation layers before all traces of human presence were buried under further fluvial deposits and volcanic tuffs.

The animal remains found at the site consisted largely of rhinoceros, bison, elephant and bear; hippopotamus, wild boar, cervidae and caprids were scarcely represented. A single find – a tooth – documents the presence of lion. In addition, the excavators discovered fragments of the bones of birds

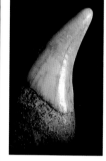

(including duck), small rodents, tortoises and fish.

Analysis of the ancient pollens found indicates that herbaceous plants were dominant in the area surrounding the site (especially grasses), as well as aquatic plants, which were favoured by the humid conditions. Few traces of wood have been found: some willow, poplar and plane, and rather less oak and pine.

The information derived from the study of the fauna and pollen gives a picture of extensive grassland with only limited tree cover; the wet environment explains the presence of sedges (*Carex*) and reed-mace (*Typha*). On the high ground were coniferous woodlands and a strip of broad-leaved thermophiles. Such an environment would most likely have been created in a climate with two annual seasons – one long and dry, the other short and humid.

Human activity is indicated by the presence of stone artifacts, made of flint and limestone. The numerous flint items are small and often have curving,

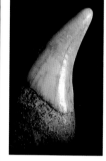

△ *The early Palaeolithic deposits at Isernia La Pineta were covered by a prefabricated building to enable the site to be excavated under cover and without interruption by bad weather. Fourteen different habitation deposits were buried under an average of 5 m (16 ft) of riverine and volcanic sediments.*

△ *A bear's tooth (left) and an elephant palate with molars (right) were part of the abundant bone remains found at the site.*

◁ *Location map: The
Palaeolithic site near
Isernia in central
Italy was discovered
during the building
of the Naples-to-
Vasto motorway.*

ISERNIA

toothed edges. What is significant is the discovery of flint flakes that fit together – indicating that they were made at the camp. Among the limestone tools (which are generally larger than those made of flint) are choppers and scrapers with wide semicircular working edges.

The stone artifacts and animal remains, grouped in dense concentrations, were found in four distinct habitation deposits, which has allowed hypotheses about the organization of the human groups to be developed. The majority of animal remains were of bison, rhinoceros and elephant, and the nature of the bone finds indicates human selection – for example, the number of vertebrae found was disproportionately low in relation to the number of crania. Also, the bones show many deliberate fractures resulting from human activity, with bones from different members of the same species often showing precisely the same pattern of damage. This is certainly connected with the techniques used to exploit the carcasses of the hunted animals, including extracting bone marrow for food.

Information on human activity at Isernia La Pineta – the choice of camp site, the search for stone to work, the making of lithic tools, the hunting and gathering, the transportation of parts of the carcasses of hunted animals, and the techniques of breaking bones to extract the marrow – has been combined with data from analyses of the sediments, bones and pollen found at the site. This has not only provided a very clear picture of the environment at the site 700,000 years ago, it has also illustrated the enormous capacity of early humans to adapt to and exploit their environment, even at this very early period in prehistory.

Functional Experimentation and Analyses

Petrographic, chemical and geological analyses showed that many of the lithic finds consisted of local flint. These studies were then used to identify appropriate material for flint-knapping experiments, which yielded two surprising conclusions.

The first is that the working of the flint was rapid and summary. A small block of flint was rested on a limestone anvil and struck sharply. This produced small flakes and left a lump, or core, of the original raw material.

Under the microscope, it was only the flakes that showed use-wear patterns, so the second conclusion is that the flint was knapped to obtain sharp cutting edges, present particularly on the flakes. It was therefore the flakes, and not the cores, that were used as tools at Isernia La Pineta. This has turned the previous concept of the tool on

◁∇ Bipolar percussion is achieved by resting a block of flint on an anvil stone and hitting it with a limestone hammerstone. Many flakes and small cores with denticulate profiles were found.

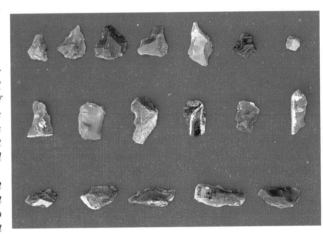

its head: the flakes, which had previously been regarded as waste products, were in fact tools, and what were thought to have been tools (the cores) were the waste-product of flint-knapping.

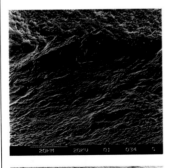

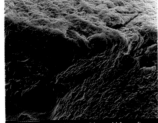

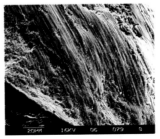

◁ The surface of the stone flakes used by archaic humans at the site became streaked and polished by use. Studying the flakes under the microscope enabled researchers to identify which parts of the tool were used, and for what purpose.

Studying the Animal Bones from Isernia La Pineta

An archaeozoological study was carried out on the animal remains from Isernia La Pineta, so as to improve our understanding of early human hunting and butchery practices. A systematic approach was adopted both in order to catalogue data accurately and also so as to try to answer a number of questions. Were the animal remains derived from hunting? Were any hunted animals selected on the basis of their species, age or sex? And how much of the carcass was actually used by these ancient humans?

The human character of the site, as well as being proved by the presence of many stone artifacts, is also confirmed by the absence of marks made by carnivores on the bones. Furthermore, the bone finds from Isernia La Pineta do not form a representative sample of the species of the time, nor are all the different anatomical parts of the animal present in proper numerical proportion. Herbivore species are well represented, but carnivores are not, and anatomical parts were clearly selected, though in a way that varied according to species. The incidence of cranial remains is relatively higher than the remains of vertebral columns and certain other bones.

It is not yet possible to speak of selective hunting on the basis of age or sex. However, the number of young animals represented is quite low; and – at least in the case of the rhinoceros – the evidence of very worn teeth suggests that the remains of elderly individuals are present.

The great age of the Isernia site has inevitably affected the state of preservation of the bone layer, to the extent that it is now difficult to distinguish traces of slaughter or butchery connected with human activity – although there are cases in which there seems to be some evidence of it. There is much more evidence of the extraction of bone marrow, many long bones and mandibles having been intentionally broken. The possibility that the brain, too, was eaten cannot be excluded, but the thinness, fragility and complex bone cavities of the retrocranium make it difficult to interpret the breaks that are often found.

To better understand the effects of impact on bones, and so work back to the techniques originally used to break them, a series of experiments was started in 1993. These used recently butchered cattle bones (anatomically the most closely comparable to bison), in particular the humerus, radius, ulna, metacarpal, femur, tibia, metatarsal and mandible.

Various fracture techniques were used, such as bipolar percussion (the bone, resting on a block of limestone, was hit with a stone, bone or wooden hammer), glancing percussion (the bone was grasped at one end and struck against a limestone anvil), and flexing percussion (the bone was held at both ends, and the middle part struck violently on a pointed anvil). The experiments revealed distinctive characteristics associated with direct percussion (large areas of impact with curvilinear edges and the production of many microflakes) and glancing percussion (sharp edges, impact zones with sometimes denticulate edges, little production of flakes and a tendency for the fracture planes to follow oblique or transverse lines). Such longitudinal fractures generally provide better access to extract the marrow and require less force. The work has shown that the type of fracture is related to several variables (the technique used, the part of the animal it is applied to, and the age of the animal).

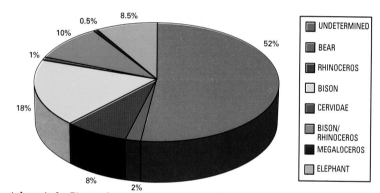

△ Isernia La Pineta: frequency, by species, of bone finds from habitation deposit 3a of sector 1 of the excavation.

The study of the site was conducted with the help of dozens of specialists. Fundamental to the study was the gathering of data. The position of finds was recorded both in terms of location (co-ordinates on a grid) and in terms of relationships to other objects. The sediments and the stratigraphy were examined in detail; samples of sediments, soils and pollen were taken for laboratory analysis; and water flotation of the soil was used to identify minute fragments and microvertebrates. The information necessary for visual and graphic records (reliefs, plans, sections, photogrammetry, photographs and filmed sequences) was also identified and selected, and written records were kept of all activity, observations and participation.

From the beginning it was clear that – because of the often substantial size and quantity of the bones, and their fragility – the palaeontological material required particular consolidation and preservation effort. This recognition was closely linked with the desire to reconstruct the habitation deposits, together with the finds themselves, in a museum. Remarkable efforts were made from the outset to consolidate and preserve the finds, and to remove them from the surrounding soil while

Habitation deposit 3a of sector 1 of the excavation, ~owing chunks of travertine and limestone, the ~mains of bison crania and (at lower left) an elephant ~sk.

Bibliography

M. Cremaschi and C. Peretto, 'Les sols d'habitat du site paléolithique d'Isernia La Pineta (Molise, Italie Centrale)', in *L'Anthropologie*, 92, 4 (1988), pp. 1017–40.

G. Guiberti and C. Peretto, 'Evidences de la fracturation intentionelle d'ossements animaux avec moelle dans le gisement paléolithique de La Pineta de Isernia (Molise, Italie)', in *L'Anthropologie*, 96 (1991), pp. 765–778.

Isernia La Pineta: un accampamento più antico di 700 000 anni, exhibition catalogue (Bologna, 1994).

C. Peretto (ed.), *Isernia La Pineta, nuovi contributi scientifici* (Isernia, 1991).

C. Peretto (ed.), *Le industrie litiche del giacimento di Isernia La Pineta* (Isernia, 1994).

Various authors, 'Nuove ricerche nel giacimento paleolitico di Isernia La Pineta (Molise)', in *Rivista di scienze preistoriche*, XLIV, 1–2 (1992), pp. 3–41.

leaving their imprints intact. There-after, the next steps were to make a mould of the surface of the excavation, complete the definitive restoration of the finds in the laboratory, and finally reposition them on the model in the museum, faithfully reproducing the original habitation deposit, with its undulations, inclinations, irregularities, and so on. Much care was also taken over the computerized archiving of the finds.

In particular, new information has emerged from analysis of the stone items and from conducting experiments in flint-knapping and comparing the results with the original finds. It was discovered that those remains that had previously been thought to be tools (the cores) were nothing but the waste from flint-knapping, while what had hitherto been interpreted as waste (the flakes) are actually what archaic humans used as tools in their daily activities (see box on p. 103).

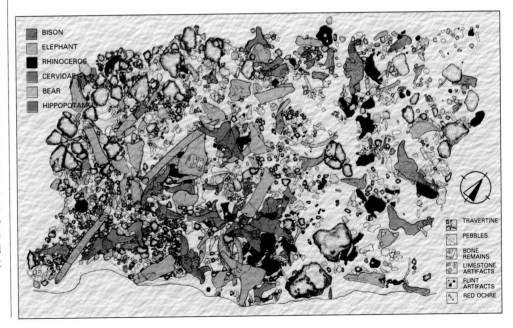

BISON
ELEPHANT
RHINOCEROS
CERVIDAE
BEAR
HIPPOPOTAMUS

TRAVERTINE
PEBBLES
BONE REMAINS
LIMESTONE ARTIFACTS
FLINT ARTIFACTS
RED OCHRE

△ *Distribution of the bone finds and lithic artifacts from a large area of habitation deposit 3a. Computer mapping and statistical study of the finds enable probable groupings or distributions to be distinguished, providing useful information about human activity at the site.*

The Great Megalithic Monuments

Europe

The term 'megalith', derived from the Greek megas ('large') and lithos ('stone'), was coined by Algernon Herbert in 1849 and adopted for impressive stone monuments spread over many parts of the world. This brief discussion will be limited to those along the Atlantic coasts of Europe and in the Maltese islands – the focus of megalith building in prehistoric Europe – and will follow the typological classification of megaliths into menhirs, alignments, stone circles, chambered tombs and temples.

It is now generally accepted that megalithic monuments belong to the Neolithic period, and that they had no single place of origin. The hypothesis advanced by V. Gordon Childe (1925), that megalith building derived from Egypt or the Aegean, has been disproved by radiocarbon dating (calibrated by means of tree-ring dating), which has shown that the European megaliths are in fact older than Egyptian pyramids or Aegean chambered tombs.

As will be seen, the European megalithic structures were probably connected with the cults of the dead and of fertility that developed during the Neolithic period. In this period farming communities dedicated a good deal of time to building imposing monuments for the dead. Some have argued that certain megalithic structures may also have functioned as astronomical observatories. However, small groups in Brittany (north-west France) and by the Tagus estuary (south-central Portugal) in the Mesolithic (c. 10,000 BC) had already been involved in an archaic form of megalith-building recognizable by large stone slabs that delimit tombs designed to contain collective burials. From the evidence of around 5,000 structures – chambered tombs and passage graves, menhirs, alignments, stone circles, statue-stelae, etc. – it seems undeniable that megalith-building reached its earliest florescence primarily in France, sometime around 4500 BC. It also appears, rather later, in Portugal (3900 BC), Spain and, towards 3600 BC, in the British Isles. The practice seems to have reached the Italian peninsula, Sardinia and Corsica from the Iberian peninsula and France. A separate and distinctive tradition of megalithic building also developed on

◁ *The menhir of Champ Dolent (Dol, France), one of the most impressive found in Europe, is 9.5 m (31 ft) high and weighs about 125 tons.*

▽ *A partial view of the famous megalithic alignments at Carnac in Brittany illustrates the grandeur of the complex. This great series of alignments consists of around 3,000 standing stones arranged in a number of separate alignments, with 10 to 13 parallel rows extending in some cases for over 1 km.*

△ *The distribution of the main megalithic
monuments so far found in Europe:
menhirs, alignments, stone circles and
chambered tombs.*

the Maltese islands, where true temples
and rock-cut tombs appear.

The term menhir is derived from the
Breton *men* ('stone') and *hir* ('long').
Menhirs are standing stones of various
sizes erected by human hands; some
are between 1 m and 6 m (3 ft and 20 ft)
high, some rise up to 12 m (40 ft). One
of the most notable is the great menhir
of Locmariaquer in Brittany. Today it
lies on the ground in four pieces, but
when first erected it must have been an
impressive sight, on account of both its
mass (it weighs about 300 tons) and its
height (23.5 m, or 77 ft).

Menhirs are found mostly in France,
but they are also present in other parts
of western Europe: in Britain, Spain,
Portugal, northern Italy (statue-
menhirs), southern Italy (Puglia),
Sardinia and Corsica. Apart from the
Breton menhirs, which date to the Early
Neolithic (*c.* 4000 BC), most of them
have been dated – on the basis of
associated material (pottery fragments,
etc.) – to the Late Neolithic (third
millennium BC), or to the Early and
Middle Bronze Age (late third to early
second millennium BC).

It is hard to determine their function.
It is not impossible that undecorated
menhirs (those not obviously depicting
a figure or object) may form a symbol of
the *axis mundi*, expressing the union

between sky and earth – or even that
they may represent phallic symbols
penetrating the body of Mother Earth in
an act of impregnation connected with
the cult of fertility. In some cases
menhirs have decoration that symbolizes the sun and water: elements that,
because of their life-generating capabil-
ities, played a highly important role in
the agrarian cultures of the Neolithic
period. In this context, the concentration of these megalithic structures
near watercourses is understandable.
The presence of menhirs near burial
monuments, or sites where rites linked
to an agrarian cult were carried out,
suggests that their function was to mark
the existence of a sacred place.
Moreover, stone, because of its im-
perishable character, sometimes
became the permanent home of the
soul of the deceased and vouched for
his or her immortality; stylized carvings
or paintings on such stones represent
the image of the deceased (statue-
menhirs).

Menhirs grouped in parallel lines form
the structures known as alignments, the
most important of which are located at

Carnac in Brittany. The longest single
alignments are about 1 km (0.6 miles)
in length, but the principal Carnac
alignments extend altogether for
around 3 km (1.8 miles), in ten to
thirteen parallel lines. There are in fact
several separate alignments, the three
main ones containing a total of almost
3,000 menhirs Menec: (1,169 menhirs),
Kermario (1,099 menhirs) and
Kerlescan (594 menhirs). Not surprisingly, these ensembles are incomplete today, as a result of the
ravages of time. There are other
alignments in Scotland and Ireland;
monuments similar to those at Carnac –
though, of course, unconnected with
them – are found also in Tibet and in
the Deccan (southern part of India). It is
not certain whether the Carnac
alignments formed a complex fulfilling
religious functions or whether they
served as an astronomical observatory
of the Stonehenge type. Alexander
Thom argued that their original
arrangement was related to the
forecasting of eclipses.

Chambered tombs or dolmens – a late
eighteenth-century term derived from

▽ *The famous and imposing chambered tomb named La Roche aux Fées in Brittany. Its
monumental portico leads to a long, rectangular chamber with walls 2m (6½ ft) high,
subdivided into four cells by stones projecting from one side.*

the Breton *dol* ('table') and *men* ('stone') – consist of horizontal slabs laid across the top of vertical stones (orthostats). They characteristically have a circular, polygonal or quadrangular chamber, sometimes preceded by an access passage. Such tombs were sometimes covered with a tumulus of earth or stone (cairn), perhaps both to signal the presence of the burial within and to protect it.

It seems undeniable that the tombs were collective, since (where the soil and subsoil were not acid) they have yielded human bones in quantities that, in some cases, seem to indicate the presence of hundreds of individuals – perhaps members of a whole family or village. Sometimes the tombs seem simply to have been ossuaries in which the bones of the deceased were deposited after being defleshed elsewhere. There are also instances of cremated remains. In some burials funerary goods have been found – weapons and utensils for agricultural, domestic and ornamental uses, along with traces of foodstuffs – to provide the deceased with all the basic necessities for the great voyage to the beyond. That many objects, some of them precious, were deliberately broken at the time of deposition provides evidence of customs recognizable in the proto-historic and historic periods.

There is also evidence in the megalithic tombs of a connection between the cults of fertility and death. By ritual propitiation, Neolithic humans on the one hand guaranteed the fertility of the earth, their only source of sustenance, and on the other protected their dead – who, once buried, acquired the vital energy needed to ensure the renewal of the seasonal cycles. The goods found in some tombs also seem to link the cult of fertility and the cult of the dead. In Portugal they included cylindrical objects of stone and bone schematically depicting the Mother Goddess, who was also portrayed on the walls of the tombs in northern Europe and clearly played the role of a female protector of the dead.

The oldest megalithic tombs have been found in Brittany – for example the passage grave under the tumulus of Kercado at Carnac, which dates to 4800 BC – although similar structures occur in the Iberian peninsula, Britain, Ireland, Germany, Denmark and Sweden. The passage graves of Brittany are sometimes decorated with carvings

△ *The grandeur of La Roche aux Fées can be clearly seen in this view, showing large horizontal slabs overlying great orthostats. This is an extraordinary example of the monumentality that Neolithic builders could achieve.*

△ *Carving on one of the orthostats of the
passage grave of Luffang (Brittany)
representing a stylized figure identified
as a deity.*

m (230 ft) long and 25 (82 ft) wide. This contained eleven Middle Neolithic passage graves built in two different phases: 3800 BC and 3500 BC (according to uncalibrated radiocarbon dating); several of the burial chambers have a circular plan and are covered with a corbelled vault.

In the Iberian peninsula (where grave goods are commoner than elsewhere) there are notable tombs in the cemetery of Los Millares (Spain), datable to the second half of the third millennium BC, and in that of Antequera (Spain), dating to the fourth to third millennia BC. Similar tombs also occur in Ireland. Of particular importance, not only for their impressive size and appearance but also for the elaborate spiral motifs carved on their stones, are the passage graves of Newgrange and Knowth (both *c.* 3200 BC) in the Boyne valley in Ireland. Each has a cruciform plan and is covered with a circular tumulus (Knowth in fact has two cruciform-plan tombs within its tumulus). At Newgrange the entrance (which leads to a passage with the burial chamber at the end) is so oriented that at dawn on the winter solstice (21 December) the rays of the sun penetrate the chamber via a narrow opening placed above the entrance.

Another type of megalithic structure found in prehistoric Europe is the stone circle, or cromlech; the latter term derives from the Breton *crom* ('circle') and *lech* ('place'), and indicates a monumental complex of menhirs arranged in a circle or semicircle. The size varies a great deal, from the small examples of Li Muri (Arzachena) in Sardinia, which have a diameter of 5 m

◁ Left: *The passage grave of Newgrange (Ireland), dating to c. 3200 BC. Bottom left: The entrance to the tomb is marked by a large slab decorated with spiral motifs and, behind, by a narrow horizontal slot above the entrance, through which the dawn rays of the midwinter sun shine down the passage beyond.*

representing polished stone axes or axe-heads along with indecipherable patterns; mostly, though, the decoration consists of human silhouettes or rather stylized parts of the human body. These may be representations of a divinity, often depicted in megalithic tombs, concerned with fertility and the protection of the dead. Brittany has a concentration of complex passage-grave structures, such as the great tumulus of Barnenez at Plouézoc'h – 70

to 8 m (16 ft to 26 ft), to the gigantic circle of Avebury in southern England, which has a diameter of 427 m (1,400 ft). Some of these circles may have had a cult and funerary function, while others may have been used as a sort of astronomical observatory.

The greatest concentration of circles is in the British Isles. The most famous of all stone circles, and one of the most evocative megalithic monuments in Europe, is the complex at Stonehenge in Wiltshire. From research conducted at the site, it is now possible to establish that the structure was built in three distinct phases.

Stonehenge 1, radiocarbon-dated to *c.* 2950–2900 BC, was a circular enclosure 100 m (328 ft) in diameter with an embankment. Around the circumference of the enclosure 56 holes were found (called the 'Aubrey Holes', after the seventeenth-century antiquary who first found them). Their function remains unclear, although fragments of cremated human bone from the next phase (Stonehenge 2, *c.* 2900–2400 BC) were found in their upper levels. In the second phase parts of the ditch were filled in and complex timber settings appeared within the enclosure.

Finally, in Stonehenge 3 (2550–1600 BC), two concentric arcs of eighty-two bluestone menhirs were erected inside the enclosure before being removed and replaced with a circle of thirty imposing blocks covered with horizontal slabs (trilithons), within which was another circle of forty bluestones and five gigantic trilithons. Within the area enclosed by the trilithons, nineteen bluestones, arranged in a horseshoe shape were added, and a large slab (4.5 × 1 m, or 14.7 × 3.3 ft) known as the 'Altar Stone' was placed at the centre of the complex. On the circumference of the enclosure four Sarsen Stones known as the 'Four Stations' were erected, perhaps for use in astronomical observations; and finally the Slaughter Stone was found near the entrance to the enclosure. Just outside the enclosure was a menhir (the Heel Stone), 5 m (16 ft) high and weighing 35 tons, which was perhaps intended to indicate the position of the rising of the sun at the summer solstice (21 June).

It is possible that Stonehenge had more than one function. That it played an important role in the sacred sphere is indicated by the circular layout, which was perhaps used for ceremonies connected with an agrarian cult. But the site could also have served as an astronomical observatory. According to some scholars, the complex may have been used for the study of solar and

△ *Computer reconstruction of the movement of the sun behind Stonehenge at the summer solstice. It is possible that this great stone circle was connected with a solar cult and the determination of calendrical time.*

lunar movements and – in connection with a solar cult – for the calculation of the seasons (the circle of thirty trilithons indicating the days of a month).

Megalithic temples occur only in the islands of the Maltese archipelago. Linked to the rock-cut tombs, which are dealt with separately (see box on p. 112), there were thirty temples, characterized by a singular and impressive architectural structure that illustrates the flourishing megalithic culture that developed during the Neolithic, between *c.* 4100 and *c.* 2500 BC (in calibrated years).

Maltese megalith building had affinities with mainland Europe but is generally considered to be an indi-genous development. Its extraordinary florescence was probably determined by the presence in the archipelago of easily worked materials, such as globigerina limestone and coralline limestone, as well as by the technical ability of the islands' inhabitants. The similarities with Europe lie in the shared capacity of prehistoric humans to erect monumental stone structures and decorate them with spiral or ocular motifs. They also include representations of the Mother Goddess, although the scale of the Maltese examples is much larger – for example, the statue in the Tarxien complex is about 3 m (nearly 10 ft) high – which differentiates them from the stylized statuettes of the chambered tombs.

△ *One of the five gigantic trilithons at Stonehenge. Its enormous size demonstrates the technical ability of the megalith-builders.*

▽ *Evocative view of the Stonehenge trilithons illuminated by the full moon.*

The Mysterious Subterranean Tombs of Malta

The building of rock-cut tombs, widely practised around the Mediterranean during the Neolithic, seems to find its most complete expression in the Maltese islands (Malta, Comino and Gozo). Here, on the island of Malta itself in the period between about 4100 and 2500 BC, prehistoric people excavated the tomb of Hal Saflieni from the living rock.

The tomb was intended for celebration of the cult of the Mother Goddess and for the deposition of many dead (the remains of almost 7,000 skeletons were found). It is a particularly complicated structure, divided into three levels and made up of rooms, small cells and alcoves that often interconnect, their walls sculpted or painted in imitation of the megalithic temples built above ground. The complex, which reaches a depth of 11 m (36 ft) and extends over an area of around 500 sq m (600 sq yd), was built using wedges and quarry picks and flint blades and scrapers, over a period of about 2,000 years. This has led scholars to argue that the uses of the three levels may have differed – and, perhaps, changed over time.

Burial deposits, bone and fragments of pottery suggest that the rooms on the first level were used for funerary purposes that seem to have been linked to cult functions – some of the finds point to a cult dedicated to the Mother Goddess. The discovery of a nude female statue and a probable phallic symbol on the second level suggest the practice of a sacred union between priest and priestess, representing male and female deities, in a rite intended to ensure the continuity of the seasonal cycle. The burial deposits on this level date to the second phase of use, when the tomb had lost its cult function and assumed a burial function; the chambers of the third level seem to have fulfilled a similar function.

The Brochtorff circle on the island of Gozo appears to share some features of the rock-cut tomb of Hal Saflieni. The circle is a complex on a single level (4–5 m, or 13–16 ft, deep), consisting of a series of natural caves and spaces used to hold the dead, and has architectural elements similar to those of the temples. The complex is surrounded by a megalithic circle dated between 3300/3000 BC and 2500 BC. The presence of obese female statuettes confirms the connection of the cult of fertility with that of the dead, while a group of quite stylized male statuettes refers to a funerary ritual.

From the current data one can argue that the Brochtorff circle on Gozo derived from the same funerary and cult needs as those that led the inhabitants of Malta to dig the rock-cut tomb of Hal Saflieni. The two structures were also contemporaneous (or, rather, both were built in the period between about 4100 and 2500 BC) and located near to temples – the Brochtorff circle close to Ggantija, and Hal Saflieni near Tarxien.

△▷ *Above:* The main chamber of the second level of the rock-cut tomb complex of Hal Saflieni (Malta). *Right:* 'The Sleeper', a statuette found in the complex.

◁ *A chamber in the megalithic temple of Ggantija (Gozo). Dated to 3600–3300/3000 BC, it is located near the Brochtorff circle (see the picture on the opposite page).*

Bibliography

A. Bonanno, *Archaeology and Fertility Cult in the Ancient Mediterranean* (Valetta, 1986).

A. Burl, *Megalithic Brittany* (London, 1985).

A. Burl, *The Stone Circles of the British Isles* (London and New Haven, 1976).

C. Chippindale, *Stonehenge Complete* (2nd ed., London and New York, 1993).

G. Eogan, *Knowth and the Passage-Tombs of Ireland* (London, 1986).

M. O'Kelly, *Newgrange* (London and New York, 1982).

C. Renfrew (ed.), *The Megalithic Monuments of Western Europe* (London and New York, 1983).

S. Stoddart *et al.*, 'Cult in an Island Society: Prehistoric Malta in the Tarxien Period', in *Cambridge Archaeological Journal*, 3:1 (1993), pp. 3–19.

△ *Plan of the Brochtorff circle (4100–2500 BC): (1) stone marking the boundary of the funerary-cult complex; (2) entrance to the circle; (3) threshold; (4) altar; (5) stone jar, similar to one found in the temple of Tarxien; (6) central zone of the sanctuary; (7) great ditches containing semi-articulated skeletons; (8) cave; (9) stone gateway similar to that at the megalithic temple of Hagar Qim; (10) statuettes of seated females representing the Mother Goddess.*

△ *Twin seated female figures, identified as Mother Goddesses, found at the Brochtorff circle site (Gozo).*

Ötzi: The Ice Man

Italy

In 1991, on the Austro-Italian border in the heart of the Alps, the mummified corpse of a man was discovered. When it was realized that he had died around 5,000 years ago the discovery provoked such public interest as to rival Priam's Treasure or the Tomb of Tutankhamun in fame and popularity. The body has been given many names: the man of Similaun, the Ice Man or, more simply, Ötzi (after the Ötztaler Alps, where it was found). The discovery has done an enormous amount to stimulate archaeological research in the Alpine area, and continues to do so.

On 19 September 1991 two Germans, Erika and Helmut Simon, during a climbing holiday in the area known as the Ötztaler Alps or the Venoste Alps, found the lifeless body of a man in a small gully near the Similaun shelter, at an altitude of 3,210 m (10,530 ft). They immediately notified the manager of the shelter, but worsening weather prevented the recovery of the body, conducted under the direction of the forensic examiner Dr Rainer Henn, until 23 September. The body was removed by helicopter and transferred to the Institute for Forensic Medicine at the University of Innsbruck and then, on the following day, to the Anatomical Institute – where it is now conserved in a refrigerated room at a constant -6°C with a humidity of *c.* 96–98%.

In the four days that separated the finding and the official recovery of the body some twenty or more people visited the find-spot. Some of them retrieved objects that were later identified as part of the Ice Man's equipment: a birch-bark container, a bow-stave, a quiver, a flint dagger and a copper axe. It was the typology of the axe and the radiocarbon dating of the body tissue which would allow Konrad Spindler, the Director of the Institute of Prehistory and Protohistory at the University of Innsbruck, to date this exceptional find to the end of the fourth millennium BC, that is to say during the Copper Age.

Given the importance of the find, Andreas Lippert (then Director of the Institute of Prehistory and Protohistory) conducted a first investigation at the gully, which enabled further objects that formed part of the equipment belonging to the mummy to be recovered. Operations were interrupted by unexpected bad weather, and within a few days the area was buried under several metres of snow. A second investigation was carried out between 20 July and 25 August 1992, again under the direction of Lippert (who had in the meantime moved to the Institute of Prehistory and Protohistory of the University of Vienna), of Dr Lorenzo Dal Ri, Hans Nothdurfter (of the Superintendency of Archaeology of the Province of Bolzano) and Professor Bernardino Bagolini (of the Department of Philology and History of the University of Trento). During this campaign, all the water produced by the melting of the ice was sieved.

Many finds were made: blades of grass, leaves, charcoal particles, and parts of insects. Also closely examined were the sediments at the bottom of the gully. As well as traces of the Ice Man's equipment, anatomical fragments were recovered (such as pieces of skin, blood vessels, head and body hair and a fingernail) and other more substantial finds: a piece from the end of the bow-stave, which had been broken during the recovery of the body, and the dead man's fur cap. Some of the objects were found lying directly on the rock – which clearly indicates that when the Ice Man

◄The gully where on 19 September 1991 a pair of German climbers found the mummified corpse of a man dating to around 5,000 years ago.

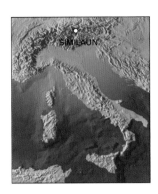

➤ *The Ice Man. A process of dehydration led to the partial mummification of his body and the preservation of the internal organs.*

sought refuge in the gully it was free of ice.

Also found during sieving were two flint objects, one of them probably a fragment of a Mesolithic type of backed point. This shows that as early as some 9,000 years ago the area was already frequented by those groups of hunters and gatherers who, as many remains in the mountains of the Trentino Alto Adige show, sometimes ventured to high altitudes (probably to hunt ibex).

At the moment of its discovery the mummy appeared to lack head and body hair – it had fallen out during the initial decay of the skin, before the process of mummification set in – but a considerable quantity of wavy, dark chestnut-coloured human hair, *c.* 9 cm (3½ in.) long, was identified on some of the clothing. On the other hand, CAT (computerized axial tomography) scans of the body revealed that the internal organs were well preserved. The anthropological analyses have shown that the Ice Man was a male who when he died had been around 35–40 years old, about 160 cm (5 ft 3 in.) in height, and weighing 45 kg (99 lb 4 oz.) – the body now weighs only 13.3 kg (29 lb 5 oz.). He had some physical peculiarities: he had a *diastema* (a small gap between the two incisor teeth), lacked wisdom teeth and had no twelfth rib. X-rays and computer tomograms

➤ *Table of plants used by Ötzi, identified by Sigmar Bortenschlager and a team at the Botanical Institute of the University of Innsbruck.*

revealed old and healed fractures of the fifth to ninth left ribs. Other fractures (third to sixth right ribs) show no callus formation and may therefore have been sustained either shortly before death or posthumously. A slight hardening of some blood vessels might have been due to a high level of blood cholesterol, and there was an indication of the beginnings of frostbite on one foot.

A particularly interesting discovery was the presence of a series of tattoos (the oldest so far known): on either side of the spine at the level of the kidneys, on the inside of the right knee, on the ankles, and on the left calf. It is difficult to understand the significance of these marks. One possible explanation is that they may have had a therapeutic purpose (like a sort of acupuncture). In fact, computer tomographic analysis of the tattooed parts of the Ice Man's body has found evidence of osteochondrosis and spondylosis, as well as the beginning of degenerative changes in the motor joints: the Ice Man must have suffered from arthritis and rheumatic pains.

Work on the body's clothing – carried out in the restoration laboratory of the Römisch-Germanisches-Zentralmuseum in Mainz, by Roswitha Goedecker-Ciolek under the direction of Markus Egg – has established that when he died the man was wearing a pair of shoes stuffed with straw, leggings, a loin-cloth, an upper garment, a cloak and a cap. Apart from the cloak

(which was made of plaited grass), the other clothes were all made of strips of fur or (in some cases) leather, sewn together with great precision and with quite regular stitching. This is clothing well suited to the harsh environment of the high mountains. The various types of skins used (goat, calf, deer and brown bear) had been treated with fat and smoked to make them less permeable.

The sewing thread was largely made of animal sinews (mostly ox), animal hair and blades of grass. In some places it was possible to identify repairs – some very coarse, perhaps made by the man himself with threads made from vegetable fibres. The staining visible in some places on the inside of the clothes indicates that they were worn with the hair side outside.

The Ice Man carried a highly functional set of equipment that included a bow-stave of yew wood, 182.5 cm (6 ft) long, and a quiver made of goat hide over a

No.	Plant	Latin name	Part used	Product
1	Yew	*Taxus baccata*	wood	bow, axe-handle
2	Lime	*Tilia sp.*	wood (branch),	retoucher, cord, bast binding material
3	Ash	*Fraxinus excelsior*	wood	dagger-hilt
4	Hazel	*Corylus avellana*	wood (stem)	U-frame of back-pack, quiver
5	Larch	*Larix decidua*	wood	boards of back-pack,
6	Wayfaring tree	*Viburnum lantana*	wood (shoot)	arrow-shaft
7	Dogwood	*Cornus sp.*	wood (shoot)	arrow-shaft
8	Birch	*Betula sp.*	bark, sap	container, glue
9	Reticulate willow	*Salix reticulata T.*	wood	fuel
10	Amelanchier	*Amelanchier ovalis*	wood	fuel
11	Alder	*Alnus viridis*	wood	fuel
12	Norway spruce	*Picea abies*	wood, needles	fuel, ?
13	Pine	*Pinus sp.*	wood	fuel
14	Elm	*Ulmus sp.*	wood	fuel
15	Juniper	*Juniperus sp.*	needles	?
16	Norway maple	*Acer platanoides*	leaves	insulating material
17	Blackthorn	*Prunus spinosa*	fruit	food

hazel-wood frame, which contained fourteen arrow shafts; two of the shafts were fitted with flint arrowheads and had threefold fletching of bird feathers at the base (all the shafts, except one, were made of viburnum wood). He also carried a group of four deer-horn tools with their pointed ends tied together with bast cord (made from the fibrous parts of some types of tree bark), an elongated and slightly curved antler point (perhaps a needle for knotting or repairing), two sinews possibly used for sewing and a length of bast cord.

Other items, too, were found next to the Ice Man. One was an axe that had an elbow-shaped haft cut from a section of yew trunk and branch, with an angle of roughly 90° between the two sections, and a blade of almost pure copper

(99.7% copper, 0.22% arsenic, 0.08% silver) glued into a fork at the end of the haft and bound with a series of leather strips. A small dagger had a flint blade fixed in an ash-wood handle with glue and thin cord made from animal sinew; a scabbard of woven bast, also found, probably belonged to it. An instrument with a shaft made of limewood with a spike of antler inserted into its centre, like the lead in a pencil, could perhaps have been a retoucher for flint tools. There were also two fungi (razor-strop fungus, or *Piptoporus betulinus*) threaded onto a strip of leather, as well as a small hide bag (a sort of belt-pouch that was fixed to the waist), which contained a scraper with 'sicklegloss', a drilling tool and a blade (all of flint), a bone awl with a broken point, and a

black mass – identified as the remains of a tree fungus (tinder fungus, or *Fomes fomentarius*), used to light fires.

The objects recovered also included two cylindrical containers made from birch bark, one of which had been used to carry live embers – it contained Norway maple leaves wrapped around pieces of charcoal (derived from species including pine, Norway spruce, larch, elm, alder) – and a back-pack frame made from a hazel rod bent into a U, its ends linked by two small larch boards secured with mortise-and-tenon joints. There were also several cords, mostly of grass, and a flat marble disc with a central hole threaded onto a strip of hide (the only non-functional item, and one to which its owner may have attributed magical powers to ward off evil).

△ *Mountaineers Reinhold Messner and Hans Kammerlander crouch beside the Ice Man. Some twenty or more people visited the find-spot in the four days between the time the body was found and its removal to the Institute of Forensic Medicine at Innsbruck. In the background at the right the yew-wood bow leans against the rock.*

The number of different types of wood used in the manufacture of the equipment (as many as seventeen) is impressive. Ötzi must have been well-acquainted with the characteristics of these woods: each item of his equipment was made from the type of wood most suitable for its purpose. It may be that the raw materials had been gathered in his home territory. If so, yew, viburnum, ash, dogwood, hazel and lime all grow in the lower valleys and reach altitudes as high as 1,600 m (5,250 ft). Only larch grows as high as the tree-line, although it also grows at lower altitudes. It can therefore be concluded that Ötzi finished making his equipment at lower altitudes and that the find-spot was not his habitual home. The finding of two grains of wheat (*Triticcum monococcum*) on his

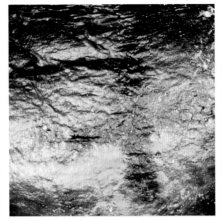
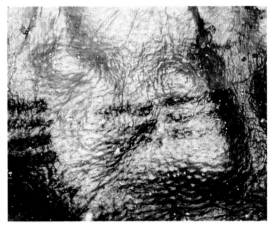

△▷ Above: *The cruciform tattoo on the inside of the right knee.* Right: *Some of the tattoos identified along the spine at the level of the kidneys. These tattoos may have had a therapeutic function, not unlike acupuncture.*

clothing confirms this. It seems, then that Ötzi came from the lower valleys, from a community with a subsistence economy (this can easily be deduced from the materials from which his equipment is made) based on farming, hunting and stock-rearing, and that he was far from his usual home at harvest time. His last journey must have occurred in late summer: this is

A Model of Interdisciplinary Research

There are now 64 research groups involved in studying the mummy, including a total of some 150 researchers of 11 nationalities – specialists in such fields of medical, biological and natural science as palaeobotany, zoology and ornithology.

That the study of such an important find has not been undertaken by a single institution is due above all to Werner Platzer (Director of the Anatomical Institute of the University of Innsbruck) and Konrad Spindler (Director of the Institute of Prehistory and Protohistory at the same university). They set out to spread the work among several teams, so gaining greater objectivity and scientific credibility in the results. This approach was followed, for example, in distributing samples for radiocarbon analysis. Five laboratories – at Uppsala, Paris, Oxford, Zurich and

Cambridge, Massachusetts – all with AMS (accelerator mass spectrometry), were sent a total of nine samples taken from the mummy and from various objects made of plant materials found on or near the corpse. The results were roughly equivalent, and by comparing them it has been possible to obtain a mean date for the mummy of 4546±17 BP (in uncalibrated radiocarbon years 'before the present') and 3352–3108 BC (in calendar years): the

mummy would therefore be around 5,000 years old.

The collaboration among scholars of different nationalities, co-ordinated by Professor Dieter zur Nedden, Director of the Department of Radiology and Computer Tomography of the University of Innsbruck, has also established new methodologies that will be applicable in fields outside archaeology – for example in cosmetic surgery. Thanks to stereolithography his team

has made a life-size, three-dimensional model of Ötzi's skull, allowing anthropologists to take more measurements than would normally be possible without damaging the mummy.

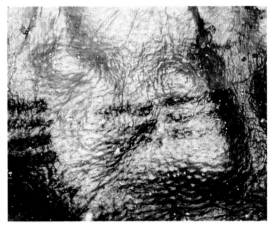

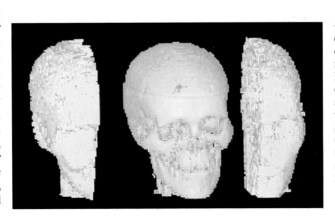

◁▷ *Left:* Three-dimensional computer representation of the Ice Man's skull. *Right:* A three-dimensional model of the skull in acrylic resin; this was produced by stereolithography from data from the CAT (computerized axial tomography) analysis. The cranium and jaw of the model can be separated.

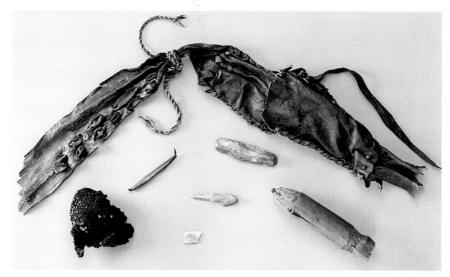

from the crystalline region of the Venoste Alps. It is, however, found in the limestone areas of southern Trentino and western Veneto around the Monti Lessini.

It is more difficult to say which culture the Ice Man belonged to. (It would be easier if at least one pottery vessel had been found with him – pottery being very culture-specific in its form and decoration.) The arrowheads, the flint dagger and the copper axe have been identified as of 'Remedello' type (so called because the first finds of this type were made at the beginning of the last century, in the cemetery of Remedello Sotto, near Brescia), which new radiocarbon dating shows was used from the end of the fourth millennium and during the whole third millennium BC. However, objects of this type are found in almost all the cultures of the Copper Age in Northern Italy. This was a period of profound economic and social changes – characterized, for example, by the manufacture and circulation in the Alpine arc of statue-stelae (monumental figures sculpted in stone with stylized features). Although difficult to interpret, they are shown with the weapons, ornaments and clothing commonly used during the Copper Age.

confirmed, for example, by the finding of a ripe sloe and stalkless maple leaves that still contained chlorophyll (and therefore must have been gathered while still green).

It is very likely that Ötzi came from, or was in contact with, populations settled in the south Alpine area. His equipment included tools made of flint – a sedimentary material completely absent

On the surfaces of these statue-stelae are depicted daggers of Remedello type, axes, halberds and 'sceptres', which could indicate a society in which such objects had a particular significance. Perhaps they were a sort of status symbol, the people who possessed them holding posts of honour in their own groups. The axe found with the Ice Man, which is similar to those shown on the stone figures, may very probably have been made by him, because the concentration of arsenic, copper, nickel and manganese in his hair (3–5 times greater than present-day levels) is explicable only as the result of contact with metalworking activities. Also, the decoration of the Ice Man's hide tunic in light and dark bands is somewhat reminiscent of the cloaks depicted on

△ Above *(clockwise from top): Small hide bag; right shoe with straw stuffing and a detail of the net of grass cords from the left shoe; birch-bark container, apparently used to carry live embers; small dagger with flint blade and ash-wood hilt with scabbard of plaited bast strips; bear-hide cap.* Right: *The yew-wood axe with its copper blade.*

△ *Ötzi and his equipment, in a reconstruction from the German weekly* Stern, *showing how he was equipped for the harsh temperatures of the high mountains.*

▷ *The Ice Man's clothing, in a reconstruction proposed by the restoration laboratory of the Römisch-Germanisches-Zentralmuseum, Mainz. From left to right: the hide belt holding up the loin-cloth and leggings; the tunic and the padded hide shoes; the bear-hide cap for the harsh temperatures and cloak made of plaited lake grasses.*

the statue-stelae. It may therefore be reasonable to conclude that Ötzi would have played an important role within his community.

As for what led him to such high altitudes, one may think of summer alpine pasture or transhumance. Such a hypothesis is supported by many finds from this period above 1,600 m (5,250 ft) in Trentino Alto Adige and by palaeobotanical analyses conducted in the Ötztal, which confirm the existence, from the fourth millennium BC onwards, of activities linked to summer alpine pasture. This is an attractive idea, bearing in mind that even today the shepherds of the Val Senales cross the Tisa pass on 14 June to take their flocks to the Ötztal pastures, and return home by the same route towards the middle of September.

The cause of the Ice Man's death remains for the moment simply a matter of conjecture. Some indications lead one to think, as Konrad Spindler and Markus Egg have argued, that he was the victim of an accident. His equipment may have been inadequate. The bow does not look finished: the marks made by the axe when removing the bark from the wood are clear, and the ends are not grooved to take the bowstring. The frame of the quiver was broken in three pieces near the mummy, as if they had been gathered together with the intention of repairing it. The same goes for the quiver's contents. No arrow was ready to be fired; only two had a flint arrowhead and both were unusable. It is therefore probable that Ötzi, knowing that he could not find flint in this area, had intended to tip the viburnum shafts with points made by working the pieces of deer antler that he had prudently brought with him. Unfortunately for him, disaster struck before he had been able to carry out any such plan.

Bibliography

P.G. Bahn, 'Last Days of the Iceman', *Archaeology*, 48 (3) (1995), pp. 66–70.

L.H. Barfield, 'The Iceman Reviewed', *Antiquity*, 68 (258) (1994), pp. 10–26.

L.H. Barfield, E. Koller and A. Lippert, *Der Zeuge aus dem Gletscher: das Rätsel der frühen Alpen-Europäer* (Vienna, 1992).

K. Spindler (trans. E. Osers), *The Man in the Ice* (London, 1995).

Various authors, *Der Mann im Eis. Neue Funde und Ergebnisse* (The Man in the Ice 2) (Vienna and New York, 1995).

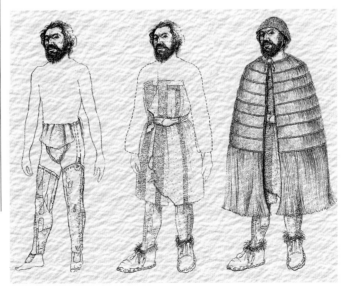

Minoan Crete and the Phaistos Disc

Greece

It was around 6000 BC that the first settlers arrived on Crete, bringing with them seeds and domestic animals, and by the end of the Late Neolithic period (3000 BC) the whole island had been occupied. Around 2800 BC a further influx of people reached Crete from the east, in particular from Anatolia. By the end of the third millennium BC the civilization we now call Minoan had begun to emerge, thanks above all to the agricultural wealth of the island and

the intrepid trading of its inhabitants. They braved the sea to reach the coasts of the Levant and Egypt, where they exchanged the island's products for raw materials, particularly metals, with which Crete was poorly endowed.

The beginning of the Middle Bronze Age (2100 BC) seems to have seen an increase in population. Existing sites grew in size, and new sites appeared. The development of small rural communities across the island, from Knossos to the area around the Gulf of Mirabello, coincided with the appearance of true towns. In western Crete – in particular at Khania and Monastiraki and Adopoulou in the Amari valley – settlements developed with features similar to those of the sites of eastern Crete, so that it is possible to speak of a cultural Koine extending over the whole island by the later Prepalatial Period

(c. 2800–2000 BC) and earlier First Palace Period (c. 2000–1700 BC). It was in this context that the first palaces developed.

These palaces are great architectural complexes, composed of groups of

buildings with different purposes (domestic quarters, kitchens, storerooms, etc.), which had economic, political and religious functions. The reasons why they evolved remain under discussion. Although the first palaces often seem to have been simple transformations of earlier structures, some scholars have seen their appearance as a result of developing contacts with neighbouring civilizations. The palatial structures of the Near East date to a much earlier period, at the end of the third or the beginning of the second millennium BC, and the Minoans' choice of a new political system and hitherto unknown architectural structures may have been influenced by their increasingly close contacts with the peoples of the Near East.

The palatial authorities controlled the surrounding territory, and agricultural produce was taken from the countryside to the palaces for redistribution, partly to those working for the rulers.

This brought the need for an accounting system that could keep the authorities informed about the movement of goods through their storerooms. Writing therefore became a necessity, and two systems developed in the First Palace Period: Linear A, whose oldest texts were found in the destruction layer of the first palace at Phaistos, and so-called 'hieroglyphic' writing, which up to now has been found mainly at Knossos and Mallia. The two have various elements in common. Both are syllabic, and both use a decimal-based system of numbers and a system of ideograms which represent objects, products or living things. Despite their similarity,

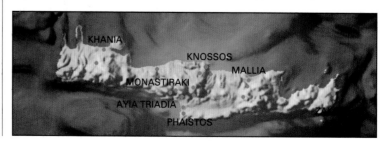

◁ *Location map of the palaces of Khani▸ Mallia, Phaistos, Zakro and other great Minoan sites of Crete.*

△ *The remains of the second palace of Mallia (sixteenth to fifteenth centuries BC). The huge jars were used to store agricultural produce brought from the surrounding area.*

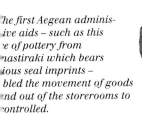

*The first Aegean adminis-
tive aids – such as this
e of pottery from
nastiraki which bears
ious seal imprints –
bled the movement of goods
nd out of the storerooms to
controlled.*

however, it does not seem that Linear A derived from the hieroglyphic writing system. During the First Palace Period the two systems coexisted, and (as the finds at Mallia show) within the same palace there were probably some scribes devoted to Linear A and others to the hieroglyphic writing.

The destruction of all the centres on the island *c.* 1750–1700 BC (Middle Minoan IIB) is generally thought to have been caused by a severe earthquake. In the immediately succeeding Second Palace Period (1700–1450 BC), the Minoans constructed new palaces. The reasons why they were able to build the magnificent princely residences of Knossos, Phaistos, Mallia, Zakro, and Khania (sometimes on the ruins of the first palaces) are linked to the prosperity Crete enjoyed and to the role it played in the political theatre of the eastern Mediterranean in this period – which also coincides with the advent of the Eighteenth Dynasty in Egypt.

Since the First Palace Period, there had been a Minoan presence along the great commercial routes that led to the coast of the Levant and the valley of the Nile. Pottery vases of Kamares ware, typical of the Minoan courts in the Middle Bronze Age, have been found in both areas. The Minoan presence is also well documented in Egyptian texts dating to periods before 1580 BC. On the other hand, Egyptian influence can be detected in various aspects of Cretan life, shown for example in the vases with pictures of cats and sphinxes found at Mallia, the small temple with a statue of a cat found at Monastiraki and the Egyptian statuette with the name of *User* found at Knossos. Under the Eighteenth Dynasty Egypt conquered the whole Syrian corridor, from Gaza to

Ugarit. It needed the resources to sustain its economy, and by now the mines of the Sudan were almost exhausted, so it was necessary to procure raw materials from other sources. The Syrian Orient was able to respond to these heavy demands and provide Egypt with gold, silver, copper, ivory and precious stones, including lapis lazuli – all of which were used in large quantities by the Egyptian workshops. However, the goods had to be transported, and it was the Minoans, masters of the sea – seen by some as Egypt's privileged middle-men – who shipped them from the Levant to the Nile.

This intermediary role brought a number of advantages and considerable prosperity. The Minoans had free access to the Syrian ports, now controlled by Egypt, and to the raw materials of the Levant (it is no accident that Syrian elephant tusks, copper ingots and flakes of lapis lazuli were found in the ruins of the palace of Zakro). And they had Egypt as a customer for the products of their craftsmen, agriculture and stock-rearing.

In the Second Palace Period, Linear A was favoured by the Minoan admin-istration: it is found in archive documents and was used for votive inscriptions found at various Minoan cult places and sanctuaries. Neither it nor the Cretan hieroglyphic writing have been read or deciphered. Most of the phonetic values that lie behind each syllabogram are unknown; there is only a limited number of signs, which makes reading and interpreting the two systems harder; and there are no bilingual texts to provide correlation between the two. Nor do we know if both were used to write a single language – or even whether the Linear A archive documents of the Second Palace Period were written in the same language as the texts of the same period that were used for votive inscriptions.

Around 1450 BC the Minoan palaces fell, and Linear A was replaced by Linear B (deciphered by Michael Ventris in 1952), which retained most of the syllabograms and ideograms of Linear A and was adapted by the Mycenaeans to write their own language, a pre-Doric Greek dialect belonging to the Arcado-Cypriot family. Archive texts in Linear B have been found on the Greek mainland at the sites of many princely Mycenaean residences, such as Mycenae, Tiryns,

▽ *The remains of the First Palace Period settlement of
Mallia (Quartier Mu), which dates to 1700 BC.*

◁ *The famous Snake Goddess of Knossos with a feline on her head-dress (sixteenth century BC). The theme of the struggle between the cat and the snake is frequently found in Egyptian iconography.*

Pylos, Thebes and Midea. This was the writing system of the court, used by Mycenaean princes to administer their territories or for activities linked to the life of the palaces; it did not survive the fall of the Mycenaean palatial world in about 1200 BC.

Up to April 1994 all the Linear B documents discovered, dating to a period between 1450 and 1200 BC, were economic in character and inscribed in clay or painted on stirrup jars. However, recent discoveries have thrown a totally new light on the history of Linear B, and have shown that it was also used for non-administrative purposes. In 1994, at Olympia, the Greek Archaeological Service found the first known example of a Linear B inscription incised in stone. The text – which dates to the seventeenth century BC (at least eight hundred years before Homer) – shows that Linear B developed on the Greek mainland in the period when the inhabitants of Mycenae were burying their rulers in cist tombs.

Also in 1994 an emergency excavation at Thebes unearthed the remains of the archive of the palace of Cadmus, where documents deal with offerings to the gods of barley, wheat, wine and olives. Many of the names previously found in Linear B texts correspond to names of gods in the Greek pantheon of the first millennium BC: Zeus, Hera, Dionysus, Poseidon, Hermes, Athena, *potnia theron* ('Mistress of Animals'). The new tablets from Thebes speak instead of the cult of a hitherto unknown deity: Maka, who has been identified with the Greek Maa Caa (Mother Earth) mentioned by Aeschylus in *The Suppliants* around 490 BC. A series of new cults are associated with that of Maka – cults of snakes, dogs, horses, bulls and birds – which are obviously chthonic cults linked to the distant past of the Mediterranean. The

△ *The great staircase that leads from the central courtyard of Knossos to the queen's apartments. The reconstructions initiated by Arthur Evans have sometimes been judged to be excessive, but they do have the merit of giving us a picture of the last phase of life of the Mycenaean palace, which dates to around 1370 BC*

discovery of the archive of Thebes thus opens a new page in the history of Greek religion.

The Phaistos Disc

As well as texts in hieroglyphic script, Linear A and Linear B, Crete has produced another very famous text: the Phaistos Disc. This was found in the palace at Phaistos in 1908 by Luigi Pernier, together with a document in Linear A, fragments of Minoan pottery and other later material, including Hellenistic sherds. It came from an area that had been occupied many times in the course of history and therefore cannot be dated precisely. The disc has a diameter of 158 to 165 mm (6.2–6.5 inches) and is 16–21 mm (0.63–0.83 inches) thick. The two faces are both inscribed, and the text was created using 45 different punches impressed

△ *The throne room of the palace of Minos at Knossos. After being the palace of the Minoan ruler, Knossos became the capital of Mycenaean Crete from 1450 BC. A Greek ruler, called Wanax in Linear B, may have controlled the whole island.*

into the soft clay – the first example of the use of movable type in history. The details and contours of the impressed shapes are very distinct, and this suggests that the punches were made of a material able to withstand prolonged use (it is clear that they were used for other inscriptions besides the Phaistos Disc). The creator of the disc incised a spiral on each side and then impressed 242 signs within their coils; the left-

> ▷ *The famous bee pendant from Mallia, found in the cemetery at Chrysolakkos, is one of the few pieces of evidence we have of the artistic ability of the goldsmiths in the later First Palace Period (1750–1700 BC).*

hand side of a sign is often obliterated by the right-hand side of the sign next to it, which means that the text reads from right to left. Side A, which has a rosette at the centre, is to be read before side B. The 242 signs are grouped into 61 words (31 on side A and 30 on side B), each separated by a line linking the coils of the spiral, and the words are grouped in turn into 17 sequences by small vertical lines placed to the left of the last sign in each sequence. At the beginning of the spiral on each face there is another vertical line (on which the point of the stylus has made five dots) linking the beginning of the text with the circumference of the disc.

The writing on the Phaistos Disc is not related to any of the other Cretan scripts, but the signs correspond to representations or objects found in Aegean culture. Thus the glove (sign 8) recalls the gloves of the boxers of Ayia Triada; the boat (sign 25) resembles a craft depicted on a ring from Mochlos; the shell (sign 20) is similar to an obsidian vase from Ayia Triada; and sign 21 recalls the impression made by a seal from Phaistos. The plumed head (sign 2), which calls to mind pictures on the walls of the temple of Ramesses III at Medinet Habu, evokes the headdress of the Philistines – one of the members of the Sea Peoples, who are said by the Bible to have come from Crete.

The Phaistos Disc was therefore probably produced by an Aegean civilization. But which one? Uncertainties about the stratigraphy of the find-spot do not allow the disc's context

123

> △ *The fresco of the 'Ladies in Blue' – revealing the women's sophisticated coiffure and splendid clothes – demonstrates the luxury of the Knossos court in the fifteenth century BC.*

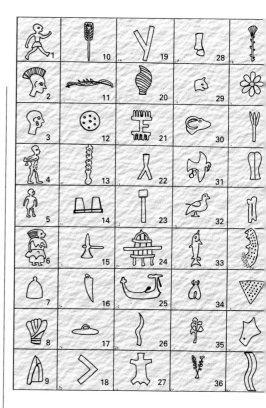

◁ *Of the images of sacred bulls found at Knossos, this* rhyton *(vase used to make religious libations) dating to the fifteenth century BC is outstanding. It was found in the Little Palace and is made of steatite with gold horns; it was filled via a hole behind the head of the animal, and the liquid was poured out through the muzzle.*

to be more firmly dated, and the archaeological parallels that scholars have been able to identify date to various points in the second millennium BC. The seal impression, which corresponds to sign 21 on the Phaistos Disc, belongs to the First Palace Period, whereas certain other objects can be attributed to the Second Palace Period: the ring from Mochlos with the picture of the boat, and the vase from Ayia Triada. Finally the plumed head, if it corresponds to the pictures at Medinet Habu, would date to the last phase of the Mycenaean palatial civilization.

The archaeological parallels with the signs of the disc therefore refer to the history of Crete from 1750 to 1200 BC. The shapes of two of the finds discussed – the ship and the vase – are particularly significant: neither can be dated to before the period 1500–1450 BC. It has therefore been suggested that the Phaistos Disc may be dated between 1500 and the end of the thirteenth century BC. If so, it is logical to suggest that the language hidden behind the syllabograms of the inscription was one used in the Aegean in that period.

What is the likelihood of the Phaistos Disc being deciphered? Since it does not carry ideographic or numerical signs – in contrast to the archive documents written in the Cretan hieroglyphic script, Linear A or Linear B – this may indicate that its text is of a non-economic character. Apart from that, all other hypotheses about the inscription are purely speculative – including the frequent suggestion that the disc carries a religious text.

It may be easier to determine the type of writing involved. Only three writing systems are found across the world: ideographic, syllabic and alphabetic. In the first, the signs consist of drawings of the objects named – a house, man or sheep is written by simply drawing it – and the signs are termed 'logograms' or 'ideograms'. Ideographic writing systems (for example, that of China) need a large number of signs to express actions or abstract concepts – not only because the objects to be represented are many, but also because abstract concepts need to be associated with them if graphic terms are used to express sentences involving verbs, adverbs, adjectives, etc.

Syllabic and alphabetic writing systems both use signs which, when grouped together, express the sound of the pronounced word. The syllabic system breaks the words into their constituent syllables, which makes the number of signs in a syllabic writing system much smaller than the number used in an ideographic system. Japanese, which consists almost entirely of open syllables (syllables that finish with a vowel) is transcribed without excessive difficulty by means of a syllabary, the *kana*, containing 48 signs and two auxiliary diacritical signs. The alphabetic system, which was created by the Phoenicians and developed by the Greeks, is the one that has been most successful, because it uses the smallest number of signs.

The number of different signs stamped on the Phaistos Disc is 45: too

△ *A reconstruction of the queen's apartments at Knossos; the* megaron *was embellished by the Dolphin fresco. The Minoan taste for flowers, animals and nature in general is clear from the wall-paintings found in the palaces of Crete – and now also on the island of Thera (Santorini), at the heart of the Aegean.*

Minoan Crete and
the Phaistos Disc

The 45 syllabograms used in the text on the ◈aistos Disc, and the two faces of the disc with the 242 ◈ressions left in the soft clay by the characters used by ◈ anonymous author. The text, composed of 61 groups ◈igns (31 on side A and 30 on side B), has not been ◈iphered. The writing is different from all other ◈tan writing systems, but the characters represent ◈haeologically identifiable objects and images linked ◈ the culture of the Aegean. The disc must date to a ◈iod between 1450 and 1200 BC.

few for an ideographic writing system, and too many for an alphabetic system. Therefore the text must use a syllabic script. However, there is no evidence available that allows this text to be related to any known writing system of the eastern Mediterranean, the Near East or Egypt. Consequently the script remains without a context, and this makes its decipherment extremely difficult. The difficulties become insurmountable if the crude reality of numbers is taken into account: the number of characters in the 61 words of the disc amounts to 242: a derisory number compared to the 30,000 characters available to Ventris when he deciphered Linear B, or the almost 7,500 characters of Linear A and the almost 1,600 of the Cretan hieroglyphic writing. It has been demonstrated scientifically that it is impossible to decipher a text of only 242 characters if one has no idea of the message it contains. The Phaistos Disc seems to be destined to preserve its mystery and fascination.

△ *The signs on the Phaistos Disc correspond to some objects characteristic of Aegean culture. The libation table placed at the entrance to the palace of Mallia resembles sign 12.*

Bibliography

K. Branigan, *The Foundation of Palatial Crete* (London, 1970).

J. Chadwick, *Reading the Past. Linear B and Related Scripts* (London, 1987).

O.T.P.K. Dickinson, *The Aegean Bronze Age* (Cambridge and New York, 1994).

G. Cadogan, *Palaces of Minoan Crete* (London, 1980).

P. Demargne, *Aegean Art. The Origins of Greek Art* (London, 1964).

J.W. Graham, *The Palace of Crete* (2nd ed., Princeton, 1987).

R. Higgins, *Minoan and Mycenaean Art* (rev. ed., London, 1981).

S. Hood, *The Arts in Prehistoric Greece* (London, 1978).

S. Marinatos and M. Hirmer, *Crete and Mycenae* (London, 1960).

P. Warren, *The Aegean Civilizations* (2nd ed., Oxford, 1989).

Cyclopean Architecture of Mycenaean Cities

Greece

*T*he full flourishing of Mycenaean civilization dates from the fourteenth century BC, in the Bronze Age, when the aristocracies of the Peloponnese and of other areas seem to have developed a definitive political, commercial and economic pre-eminence in the Mediterranean world.

Δ *The so-called 'funeral mask of Agamemnon', from Shaft Grave V of Grave Circle A at Mycenae (sixteenth century BC). (Athens, National Archaeological Museum)*

Modest centres (almost always situated on high ground within sight of plains or valleys, and generally not far from the sea) evolved into urban settlements of a type not dissimilar to Minoan palace-towns and rather reminiscent of the medieval quarters clustered around a feudal castle. Expansion came with a prosperity that sprang from a close link between manufacturing (including high-quality, sophisticated pottery and metalwork) and trading that covered the whole Mediterranean, and led to considerable economic and cultural interaction. The effects can be seen in many of the places celebrated in the stories of Homer – in Mycenae, Argos, Tiryns; at other sites, especially in the Argolid, such as Laconia and Messenia; and at Thebes and in Attica.

The palaces remained faithful to the ancient model of the megaron, but the number and size of their rooms increased. Porticoed courtyards, propylaea (gates) and service areas were added, and they became surrounded by houses, probably reserved for dignitaries with political and military roles. The area enclosed by the city walls expanded, too, and workshops and storerooms were included within the city. For gateways in the walls, the Phrygian model of the *scea* gate was adopted: a gate set into the circuit of the walls at right angles, and approached from outside by a long, narrow entrance way. The cemeteries took on a monumental character, and the tombs of the mighty were filled with goldwork and precious ornaments – clear signs of the wealth and prestige acquired by the dominant families.

Mycenae is exceptional, because its swift decline and abandonment at the end of the second millennium BC have preserved its essential characteristics. Its site – on a steep hill overlooking the fertile plain of Argos and the Gulf of Nauplia, with its back protected by two mountains and steep valleys – is typical of the settlement locations chosen by a warrior society.

The acropolis of Mycenae has two city walls. The first dates to the middle of the thirteenth century BC and was built with 'cyclopean' masonry (huge, uncut blocks of stone with a filling of smaller stones and rubble); the second and larger wall, of the twelfth century BC, was built of almost regular rows of dressed rectangular blocks. The later wall, which also encloses Grave Circle A (the tombs were excavated by Heinrich Schliemann in 1876) has only two entrances: the splendid Lion Gate (actually two lionesses) and the north gate, both of them of *scea* construction. In the north-east sector towards the mountain,

Δ *Virtual reconstruction of Mycenae, showing the main architectural features of the acropolis. (1) Lion Gate; (2) granary; (3) Grave Circle A; (4) aristocratic houses; (5) shrine; (6) Tsountas House; (7) Royal Palace; (8) House of Columns; (9) north gate; (10) postern.*

*Cyclopean Architecture
of Mycenaean Cities*

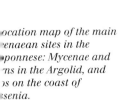

*...ocation map of the main
...enaean sites in the
...ponnese: Mycenae and
...ns in the Argolid, and
...s on the coast of
...senia.*

TIRYNS ○ MYCENAE
○ PYLOS

posterns and secret exits, visible to the inhabitants, were almost imperceptible to anyone approaching from outside. The Lion Gate is one of the masterpieces of Mycenaean architecture. It consists of two vertical piers with a massive lintel, thicker in the centre than at the ends, set on top. The large, dressed rectangular blocks of the wall above are shaped and corbelled in such a way as to transfer weight out towards the ends of the lintel, leaving a triangular tympanum above it, which was filled with a relief decoration of lionesses on either side of a column.

The most impressive example of Mycenaean fortification is the intact city wall of Tiryns, which dates to 1250 BC. The external wall, which reached a thickness of 8 m (26 ft), surrounded the palatial complex; it had posterns and a single gate of *scea* type. The palatial complex was centred axially on the great throne room of the megaron which – like those at Pylos and Mycenae – had a massive central hearth surrounded by a low, painted moulding and set between the four wooden columns that held up the roof. Around the megaron, which also included a bathroom, were service areas, cisterns and a formidable system of covered galleries for defensive purposes. The Mycenaean technique for building galleries and covered corridors is notable for its use of the principle of the weight-relieving triangle to create a false arch by means of corbelling: superimposing large blocks, each projecting slightly beyond the one below, until the two sides of the vault meet, at which point two vertical elements disperse the reciprocal counter-thrust along the walls. It is at Mycenae, though, that the most surprising vaulting of this type can be seen: over 90 m (295 ft) of galleries

with rock-cut steps descending to a subterranean cistern that guaranteed a protected water-supply in time of siege.

Thanks to the excavations at Pylos, in Messenia, it is possible to visualize a typical Mycenaean palace, centred on its megaron and consistent with, for example, Homer's description of Ulysses' home in Ithaca. The palace of the legendary Neleus and Nestor had no defensive structures and was like a country estate, closely bound up with the exploitation of the surrounding fertile land and with various manufacturing activities; a picture of these

activities emerges from the palace accounts (written in Linear B script on clay tablets), which survive because the tablets were baked in the fire that destroyed Pylos towards 1190 BC. Succeeding one another on a longitudinal axis were a gate flanked by guard rooms and by the royal archives, a court like the (much larger and porticoed) one at Tiryns, a double

vestibule, and the megaron, with its hearth and four columns and a throne placed in the middle of the right-hand wall. The existence of stretches of stairway suggests a two-level arrangement, with galleries and rooms lit by high ceilings. All around the megaron stairways and corridors led to minor rooms with residential and service or storage functions. Stone was used for load-bearing up to modest heights, but the lightness of the other building materials – wood and fine plaster – would have allowed the buildings to reach much higher.

A first attempt to create a non-physical reconstruction of the buildings and of the rich painted decoration of the Mycenaean royal palace at Pylos was made in the mid-twentieth century, by the draughtsman, Piet de Jong. The hypotheses developed from the archaeological data have been used to create a fine exhibition in the small, but very rich, Archaeological Museum of Chora

△ *The famous Lion Gate at Mycenae (end of
the fourteenth century BC). In the relief on
the tympanum the figures flanking the
column are actually two lionesses.*

127

▷ *Axonometric view of the tholos tomb known as the 'Treasury of Atreus' (fourteenth century BC). Note the long* dromos, *the tholos chamber and the funerary chamber at the side.*

Trifilias, not far from the excavations.

Still looking at civic architecture, there are some notable buildings at Mycenae. Within the city wall, along the southern flank of the hill, are the House of the Warriors

△ *The entrance of the 'Tomb of Clytemnestra' at Mycenae (fourteenth century BC). This is another tomb to which the name of a member of the House of Atreus has been attached.*

and, higher up, the House of Columns; very convincing reconstructions for these have recently been proposed. Outside the wall there is the House of the Oil Merchant, which shows that 'middle-class' residences were built near the palace (it also yielded archive tablets written in Linear B).

The funerary structures built by Mycenaean architects are also impressive. Cist and pit tombs were succeeded, around 1400 BC, by rock-cut chamber tombs – of which there are examples at Midea, Dendra and in the Argolid, as well as in Messenia, Laconia and Attica and on Kephallonia. Generally composed of a square funerary chamber with sides around 6 m (19 ft) long, preceded by a short access corridor (dromos), their adoption would seem to reflect the influence of Egyptian models, known to the Mycenaeans as a result of their close relations with Egypt.

However, it is after the middle of the fourteenth century BC that the most original Mycenaean funerary monuments appear – enormous circular tholos tombs, perhaps derived from a Cretan archetype that then developed autonomously in Messenia from the sixteenth century before being introduced in the Argolid, where the finest examples are found. The so-called 'Treasury of Atreus' at Mycenae is a magnificent example. Its tholos is preceded by a dromos 36 m (118 ft) long and 6 m (17 ft) wide, flanked by walls that increase in height and are made of enormous dressed rectangular blocks set in regular rows. At the end of the dromos stands an impressive monumental façade containing a door over 5 m (16 ft) high and almost 3 m (10 ft) wide. The whole façade has been reconstructed as closely as possible to the original, and Minoan influence on the architecture is discernible. The weight-relieving triangle is clearly

△ *An interesting example of Mycenaean pottery, this* rhyton *(libation vase) shaped like a bull's head imitates more refined versions in stone and precious metals.*

visible above the architrave of the door. The great circular tholos chamber is over 13 m (42 ft) high and is 14.5 m (47½ ft) in diameter. It is built of concentric rows of stone blocks, the inner face of each projecting a precise and regular distance beyond the row beneath, until the keystone that locked the structure was reached. The faces of the blocks were dressed, shaped and

stuccoed to achieve the perfect curve of the false dome. The small funerary chamber lies to one side of the tholos chamber, cut into the rocky bank from which (on the outside) the dome emerged, its earth covering sloping down and along the sides of the dromos. In some cases, for example in the famous Tomb of Aegisthus (also at Mycenae), whose tholos has collapsed, the access corridor was cut into the rock along with the circular chamber.

There is a great deal of archaeological evidence to attest the high level of art and technology achieved in Mycenaean art, but the fragments of frescoes at Mycenae, Tiryns and Pylos can only convey a minimal idea of the brilliant polychromy of the palaces. Much more exciting are the splendid objects created by the metalworkers, such as the famous funerary masks (including the one erroneously attributed to Agamemnon), the daggers decorated with damascening and niello, the great ritual zoomorphic vases (*rhyta*), the Vapheio cups and the abundance of jewels deposited in royal and aristocratic tombs. Nor should one forget the superb pottery ornamented in a decorative style that was increasingly based on rationalistic stylization.

Bibliography

J. Chadwick, *The Mycenaean World* (Cambridge and New York, 1976).
O.T.P.K. Dickinson, *The Aegean Bronze Age* (Cambridge and New York, 1994).
G. Mylonas, *Mycenae and the Mycenaean Age* (Princeton, 1966).
W. Taylour, *The Mycenaeans* (London and New York, 1983).
J.B. Wace, *Mycenae: An Archaeological History and Guide* (Princeton, 1949).

◁ *A work that epitomizes the warlike character of Mycenaean society, this fresco from Tiryns (1350 BC) depicts a warrior. (Athens, National Archaeological Museum)*

▽ *Virtual reconstruction of the megaron of Mycenae, showing the great hearth between the four central columns. The colours and decorative scheme are hypothetical.*

△ *This lively and imaginative drawing by Piet de Jong is a hypothetical reconstruction of the megaron of the Mycenaean palace at Pylos, in Messenia.*

Bologna: Home of the Villanovans

Italy

Pliny the Elder, in the first century AD, called Iron-Age Bologna princeps Etruriae and credited it with a major role in the early history of the Etruscans and ancient Italy. The city lies on the southern edge of the Po plain, where the river Reno leaves the Appenines, and is protected by the hills of the Osservanza. It was founded around the ninth century BC, the time when so-called Villanovan culture developed there. The term 'Villanovan' has been used for the archaeological manifestations of the Etruscan culture during the Early Iron Age (ninth to mid-seventh centuries BC) ever since the type site at the cemetery of Villanova di Castenaso (Bologna) was discovered in the nineteenth century AD.

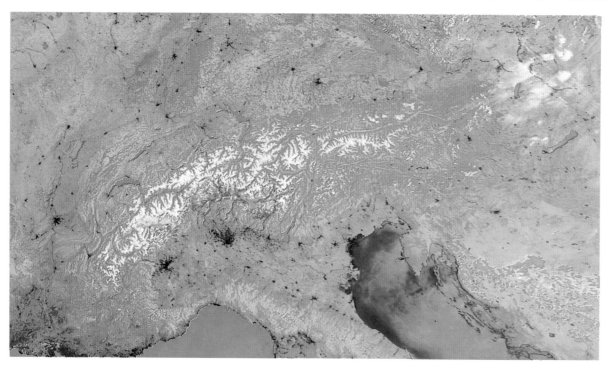

▷ *Terracotta firedogs in the form of horse protomes, decorated with alternating concentric circles and impressed stylized aquatic birds (seventh century BC). Most of the settlement evidence for Villanovan Bologna was found between AD 1872 and 1890, in the course of town-planning and building schemes.*

The first inhabitants of Bologna were a demographic mixture of people from northern Etruria and local population groups. The area had abundant economic potential (for agriculture, stock-rearing and commerce), and the city's position in the Po valley enabled it to trade with the whole of peninsular Italy and northern Europe, and with the eastern Mediterranean via the Adriatic ports. As early as the eighth century BC the Villanovan centre had developed into a settlement of some size, divided into separate villages, and (presumably in the seventh century) extended over a total of more than 300 hectares (740 acres). A comparison with Rome – which in the seventh and sixth centuries BC occupied some 150 hectares (370 acres), and in the fourth century some 284 hectares (700 acres) – makes clear just how large the Villanovan settlement of Bologna was.

Archaeological evidence reveals a striking hierarchical relationship between the central settlement and those of the periphery, which did not seem to undergo substantial change over more than three centuries. Such stability would certainly have reinforced the position of the primary centre, but not to the detriment of the scattered population – which in fact was able to develop and find new incentives through control of communication and trade routes. The initial colonization, with settlers arriving from outside, must have been followed by a convergence of population and demographic mixing within and around the city's territory.

It is more difficult to determine whether centres of intermediate size existed; if they did, then there would have been further hierarchical relationships between the settlements in the area. In a subsistence economy or a self-sufficient economy, such as that of the Villanovan culture in its early

◁ *Satellite image of the Po valley with Bologna near the centre. Recent finds suggest that the major increase in the Villanovan population occurred largely at sites that emerged between the ninth and the first half of the eighth centuries BC. The majority of new buildings were built between the end of the eighth and the seventh centuries, and 90% of the settlements datable to the sixth century BC were established in earlier periods – which suggests a contraction of population in this period and almost no increase in the number of settlements.*

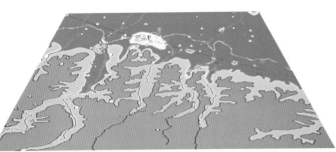

stages, one of the most urgent needs is efficient and reliable distribution of resources. Evidence has yet to be found of increasing organization in the area, concerning, for example, the movement of agricultural produce, goods and services between the various zones.

▷ *The settlement network in the Bolognese plain in the Villanovan period. This computerized picture includes the data so far known for the territory.*

Grave goods show that in the second half of the eighth century BC social diversification and the accumulation of wealth became more marked. This was certainly associated with land division and ownership, for the sites of the Bolognese cemeteries substantially reflect the allotment of land in various different areas. They also reflect the 'Orientalizing' influence, which spread to Bologna in the later eighth century BC – important evidence of which has been found in the form of monumental structures, such as the funerary stelae called the 'Proto-Felsinian stones'. It is significant in terms of settlement structure that the stelae occur not only in the main centre but also the rest of the territory, as is clear from the finds (mostly datable to the seventh century

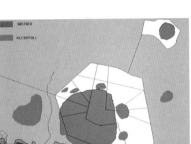

◁ *The development of the settlement of Bologna in the Villanovan period. The settlement area, shown at the centre in red, covered an area of over 300 ha (740 acres) and was surrounded by the cemeteries.*

BC) from Saletto, San Giovanni in Persiceto, Crespellano and Casalecchio di Reno. The relative importance of the surrounding territory in relation to the city in this phase is still best indicated by finds of this type (stelae and cippi): from a total of over 2,500 tombs, only sixteen examples have been found in Bologna itself, while a third come from the surrounding territory.

The examples of the Malvasia Tortorelli stone and the Via Tofane stele, in particular, show that the new Orientalizing artistic language was probably brought to Bologna not through the imitation of imported models but directly, by foreign craftsmen themselves. The data available to us clearly suggest that, at this time and in this area, the social evolution of the culture had produced a rural aristocracy. Confirmation of this is provided by the cemetery of Casteldebole, immediately west of Bologna, where particularly sumptuous grave goods – significantly including swords – prove the existence of ranked social classes in the peripheral areas. The location of the majority of the monumental stelae both in the plain and on the plateau also

indicates the close supervision of the agricultural zones, which probably derived their importance from privileged access to the primary centre.

On 17 January 1877, while a drain was being dug in the area of the present-day Piazza San Francesco, in the centre of Bologna, a large jar was found sitting in the middle of a Villanovan hut floor. It was 125 cm (49½ in.) high and 95 cm (37½ in.) wide and contained 14,838 bronze objects and three of iron, all apparently arranged with care. These (some of which were used and worn out) included weapons, tools, utensils, fragments of pottery, cut sheets of metal, metal slag, casting residues, brooches, daggers, knives, spearheads, pieces of swords, files, rasps, saws, awls, scythes, chisels, razors, an anvil, horse harness, rings, bronze vessels, nails and axes (the last in large numbers: 4,073 pieces). All the material is datable between the end of the Bronze Age and the beginning of the seventh century BC, and some pieces bear letters or alphabetic signs, perhaps

△ *A cremation tomb, showing the urn for the ashes and its inverted covering bowl protected by a small structure of sandstone slabs (ninth century BC). (Bologna, Civic Archaeological Museum)*

◁ *Plan of Tomb 25 of the cemetery of Casale di San Lazzaro (seventh century BC). The burial was covered by a small tumulus of earth.*

used for counting or identification. The San Francesco hoard, the largest such find in Italy, is a valuable source of information about the daily life and technological knowledge of the period.

Since the hoard was discovered there has been considerable debate about its interpretation. Was it a votive deposit, the store of a foundry, or something else? In fact this accumulation of objects – many of them obsolete, worn-out and thus unusable – may well have served as a store of valuable and

▷ Computerized relief plan of a Villanovan hut, made during the course of excavation.

recyclable metal. The Bolognese hoard may be considered as a sort of primitive 'national bank': an accumulation of communal wealth in the form of metal to be traded and exchanged. Metallurgical analysis of the objects – finished, half-worked and used – has produced no evidence of metal-casting *in situ.*

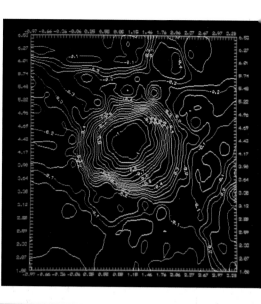

The Villanovan Hut

The archaeologist faces difficulties in proposing reliable reconstructions of buildings dating to the Early Iron Age (ninth to eighth centuries BC) because these buildings, made largely of perishable materials, only leave 'negative' traces in the ground: ditches, holes, small channels, soil disturbance, foundations or accumulations of earth.

Suggestions for reconstructing Villanovan huts are therefore based both on the patient gathering of data during excavation and on comparisons with clay models of huts found in tombs, where they were used to hold cremated remains.

△▷ Model of a reconstructed Villanovan hut datable to the eighth and seventh centuries BC.

The hut could be elliptical, circular or rectangular in plan, and generally consisted of one room, although it could have two or three separate internal areas. It had supporting posts both inside and outside the structure, with walls of wattle and wooden frames covered with clay (daub). In some cases there was a short porticoed entrance. The floor could be of beaten earth or, more frequently, of planks which covered an underground space. The most obvious structural element in the foundations of the hut is a pit that sometimes reaches a depth of more than 2 m (6½ ft) below floor level. This

underground space is unrelated to the height of the hut, and it has been suggested that it was intended for storing goods (a cellar). It was reached through a trap-door in the floor. The hut's roof was made of branches, wood and clay, with a central opening to let out smoke.

Inside, at the centre, was the hearth with its terracotta firedogs and ovens; the furnishings were on the whole modest and consisted of wooden furniture, vessels for eating and drinking, pans and kettles. The largest containers, the dolia, in which foodstuffs were stored, were kept under the floor.

The cemeteries, which are arranged in clusters around the settlement of Bologna, contained over 4,000 tombs. Each cluster related to a different area of settlement. The largest were in the westernmost sector, beyond the river Ravone, and consisted of the cemeteries of Benacci, Benacci-Caprara, De Lucca, Melenzani, Romagnoli, Cortesi, Nanni Guglielmini, Arnoaldi, Stradello della Certosa and Aureli. In the south-east area is the Arsenal cemetery, while in the eastern area there are the cemeteries of San Vitale and Via Savena (linked with the oldest part of the settlement) in the areas of the Piazza della Mercanzia and Via Savena. To the north there are only traces of small cemeteries.

◄ *Bronze jewellery of the end of the seventh century BC (Bologna Civic Archaeological Museum).* Left: *Pair of brooches from Tomb 11 of the Aureli Cemetry.* Below: *Leech fibula.*

The Villanovan culture is distinguished by cremation burials in urns of biconical shape that were covered with inverted bowls. This type of interment was abandoned around the middle of the sixth century BC, in a change which marks the transition from the Early Iron Age to the historical period proper.

The typological evolution and the wealth of the grave goods provide fundamental information for dating, but they also give us at least some idea of the ideology, economic development and structure of Villanovan society. In the ninth century BC the tombs generally contained rather modest grave goods, reflecting a largely egalitarian society: for the most part, only a biconical urn and covering bowl. In the first half of the eighth century other vessels begin to appear, among them bowls, mugs and cups, along with bronze items: fibulae and, in women's tombs, bronze belts with embossed and engraved decoration. Men's tombs typically contain razors and horse bits (the latter a symbol of aristocratic power). From the second half of the eighth century BC the grave goods are augmented with accessory vessels, such as banquet services and vases decorated with geometric motifs and metal strips that illuminate the dark, burnished surface of the pottery. Weapons are rarer in male tombs, occurring only in exceptionally rich burials, but razors, serpentine fibulae, knives and dress pins are typical. Female tombs are characterized by the presence of thread spools, spindle whorls, and serpentine fibulae with bows of bronze wire threaded with bone

△ *Pair of horse bits with bronze phalera from Tomb 34 of the Benacci-Caprara cemetery (eighth century BC).*

and amber discs and glass-paste beads. Towards the end of the eighth century BC and for the whole of the seventh century the grave goods reflect Orientalizing influences and iconography – part of a complex historical and artistic phenomenon that involved the whole Mediterranean at this period. People of the Villanovan culture acquired and reworked objects and motifs from the Near East. Such objects, both imported and locally made, were highly valued by the Etruscan aristocracy and were paraded and exhibited on ceremonial occasions, so that their presence among grave goods serves as an indicator of the prevailing ideology. The new decorative repertoire now included palmettes, lotus flowers, rosettes, real and fantastic animals and human figures, as well as geometric motifs. All these motifs were impressed, engraved or applied in relief on both pottery and bronze vessels. From the last decades of the seventh century BC to the middle of the sixth there was a progressive change in the funerary goods, with the biconical urn being replaced in

▷ *Sandstone cippus-altar 1.9 m (6¼ft) high found in Via Fondazza. It is decorated with plant motifs, palmettes and lotus buds and dates to the seventh century BC.*

some cases by a dolium – an urn of ovoid form.

Examples of writing in the Etruscan language are very rare in Villanovan Italy. The first graphic marks on pottery and bronzes are simple alphabetic signs: in the San Francesco hoard there are more than one hundred alphabetic graffiti and one inscription relating to a name.

One of the earliest and longest Etruscan texts known came from Bologna and was incised on a pottery amphora from the Melenzani cemetery, datable to the seventh century BC. It is an inscription, running from right to left in a spiral, incised in the raw clay prior to firing. The thirty words of the text are difficult to interpret, but the name of the woman who received the vase as a gift has been identified (Venus), as has the name of one of the donors (Remesalu, perhaps her husband) and that of the craftsman (Remiru) who made the amphora and incised the inscription. The orthography suggests that the

△ *Gilded silver plaques, decorated with heads with triangular faces and Egyptian-type hairstyles, from Tomb 11 of the Aureli cemetery (end of the seventh or beginning of the sixth century BC).*

inscription was written by a craftsman from northern Etruria. Apart from its linguistic significance, this inscription also provides the important information that at the end of the seventh century BC the aristocracy of Bologna wrote in Etruscan and was without doubt culturally Etruscan.

Recent excavations of Villanovan cemeteries and settlements in the Bolognese plain are providing increasing amounts of data, previously unavailable, which is very useful for reconstructing the typology of the settlements of the Early Iron Age. The villages in the plain seem to have certain common characteristics. They were located overlooking water courses, arranged in distinct settlement clusters with their own

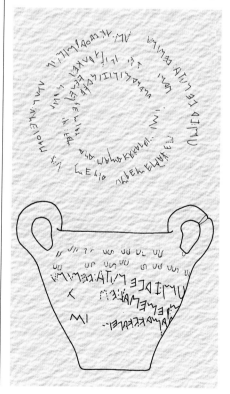

cemetery area, and carefully oriented to the north. The huts have various different plans, from the typical square form to ovoid or ellipsoid. The size of the huts, which are almost all quite small, covering an area from 6 to 10 sq m (65 to 108 sq ft) and not more than 25–30 sq m (270–320 sq ft), implies that each building was used by only one family.

Within the settled areas there must have been open zones with no buildings, which were probably used as fields for cultivation, pasture and for the control of animals. At the centre of the complex were areas dedicated to industrial and craft activities, indicated in excavations by traces of the working of bone and antler and by pits equipped for metalworking. Not far away were rubbish pits, and pits for storing water, foodstuffs and other commodities.

The organization of the sites also included ditches that served as drains

▽ *Small amphora with Etruscan inscription of at least thirty words, from the cemetery of Melenzani (seventh century BC).*

◁ *Bronze situla from the cemetery of Certosa (mid-sixth century BC), decorated with scenes of warriors, processions and rows of animals.*

*Bologna: Home of the
Villanovans*

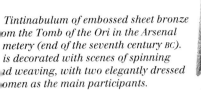

*Tintinabulum of embossed sheet bronze
from the Tomb of the Ori in the Arsenal
cemetery (end of the seventh century BC).
It is decorated with scenes of spinning
and weaving, with two elegantly dressed
women as the main participants.*

and as systems for water distribution. These are of wedge-shaped section, some 4–5 m (13–16 ft) wide at the top, over 2 m (6½ ft) deep, and with markedly convex walls. They seem to belong to a complex system of channels designed to control water in the area and perhaps also the allotment of land. The settlement system, which also remained in use as a model in the next phases of the sixth and fifth centuries BC, shows considerable planning and organization of the territory and an advanced use of techniques for controlling and exploiting the land. From the little palaeobotanical data available, it is possible to classify those settlements that have been examined as mainly rural in character, occupied primarily with rearing sheep (for wool) and pigs and (to a lesser extent) bovids and ovicaprids (for meat). The diet was supplemented by bird-catching, hunting and also fishing. In the absence of comparative pollen analyses, a study of the faunal data shows a fairly widespread population living in damp, forested areas.

Summing up the data from the area between the river Panaro to the west, and the river Idice to the east, it is apparent that there was a progressive growth in settlement between the ninth and eighth centuries BC. From the second half of the eighth and throughout the seventh century BC the increase in the number of sites becomes particularly striking, but it ended with a reorganization and reduction in settlement during the sixth century BC.

Bibliography

L. Barfield, *Northern Italy before Rome* (London, 1971).

G. Bartoloni, *La cultura villanoviana. All'inizio della storia etrusca* (Rome, 1989).

G. Bermond Montanari (ed.), *La formazione della città in Emilia Romagna*, exhibition catalogue, II (Bologna, 1987).

M. Forte, and P. Von Eles (eds), *La pianura bolognese nel villanoviano.*

Insediamenti della prima età del Ferro (Florence, 1994).

R. Peroni, *Introduzione alla protostoria italiana* (Bari, 1994).

J. Reich, *Italy before Rome* (Oxford, 1979).

N. Spivey and S. Stoddart, *Etruscan Italy* (London, 1990).

M. Zuffa, 'La civiltà villanoviana', in *Popoli e civiltà dell'Italia antica*, 5, 1976, pp. 199–363.

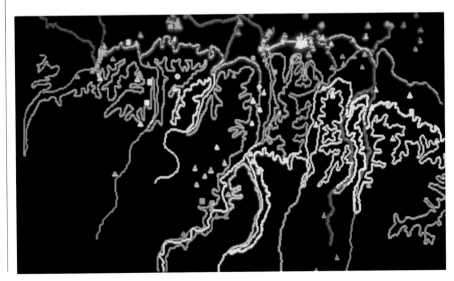

△ *The Bologna area in the Villanovan period, shown on a map generated by computer using a Geographical Information System (GIS). The GIS makes it possible to set the archaeological sites in context, taking into account the evolution of the landscape, the geomorphology and the spatial relationships of the various elements.*

Amber and Gold: The Etruscan Trading Centre of Verucchio

Italy

One morning Helios gave in to the demands of his son Phaethon and let him drive the chariot of the Sun. Phaethon wanted to show off to his sisters Prote and Clymene, but he lacked the strength to control the wild dash of the white horses that the two women had harnessed to the chariot. He let it run, first, so high in the sky that all the mortals on earth shivered with cold, and then so close to the earth that the fields were scorched. Zeus, in a rage, killed him with a thunderbolt and he fell into the Eridanus river. His grieving twin sisters were transformed into poplars, or alders, growing along the banks of rivers and crying tears of amber.

This version of the Greek myth is a good introduction to the subject of the circulation of amber in prehistoric and proto-historic Europe. Since amber is of organic origin, it cannot really be called a mineral. It is a resin that flowed from various species of coniferous tree during the Tertiary Period and was subsequently fossilized; the best-known variety, that from the Baltic, comes from a species of pine. The material is very light, warm to the touch, and is magnetized by stroking. It varies in transparency and opacity, and occurs in many shades of yellow, red and brown. Yellow amber is mainly found

▽ *The amber routes of pre- and proto-historic Europe: the routes branch out from the north European deposits and extend to large parts of the Mediterranean basin. The amber trade flourished in the Bronze and Early Iron Ages.*

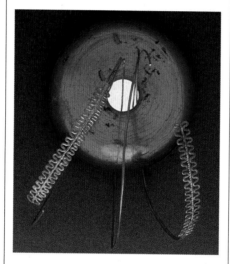

in northern Germany (Schleswig-Holstein), in Denmark (Jutland) and on the southern shores of the Baltic

(Poland). Less substantial deposits occur in southern France, Italy, Spain, Syria and Romania. In Italy the known deposits, which are rather poor, are in Sicily and in the Apennine ranges of Emilia and Romagna – but they were not known or exploited in antiquity. In the Early Iron Age, Verucchio (near present-day Rimini) was one of the most important European centres for the trading and working of amber, acquiring the fossilized resin in its raw state from the Baltic area and selling it on as precious and elaborate finished objects. In this sense we can speak of a real amber technology.

△ *Earring from Tomb 23, Moroni property, at Verucchio (seventh century BC). The disc pendant of amber is threaded on thin gold spirals.*

From early in prehistory amber was much prized and became a commodity of great prestige, particularly appropriate for princes and rulers. In the *Odyssey*, for example, one of the most important gifts brought by Penelope's suitors was an amber and gold necklace 'like the sun' (*Odyssey*, XVIII.295–6). In antiquity amber was also believed to have therapeutic and apotropaic properties (see, for example, Pliny's *Natural History*, XXXVII.xi.44). In the historical period Herodotus and Pliny discussed the Nordic amber trade. In particular, Pliny (*Natural History*, XXXVII.iii.43–4) traced the amber route which a Roman horseman in the time of Nero must have travelled: it ran from the Baltic shores of Germany to Carnuntum (present-day Bratislava on the Danube), then via Pannonia to the Venice area, ending at Aquileia. From the prehistoric period the amber trade covered a large part of Europe and the Mediterranean, bringing the great continental cultures into contact. The recorded myths agree that amber was found in the Elektrides islands (the Latin word *electrum* means 'amber'), located by some writers at the mouth of the Po or in the upper Adriatic. Even in prehistoric times, there is evidence in this region of the working, redistribution and trading of raw amber coming from northern Europe.

Verucchio was part of the territory of Etruscan rulers from the ninth to the mid-sixth centuries BC and Rimini was the stronghold of the Malatesta family in the medieval period. It stands on a

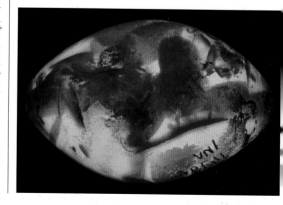

△ *Amber decoration of a fibula from Tomb 118, Lippi property (seventh century BC). The resin contains plant fragments, which intensify the colour.*

VERUCCHIO

*Amber and Gold: The Etruscan
Trading Centre of Verucchio*

The main amber deposits are in areas (Scandinavia, Denmark, the Baltic region) that were covered by extensive coniferous forests in the Tertiary Period.

massive limestone outcrop over 300 m (1,000 ft) high – the last obstacle that the river Marecchia must pass before spreading across the plain to reach the sea. This large and naturally fortified site is reminiscent of sites on the tufa cliffs of Tyrrhenian Etruria (northern Latium, Umbria and Tuscany). It may be that the first Etruscans at Verucchio,

and, a little further away, the Veneti. This explains the fortification of the site and the significant presence of many weapons in the princely tombs. It dominated a large territory of small settlements, but (lying on the spurs that dominate the coastal plain and commanding the Marecchia valley and Viamaggio pass) it also controlled the land routes from the Adriatic and the Po to Central Italy, the Tiber valley and southern Etruria (Veio and Tarquinia). In the larger context of the amber trade in the prehistoric and proto-historic periods, this Etruscan outpost not only controlled land communications, its access to the sea linked it also to south-central Europe and the eastern Mediterranean. As a node on important trade routes it must have had ware-

house facilities for merchants and craftsmen, some of whom were dependent on the local aristocrats.

Verucchio's location, close to a river but not directly on the coast, is similar to that of Frattesina – which is also some way inland and lies close to the Po and the most important navigable river systems. In its earliest phase Verucchio may have been in contact with Frattesina, directly or via shared trade routes. At all events, on the Adriatic coast Verucchio inherited the role previously held by Frattesina of an autonomous centre involved in the trading, working and redistribution of amber. Its closeness to the sea and control of trade routes means that there must have been an important port nearby. Although archaeological proof is still lacking, its site may be identified as that of present-day Rimini, whose Latin name of Ariminum probably reveals an earlier Etruscan ancestry as Arimna. Rimini, the Romans' strategic choice as the first colony of Cisalpine Gaul in 268 BC, was perhaps a landing place for coastal trade from the Geometric period onwards.

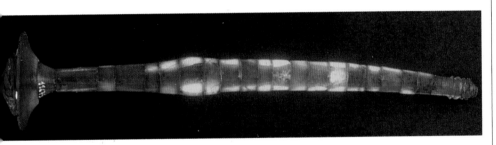

presumably coming from southern Etruria in the ninth century BC, chose this strategic site partly for its resemblance to the volcanic landscape of inland Etruria.

About 15 km (9 miles) from the sea, the site would have enjoyed all the advantages of great coastal city-states in the Iron Age: it was sufficiently protected from the seaborne dangers but close enough to the sea to benefit from commercial contacts, trade and transport. The important harbour that must have existed at the mouth of the Marecchia, on the site of present-day Rimini, allowed the landing of precious cargoes from the east Mediterranean and from continental Europe.

In relation to the Etruscan centres of the central Po valley and Tyrrhenian Etruria, Verucchio was an enclave, a frontier territory surrounded by populations with different languages and cultures: the Umbrians, the Picenians

△ *Distaff from Tomb 47, Lippi property (mid-seventh century BC). The amber discs are decorated with minuscule geometric incisions.*

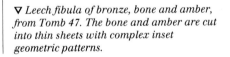

▽ *Leech fibula of bronze, bone and amber, from Tomb 47. The bone and amber are cut into thin sheets with complex inset geometric patterns.*

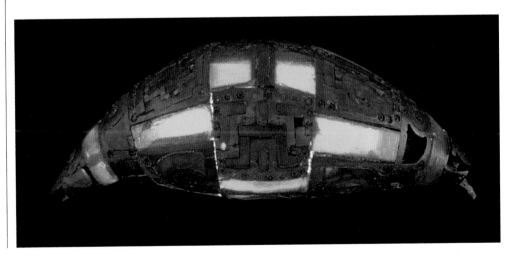

◁ *Reconstruction of an arc fibula with a bow made of bone discs at the centre with amber insets, and amber discs at the ends: (1) pieces of amber decorated with pigment and incised decoration; (2) sheet of tin; (3) curved bronze sheet; (4) amber disc with perforations; (5) narrow strips or threads fixing the discs in place; (6) bronze wire on which the discs are threaded.*

▽ *Pie chart showing the presence of amber in the tombs. It has been found that amber is particularly common in female tombs.*

The prestige and the craftsmanship of the objects found in the tombs at Verucchio indicate the existence of highly skilled craftsmen supplying the needs of a princely class. Amongst them were sculptors, weavers of fine cloth, bronze-workers and other metal-workers, and carvers of wood, ivory, bone and amber; some of them probably came from Etruria proper. From the end of the eighth century BC the Etruscan aristocracy showed off its political power by offering masterpieces of its metal technology to the great Greek sanctuaries – for example the Etruscan bronze shields found at Olympia and Samos.

Amber occurred in the tombs of Verucchio as early as the ninth century, but became increasingly common in the succeeding centuries, and was most abundant in the Orientalizing period

(seventh century BC). This obviously suggests a marked increase in the purchasing power of Verucchio's aristocratic leaders as a result of their close links to the main international markets. Amber items are overwhelmingly present in female tombs. The high standard of craft production shows that Verucchio was a major centre for the working and distribution of amber, which arrived in bulk in its raw state and went back on to the market as high-quality finished artifacts. It is therefore probable that here was a full-scale amber industry there, meeting not just the needs of the local rulers and aristocracy but also those of a much wider market. During the Orientalizing period the distribution of amber at Verucchio and in Etruria followed routes already used during the prehistoric period, but the evolution of an aristocratic culture must have favoured the exchange of luxury goods

and gifts between high-ranking individuals of different cultural groups. Such exchanges certainly involved items made out of and decorated with amber – rare gems of distant provenance.

TOMBS WITHOUT AMBER 5.26%

TOMBS WITH AMBER 94.74%

In the tombs found at Verucchio many different materials are decorated with amber, and a variety of different manufacturing techniques are involved. For example, fibulae could be made from one or more of a range of materials: bone, ivory, bronze, iron, amber and glass paste (though glass paste and amber never appear on the same object). Where different materials were combined in one object, a complex series of techniques had to be used to create it.

It is likely that much amber working was carried out when the material was hot, so as to avoid wasting too much of it and so as to achieve better results

▽ *Dragon fibula with gold double pin, from Tomb 89, Lippi property. It weighs 30.45 gm, has a central rosette with stamped and granulated triangles and an embossed catchplate. The granulation consists of 436 grains of between 0.1 and 0.2 mm in diameter; the catchplate and the bow were cast in three separate pieces.*

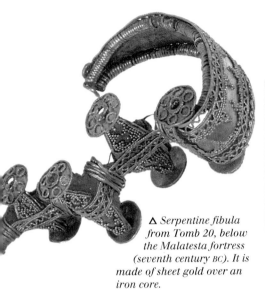

△ *Serpentine fibula
from Tomb 20, below
the Malatesta fortress
(seventh century BC). It is
made of sheet gold over an
iron core.*

when cutting and modelling. Depending on the decorative effects (of form, colour or transparency) desired, and on the materials to be combined with it (bronze, bone or ivory, for instance), amber was 'shaped' by various techniques. For example, on a distaff made of twenty-three cut, moulded and perforated amber beads threaded onto a bronze pin, the top bead (in the shape of a truncated cone) and the two discs above are all made of amber, while between the two discs is a thin bronze disc cast integrally with the end of the pin. This object is notable for the fact that, due to the transparency of the amber, through each bead one can see complex decorative motifs – meanders,

buds and other vegetal forms. No specific analyses have been carried out, but it may be that around the central bronze shaft of the distaff there is an armature, of bone or bronze, on the surface of which these motifs were incised or painted. Another item of particular interest is a bronze knife with a hilt decorated with two amber beads and four ivory discs. Most striking is the decoration of complex meanders that is visible through the transparent amber – and seems to be stamped within it.

In fibulae with bows of bronze wire threaded with amber and bone (composite bows), the amber insets are often numerous and create a rich decoration. A number of fibulae with composite bows made of a framework of bone cut to hold amber insets have been found in tombs; one has more than 300 small cruciform insets, and almost thirty larger rectangular insets, all of amber. Finished objects little more than 10 cm (4 in.) long can be made of 350–400 pieces. The parts in bone are made from bovine ankle-bones, cut into rectangular and trapezoidal shapes and then smoothed to give the convex profile of the leech-bow fibula. The settings cut for the smaller amber insets have tiny circular holes in them (nearly always five in each), presumably for securing the insets. The larger amber insets, trapezoidal or rectangular, are

∇ *Detail of the fibula shown on the left. The gold sheet that covers the iron core is held in place by a pair of twisted gold wires. The twist increases the flexibility of the wire and also supports the granulation; the eight lateral discs are fixed to the bow of the brooch with small hooks. The decoration is in granulation and filigree.*

not set so deeply into the bone, but are slotted into shallow, broad cuts in its surface. In most bone-and-amber fibulae the ends are plugged with disc-shaped amber beads that have a circular hole through the centre to hold the bronze wire of the bow.

Yet another technique of fibula decoration involved a series of lozenge- or almond-shaped beads of amber, sometimes alternating with bone discs decorated with amber insets. Running through each bead is a series of small perforations for the very fine threads that hold the discs (and the brooch) together; the perforations create a pleasing decorative effect of horizontal lines within the translucent amber. At Verucchio amber beads were also set into the handles of *kantharos*-shaped cups and into a variety of ivory objects, such as conical buttons, belt hooks and handles.

The greatest quantity of precious metals to be found in Etruria dates to the Orientalizing period (towards the end of the eighth century BC and during the

◄ *Detail of the dragon fibula from Tomb 89. Note on the central rosette, the granulated decoration of triangles pointing towards the centre.*

The Bronzes

Archaeometry involves chemical and physical analyses of ancient artifacts to determine, among other things, the technology used to make them and where they were made. The analysis of bronzes and ancient metalwork in general (archaeometallurgy) is aimed in particular at the study of alloys and casting techniques. Two types of analysis have been carried out on the bronzes from Verucchio: atomic absorption spectrometry (which allows the chemical components of the metal to

◄ High handle of cast bronze from Tomb 3, Le Pegge site. It consists of a disc with a figure and two birds, held up by a bronze figurine.

be identified and quantified) and electron microscopy. The first results show that the Verucchio bronzes have a much higher level of tin (rather than the cheaper lead) than those of the seventh and sixth centuries BC found in Tyrrhenian Etruria. The analyses of horse-bits, frequently found in the tombs as symbols of power, show that different alloys were used for the snaffles that carry the reins, and the cheek-pieces, both of which are decorative elements. This information helps our understanding of how far the specialization and technological expertise of the craftsmen had developed and, at the same time, of the economic power of their rulers.

techniques, they represent strikingly the prestige and power of the rulers of Verucchio, and the city's importance in the great trading systems of the Orientalizing period. No notable concentrations of gold have been found – rather gold items have come to light singly or in small groups, in very richly furnished tombs – but the finds show that in this period particular attention was being given to the search for new design ideas.

The main classes of goldwork are serpentine and dragon fibulae, and decorative plaques with stamped decoration, which were used for decorating cloth. They demonstrate all the manufacturing techniques that were used, particularly in the Orientalizing period:

◄ *Detail of sheet-gold plaque from Tomb 18, below the Malatesta fortress (seventh century BC). It is part of a group of gold plaques that decorated the clothing of the deceased: they were elongated triangles with straight and concave sides, and were decorated with stamped human heads, round bosses, monkeys, snakes and geometric motifs*

seventh) and was concentrated almost exclusively in the tombs of high-ranking individuals. The innovations of this period – attributed to contact between traditional local metallurgy and the craft techniques of the Near East – led to the introduction of ornamental techniques such as granulation and filigree, which were put to use in the service of the new vocabulary of forms and iconography.

There are relatively few gold objects in the tombs at Verucchio, but some of them are remarkable. Showing a complete mastery of manufacturing

▷ *An almost complete sheet-gold plaque from Tomb 18. It has stamped decoration of alternating human faces and round bosses.*

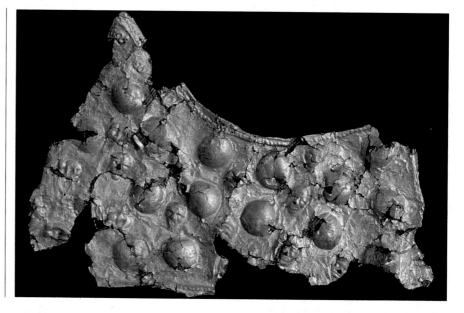

*Amber and Gold: The Etruscan
Trading Centre of Verucchio*

◄ *Wooden throne from Tomb 89,
below the Malatesta fortress. It is
decorated with bronze studs and
carved scenes of the working and
transportation of wool and of
domestic life.*

Bibliography

L. Bonfante, *Out of Etruria* (Oxford,
  1981).
L. Bonfante (ed.), *Etruscan Life and
  Afterlife* (Detroit, 1986).
M. Forte (ed.), *Il dono delle Eliadi:
  ambre e oreficerie dei principi etruschi
  di Verucchio*, exhibition catalogue
  (Rimini, 1994).
  G.V. Gentili, 'Il villanoviano
    verucchiese nella Romagna
    Orientale e il sepolcreto Moroni', in
    Studi e documenti di Archeologia, I,
    1985.
G.V. Gentili, 'L'età del Ferro a
  Verucchio: cronologia degli scavi e
  scoperte ed evoluzione della
  letteratura archeologica', in *Studi e
  documenti di archeologia* II, 1986,
  pp. 1–41.
N. Negroni Catacchio, 'L'ambra:
  produzione e commerci nell'Italia
  preromana', in *Italia: omnium
  terrarum parens* (Verona, 1989),
  pp. 659–96.
N. Spivey and S. Stoddart, *Etruscan
  Italy: An Archaeological History*
  (London, 1990).

solid casting, cutting, granulation, filigree, stamping and chiselling.

The casting techniques involve the
use of both re-usable moulds and the
lost-wax method. In the first method,
the mould – made of two or more pieces
– forms a negative of the shape to be
reproduced, with a hole or channel into
which the liquid metal is poured and
another to let air escape as the mould is
filled. Most commonly, however, the
Etruscans used the lost-wax method.
Here a one-piece wax model is made of
the object to be moulded, including the
inlet and outlet channels for the molten
gold and the escaping air. This model is
then enclosed in wet earth or clay.
When this has dried, the mould is
heated to liquefy the wax, which is
poured away, and the molten gold is
poured in from a crucible. The gold fills
the space that the wax model had
occupied, exactly reproducing its shape.
Finally, when the metal has cooled and
solidified, the mould is broken in order
to extract the casting. Since this means
that the mould is not re-usable, any
casting made by the lost-wax method is
a unique piece.

▷ *Detail of the throne shown above. The
scenes are arranged in bands, a common
feature of decorative schemes in the
Orientalizing period.*

Princely Daunia

Italy

*D*aunian civilization lasted for over seven centuries, from the Early Iron Age (ninth century BC) until the area was Romanized in the third to second centuries BC. It was a cohesive culture, rather resistant to outside influences. According to historical sources, the region known as Daunia was part of Apulia, on the east side of south central Italy. It covered the present-day province of Foggia from the river Fortore to the Ofanto (including the Gargano promontory), the south-east strip of the Ofanto basin (in Bari province) and the Melfi area of the middle Ofanto and upper Bradano valleys. The different geological and environmental character of each area affected the type and distribution of settlements.

The rise of powerful aristocratic groups, the *principes* of Daunia, transformed a basically egalitarian society into one that was strongly hierarchical. Between the second half of the seventh and the beginning of the sixth centuries BC, this led to the building of the first tombs of high-ranking people, and later (in the late sixth and the fifth centuries BC) to the construction of princely residences: the 'palaces'. Archaeological data shows that there was a serious crisis of aristocratic ideology during the fifth century BC. However, the *principes* survived, and – thanks to their receptiveness to Hellenizing models – in the fourth and third centuries BC (and up to the complete Romanization of the territory) they were responsible for the development of proto-urban and then of urban architecture. In fact Daunia, in contrast to other Italic populations, became an urban civilization quite late – not until the fourth to third centuries BC, when the area was already being influenced and dominated by Rome.

For a large part of the Iron Age there were two characteristic types of settlement in the region. The first, scattered over the coastal plain and the foothills behind, was the open village consisting of groups of unfortified huts. The second type consisted of villages set in defensive positions on the hills on sites that were naturally well fortified; these, too, consisted of groups of huts, often alternating with areas dedicated to manufacturing and grazing.

Overall, the organization of the territory seems to have taken the form of small villages or small groups of houses with a common economic role. These settlement micro-units shared large areas used for cultivation and craft activities, and the relationships between them seem to have been those of equals, not involving hierarchies of dependence or dominance. Each territorial nucleus would have had its own specialized role in the economy of the region, determined partly by the specific characteristics of its site and partly by the overall needs of the system. Up to about the fourth century BC no complex hierarchical divisions are detectable, but there was a basic spatial pattern, with central settlements of about 50–80 hectares (120–200 acres) in size and smaller agricultural villages of 1–5 hectares (2–12 acres). The latter were open villages – with all the land and houses visible from the centre, which provided easy internal communication – and generally it would have taken no more than two or three hours to walk from one to another.

This system of villages was more than sufficient to control the territory and manage the resources, so Daunian territory was not in need of urbanization to improve its organization. The adoption of an urban system of settlement and the political aggregation into a region with a newly built city for its centre must have been the result of outside influences. The urban model developed at a time (in the second half of the fourth century and the third century BC) when the whole of Daunia had been completely Hellenized but was under threat from the expansion of the Samnites, and subsequently the Romans.

▽ *Plan of the rock-cut Varrese tomb at Canosa (fourth century BC), with central lobby and five chambers.*

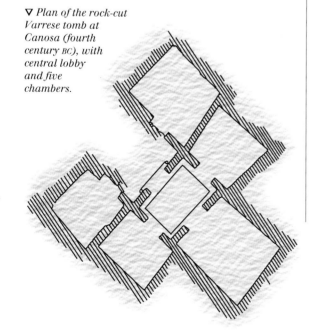

△ *Computer reconstruction of the archaeological landscape of Ascoli Satriano (Foggia) in the Iron Age, based on contour lines. The settlement areas are indicated in blue.*

MICRORILIEVO GEOMORFOLOGICO 3D

SOPRA 450
436 - 450
422 - 436
408 - 422
394 - 408
380 - 394
366 - 380
352 - 366
338 - 352
324 - 338
310 - 324
296 - 310
282 - 296
268 - 282
254 - 268
240 - 254
226 - 240
212 - 226
198 - 212
183 - 198
SOTTO 183

QUOTE

➤ *Location of the most important settlements of ancient Daunia. The Daunian territory was quite large and complex, and a diverse settlement pattern developed over several centuries.*

MONTE
SARACENO
TIATIO
ARPI○ ○SIPONTO
ORDONA○
○ CANOSA
MELFI○

For most of the Iron Age, Daunian settlements were open villages consisting of huts made of dried vegetation, straw, clay and wood. The hut plan evolved slowly from rectangular buildings of rectilinear or apsidal plan, as at Salapia (tenth to ninth centuries BC), to circular or elliptical structures (seventh to sixth centuries BC), as in many settlements at Arpi, Cupola, Ordona, and Lavello.

What became the most common type had a central hearth, pebble foundations and external posts supporting the roof, plus – sometimes – a short entrance portico. The transformation of proto-historic house-huts, made of perishable materials, into an 'urban' type of building, was a long-drawn-out, uneven process (in some

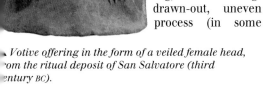

▲ *Votive offering in the form of a veiled female head, from the ritual deposit of San Salvatore (third century BC).*

➤ *Computer mapping of the Daunian settlement at Villa Faragola (eighth to fourth centuries BC). Left: a three-dimensional projection. Centre: the structures plotted on the ground. Right: micro-relief of the site.*

The Funerary Stelae

Typical of the Daunian culture are funerary stelae: anthropomorphic sculptures used as burial markers. Made from slabs of soft limestone, they were most used between the seventh and sixth centuries BC, when the proto-historic settlements of the region were at their height. The lower, unworked, part was set into the ground, and the projecting upper part was carved with anthropomorphic forms. The figure of the deceased is shown wearing a garment similar to a priest's cassock and often carries personal objects or weapons, and stelae might also be decorated with geometric motifs and figurative scenes.

The figurative decoration represents scenes of daily life: fishing, hunting, sailing and domestic activities – such as spinning and milling grain – and magico-religious rites. Also depicted were funeral games and the final voyage of the deceased, in heroic mode, for the other world. The details on the stelae were finely incised and finished with red and black pigments.

△ Stele of a Daunian woman (sixth century BC). Note the ornaments, the arms and the geometric and figurative motifs that decorate the reverse.

The stelae of male burials are distinguished by their shape, with four rectilinear sides, and by the absence in the depiction of the deceased of personal ornaments and the presence, in many cases, of weapons and armour (short sword, shield, pectoral). The stelae of female graves are embellished with brooches, pendants and necklaces; the deceased are shown with their arms folded on their chests and wearing gloves, and they have two notches at the sides of the neck, which gives them a long-necked look.

The depictions on this type of monument are stylized and intended not so much to represent a deceased's features as to assert their identity and demonstrate their social and political roles, thus endowing them also with apotropaic virtues that were indispensable for the voyage to the other world. Quite apart from the forms and the iconography, such funerary manifestations must have been confined to the privileged classes, whose ideology is revealed above all in funerary rites.

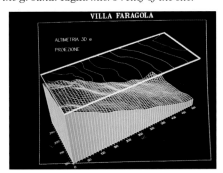

VILLA FARAGOLA

ALTIMETRIA 3D 6
PROIEZIONE

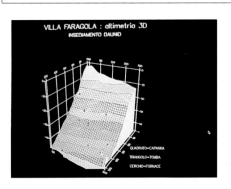

VILLA FARAGOLA : altimetria 3D
INSEDIAMENTO DAUNIO

QUADRATO=CAPANNA
TRIANGOLO=TOMBA
CERCHIO=FORNACE

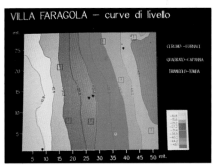

VILLA FARAGOLA – curve di livello

CERCHIO=FORNACE
QUADRATO=CAPANNA
TRIANGOLO=TOMBA

▷ *Daunian sub-geometric jug from Tomb II at Ordona, probably made at Canosa (second half of the sixth century BC).*

places huts remained in use for a long time), that seems to have started towards the end of the sixth century BC and taken place mostly during the fifth century. Thereafter houses were built to a rectangular plan on a base of stones mixed with clay, and their walls were made of wood and mud bricks topped by a tiled roof – sometimes decorated with palmette antefixes of Greek ancestry (as at the sites of Banzi, Canne, Ordona).

Public buildings were an exception to this process of evolution. At Canosa, in the area called Toppicelli, a building from the second half of the sixth century BC – identified as a shrine of Greek type – was built in large squared blocks and decorated with architectural terracottas of Hellenic derivation. At Lavello (and probably also at Tiati and Ascoli Satriano) real palatial complexes were built that must have had a politico-religious role, combining the civil and sacred. The palace of Lavello

is transitional in its architecture, with foundations and walls of stone rubble and wooden posts consolidating the walls and supporting a roof that was originally covered with perishable materials. Internally, it consisted of a large, elongated rectangular room with a vestibule at the entrance. Both the shrine (a Greek building type) and the palaces, which represent an evolution of the local architecture, can be seen as late examples of the proto-urban architecture of an earlier period, when the palatial complexes had stood, grand and isolated, in the Etruscan countryside.

The appearance of this 'solid' architecture, first in public buildings and then in private houses, is partly attributable to external cultural influences, as is shown by the spread of architectural terracottas of Greek and Etrusco-Campanian type. Circular gorgon-head antefixes derived from Magna Graecia, are found in the Melfi area, which was influenced by the Greek colonies on the Gulf of Taranto, while antefixes of Etrusco-Campanian type, in the form of a haloed head, are characteristic of central and northern Daunia (Lucera, Arpi, Tiati), which had

contacts with Etruscanized Campania. Since there are no urban models for the greater part of the Iron Age, we can only see this type of civil-cum-religious public building (shrines, *naiskoi*, temples and palaces) as serving to centralize daily activities in the social and political spheres. In the eighth to seventh centuries BC most of the Daunian settlements do not seem to have been amenable to external influences. From the sixth to fifth centuries BC, however, the area became increasingly receptive, as a result of the Hellenizing influence of the Greek colonies on the Gulf of Taranto – as finds of *inter alia* Ionian cups, black-glaze cups and other black-glaze pottery show.

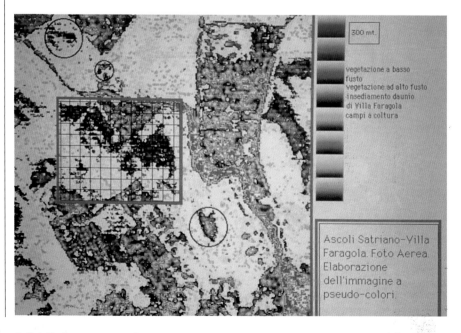

△ *Detail of a computer-enhanced aerial photograph of Ascoli Satriano. In the grid at the centre, a dark shadow marks an area of huts of Daunian date (eighth to fourth centuries BC). The colour palette on the right distinguishes the different types of land and structures detectable on the ground on the basis of their 'reflectance'.*

△ *Computer-enhanced aerial photograph of Ascoli Satriano, which has allowed unexplored and buried sites to be located.*

Recent research in the area of Ascoli Satriano has revealed the prosperity and the economic growth of the territory. Not only was the area's cultural receptiveness transformed but a new and extraordinarily vital productivity is detectable throughout the fourth century BC. It seldom extended beyond Daunian territory, but the presence of a wide variety of artifacts (even quite luxurious ones) in small agricultural centres presupposes that a complex distribution system must have existed. In this phase changes in public and private building and the strong Hellenizing stimulus contributed decisively to the formation of cities. Fortified urban centres were founded, surrounded by walls and with planned streets; space was allocated for private houses, which were no longer isolated and separate, and for civil and religious public architecture. Urbanization and demographic concentration led to the depopulation of the countryside, and by the end of the fourth century BC the scattered villages were largely abandoned and replaced by isolated

Detail of walling in opus mixtum *at Ordona (ancient erdonia). Excavations at the site have revealed not only the pre-Roman settlement, but also the Roman ntre (from the end of the fourth century BC).*

farming estates. In the process, primary centres that already had a central role – such as Canosa, Canne, Ascoli and Ordona – turned into urban centres, and absorbed the minor settlement areas scattered through the territory.

At Canosa and at Canne the urban revolution led to the abandonment of

▷ Panorama of the excavations at Herdonia, with a view of the forum and the basilica (the latter is of Augustan date and had walls in opus incertum *and a central colonnade).*

the pre-urban and archaic villages and the ancient temples and manufacturing complexes, in favour of more extensive and easily defended settlements around the acropolis. Something similar occurred at Ordona (ancient Herdonia), in the area that represented the main nucleus of Daunian settlement, where a city was founded at the end of the fourth century BC that later grew into the Roman city. The hill was fortified with a an earthen rampart reinforced with a wooden framework (another rampart, with a ditch, replaced this at the beginning of the third century BC). A different technique was used to build the city wall of the Latin colony of Luceria (315 or 314 BC) out of cut sandstone blocks.

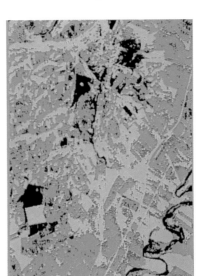

△ *Computerized predictive map of Ascoli Satriano. Digital analysis has made it possible to locate previously unknown sites.*

The last example of public architecture in Daunia is the temple of San Leucio at Canosa, datable between the end of the fourth and the beginning of the third centuries BC. It is a majestic building on a high moulded podium, with monumental stairs and an Ionic-style colonnade topped with a Doric frieze of metopes and triglyphs; the capitals of the cella represent male and female heads decorated with volutes and acanthus leaves. The temple's monumentality and the wealth of its decoration testify to the economic success of the princes of Canosa, but the building may be seen as demonstrating the transition from the Daunian culture to the Roman.

Bibliography

L. Bonfante (ed.), *Etruscan Life and Afterlife* (Detroit, 1986).
La civiltà dei dauni nel quadro del mondo italico: Atti del XIII Convegno di studi etruschi e italici, Manfredonia 21–27 June 1980 (Florence, 1984).
E.M. Iuliis, *La ceramica geometrica della Daunia* (Florence, 1977).

E.M. De Iuliis, 'L'origine delle genti iapigie e la civiltà dei Dauni', in *Italia omnium terrarum alumna* (Milan, 1988), pp. 593–650.
E.M. De Iuliis, *Gli Iapigi. Storia e civiltà nella Puglia preromana* (Milan, 1988).
M.L. Nava, *Stele Daunie*, vol. I (Florence, 1980).
N. Spivey and S. Stoddart, *Etruscan Italy: An Archaeological History* (London, 1990).

Entella: A Long-lived Fortress City

Italy *The ruins of this ancient city lie on the spectacular and precipitous Rocca d'Entella, to the west of the river Belice sinistro in western Sicily. It was occupied from at least the fourth century BC until 1246, and was initially a Greek colony but was later ruled from Campania, Syracuse and Carthage, before coming under Roman control. In post-Roman times it was occupied by Arabs, who were expelled in the thirteenth century AD. Recent archaeological research has identified part of the city wall, parts of the Greek and Arabic cemeteries, a public granary of Hellenistic date and various monumental structures of the Norman and medieval periods.*

the Roman empire Sicily fell to the Vandals and was later ruled by the Byzantines, before being taken by the Arabs in the ninth century. Arab rule was ended in 1197 by the Holy Roman Emperor Henry VI, and a rebellion by the remaining Arab inhabitants of Entella provoked harsh repression from Emperor Frederick II, who in 1225 and 1246 deported the survivors to Apulia, thus bringing the city's life to an end.

Some decrees of Entella – written on bronze and dating to the time of Agathocles, tyrant of Syracuse, at the end of the fourth century BC – were discovered by clandestine excavations in the 1970s. They have provided valuable information about events that took place in the city, its alliances, regulations, calendar, and some of its buildings (among them were a temple of Estia, a theatre and a council chamber). Archaeological research begun in 1983 by the Scuola Normale Superiore of Pisa has so far concentrated on the Hellenistic period (fourth to third centuries BC), from which a large public food store has come to light, and the Arab/Norman period, which has yielded the remains of two fortifications and a Muslim cemetery (the first found in Sicily).

The Archaic city wall was rebuilt in the Hellenistic period and enclosed an area of around 40 hectares (100 acres) accessible only via two gates opening on to the north slope. Combined with the imposing natural defences of the Rocca d'Entella, surrounded on most sides by high, rocky escarpments, this made Entella a particularly well-fortified city.

The system of fortifications has been identified – by aerial photography, by surface survey and by excavation – on the north side, the only side where there are no precipices. Here the city wall is preserved not only on the central rocky massif, but also in the

With Segesta and Erice, Entella is one of the three major cities, originally founded by settlers from northern Anatolia, which retained their own cultural traditions and language over a long period, even when they used a Greek alphabet derived from the colony of Selinunte on the south coast of Sicily. Called *Elimi* ('eaters of Italian millet') by the Sicilian Greeks, after their preference for this cereal, these settlers were in close contact with the Greek world, especially in the fifth century BC; their main city, Segesta, was allied with Athens against Syracuse.

Entella seems initially to have enjoyed political autonomy – thanks to good relations first with the Phoenicians in Sicily and then with the Carthaginians. However, in 404 BC, the year in which the Athenian expedition to Sicily failed, Campanian mercenaries took it. The city subsequently passed a number of times between Campanian, Syracusan and Carthaginian rule (minting its own silver and bronze coinage in the fourth century BC) until it ended up under Roman control at the time of the First Punic War (264–241 BC), and thereafter it declined. After the end of

△ *The north-west part of the city wall. Built in straight sections with bastions, it dominates the landscape.*

▷ *Gold ornament in the form of a crescent moon, from a Hellenistic tomb in the cemetery of Entella. Despite clandestine excavations in the past, precious objects of great craftsmanship were found intact in the cemetery.*

◁ *Location map:
Entella lies in the
interior of western
Sicily. It was founded
by settlers from
Anatolia in the later
prehistoric period.*

deep north-east and north-west valleys: the natural access routes to Entella from the main Belice valley. On the north-east side the wall, although no longer continuous, is traceable across most of the valley; it was built in straight segments linked by two (or perhaps three) bastions, one of which was circular. It has been suggested that there was a gate in this stretch of wall, but it is no longer visible on the ground, due to substantial rock falls from the overhanging spurs.

The central massif of the Rocca d'Entella was entirely enclosed within the perimeter fortifications. Lengths of wall are also detectable in the steepest sectors, and at the east end a large square bastion can be made out. In the north-west valley the wall has been identified for about 120 m (130 yards), connecting the central massif to a square bastion with a small gate behind it. A little further west there was another, semicircular, bastion set on a rocky outcrop, and in the lower part of the valley there may be another gate, protected by bastions on both sides – the

arrangement of the walls found in recent excavations seems to indicate a non-frontal type of entrance. West of this, the wall extends halfway up the hillside in straight runs reinforced with bastions at the points where it changes direction.

In the sector so far investigated, the walling dates to the Archaic period, not later than the mid-sixth century BC. Substantial rebuildings, of uncertain date, are indicated by differences in the building technique that can be seen on some stretches: the west bastion is built of rough-hewn blocks of chalk using dry-stone technique with earth as a binder, while the external wall of the east bastion is made of large, squared blocks of chalk and limestone laid in regular rows of Flemish bond. There are differences of technique between the lower and upper parts of the square bastion at the east end of this sector of the wall, which indicate rebuilding, probably during the Hellenistic period. There are no traces of re-use during the medieval period; evidently the defences fell into disuse, and the medieval fortifications were built inside the circuit of the ancient city wall, enclosing a smaller area.

Defensive devices – difficult to date but definitely not medieval – were also found on the steep sides of the acropolis, at least in the sectors where access might have been possible. Stretches of fortification protected the access to the

△ *The entrance to the public granary. It consisted of a large stairway which linked an open space lying at the back of the building with the grain storage rooms.*

plateau of the city at points where stairs had been cut into the rock leading down to the cemeteries below, while remains of the wall and of a square tower are visible on the south side.

Along the east flank of a deep, north-ward-sloping valley flanking the Rocca d'Entella – which forms a natural access point to the ancient city and was protected by one of the gates in the city wall - a public granary of the Hellenistic period has been completely uncovered. Excavations in this area have revealed not only the structure of the building but traces of previous settlement and parts of a chalk quarry worked in antiquity and used for settlement in the medieval period. There is clear evidence of a suspension of use during the Roman late Republican and Imperial periods and in early post-Roman times.

The Hellenistic granary building is located at the back of an upper terrace,

◁ *Part of the public granary built at the end of the fourth century BC. The building faced a large open space, probably the agora.*

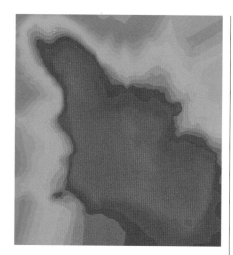

△ *Computerized digital images of the area:* Above left: *a relief model of the terrain (darker colours indicate the highest areas).* Above right: *an aerial photograph of the site.* Bottom: *a complete three-dimensional model in which it is possible to move virtually.*

artificially cut into a rocky outcrop that had been smoothed out during the construction of the perimeter walls. It was divided into northern and southern sections by a stairwell, with the larger section (composed of five adjacent rooms) running north–south and the smaller (of two rooms) stretching east–west. The roof – made simply of pantiles laid on the so-called 'Laconian' system and supported on wooden beams – may have had a single slope, facing the valley. There is nothing to suggest that the building included a second floor.

It was certainly built after the middle of the fourth century BC (and, in all probability, in the last quarter of that century), but the north section was burnt during the first decades of the third century BC. After this, the first two rooms of the northern section unex-

pectedly collapsed – sealing in evidence of the activities that had taken place in them – and the other rooms were abandoned and their contents removed (except for the large grain containers, which clearly could not be squeezed through the doorway). Then the walls began to fall down, and total collapse must have taken place progressively in several stages, one of which may have involved an earthquake.

The presence of *pithoi* in at least three of the rooms allows the building to be identified as a public granary, like others found in Sicily, for example at Monte Adranone and at Serra Orlando (ancient Morgantina). The elongated rectangular plan with rooms aligned

along a single axis, is perhaps most similar to the complex at Morgantina, notwithstanding its later date of initial construction. The designation of some of the rooms as 'domestic' can probably be justified on the grounds that they were rooms of mixed use – as offices and living quarters – for the magistrates responsible for the public distribution of grain.

To the south-east of the building there was a chalk quarry (from which the material for building the granary came), and in the foundations of its perimeter wall a small group of votive objects was found – placed there as a sacrificial offering at the start of the building work.

Cemetery A at Entella (so called to distinguish it from other cemeteries found during the surveying and excavation at the site) occupies a vast natural terrace below the southern face of the acropolis. Its location, outside the city wall, beside an access route and presumably close to a gate, reflects a pattern common in the ancient world. The majority of the burials so far found reveal a degree of superimposition that bespeaks extensive use of the cemetery, not only in the later pre-Hellenic period (the end of the fourth century and the third century BC) but also many centuries later in the medieval period (eleventh to thirteenth centuries AD). The later pre-Hellenic tombs were single inhumations, with the deceased always laid in flat on the back. In spite of the damage caused by severe tomb-robbing, quite a broad range of tomb types has been identified, from simple trench graves to the monumental underground chamber made with large limestone slabs. Funerary equipment

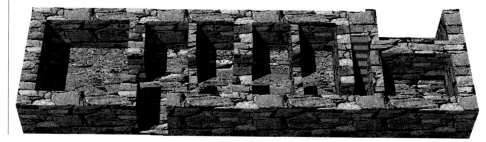

△ *Computerized axonometric reconstruction of the public granary, produced by means of solid-modelling and computer graphics. The texture of the walls was produced by digitally sampling the cut stones found at the site.*

The Decrees of Entella

△ The ninth decree, in which Entella expressed its goodwill towards Segesta for the freeing of men and women from an enemy.

In the 1970s, clandestine excavators using metal-detectors unearthed unusual documentary evidence from the city, in the form of a series of decrees issued by Entella in the time of Agathocles, tyrant of Syracuse, apparently between 312 and 306 BC. Of the nine decrees so far known, one (Decree III) relates to another, as yet undiscovered Sicilian city: Nacona. The texts were intended to be publicly posted in the council chamber (Decrees IV, V, VII, VIII, IX) and in the temple of Estia (Decrees I, II and VI) of Entella.

The presence among them of the decree from Nacona reinforces the hypothesis that the decrees were never posted, but remained near the workshop of the bronzesmith who made them until they were found. The rapid and unforeseen return of the Carthaginians to the city presumably prevented the posting of the decrees, in which various cities of Sicily were thanked for help given on a variety of occasions (for example in the war against the Carthaginians).

Written in the Doric Greek dialect of Sicily, they represent the major evidence available today for the study of this dialect. As well as providing evidence of interstate relations between Entella and Segesta, Enna, Assoro, Gela, Erbita, Petra, Makella, Schera and Cutattara, the decrees even reveal the name of a previously unknown site: Cutattara. From the decrees emerge details about Entella's institutions and its history: the archonship and the hieromnemonate; the city's calendar; the role of the popular assembly; a serious famine which both the city and its private citizens offered their help to relieve; the presence of an agent of Agathocles in the city; and the Oscan and Greek names of the inhabitants. No less important, however, are the data on town-planning, which indicate that in the Hellenistic period Entella had a theatre, a temple of Estia and a council chamber.

Only the ninth of the Decrees of Entella is conserved in Italy (in Palermo); all the others are now in foreign collections.

for funerary purposes in other periods as well. However, it was not always used exclusively as a cemetery: the remains of a kiln, doubtless used to make indigenous pottery with painted geometric decoration, as well as traces of other structures imply the presence in the Archaic period of structures connected with pottery manufacture.

Limited trenches excavated a few tens of metres to the west of Cemetery A have produced a stratigraphic sequence of prehistoric pottery (mostly related to the Thapsos-Milazzese horizon of the Middle Bronze Age) and abundant Archaic material of Greek type, which provide evidence of contacts with the wider world from as early as the final decades of the seventh century BC.

Bibliography

Various authors, *Entella. Ricognizioni topografiche e scavi 1983-1986*, ASNP, S. III, XVI, 1986, pp. 1075–174; ... *scavi 1987*, ASNP, S. III, XVIII, 1988, pp. 1469–1556.

Various authors, *Entella. Relazione preliminare della campagna di scavo 1988*, ASNP, S. III, XX, 1990, pp. 429–552; ... *scavo 1989*, ASNP, S. III, XXII, 1992, pp. 627–759; ... *scavo 1990-1991*, ASNP, S. III, XXIV, 1994, pp. 85–336.

Various authors, *Alla ricerca di Entella* (Pisa, 1993).

Various authors, *Entella I* (Pisa, 1995).

consisted almost exclusively of pottery vessels and of alabaster unguent containers.

There is only one type of tomb dating to the medieval phase, a period in which the city was occupied by Muslims. This is a simple trench with no stone facing or cover and containing no grave goods, with the body of the deceased laid on its right side, the face turned towards Mecca.

Two indigenous burials – in a trench and in a small cave – dating to the second half of the seventh century BC, and three secondary cremations from the late Republican period (before 31 BC) – associated with a base interpreted as an offering table – show that at least part of the terrace was used

◁ Photographs, such as this one of the Hellenistic public granary, have aided the creation of digital images tested on models of the site.

The Acropolis of Athens

Greece

Regarded for centuries as the quintessential symbol of Greek culture and civilization, the Acropolis of Athens, with its monumental architecture, is undoubtedly one of the most influential complexes of buildings from antiquity. In it, philosophical concepts, ethical and religious values, political will and outstanding human skills converged to produce something that has been fittingly defined as 'an experiment in perfection'.

The Acropolis plateau stands 156 m (512 ft) above sea level, on a ridge that runs from east to west, and its steep and rocky slopes overlook the chaotic modern metropolis. It was first occupied in the Neolithic period, housed a fortified citadel in the Mycenaean era, and, in the Geometric period, became the religious heart of the *polis*: the principal cult site and a sanctuary of the eponymous goddess of the city, Athena. According to myth, Athena appeared here to King Cecrops and defeated Poseidon in a contest for the patronage of Attica, countering the sea god's gift of a horse (an obvious instrument of war and the symbol of an oligarchic society) with her own special gift of an olive tree, which represented honest hard work, trade in the products that it yielded, and the peace necessary for

both. The Acropolis also accommodated sacred areas dedicated to other divinities – such as Zeus, Artemis and Poseidon – and to heroes, such as Erechtheus.

Monumental building on the Acropolis began in the sixth century BC: first under the tyrant Pisistratus, who instituted the Panathenaia (a festival in honour of the goddess, celebrated every four years), and then under his sons, Hippias and Hipparchus. A Doric temple was erected in the space that now lies between the Parthenon and the Erechtheion, and facing them minor votive chapels and a first version of the Propylaea appeared.

It was, however, in the fifth century BC that the great era of systematic monumental building took place that has since made the Acropolis famous.

△ *Detail of a statue of Athena, the wise and warlike goddess who won the contest with Poseidon for the patronage of Attica and Athens.*

The first stages consisted of renovation programmes undertaken by the democrats, first conservatives and later 'progressives', who held power in the aftermath of the Persian Wars. Everything that had been contaminated by the presence of the hated 'barbarian' invaders (cult and votive statues, *kouroi* and *korai*, altars and temple complexes with their rich architectural decoration of stone or painted terracotta) was buried in the gigantic purificatory pits of the so-called 'Persian reclamation', discovered and excavated in 1886–7.

The advent of Pericles (*d* 429 BC) on the political scene and the increasingly imperialistic policy of Athens towards the Greek world and the Mediterranean – which coincided with great developments in philosophy, arithmetic and

◁ *The Parthenon seen from the hills to the south-west, a vantage point that shows its harmonious proportions to advantage.*

geometry – determined the final version of the monumental programme. The prevailing politico-religious ideology was focused on a proper celebration and exaltation of the goddess Athena, the city of Athens and its citizens, their institutions, their religious and political beliefs and their pan-Hellenic orientation.

The Acropolis complex was, therefore, born of the will of Pericles but sustained by the extraordinary democratic ethos of the city, and it coherently expressed in artistic terms the spiritual outlook, the rationale and the values of its inhabitants. Building began in 449 BC with the renovation and enlargement of the temple of Athena. This endeavour crystallized the inspiration of Pericles, the architectural genius of Callicrates and Ictinus, and the creativity of the greatest artist of antiquity, Phidias, who supervised the works and executed the sculptural decoration with the help of a highly efficient workshop.

Today, after centuries of plundering, damage and degrading re-uses, the splendour of the Parthenon still reflects the fundamental and yet complex purity

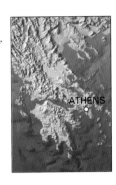

▷ *Location map: For Athens, the location of its port of Piraeus – which lies 10 km (6 miles) south-west of the city-centre – favoured its commercial expansion towards the east and south, including trade with Egypt.*

and perfection of its design. Ictinus, created a grandiose Doric octastyle peripteral temple (of eight by seventeen columns) in which every single space, measurement and element was the result of proportional calculations related to aesthetic requirements. For example, in the colonnade, whose columns are thicker than usual and closer to the walls of the cella, the ratio between the lower diameter of the columns and the intercolumnar spacing is the same (4:9) as

that between the width of the stylobate and its length. Such calculations also underlie the harmonious modulation as well as the height and slenderness of the Doric colonnade in the cella, which created a particular sense of space. Also used recurrently throughout the complex are the golden section and sequences of measurements corresponding to progressive square-roots, which prefigure the theories in the *Theaetetus* and the *Timaeus* of Plato in the next century.

Still more arresting are the logic of the siting and the system of optical correction adopted by the architects to enhance the harmony of the Parthenon. The northward expansion incorporated the base of the temple begun *c.* 490 BC and destroyed by the Persians *c.* 480–479 BC. The choice of site enhanced

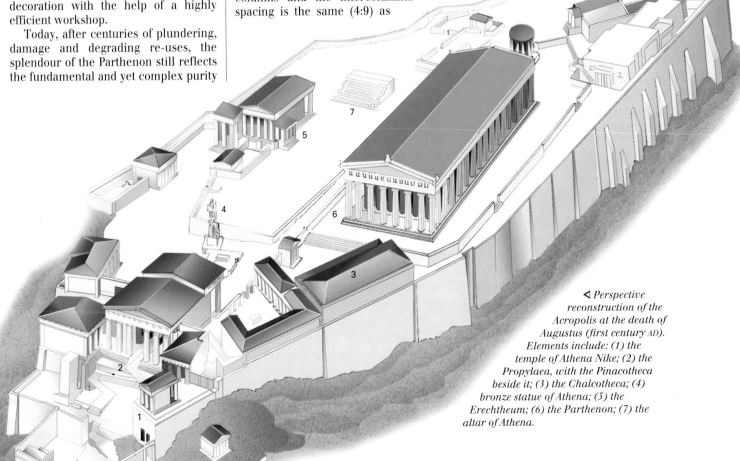

◁ *Perspective reconstruction of the Acropolis at the death of Augustus (first century AD). Elements include: (1) the temple of Athena Nike; (2) the Propylaea, with the Pinacotheca beside it; (3) the Chalcotheca; (4) bronze statue of Athena; (5) the Erechtheum; (6) the Parthenon; (7) the altar of Athena.*

△▷ *The Parthenon seen from the west, the side facing the Propylaea. A three-quarter view shows the elegance of its proportions, as does the image on the right, which is a complete virtual reconstruction of the monument.*

was usual in the Doric order – were inclined slightly inwards, while the stylobate was built with a slight convexity, being 6 cm (2.4 inches) higher in the centre than at each end of the short sides.

The decoration of the temple was laden with religious significance and political values in the highest sense. It was embellished like a treasure-chest – into which Phidias placed one of his greatest masterpieces, the Athena Parthenos (only the faintest impression of which can be provided today by a reduced-scale Hadrianic marble replica known as the Varvakeion Athena). And it was Phidias, with a close-knit and highly skilled team of collaborators, who

the perspective effect of precession when the building was seen, on the right in three-quarter view, by a viewer coming through the Propylaea from the Sacred Way (along which the procession snaked at the Panathenaic festival in honour of the goddess). On the other hand, because of the particular structure of the Doric order and the imperfections of human eyesight, this viewpoint could induce a distorted visual perception of the temple and its proportions. Therefore, in order to counteract an impression of 'elongation' of the building, and of a

slight sagging at the centre of the stylobate, the columns – which incorporated the convex swelling part of the way up the columns (entasis) that

◁ *A detail of the east face of the Parthenon, with a part of the pediment showing a horse from the chariot of Selene and, underneath it, a metope with a scene from the battle of the gods and giants (gigantomachy).*

conceived and executed the whole decorative scheme. The pediments represented the birth of Athena from the brow of Zeus and the contest between Athena and Poseidon for patronage of the city, in the presence of the mythical king Cecrops. The metopes show the usual allegorical oppositions of Good and Evil, Law and Anarchy, in the form of Athenians fighting Amazons, Greeks fighting centaurs, gods fighting

giants, and Greeks fighting Trojans (a metaphor for the recent Athenian defeat of the Persians, and so of the triumph of justice over barbarism). The extraordinary Ionic frieze around the exterior of the cella – solemn and intense, and combining sculptural lyricism with naturalism and harmony – portrays the Panathenaic procession in honour of the goddess. At the end, the whole city, with all its inhabitants ordered in their social groups, presents itself for inspection by the gods of Olympus.

In 437 BC, a year after the main structure of the Parthenon was finished and while the sculptural decoration (probably involving the co-operation of all the major artistic workshops in Athens) was still going on, work began on rebuilding the single entrance to the Acropolis – the Propylaea – through which the Sacred Way passed on to the western edge of the plateau. This project, carried out by the same workers who had built the Parthenon, was directed by another great architect, Mnesicles, and was left incomplete when the Peloponnesian War broke out in 431 BC.

It was not an easy job to create an entrance of suitable proportions, elegance and sobriety to complement the massive structure of the recently completed temple. It had to fit into an asymmetrical and constricted site and, in addition, had to respect the existing monuments and sacred spaces. However, Mnesicles conceived a structure, preceded by a steep and impressive flight of steps, that stood on the edge of the plateau, adapting itself to its rocky ruggedness while at the same time 'taming' it by means of the accuracy of all the proportional relationships and the precision of the dimensions of every single component. A Doric hexastyle pronaos solemnly announced the entrance to the sacred *temenos* of Athena's sanctuary. It

consisted of an elongated vestibule, subdivided by two rows of three particularly slender Ionic columns. At the end stood a wall with five gateways opening at the top of flights of five steps (the middle gateway has a ramp for horses, processional carts and animals) that mark the break of the contour and harmonize the change in slope. As the visitor moved on, a Doric colonnade identical to that at the lower end of the Propylaea framed Phidias' colossal bronze statue of Athena – 7 m (23 ft) high – and revealed the harmonious perspective of the Parthenon: the visual

△ *The Propylaea from below. In this monumental gatehouse, Mnesicles solved the difficult
problem of creating a suitable entrance to the sanctuary of Athena on an awkward site. On
the right is the temple of Athena Nike, built according to plans by Callicrates.*

△ *The small temple of Athena Nike. This project by Callicrates, put forward for the Acropolis as early as the time of Cimon, was first implemented on the banks of the Ilissus (a few eighteenth-century drawings are our only record of this), and it was not until the last quarter of the fifth century BC that financial support was forthcoming and space was found for it on the acropolis.*

reference-point of the whole Acropolis. On either side of the front of the Propylaea stood two small porticoed wings, one of them (the northern one) leading into a rectangular space behind it: the Pinacotheca, where famous paintings were preserved.

Just outside the Propylaea, on a terrace beside its southern wing, a graceful small temple dedicated to Athena Nike was built between 424 and 410 BC. The architect may have been Callicrates, who devised for it a highly original amphiprostyle plan – with Ionic columns placed only at the back and front of the temple. This revived and modified a project devised about thirty years earlier that had been 'diverted' into a small temple dedicated to Demeter and Kore (or Persephone) built on the banks of the Ilissus.

The frieze on the Temple of Athena Nike depicts the themes of combat and assembly. A balustrade surrounding the terrace on which the temple stood (to prevent the faithful falling on to the slopes of the Acropolis below), finely sculpted in relief by a follower of Phidias, depicted a series of personifications of Victory, clad in fluid draperies.

The last building constructed on the Acropolis towards the troubled end of the fifth century BC was the Erechtheum, located to the north of the Parthenon close to the site of an ancient temple serving a variety of very ancient cults. It was built between 421 and 405 BC (by either Callicrates or Mnesicles) and had an unusual and complex plan, presumably dictated by the ritual and formal demands of the cults involved. The temple was divided into two principal chambers set at different levels determined by the sharp rise in ground level from west to east. The statue of Athena Polias, an ancient, primitive portrayal of the goddess, was kept in the western chamber, which also housed the cults of Poseidon-Erechtheus, Butes (the son of the king of Athens), Hephaestus and the

serpent-king Erichthonius. Before the west front stood the sacred olive tree traditionally regarded as the one given to the city by Athena during her contest with Poseidon; and on the northern side a portico with six Ionic columns protected the mark left in the rock by Poseidon's trident when, according to legend, he made a salty spring gush forth. From the south side of the building a delicate loggia supported by caryatids projected to enclose the mythical tomb of Cecrops. The decision to support the roof of the loggia with statues of young women wearing the peplos, instead of using columns, accords with an intention to mingle the elegance of the Ionic taste with the formal perfection of the artistic vocabulary of Phidias – here interpreted by one of his best followers, probably Alcamenes. What is most interesting about the Erechtheum is the inter-locking rhythm of the volumes of the building, which does not rest on a single flat foundation, because of differences in the ground-level and the need to preserve certain points that had been consecrated *ab antiquo* by various

▷ *Detail of the entablature of the small temple of Athena Nike and its frieze. This building is one of the most harmonious uses of the Ionic order; the capitals are particularly elegant.*

Bibliography

G. Jouven, *L'architecture cachée. Traces
   harmoniques* (Paris, 1979).
G.P. Stevens and J.M. Paton, *The
   Erechtheum* (Cambridge Mass.,
   1927).
W.B. Dinsmoor, jr, *The Propylaea to the
   Athenian Akropolis* (Princeton, 1980).
I. Jenkins, *The Parthenon Frieze*
   (London, 1994).
M. Robertson, *The Parthenon Frieze*
   (Oxford, 1975).
J. Boardman and D. Finn, *The
   Parthenon and Its Sculptures*
   (London, 1985).
F. Brommer, *The Sculptures of the
   Parthenon* (London, 1979).

divine manifestations. The asymmetries
and the diversity of the Archaic cults
were drawn together by the lightness
and elegance of the Ionic style into a
coherent and yet not monolithic whole.

The Acropolis was revered both as a
holy place and as an extraordinary
open-air museum of Hellenic philosophy, politics, culture and art (even the
Romans wanted to erect a small circular
temple there, dedicated to the cult of
Rome and Augustus). Today, by virtue
of the richness of its temples and their
decorations, it serves also as an unusual
laboratory for experimental and virtual
archaeological research that is building
on more than a century of excavations
that have disentangled the chronological succession of its buildings.

△ *The Loggia of the Caryatids, on the south
side of the Erechtheum. This Ionic revival of
the Late Archaic use of caryatids was most
probably the work of Alcamenes, a pupil of
Phidias.*

▷ *Virtual reconstructions of the caryatids of
the Erechtheum (left and right), compared
with the actual remains of one of the
originals (centre). The caryatids on the
Acropolis today are casts; to protect them
from the notorious atmospheric pollution of
modern Athens, the originals are now in the
Acropolis Museum, while the best-preserved
is in the British Museum.*

Delphi: The Navel of the Ancient World

A place of extraordinary fascination, Delphi lies in the Phocis region, at a height of 570 m (1,870 ft) on the slopes of Mount Parnassus, at the junction of ancient communication routes. It is suspended halfway between the Phaedriades ('shining rocks') and 'the sea of olive trees', which tinge the valley below with shimmering silver for kilometres, as far as the Gulf of Itea.

The renowned sanctuary of Apollo arose in the Geometric period (tenth to ninth centuries BC) on a pre-existing Mycenaean site used for chthonic cults. The relatively modest complex dedicated to Athena Pronaia was built later, at a lower level, on an artificial terrace. As at numerous other pre-Hellenic religious centres, the cult of a proto-historic deity was replaced by that of a god from Olympus, a metaphorical reflection of the arrival of the new Indo-European masters of Greece. However, the legend of Apollo's victory over Python, the serpent-dragon son of Gaia (the great Earth Mother) and guardian of a rocky cave in which vapours intoxicated men and endowed them with prophetic powers, is particularly significant. Apollo's triumph was 'necessary violence' applied to the ferocious primitiveness symbolized by Python – a catharsis that expressed the triumph of established civilization and law over the barbarism of the 'Dark Ages' and the establishment of reason and equilibrium, wisdom and creative genius as prerogatives and gifts of the god. Apollo inherited the protective powers of the mysterious, primitive, natural force that sprang from the cave, delegating oracular pronouncements to a priestess, the Pythia, whose inarticulate cries were interpreted by a suitably chosen group of priests. It is therefore easy to understand the reasons for the religious and political centrality of Delphi, the 'navel of the world', especially in the seventh and sixth centuries BC: all the acts of the Greek people, from the foundation of colonies to wars between city-states, were legitimized or prohibited by the word of the god, via prophecies and responses.

The impressive ruins of the sanctuary of Apollo and Athena testify to Delphi's importance. They included imposing buildings (a stadium, theatre, gymnasium and hostels) used for the Pythian Games: a kind of 'championship' of artistic and sporting disciplines performed in honour of the god every eight (later four) years. In the disorder appropriate to eternally sacred (and therefore untouchable) cult sites, these buildings stood side-by-side with structures of pure embellishment and works of art, altars and so-called 'treasuries' (*thesauroi*): temple-deposits of precious offerings, which also reflected the propaganda of many city-states from Asiatic Ionia to the Cyclades, and from colonies in Attica and the Peloponnese.

No Greek archaeological site is better endowed with sanctuaries – especially the major ones, such as those of Delos, Olympia and Dodona. This makes it, as it were, an extensive horizontal stratigraphy. Within the sacred enclosure (temenos), which is still visible today, everything was the exclusive possession of the god. Along both sides of the Sacred Way, winding its way up the hill, there was a succession of works by

△ *Aerial view from the east of the sanctuary of Apollo at Delphi. From left to right, along the slopes of Mt Parnassus: the Treasury of Athens (490–480 BC), beside the Sacred Way; the Temple of Apollo (373 BC) in the centre; and the theatre (fourth century BC).*

*masterpiece of
...ssical bronzework,
... famous Charioteer
...icated to Apollo
... the tyrant
...yzalos of Gela
...er his victory in the
...hian Games (474 BC).
...elphi, Archaeological
...seum)*

largest opening to the south-east – at the level of the Roman agora, where there were porticoes with shops selling votive offerings and souvenirs. Here the Sacred Way begins.

From the arrangement of numerous statue pedestals – erected by various Greek cities between the fifth and the fourth centuries BC to commemorate important events in their history – it is possible to get a vague idea of the shining sequence of votive monuments, frequently of bronze, that embellished the god's precinct from the first ramp. In contrast to the planning of the great Hellenistic acropolises, this sequence was not co-ordinated by the clever management of architects or planners; it was determined by the casual correspondence and occasional conflict of images arising from the propaganda

◁ *Location map: Delphi lies in the Phocis region of central Greece. Considered the navel of the world (the omphalos offered to Cronos and refused by him, was venerated here in the shape of a conical stone), by the Geometric period (tenth–ninth centuries BC) Delphi had become a cult site for Apollo and the renowned oracle.*

of one state or another. It was largely motives like these that initiated the series of *thesauroi* dedicated to the glory of Apollo by the city-states of the Greek world: Sicyon, Thebes, Megara, Syracuse, Cnidus, Corinth – and others of uncertain identity, of whose treasuries there remain, unfortunately, only faint traces, sometimes with fragments of architectural or sculptural decoration.

architects and artists (from the sixth century BC to the fourth) working to the order of governments, tyrannies and, later, monarchs and high magistrates. There are no signs of an overall plan, for buildings of very different eras occupy adjacent sites with no consideration for the existing layout. Neither are there any traces of modification or demolition: at Delphi, as at other sanctuaries, buildings were added (filling up any vacant site that could still be built upon without jeopardizing the stability of other structures) but never removed, and buildings that time or disasters had destroyed or damaged were repaired or enlarged. The sacred enclosure was built during the sixth to fifth centuries BC using large polygonal and square blocks. It contained nine gates, the

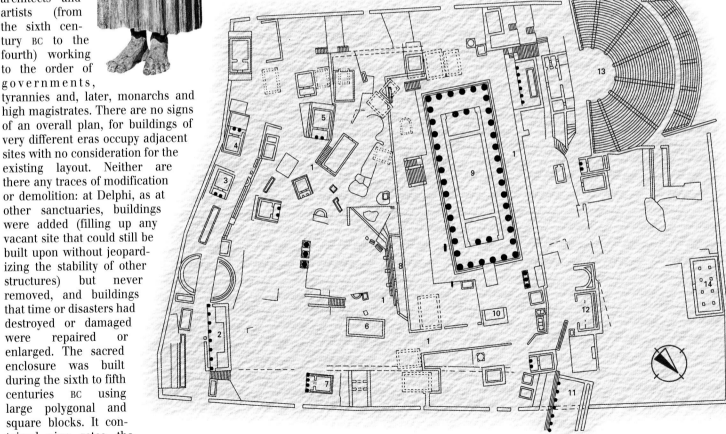

△ *Plan of the sanctuary of Apollo, showing the principal buildings inside the temenos and along the Sacred Way: (1) The Sacred Way; (2) the Spartan votive of Egospotami; the Treasuries of (3) Sicyon, (4) Siphnos, (5) Athens, (6) Corinth and (7) Massilia; (8) the Stoa of the Athenians; (9) the Temple of Apollo with (10) the altar in front; (11) the Portico of Attalus I and (12) the votive of Daochus II, the work of Lysippos; (13) the theatre; (14) the Cnidian Lesche, originally decorated by the great painter Polygnotus of Thasos.*

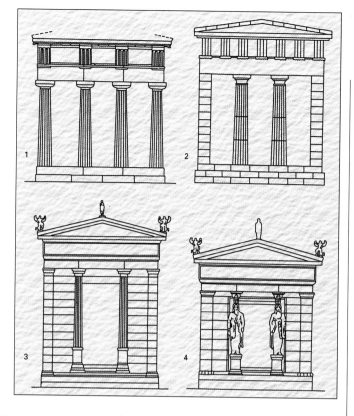

▷ *Reconstructed façades of four of the Treasuries: (1) that of Sicyon (560–550 BC), a pseudo-tetrastyle Doric prostyle, with the triglyph of the frieze centred over the columns below; (2) that of Athens (490–480 BC), a Doric distyle in antis, with deeper triglyphs centred on the underlying columns and on the intercolumniation; (3) that of Massilia (530 BC) in the sanctuary of Athena Pronaia, an Ionic distyle in antis, with Aeolian capitals and an elegant acroteria; (4) and that of Siphnos (530–520 BC), an Ionic distyle in antis, with two caryatids and acroteria.*

In contrast, the Treasuries of Siphnos and of Athens represent two notable testimonies to Archaic and Classical sculpture. The first was a small Ionic temple, distyle *in antis* but, unusually, with the columns of the pronaos replaced by two elegant caryatids. Today, only its foundations survive *in situ* (the remains of the rest of the structure are in the Delphi Archaeological Museum). Built in 530–525 BC, it is one of the most important examples of mature Archaic architecture. On the north and east sides of the frieze there is a gigantomachy rendered with great liveliness and a bold use of space.

The Treasury of Athens, erected soon after the battle of Marathon (490 BC) for the display of some of the booty taken from the Persians, has undergone a scrupulous reconstruction and restoration and stands almost intact in its original position. This, too, is a small distyle *in antis* temple (it was barely larger than the Treasury of Siphnos), but it uses the Doric order. The simple harmony of its proportions is set off by a sober frieze of metopes alternating with triglyphs that depict the Battle of the Greeks and the Amazons, the Exploits of Theseus and the Labours of

Hercules, all in a Classical style that still incorporates Late Archaic elements.

Unfortunately, only in virtual reality is it possible to reconstruct the complete setting of the area of the Treasuries that was so charged with political messages. (After its crushing defeat of Athens in the Peloponnesian war, Syracuse built its own Treasury opposite the small Athenian temple that had become a symbol of Greek independence!)

The most important building in the temenos was, of course, the Temple of Apollo. What can be seen today is the remains of the sixth phase (373 BC) of the Temple (which followed the dimensions of its Archaic predecessor). These reveal a classic example of a Doric peripteral hexastyle temple made of limestone and tufa and measuring about 60 × 23 m (197 × 75 ft). Its columns of plastered tufa rested on a stylobate with three steps sitting on a massive artificial substructure. The cella, peristasis, pronaos and opisthodomus contained both works of art and objects of cult and historical significance, and this gave the temple building and its surroundings a secondary role as a museum of sacred art: something often found in the major Greek sanctuaries. Its size must have imposed itself upon the surrounding buildings, drawing visual attention towards the 'house of the god', which, significantly, was sited about halfway between the two springs and the rock that tradition has linked with the oracular ritual of the Pythia.

In the western corner of the temenos, almost overhanging the terrace on which the temple sits, is the theatre. This is in an excellent state of preservation (only the stage building has disappeared) and is cut into the slope of the hill in accordance with

▷ *The reconstructed Treasury of Athens (490–480 BC), decorated with Classical-style metopes that show some Late Archaic elements.*

Greek custom. This would have been approached via elegant, frescoed porticoes and exedrae adorned with sculptures and votives (a well-known example is that of the tyrant Polyzalos of Gela, dating to 475 BC, from which there survives the splendid Charioteer, now preserved in the Delphi Archaeological Museum).

Outside the temenos lay the stadium, partially dug into the slope. It was about 180 m (590 ft) long and was surrounded by tiers of seats on a high podium probably protected by railings. The athletic and horse-racing competitions of the Pythian Games contested here could have been attended by crowds of at least 70,000 spectators.

The sanctuary of Athena Pronaia, despite its more modest dimensions, preserves the remains of one of the most fascinating buildings of ancient Greece, the Tholos. It was the masterpiece of the Phocian architect Theodorus and was built in 380–370 BC and was a rather rare type of circular temple, perhaps traceable to prehistoric ritual traditions. Its essential characteristics – proportion, adherence to mathematical formulae, and style – are clearly Attic, with its external peribolus of twenty Doric columns following the classic rhythms codified by Ictinus, the architect of the Parthenon. Complex innovations can, however, be seen in the organization of the modest internal space and in the application of the Corinthian order to the ten columns of the cella, touching but not integral with the wall and standing on a high socle of dark Eleusinian limestone that contrasts with the white Pentelic marble of the columns themselves. The Doric frieze (repeated on the external wall of the cella), the original coffered ceiling of

the peristyle, and the acroteria also show a decorative inspiration transcending canonical models and introducing the architectural language and eclecticism Hellenism was to make its own.

Finally, at least some of the works housed in the Delphi Archaeological

found north-west of the temple, which were probably contemporary replicas of original bronzes by Lysippos.

Museum must be mentioned as what must have been major visual reference points within the sanctuary: a sphinx that decorated the top of a column about 12 m (39 ft) high, erected south of the temple as a votive offering by the people of Naxos in about 560 BC; a column, originally 13 m (43 ft) high, with a group of dancing *korai*, dedicated by the Athenians in 325 BC and found near the temple; and the splendid statues donated by Daochus II,

Bibliography

Fouilles de Delphes (series ed. by French School of Archaeology in Athens).
H. Berve, G. Gruben and M. Hirmer, *Greek Temples, Theatres and Shrines* (London, 1963).
H.W. Parke and D.E.W. Wormell *The Delphic Oracle* (Oxford, 1956).
H.W. Parke, *Greek Oracles* (London, 1967).
V. Petrakos, *Delfi* (Athens, 1979).

△ Top left: *The remains of the east side of the temple of Apollo as it is today.* Above: *The same view but with the temple shown in a virtual reconstruction; the access ramp and the altar of Apollo are in the foreground.*

Olympia: Home of Zeus

Greece

*T*he archaeological park of Olympia lies peacefully in the heart of Elis, in a short valley at the confluence of the rivers *Alpheios and Kladeos. It sits just under a low hill, covered with pines and shrubs that on hot summer days, fill the place with resinous aromas. This was the ancient sanctuary of Zeus where all Greeks united to venerate the true gods and celebrate an ethnic and cultural identity that went beyond the political divisions between city-states.*

The origins of this cult centre go back to the end of the second millennium BC. It enjoyed a dual status as a sanctuary and as a point of peaceful convergence for the whole of Hellas during the four-yearly Olympiads. (The Olympiad was a sacred truce during which the various city-states sought a solution to their conflicts and differences through the guidance of Zeus, rather than – as at Delphi – through the mystic ambiguity of Apollo's responses transmitted through the Pythia.) However, from 2800 BC a community settled permanently on Mt Kronos and in the area of the *Altis*: the sacred grove of plane-trees, olives, oaks, poplars and

pines, around which the cult enclosure, the temenos, developed.

Precisely because of its remote origins, Olympia, like many sanctuaries, was a point of convergence for cults and myths that involved various figures associated with Zeus. These included Hercules, who brought the sacred olive tree from the land of the Hyperboreans and instituted the Olympic Games in memory of Pelops and in honour of Zeus, and the river-god Alpheus, whose love for the nymph Arethusa in Syracuse symbolized the spiritual bonds with the Greeks of the West. The cult of the Phrygian hero Pelops (who gave his name to the entire region: Peloponnese

means 'island of Pelops') affirmed the sanctuary's links with the eastern lands colonized by the Greeks even before Italy and Sicily and celebrated his defeat of the cruel King Oenomaus in a chariot-race, asserting the values of justice, humanity and respect for the divine laws. And Hera, the wife of Zeus, had a temple here at a time when, the according to proto-historic custom, the ruler of Olympus was venerated at a simple open-air altar, of which nothing has survived, in the sacred grove of the *Altis*.

▷ *Aryballos for perfumed oil in the form of a kneeling athlete crowning himself with the victor's ribbon (sixth century BC). The receptacle which he carries on his head must have contained the oil with which an athlete anointed himself before and after the contests. (Athens, Agora Museum)*

The layout of the sacred buildings and the surrounding complex that accommodated the athletes and visitors, as well as the pilgrims and delegations who flocked here even when the Olympic Games were not being held, does not have the spectacular scenic quality of Apollo's sanctuary at Delphi. However, the importance of the complex is reflected in its vast size and the monumentality of some the buildings which stood out from the numberless works of art, votive offerings, chapels and treasuries that spread over the whole area between the seventh century BC and the fourth century AD, when the Roman Emperor Theodosius I's prohibition of the pagan cults and the suppression of the games sounded Olympia's death knell.

△ *Aerial view of Olympia from the east. In the foreground is the River Kladeos; immediately beyond are, from left to right, the gymnasium, palaestra, workshop of Phidias and Leonideum. In the centre lie the remains of the temples of Hera (left) and Zeus. The stadium in which the Olympic Games took place can be seen in the far distance.*

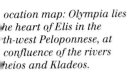

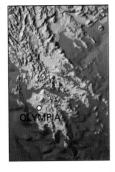

ocation map: Olympia lies
he heart of Elis in the
th-west Peloponnese, at
confluence of the rivers
heios and Kladeos.

One can visualize the grandeur of some of the buildings from the scale-model reconstructions of the sanctuary, made in recent decades, that are displayed in the splendid Archae-ological Museum recently set up not far from the ruins of the gymnasium. (This was a vast rectangle, enclosed by four porticoed structures, that was intended for the training of the athletes, as was the nearby palaestra.)

An ancient sanctuary is a dense horizontal 'stratification' of buildings that (in contrast to the more straight-forwardly functional city) is determined only by rules of a ritual nature. Consequently, in examining the image of Olympia, and that of other great Hellenic religious centres, we should

▽ *Plan of the sanctuary at Olympia. (1)*
Temple of Zeus; (2) Temple of Hera; (3)
Palaestra; (4) Leonideum; (5) Philippeum.
There is no detectable overall plan for the
layout, despite the presence of such
'rationalizing' elements as (6) the Portico of
the Echo and (7) the terrace of the
Treasuries.

not forget that its final appearance was forged after the time when it was at its peak. At Olympia, this means that the archaeological evidence extends from the orientalizing phase of the Archaic to the Hellenistic and Roman periods, by way of embellishments from the Classical age carried out by Libon (architect of the temple of Zeus), Phidias (sculptor of the colossal statue of Olympian Zeus in the cella of that temple) and other first-rank sculptors, such as Praxiteles and Peonio.

Despite its mutilation, the Temple of Zeus is still imposing and monumental, and is still the visual reference point for the entire complex. A Doric hexastyle peripteral temple, it was built in the fourth decade of the fifth century BC of local shelly limestone coated with stucco. Its decoration included two famous pediments about 26 m (85 ft) long by the anonymous Master of Olympia, which are masterpieces of Greek art in the transitional phase from Archaic to Classical, and twelve metopes on the pronaos and the opisthodomus that depict the Labours of Hercules. The earthquakes that have hit the region over the centuries, together with devastating flooding of the rivers Alpheios and Kladeos after the sanctuary was abandoned at the beginning of the fifth century AD, have toppled the architrave and the weighty

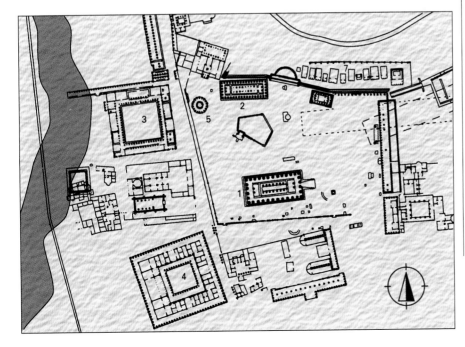

columns of the peristasis, whose drums and capitals lie scattered at the foot of the high steps of the stylobate.

Probably in no other temple in the Greek world does the pediment decoration achieve such a religious intensity and such density of meaning. It was enhanced by vivid colours (which today, unfortunately, can only be reconstructed in virtual reality) typical of Greek art and so different from the icy whiteness imagined by the Neo-classicists. On the eastern pediment, on either side of the manifestation of Zeus – which occupied the centre of the scene – the contest between Pelops and Oenomaus (after which the victorious Pelops would marry Oenomaus'

△ *A masterpiece of the Severe Style, probably produced*
by a Corinthian workshop, this ceramic acroterion
(from a temple?) of The Rape of Ganymede dates to
480–470 BC. (Olympia, Archaeological Museum)

daughter Hippodamia and end his reign of cruelty) is captured at a psychological moment, a little before the challenge. The tension surrounding the contest, of which the god is the holder and guarantor, unites all those present except for the arrogant king of Pisa in Elis, who is blind with inhuman and violent pride. It seems to isolate them in

North of the Temple of Zeus the Temple of Hera was built at the end of the first half of the seventh century BC. This was a Doric hexastyle peripteral temple, rather elongated in plan, with rich architectural decoration of painted terracotta. Even though it already possessed precious votive offerings, after the inauguration of the main

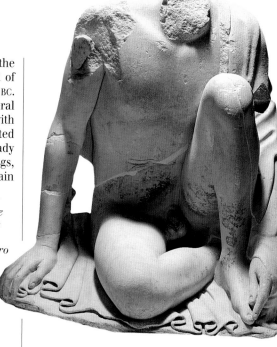

▷ *A figure from the east pediment of the Temple of Zeus: the Ephebe, possibly representing the hero Arcas. It dates to 460 BC. (Olympia, Archaeological Museum)*

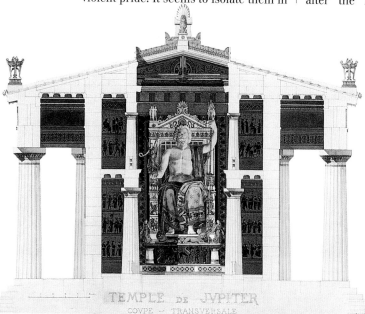

◁ *In this fanciful reconstruction by V. Laloux (1883), a vertical section through the Temple of Zeus gives an idea of the appearance and effect of the colossal statue of the god created by Phidias.*

TEMPLE DE JVPITER
COVPE ~ TRANSVERSALE

temple it was transformed into a sort of spectacular open-air museum for sacred art, which also continued to function as a sanctuary. As the remains of stone pedestals from every era testify, its buildings were crowded with statues of heroes, victorious athletes, divinities and politicians who (in a self-serving act that smacked as much of propaganda as devotion) offered images of themselves to the sanctuary. The famous group of

poses that are static but tense, and simple but telling gestures betray the characters' states of mind: the disturbance of the elderly soothsayer who 'sees' the outcome, twisting his beard as he stares at Oenomaus; the divinely inspired foreknowledge of Hippodamia, who makes a ritual gesture appropriate to a wedding); and the confused restlessness of the common folk – expressed in a young stable boy, who plays with his big toe without looking up. On the western pediment, on the other hand, the dynamism of the lines guides the viewer's eyes across the savage battle between the Lapiths and the Centaurs, fought out in the presence of Apollo, which can be read as a grand metaphor of the eternal conflict between Good and Evil, Justice and Injustice, Reason and Instinct.

△ *A virtual reconstruction of the east front of the Temple of Zeus conveys something of the imposing sight that would have greeted visitors as they approached its high stylobate.*

Hermes and Dionysus was found here; controversially attributed to Praxiteles, but in any case a masterpiece of Late Classical art, it can be seen today in the Archaeological Museum.

Other buildings of notable importance are spaced in the *Altis*. In a slightly raised position, on a terrace dug at the foot of Mt Kronos, stand the remains of a line of Treasuries. These were the

The remains of the temple of [He]ra (seventh to sixth centuries [BC]). The original wooden columns [w]ere only replaced by stone ones [w]hen they had become very [di]lapidated. The drums and [ca]pitals, therefore, date from all [th]e periods from Archaic to [R]oman.

votive chapels in which, over the course of centuries, such famous cities as Sicyon, Sibari, Cyrene, Selinus, Megara, Gela, Byzantium, Metapontum, Syracuse and Epidaurus (and others unidentified) deposited gifts in honour of the god, in everlasting testimony of both their gratitude and their power.

A line of sixteen statues of Zeus stands at the foot of this terrace, sited so as to overlook the athletes and the public on their way to the entrance to the stadium (which could hold 45,000 spectators on its terraced slopes). These statues were paid for with money from the heavy fines inflicted on athletes who were responsible for attempts to win by cheating. Also of interest is the Philippeum – a small, circular monopteral temple. This elegant building, erected by Philip II of Macedon after his victory at Chaeronea (338 BC) and

completed by Alexander the Great, had an Ionic peristasis and Corinthian columns on the inside. It contained five gold and ivory statues representing the Macedonian conqueror and members of his royal family – lost masterpieces by Leochares, which can perhaps be reconstructed by reference to the five miniature ivory heads found in the tomb of Philip II at Vergina.

Among the other elegant and functional buildings were the Leonideum – a kind of luxury hotel in the heart of the Sanctuary, which was embellished by gardens with fountains – as well as numerous sporting structures, such as the palaestra, the gymnasium, the baths and the thermal baths.

△ *West pediment of the Temple of Zeus, depicting the battle of the Lapiths and Centaurs. It dates to 460 BC. (Olympia, Archaeological Museum)*

Bibliography

Olympische Forschungen und Berichte über die Ausgrabungen in Olympia (published by the German Archaeological Institute in Athens).

L. Drees, *Olympia: Gods, Artists and Athletes* (London, 1968).

J. Swaddling, *The Ancient Olympic Games* (London, 1980).

A. Yalouris, N. Yalouris, *Olympia: Guide to the Museum and Sanctuary* (Athens, 1987).

▽ *Virtual reconstruction of the east front of the Temple of Hera. The Archaic characteristics of the building, erected in the seventh century BC and completed in the sixth, are visible: the heavy structure, modest height, and simple decoration.*

The Royal Tombs of Macedonia

Greece

*I*n 1988 an exhibition entitled 'Art of the Macedonians from the Mycenaean Age to Alexander the Great' was held in Bologna. It brought to the world's notice what a wealth of works of art ancient Macedonia possessed, even before it established the hegemony over the whole of Greece that was confirmed in 338 BC by the Battle of Chaeronea in Boeotia. The capitals of Philip II and Alexander the Great and their successors have, however, remained potent poles of attraction for scholars; Aegae (near present-day Vergina) and Pella are archaeological sites of enormous interest, as are the royal and aristocratic necropoleis of Vergina, Lefkandi, Thessaloniki and Dion.

The Macedonian tombs are some of the most interesting architectural monuments in the whole of Greece between the fourth and second centuries BC. They are underground constructions, covered with earthen tumuli, made of the soft local tufaceous stone and coated with a thick layer of plaster that imitated the brilliant sheen of polished marble (white or, when it was intended to emphasize the architectural framework, polychrome). Typically the plan consists of a simple chamber,

▷ *Axonometric 'exploded view' of a tomb in the Macedonian necropolis of Dion which shows the typical structure of these monuments: the funerary chamber, roofed with a barrel-vault, is preceded by a vestibule that has a façade decorated with a tympanum and a Doric frieze in fresco.*

▽ *Gold crown with lanceolate foliage, berries and flowers (350–300 BC) from Tomb B at Derveni. (Thessaloniki, Archaeological Museum)*

or an antechamber and funerary chamber, roofed with a barrel vault (whose origin and chronology have been much debated) and preceded by a temple-shaped façade, with columns and architraves that are often of the Doric order. The façades and some of the interiors were decorated with painted friezes that, when still visible, show the

elegant and vivacious polychrome of Late Classical and Hellenistic painting. They were the final resting places of rulers, local archons and their *hetairoi* ('companions'), who were buried there in costly urns and accompanied into eternity by extremely rich grave goods. The large number of burials shows that these were family tombs that contained the mortal remains of successive generations.

An overview of the Macedonian tombs begins with the famous royal tombs of Vergina, discovered by Manolis Andronikos in 1977 in an area already noted for its large number of high-class burials. Defined as a 'cist' despite its small dimensions – 2.9 × 4.3 × 3 m (9½ × 14 × 9¾ ft) – Tomb I must have

contained precious grave goods that were lost to the raids of tomb-robbers, but interesting frescoes remain on three of the interior walls. A band of pairs of griffins face-to-face, alternating with flowers forms the lower border of squares containing refined images of female figures (whose origins Andronikos correctly identified in the late fifth-century BC style of the elegant

Location map: Vergina, ancient Aegae, lies in the heart of Macedonia in northern Greece. The military expansionism of Philip II and Alexander the Great brought the region – traditionally considered to be on the periphery of Greece – into the centre of Hellenic political history.

lekythoi) on a white background. These include a rare scene of the Rape of Persephone in which Hermes runs in front of the chariot of Pluto, who has captured the desperate Persephone from under the frightened eyes of her friend Cione. The brilliant colours, the assured nature of the design, and the dramatic inspiration that pervade the frescoes suggest an attribution to Nikomedes, the famous painter of the mid-fourth century BC.

Tomb II, nowadays identified with certainty as the tomb of Philip II, was miraculously intact. It measures 9.1 × 5.6 × 5.3 m (29¾ × 18⅛ × 17½ ft) and has two chambers set on a single axis. The portico façade has a double-door framed by elegant Doric columns surmounted by a coloured epistyle and a frieze of a hunting party, with men on foot and on horseback (one of whom seems to have been intentionally depicted in a portrait style) and wild animals. The artistic quality is truly exceptional, and these paintings were probably executed *in situ* for this burial. The two chambers, which were covered by a barrel-vault, contained a rich assemblage of grave goods. The objects found in the tomb in the same

△ A pair of naturalistic bronze greaves (350–300 BC), part of a suit of armour from Tomb A at Derveni. (Thessaloniki, Archaeological Museum)

position that they occupied when the grave-diggers closed the doors (as they thought, for ever) can still provide stirring images.

The tombs of Lefkandi, between Edessa and Veria, are also famous, in particular the so-called 'Great Tomb' or Tomb of the Judgment, which dates to the reign of Alexander the Great (336–323 BC). This tomb measures about 10 × 8 m (33 × 26 ft) and is preceded by a rectangular antechamber which is larger than the mortuary chamber. It is of a more widespread Macedonian tomb type with a barrel-vault that extends

▽ The extraordinary marble throne, with rich carved and painted decoration, from the tomb of Eurydice (325–300 BC). The panel on the back depicts Hades and Persephone in Glory – a completely new funerary theme in Greek art.

over both chambers, a structure of soft limestone, a façade resembling a tetra-style *in antis* temple arranged on two registers, and richly decorated and crowned by a pediment. The impressive architectonic and painted decoration includes motifs of great interest.

The lower register of the façade is divided into five bays – the widest corresponding to the door – by four Doric semi-columns. The upper halves of the lateral panels contain four frescoes, in an excellent state of preservation, that depict a subject rarely seen elsewhere in Greek art: Hermes, in his role as conductor of spirits to the underworld, presenting the dead man for the inspection of Janus and Rhadamanthys, the judges of Hades. The upper register of the façade contains seven false windows with double studded shutters separated by six Ionic half-columns. Between the two registers run two friezes: one of Doric order with alternating triglyphs and painted metopes, and above this a continuous painted stucco frieze of Ionic type. The first contains eleven metopes with scenes from the Battle of the Lapiths and Centaurs; the second contains a violent and dramatic battle between the Macedonians and the

Persians. The latter can be seen as related to the battles between Greeks and Persians, or Achaeans and Trojans, that often appear on the sculptural decoration of Archaic and Classical Greek sacred buildings, standing as metaphors for the conflict between Good and Evil, Justice and Injustice – but it also alludes to the aristocratic (and hence 'heroic') condition of the deceased, and as a

△ *Right: Bronze-plated crater encrusted with silver (c. 330 BC) from Tomb B at Derveni: on one side (side A) a scene of the wedding of Dionysus and Ariadne is embossed between dancing satyrs and maenads. Left: Detail of the volute of one of the handles, finely decorated with a head of Hercules in a circular frame. (Thessaloniki, Archaeological Museum)*

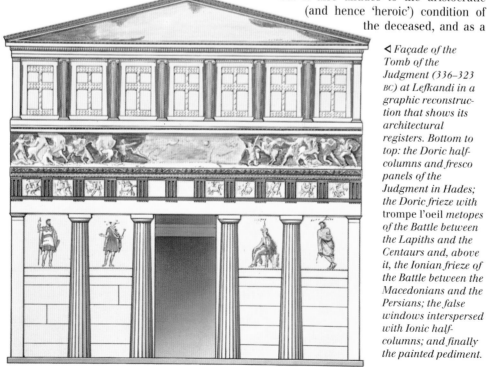

◁ *Façade of the Tomb of the Judgment (336–323 BC) at Lefkandi in a graphic reconstruction that shows its architectural registers. Bottom to top: the Doric half-columns and fresco panels of the Judgment in Hades; the Doric frieze with trompe l'oeil metopes of the Battle between the Lapiths and the Centaurs and, above it, the Ionian frieze of the Battle between the Macedonians and the Persians; the false windows interspersed with Ionic half-columns; and finally the painted pediment.*

melancholy *memento* of the brutality of Death.

Other notable tombs at Lefkandi are the Kinch tomb, named after the Danish scholar who first studied it, and the tombs of Lyson and Kallicles, named after the inscriptions which accompany them. Important monumental complexes have been excavated in the surrounding area and, although they have yet to be thoroughly interpreted, they certainly formed part of residential settlements connected to these sumptuous burials.

In the autumn of 1977 a Greek archaeological team under Manolis Andronikos discovered two intact tombs during excavations at the necropolis near a small Macedonian village called Vergina, not far from the remains of the

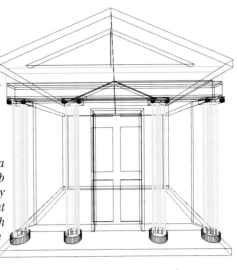

Macedonian Funerary Architecture

That all the Macedonian tombs excavated before 1977 had already been violated has led many scholars to base proposals for dating them exclusively upon architectural and structural factors. This has inevitably led to errors that have been recognized in the light of recent discoveries. Unreliable results have been derived from the proportional relationship of the height of the tomb and the circumference generated from the radius of the barrel-vault, and from typological comparisons of architectonic decoration that, in the soft and coarse stucco-covered limestone of the local tradition, in most cases differs from tomb to tomb. There are, therefore difficulties in proposing a hypothesis of an internal evolutionary sequence for this class of architectural monument, of which the vault and the façade are the distinctive elements.

The first example of a barrel-vault in a Greek tomb is that of the funerary chamber of Philip II at Vergina (336 BC), which dates to before the end of the fourth century BC. Traditionally this has been seen as justifying the theory that this tomb type was derived from the East after Alexander the Great's expeditions – as though the Greeks had not had occasion to absorb earlier eastern architectural models or were incapable of elaborating the arch, the barrel-vault and funerary pictorial decoration for themselves. Starting from analysis of four passages – from Sophocles, Plato, Seneca and Pliny the Elder – that have been undervalued by previous critics, Manolis Andronikos has suggested that the Macedonian vaulted tomb was indigenous. He points out the correspondence between Plato's writings and the appearance of Tomb II of Vergina – which was, moreover, similar to the first, provisional, tomb of Alexander the Great as described by Diodorus Siculus. It seems certain that, after increasing the size of their cist tombs to monumental dimensions, the Macedonian architects developed vaulted roofing in the middle of the fourth century BC to meet the engineering problems of yet more imposing structures. These they completed with sculpted and painted façades, for which we still have no recognizable internal evolutionary sequence, although they share common elements, such as the delineation of an access portico, a real propylaeum to define the funerary nature of the structure, and elegantly articulated friezes and pediments.

◁△ Virtual reconstructions of the façade of a Macedonian temple-style tomb (350–300 BC) excavated by K.A. Rhomaios on the edge of the Vergina plateau.

ancient royal palace of Aegae. One of these – Tomb II, which has a double chamber – was identified as that of Philip II, the Macedonian ruler who put an end to the independence of the Greek city-states, and the man who was Alexander the Great's father. The discovery aroused enormous interest throughout the scientific world.

Andronikos' proposed identification was given a cautious reception, though – despite the rich grave goods of gold, silver and bronze concealed behind the tomb's two marble doors, which fully supported the notion of its belonging to the royal family.

According to some, the two deceased (there was an urn in the antechamber containing the cremated remains of a

▷ Gold mask (350–340 BC) from the tomb of Philip II at Vergina, showing how the face of the Medusa evolved from the terrifying Archaic forms to the more human unease of Late Classical forms – something also found in contemporary pottery. (Thessaloniki, Archaeological Museum)

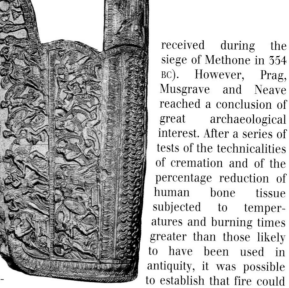

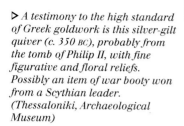

▷ *A testimony to the high standard of Greek goldwork is this silver-gilt quiver (c. 350 BC), probably from the tomb of Philip II, with fine figurative and floral reliefs. Possibly an item of war booty won from a Scythian leader. (Thessaloniki, Archaeological Museum)*

woman) were Philip III Arridaeus – half-brother of Alexander the Great, who succeeded him in 323 BC – and his wife Eurydice. Such objections were subsequently invalidated by palaeo-anthropological and palaeo-pathological research carried out on the male skeleton by a group of English scientists, but the episode did show that even the most acute and well-argued evaluations can be deceptive if based primarily on literary sources. The first investigations of the human remains, carried out by Xirotiris and Langenscheidt in 1981, produced no significant data that linked the cremated remains with what the narrative sources had to say about Philip II's physical appearance (he had lost his right eye and had his face disfigured by an arrow wound received during the siege of Methone in 354 BC). However, Prag, Musgrave and Neave reached a conclusion of great archaeological interest. After a series of tests of the technicalities of cremation and of the percentage reduction of human bone tissue subjected to temperatures and burning times greater than those likely to have been used in antiquity, it was possible to establish that fire could not have been the principal cause of the asymmetries and anatomical peculiarities of the skeleton.

Direct study of the cranium also revealed an essential chapter in the life of the deceased person. Clear signs of bone regeneration on the upper right orbital arch indicated a probable lesion, and confirmation of this came from deformities and traces of fracture on right-hand cheek-bone and the right-hand side of the jawbone, and from adjustment phenomena relating to mastication detectable on the jaw. From a cast of the skull it was evident that the face had been disfigured by a devastating wound to the right eye and to the surrounding region, caused by the violent penetration of a blunt instrument many years before death. Accurate reconstruction of the face, on the basis of the cast of the skull showed how he must have looked: a horrendous scar ran transversely over where the eye had been and linked up with a large hollow extending over a large part of the orbital region and the cheek-bone. Determining the shape of the nose, based upon numerous previous experiments, and adding the characteristic hair and beard of the Macedonian sovereigns, created a portrait that was extraordinarily close to all the images of Philip II found on statues, coins and medals – and above all to the lovely miniature ivory head also found in Tomb II of Vergina, which now became identified with man who defeated the Greeks at Chaeronea.

The skeleton of Vergina really is that of Philip II of Macedon, therefore, and it carries proof of the serious wound that he suffered in 354 BC, which caused the total loss of his right eye and the disfigurement of the surrounding part of his face. Prag's observations favour the best-known version in the historical sources, according to which the king, raising his head too far while inspecting his catapults, was hit by an arrow from an enemy archer on the walls of the besieged city of Methone.

Tomb II at Vergina is also of fundamental archaeological interest for its sumptuous structure and rich funerary goods. Through the Doric façade, which has a painted zoomorphic frieze with a single hunting scene, a marble double door decorated in relief with false studs opens into an axially aligned antechamber and funerary chamber. In the latter, together with the gold *larnakes* (funerary urn) containing the remains of a woman, precious jewellery was found, including a thin sheet of gold bearing the eight-rayed Macedonian star in relief, a quiver of silver-gilt and five miniature ivory heads up to 3 cm

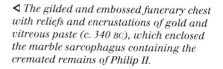

◁ *The gilded and embossed funerary chest with reliefs and encrustations of gold and vitreous paste (c. 340 BC), which enclosed the marble sarcophagus containing the cremated remains of Philip II.*

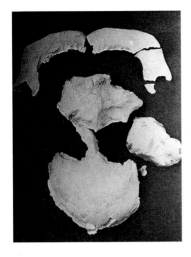
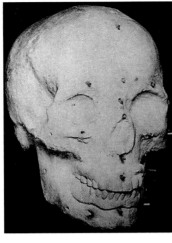
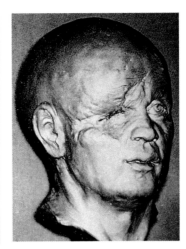
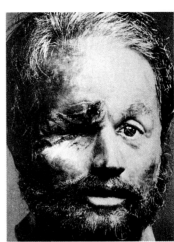

(1.2 in.) high representing members of the royal family – among whom Philip II, his wife Olympias and son Prince Alexander III are firmly identifiable. The last could be a small but equally priceless version of the lost statues that Philip commissioned from the great sculptor Leochares for the Philippeum, erected in the sanctuary of Olympia to commemorate his victory over the Greeks at Chaeronea.

Also found in the tomb were a bronze sword with a wooden sheath veneered in ivory, the remains of an iron cuirass lined with cloth and leather and trimmed with bronze plates decorated with gold, a parade shield to rival the mythical shield of Achilles, described in the *Iliad*, in the variety of scenes and themes depicted on it and the extraordinary richness of the materials used. These finds provide a vivid picture of the refinement and luxury that had been characteristic of the art of Macedonia since earlier centuries. (The Archaeological Museum in Thessaloniki houses finds of exceptional interest and value from the classical necropolises of Sindos and Haghia Praskevi.)

Bibliography

M. Andronikos, *The Royal Tombs of Vergina* (Athens, 1980).

M. Andronikos, 'Some Reflections on the Macedonian Tombs', in *Annual of the British School at Athens*, 82 (1987), pp. 1–16.

J. Boardman (ed.), *The Oxford History of Classical Art* (Oxford, 1993).

Various authors, 'The Skull from Tomb II at Vergina: King Philip II of Macedon', in *Journal of Hellenic Studies*, CIV (1984), pp. 60–78.

Various authors, *Arte dei Macedoni dall'età micenea ad Alessandro Magno*, exhibition catalogue (Bologna, 1988).

△ *Four stages in the reconstruction of the face of Philip II, disfigured by the injury to his right eye suffered in 354 BC during the siege of Methone.*

△ *Small ivory head of Philip II, from the funerary couch in his tomb at Vergina. Its resemblance to the reconstruction above is noticeable. (Thessaloniki, Archaeological Museum)*

◁ *Iron cuirass (c. 350 BC), decorated with bronze and gold plaques, from the grave assemblage of Philip II. (Thessaloniki, Archaeological Museum)*

Rome's Urban Landscape

*I*mperial Rome could call itself a metropolis in the modern meaning of the term – that is to say, an enormous urban agglomeration with many of the problems we complain of in today's cities: traffic, overcrowding, pollution, fire danger, hygiene, public order, poor road conditions, poverty, high cost of accommodation, and so on. It was a city of between one and one-and-a-half million inhabitants and faced urban management problems of extraordinary complexity. Some of the architectural and planning solutions that were adopted by some emperors produced notably pleasant and effective results, but the great urban transformations of the Rome of the Caesars never really solved the city's fundamental shortcomings. Today, as living conditions deteriorate in Rome and other urban centres, we can perhaps console ourselves with the knowledge that the inhabitants of ancient Rome had the same problems on their minds as we have, and that some things never change.

▽ *Model of ancient Rome. The Circus Maximus and the circuit of the Etruscan wall lie in the centre. These were some of the city's oldest public buildings. Urban problems arose from the start, when the settlement adapted itself to the topography of the seven hills.*

△ *Bust of the Emperor Hadrian (AD 76–138). A connoisseur of Greek culture, Hadrian built a luxurio[us] Imperial villa at Tivoli between AD 125 and 138.*

The problems of the city

Rome's problems began almost when the city began – from the moment when the settlement developed in a sprawl over an area consisting of seven hills. When, in Imperial times, it was eventually decided to institute a more rational plan, it already seemed too late. By then any plan had to take into account the existing late Republican city as well as the peculiarities of the site (the seven hills). These constraints prevented a systematic overall plan from being adopted, so it was mainly 'surgical' rebuilding and urban modernization that could be undertaken. One of the few (and in part missed) opportunities for urban and architectural renovation and regularization occurred under Nero, after the disastrous fire of AD 64.

Splendid examples of experimental architecture and building are more often found in the provinces or on the

*Rome's Urban
Landscape*

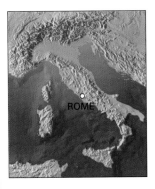

◄ *Location map: Rome
lies in the lower Tiber
valley. The river was
the city's principal
commercial artery.*

periphery of the Empire, where the constraints of space and population were less intense and the feasibility of planned development was greater. The urban history of imperial Rome is one of schemes involving major demolition before rebuilding could begin – from the construction of the Imperial Fora by Caesar and by emperors down to Trajan (first century BC to first century AD) to the opening of the Via Nova between the Aventine and Caelian hills (under Caracalla in the second century AD) and the building of Aurelian's walls in AD 271. The grandiose urban renewal schemes of emperors such as Augustus

(who divided the city into fourteen regions), Nero (after the fire of AD 64) and Trajan, amongst many others, created magnificent harmonies and architectural memorials, but did not substantially deal with the city's most obvious shortcomings.

There was a chronic problem of street space. The streets were narrow, and the large volume of traffic circulated slowly and barely succeeded in reaching the centre at all. Obstruction of the streets also created serious problems for the movement of vehicles and, above all, created a very serious fire risk – which was increased by the

indiscriminate use of wood in the construction of the *insulae* and many other buildings.

The city had a fire service, made up of 7,000 *vigiles* based in local barracks, traces of which are still detectable today. There was no public transport system except for hired litters or sedan

△ *Rome in the fourth century AD: (1) Forum Romanum; (2) Forum of Trajan; (3) Circus Maximus; (4) Flavian amphitheatre (Colosseum);
(5) Stadium of Domitian; (6) Imperial palaces; (7) Temple of the Divine Claudius; (8) Temple of Jupiter Capitolinus; (9) Pantheon;
(10) Mausoleum of Hadrian; (11) Mausoleum of Augustus; (12) Baths of Caracalla; (13) Baths of Trajan; (14) Baths of Diocletian;
(15) Porticus Aemilia; (16) Horrea Galbana; (17) Castra praetoria; (18) Aurelian's Wall.*

chairs, carried by slaves, which served as taxis. Water was supplied to the majority of the population via the fountains, but to have piped water in one's own house was a personal privilege granted as a favour by the emperor himself. As for burials, public cemeteries did not exist, nor were areas set aside for this purpose; one could be buried on one's own property, provided it lay outside the *pomoerium*, the formal boundary of the city. The only known example of public intervention in this sphere is the transformation of ancient cemeteries into parks by Augustus and Maecenas.

One of the Imperial city's chronic problems was sanitation, especially in hygiene and quality of environment. No adequate solutions were ever found for overcrowding and urban agglomeration. Lack of comfort in the houses, lack of air and light caused by tall buildings, and meagre street space created environmental conditions that became extremely difficult in times of emergency (epidemics, fires and riots). These problems were all the greater because until the fourth century AD Rome had no public hospitals, asylums or hospices (with the possible exception of the sanctuary of Aesculapius on the Insula Tiberina) – and during the time of Gallienus (AD 253–68) a plague killed at least 5,000 people per day in Rome and the surrounding villages. Only at a late stage and through private initiatives (frequently Christian) were sanitary support structures established. The first project of this type was the hospital established by Fabius in AD 380, in a country house situated on the outskirts of Rome.

Another grave deficiency in Roman urbanism was the absence of a system of street signs: only the most important roads – in particular the *vici* – were signed. Apart from public and religious areas and buildings, the Fora and monuments, the residential areas all looked the same: uniform façades, straight roads and dim lighting. As a result, the names of locations were improvised – for example from the name and profession of the proprietor, from the number of houses or blocks away from well-known urban sites, from the signs of shops and commercial premises or, in the case of the better houses, from their insignia or external decoration. Notables and important people, being the owners of *domae* (private residences), were easily traceable simply from the number of the residential district.

Despite the total lack of museums in the modern sense (deliberately enclosed spaces for the public display of works of art), open-air exhibition areas were established, as in the Forum of Augustus, the Forum of Peace, in bath-houses, in the Gardens of Agrippa, at the Campus Martius, and in the Gardens of Caesar in Trastevere. In the Imperial era, baths and porticoes were the best public spaces for displaying works of art. The most famous was the Portico of Octavia, in which the collections were divided between the central area, the outer colonnade, the *schola*, and the two temples of Jupiter

△ *The Forum Romanum as it is today. It was the cent of the political, commercial and legal life of ancient Rome, but as the city's population increased it became too small.*

Stator and Juno. Equally numerous, if less frequented, were exhibitions held indoors: in temples, such as those of the divine Caesar, the divine Augustus and Concordia in the Forum; in civic buildings, such as the Curia of the Comitium; in the theatres of Marcellus, Pompey and Balbus, in the Imperial Palace on the Palatine, and in the *Domus aurea* of Nero. However, most of these collections were accessible to the public only with difficulty; Pliny the Elder (*Natural History* XXXV.x.29) speaks of the *Domus aurea* as the 'prison' of the paintings of Fabullus.

The urban history of Imperial Rome ends with the fall of the eastern Roman Empire in AD 476, when the Ostrogoth kingdom took over the administration of the city. After 537–8, when Vitigis, king

◁ *Virtual reconstruction of the Forum Romanum. To the north of it, in 46 BC, Julius Caesar built a new Forum, and other emperors, from Augustus to Trajan, followed his example.*

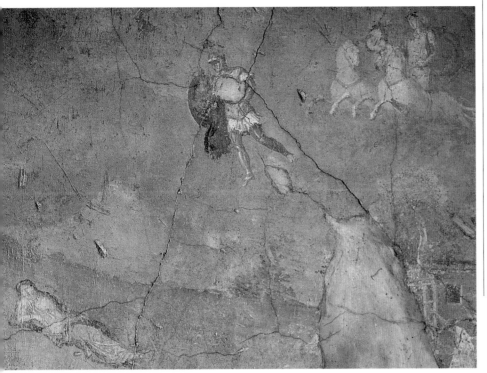

of the Ostrogoths, besieged Rome and destroyed its aqueducts, the city had to be content to draw all its water from the Tiber for the next millennium.

The earliest Rome

Between the fourteenth and the end of the eleventh century BC, the first settlements of what was to become Rome developed between the Palatine and the Capitoline. Initially these were small communities perched on higher ground all round the Velabrum marshes and linked by tracks. Between the end of the eleventh and the second quarter of the eighth centuries BC (the time of the *populi* and of the leagues), the community divided into juridical-sacred leagues established on the hills, and created out of the sparse villages a real community state – in other words, an embryo of future urban civilization. Between the middle of the ninth and the second quarter of the eighth centuries BC (and hence before the foundation of Rome), the *Septimontium*, a federation of villages united by juridical-religious laws, was established in a defined territory. During this period the inhabitants underwent an extraordinary process of growth that bonded together the different tribal groups.

➤ *The Capitoline Wolf (c. 450–430 BC), a fine example of early Roman bronze sculpture. According to Cicero's account, the image of the animal (a symbol of Rome's origins) was displayed on the Capitol. It has not been repaired since it was struck by lightning in 65 BC.*

What did this forerunner of Rome look like? We must imagine a rugged landscape of valleys and gorges with rocky streams and tortuous roads climbing over hills and running alongside the ancient houses. Age-old woods of oak, beech, ilex and cypresses covered the hills, but the valleys and the slopes were densely covered with a scrub of myrtle, fig, laurel and brambles. Some places were consecrated to nymphs or divinities, such as springs or caves – including the Lupercal grotto above the Velabrum, where, according to myth, Romulus and Remus were raised. The villages of the *Septimontium* must have been autonomous agglomerations of houses surrounded by gardens and fields, animal pens and workshops producing ceramics and metalwork.

In the second quarter of the eighth century BC (the traditional date of Rome's foundation was 753 BC) the community state became a city-state, with a real urban territory marked by the Palatine and by the line of the *pomoerium*. Access to the Palatine was forbidden to armed troops, and the hill became a 'prohibited' zone under the control of a single political authority. The Etruscan rite of the foundation of the city, (accomplished, according to legend, in the course of a day by the augur-king Romulus under the protection of Jupiter) gave the Palatine absolute supremacy over the urban area, making it a centre of power. This led to Rome developing outwards from its core, the Palatine, in complete contrast to other cities of the ancient world – for example, the Greek cities. In terms of the planned synthesis of separate villages, Rome in the age of Romulus could already be defined as one of the most important settlements of the western Mediterranean. As early as the eighth century BC, the Forum Boarium ('cattle-market') was its main square and principal market-place. During the reigns of Ancus Marcius (640–616 BC) and Tarquinius Priscus (616–578 BC) we can identify the first town-planning schemes – of which traces remain in the valley of the Forum, such as the first paving (625 BC) and the first Regia (palace), which took the shape of a house. It was in this period that huts of posts, planks and clay were replaced by houses with masonry walls and tiled roofs.

◄ *Fresco from Nero's* Domus aurea *in Rome representing the origins of Rome: Mars descends from the sky to impregnate Rhea Silvia, who lies asleep.*

◁ Polychrome terracotta antefix with a woman's head, found in Rome-Tre Fontane. This splendid decoration was positioned on the gable-end of a roof to seal the end of the course of ridge tiles.

In the reigns of Tarquinius Priscus and Servius Tullius (that is, between the end of the seventh and the middle of the sixth century BC) great public works were undertaken: streets, squares, buildings, sewers and canals. The draining of the marshes and the channelling of the water allowed further settlement in the valley, which led on to the coalescence of the separate villages. These new schemes included the reclamation of the site of the Forum Romanum (as a result of the building of the Cloaca Maxima), which became the new political, religious and administrative centre. The rebuilding of the Regia, the building of the Curia and the development of the square used for the citizens' assemblies are attributed to Tarquinius Priscus. In the Forum Boarium, Tarquinius also erected the temples dedicated to Fortuna and *Mater Matuta*.

The 'House' of Romulus

Recent excavations carried out by the archaeological Superintendency of Rome on the south-west slopes of the Palatine have uncovered a village of early Iron Age huts. Of these there remain the post-holes for the wooden uprights and the floors dug into the tufa; the super-structure of the huts, which can no longer be recon-structed, must have consisted of a framework of branches and straw bound together with clay. The site lies in a position controlling the ford over the Tiber near the Insula Tiberina.

The singularity of the find stems from the fact that one particular hut remained unaffected by later structures of Roman date; in fact, there is a shrine around it: an area of respect and veneration. Furthermore, the hut and shrine are close to the house of Augustus and the temple of the Magna Mater *(Cybele)*, and must certainly have still

been visible and well pre-served in Imperial times. Whose, then, was this hut and why was it so carefully preserved for so long? We know from ancient sources that the hut ('house') of Romulus – or rather a building that was venerated as such – was preserved in this area of the Palatine. We also know that up to the fourth century AD this shrine preserved a straw hut, a symbolic building that, when it burnt down or deteriorated was restored or rebuilt.

The significance of the discovery was that, in all probability, this shrine preserved the cult site par excellence: the house of Romulus. The identification is not so speculative as it seems if we think of the very relevant comparison that can be made with the myth of the tomb of Aeneas at Lavinium. In this case too, the great antiquity of the cult of the Trojan hero on the coast of

Latium has been clearly shown, leaving aside the historical reality of the event. Research results from the excavations on the Palatine have shown that the only part of the area in question to remain unaltered by later urban development was that of the shrine. It was to remain untouched both in the late Republican era, when the temple of the Magna Mater was built, and in Imperial times, when shops were put up. From the stratigraphy it is quite clear that this ashlar built structure was never violated or destroyed, and throughout the Roman period remained a memorial site, a reminder of Roman origins. It is significant that Augustus – who so strongly promoted his own image as the 'refounder' of the city – erected his own house close to the first 'house' of Rome: that of Romulus.

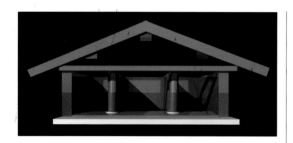

What did Rome look like in this era? By now houses had spread everywhere: on the hills, in the valleys, along the Sacred Way, in the Forum, on the slopes of the Palatine. They consisted of several adjoining rooms and had porticoes, en-closed courtyards and decorated roofs.

△ Virtual reconstruction of the Temple of S Omobono. The building was erected in the second quarter of the sixth century BC on a site once occupied by proto-historic huts.

For an idea of the rich architectural polychromy and sumptuous furnishings we can look to the Etruscan chambered tombs of Cerveteri, such as the Tomb of the Shields and Seats. In all probability, sacred architecture did not differ much from the domestic architecture, as is attested by the two archaic phases of the temple of S Omobono (attributed to Servius Tullius), which have an almost square plan with three adjacent cellae with porti-coes. The houses, then, were richly adorned with architec-tural decoration in polychrome terra-cotta, and they did not generally exceed an area of 10 × 20 m (33 × 66 ft), including the courtyard. Only at a

later stage did sizes increase, as shown by recent discoveries on the slopes of the Palatine under the Arch of Titus, where houses measuring 35 × 19 m (115 × 62 ft) with vast courtyards have been unearthed. Further urban initiatives can be traced in the building of cisterns, made of blocks of tufa, to collect rainwater. By the end of the Archaic era the urban landscape of

▷ Small ivory lion with an archaic Etruscan inscription, found near the Temple of S Omobono (the first building in the sacred area).

Rome had acquired a definitive architectural and territorial form. This included the houses of ordinary citizens, with tiled roofs, patricians' houses with towers, and the houses of the gods (such as the temple of Jupiter on the Capitoline, and those of *Fides*, Juno Lucina and Luna on the Aventine) sparkling with polychrome decoration. All the same, the streets, the paved squares, the ashlar walls and most of the urban landscape still largely followed the contours of the ground, and the underlying topography was not yet modified by major earth-moving and architectural engineering.

The definitive delineation of the urban area came with the building in the fourth century BC of the city wall: an imposing structure of tufa ashlars with a perimeter of 11 km (6.8 miles), crossing hills and cliffs, neatly separating the city from the countryside. This was decisive, not only for the definition of the urban area but also for the political and religious legitimacy of the city. It has been calculated that in this period Rome could have housed about 30–40,000 inhabitants distributed over an area of 300 hectares (740 acres), making it one of the largest cities in the western Mediterranean. In a further assertion of the urban political identity, Tarquinius Superbus built the temple of Jupiter Capitolinus, the foremost divinity of the city and protector of the Roman people. This was a grandiose temple in ashlar, 55 × 53 m (180 × 174 ft), with six columns on its façade and a triple cella, symbolizing the triad of Jupiter, Juno and the city's tutelary deity Minerva.

Augustan Rome: The city of fourteen regions

At the end of the Republican era the official limits of the city were formed by the *pomoerium*. In 7 BC Augustus extended the city limits to include the suburban zones (*pagi*) that formed the outer rim of the city. This greatly increased the urban area, which was

△▽ Above: *Virtual reconstruction of* insulae, *high-rise apartment blocks.* Below: *Model of* insulae *at Ostia. These are particularly sumptuous examples. Every* insula *was divided into lodgings (*cenacula*), which were rented.*

therefore divided into fourteen administrative regions – from which the city would take its name of *Urbs XIV regionum* (city of fourteen regions).

One of the major difficulties that Augustus encountered in his restructuring was the urban imbalance inherited from the Republican era. The city's historical and geographical centre was on the Palatine, surrounded by the other hills, and the principal north–south transport artery, known as the *cardo*, was formed by the Via Appia and the Via Flaminia. In place of a *decumanus* – a single east–west artery – a number of different routes led from the centre towards the periphery. Each of the administrative regions represented a different district: seven pomoerial and seven extra-pomoerial. From the time of Augustus to the end of the Imperial era the city expanded in two directions: to the east in the age of Aurelian, due to the creation of the new city wall, and to the west, in the Transtiberina area, between AD 136 and the fourth century. The city of the fourteen regions reached its maximum extent in the fourth century AD, spreading over an area of 1,800 hectares (4,450 acres).

▽ *Virtual reconstruction of the interior of a* domus, *a luxurious Roman house. In the centre is the* impluvium, *a small pool in the atrium for collecting rainwater.*

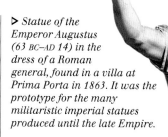

▷ *Statue of the Emperor Augustus (63 BC–AD 14) in the dress of a Roman general, found in a villa at Prima Porta in 1863. It was the prototype for the many militaristic imperial statues produced until the late Empire.*

Communications with the world

'It was not without reason that the gods and men chose a place like this for the foundation of their city. A place with healthy hills and a river to transport agricultural produce from the interior and receive goods arriving from the Mediterranean; a place close enough to the sea to benefit from it, but not so close as to be exposed to the incursions of foreign fleets.' This was Livy's view (V.54) of Rome's strategic position and outstanding development potential.

An important factor was Rome's location at the point of convergence of

the most important communication routes of the Early Iron Age, which met in the Latin, Etruscan and Sabine settlements around the main ford across the Tiber, by the Insula Tiberina. The sea was a relatively short distance away downstream, which facilitated communication with the rest of the ancient Mediterranean, while by land a road system connected the city with Ostia, Ardea, Labici, Tusculum, Praeneste, Gabii, Tibur and Nomentum in the Archaic era. At the end of the fourth century BC a network of road communications developed for long journeys – which ultimately would cross the territory of over thirty of today's nations. The Roman road system (which began with the construction of the Via Appia, the Flaminia, the Salaria, the Cassia, the Aurelia and the Emilia) would become truly impressive, but it was the waterways that opened up for Rome the commercial horizons of the Mediterranean.

A combination of land and sea transport enabled 250,000 tons of Egyptian grain per year to be imported, and opened trade routes to the East Indies, the Persian Gulf and the Red Sea. Figures from the time of Diocletian (AD 284–305), for example, show that it was cheaper to move grain from one part of the Empire to another by sea than to transport it on wagons for hundreds of miles. Any type of load could go by water: columns, blocks of marble, statues, sarcophagi and large obelisks, as well as fine materials, ceramics, fabrics, glass, jewels, wine and foodstuffs. The most important sea routes – combining long-distance voyages with local coastal and river navigation – connected Rome with the

great cities of the Mediterranean: Antioch, Alexandria, Caesarea, Carthage, Cadiz, Tarragona, Narbonne, Marseilles and Arles. The routes were varied, using different transhipment points, according to commercial objectives.

The *insulae*

One of the elements of ancient Rome that seem to link it to our own cities was the *insulae*: high-rise houses and apartment blocks divided into lodgings or apartments (*cenacula*) that were rented out to tenants. The term *insula* ('island') originated with the first houses of this type, which were single units with free space around them and a vegetable garden. Later, under the pressure of urban agglomeration, the individual residences with attached spaces disappeared, making way for large, multi-storey buildings that nonetheless were still referred to as *insulae*. Over time, such buildings came to epitomize the inescapable urban necessity of making the maximum possible use of ground area, as over-crowding and shortage of housing in Imperial Rome led to increasing numbers of multi-storey buildings, the use of cellars and basements for residential occupation and progressive reductions in the size of rooms and lodgings.

The most common type of *insula* was like a barracks, an enormous block subdivided into large numbers of lodgings and apartments. These could be four or five floors (or more) in height, with shops on the ground floor and roof gardens or attics at the top. In general, however, the *insulae* were of more modest proportions, having a façade 6–12 m (20–40 ft) wide with one entrance for the ground-floor shop and another leading to the stairway to the rest of the building. Each apartment or lodging within the building was usually

△ *Computer reconstruction of the 'geometric centre' of ancient Rome: the Triumphal Way, the Arch of Constantine and, on the right, the Flavian amphitheatre, later called the Colosseum.*

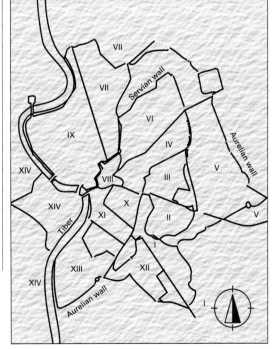

▷ *The fourteen regions into which Augustus divided Rome: (I) Porta Capena; (II) Caelemontium; (III) Isis and Serapis; (IV) Templum Pacis; (V) Esquiliae; (VI) Alta Semita; (VII) Via Lata; (VIII) Forum Romanum and Magnum; (IX) Circus Flaminius; (X) Palatium; (XI) Circus Maximus; (XII) Piscina Publica; (XIII) Aventinus; (XIV) Transtiberina.*

rented separately, the price varying according to its dimensions and standard of internal appointments. The smallest type of *insula* was the *taberna*, a small shop or workshop premises that could serve as a workspace or a habitation, or both. In Imperial Rome increasing shortage of lodgings and lack of building space pushed these buildings ever upwards, to heights of up to 30 m (100 feet), creating considerable risks of structural instability and fire.

The baths

Some of the most entertaining and sophisticated places in the Imperial city were the great bathing establishments, which combined functionality, a healthy environment and architectural splendour. The size of these complexes enabled them to accommodate an extraordinary number of people: up to 1,600 could enjoy the services offered at the Baths of Caracalla, and another 3,000 those of the Baths of Diocletian. In addition to the irresistible attraction of immersing their bodies in hot and cold baths and of sweltering in steam-rooms, the public could find further stimulation in the other recreational activities, both physical and intellectual. For example, they could tune their muscles in a small stadium and a *palaestra*, while in

▽ *Plan of the Baths of Caracalla:*
(1) natatio (pool); (2) frigidarium;
(3) tepidarium; (4) caldarium;
(5) palaestrae; (6) exedrae;
(7) cistern.

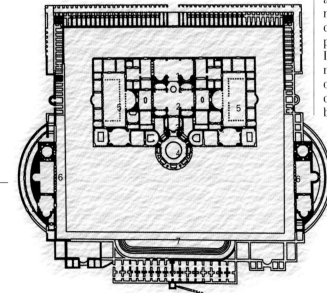

libraries, conversation rooms or auditoria for theatrical or musical performances they could devote themselves to reading, listening and cultural activities and entertainment. At the baths, as in a modern multi-purpose centre, they could also find restaurants and shops providing high-quality service. In the Imperial age the baths also became the museums of the city, and a great many of the large works of art which have come down to us were preserved in bath buildings. The *Laocoon* of Agesander, Athanodoros and Polydoros of Rhodes, as well as *Pluto and Cerberus*, were found near the Baths of Trajan, for example; the *Farnese Bull* and the *Farnese Hercules* were found in the area of

the Baths of Caracalla; and the colossal statue of *Castor and Pollux* was found near the Baths of Constantine.

In AD 212 a branch of the aqueduct of the Aqua Marcia was built at the same time as the Baths of Caracalla, so as to supply them with water. The monumental bath-house complex was inaugurated in AD 216 and was opened to the public free of charge. Its patrons were predominantly the *plebes* living in the adjacent quarter, who found it rather inconvenient to reach the services situated in the distant city centre. The baths fell out of use after Elagabalus and Severus Alexander in the middle of the third century, were restored under Aurelius and Diocletian

△ *The caldarium of the Baths of Caracalla was a large space roofed with a cupola and containing seven hot-water baths, with a very large and circular eighth bath in the centre.*

Hellenistic original (or copy of an earlier original) of the Torture of Dirce, better known as the Farnese Bull, a colossal marble group discovered near the Baths of Caracalla. Amphion and Zethus are about to tie their stepmother Dirce to a furious bull. (Naples, National Museum)

Bibliography

A.M. Liberati and F. Bourbon, *Splendours of the Roman World* (London and New York, 1996).

R. Bianchi Bandinelli, *Rome: The Late Empire* (London, 1971).

R. Bianchi Bandinelli, *Rome: The Centre of Power* (London, 1969).

T. Cornell and J. Mathews, *Atlas of the Roman World* (Oxford and New York, 1982).

M. Cristofani (ed.), *La grande Roma dei Tarquinii*, exhibition catalogue (Rome, 1990).

M. Grant, *The Roman Forum* (London, 1970).

R. Lanciani, *The Ruins and Excavations of Ancient Rome* (London, 1897).

C. Moatti, *The Search for Ancient Rome* (London and New York, 1993).

C. Scarre, *Chronicle of the Roman Emperors* (London and New York, 1995).

Various authors, *Storia di Roma. L'impero mediterraneo* (Turin, 1990); *... Caratteri e morfologie* (Turin, 1989); *... Roma in Italia* (Turin, 1988).

J.B. Ward Perkins, *Roman Imperial Architecture* (Harmondsworth, 1981).

towards the end of the century, and again under the Ostrogothic king Theodoric in the early sixth century, and were in use until 537, that is up to the occupation of the Goths. In the sixth and seventh centuries part of the site was used as a necropolis.

The complex consisted of a large central building, measuring 220 × 114 m (240 × 125 yd), surrounded by a partly colonnaded monumental enclosure of 337 × 328 m (370 × 360 yd). The central building, the bath-house, had two symmetrical side sections linked by a central portion that was articulated in a sequence of *caldarium, tepidarium, frigidarium* and *natatio.*

The *caldarium* (hot room) was a large circular room with a cupola supported by eight pillars. It contained seven baths, with an eighth, very large and circular, bath in the centre. The *tepidarium* (warm room), a small space with two baths and niches for statues, communicated with the *frigidarium* (cold room), a vast space roofed with three barrel vaults supported by pilasters and granite columns. Finally, the *natatio* (swimming pool), which could contain up to 1,400 cu m (308,000 gallons) of water, lay in the centre of the north-east side, in front of an elegant series of columns and niches for statues.

The complex hydraulic system required to distribute the water filled two underground levels: from the upper level pipes channelled the water to the baths and the fountains, and on the lower level the waste water flowed directly to the large sewer south-west of the complex.

▷ *Computer reconstruction of a* caldarium *(hot room), in this case embellished with splendid marble pavements.*

Pompeii: The Time-machine

Italy

*I*n *Pompeii life stopped on 24 August* AD *79, when a dramatic eruption of Vesuvius buried the whole town in volcanic ash and asphyxiated its inhabitants, leaving to the world a site apparently in chronological suspension – 'frozen' in time, almost as if it had been the target of a nuclear explosion.*

At the time of the eruption Pompeii was a provincial resort with a population of about 10,000. It was not a large political and cultural centre, but a small country town, surrounded by vineyards and orchards, lying at the mouth of the Sarno and close to the sea (the eruption moved the coastline more than 1½ km,

or 1 mile, seawards) – an ideal position from the point of view of regional communications and trade. However, the world fame that the site has attracted owes more to the extraordinary conditions of its discovery and preservation than to its importance in Roman times.

Although it was sporadically occupied in the early Iron Age, the origins of the settlement date to the first half of the sixth century BC, when the first enclosure wall was built in ashlar, encompassing an area of some 60 hectares (150 acres). Various items of Etruscan manufacture (such as *bucchero* pottery), dating to the end of the sixth century and the fifth century BC, have been found at Pompeii, but these imply commercial contacts with the Etruscan-dominated Campanian area, rather than Etruscan occupation. In fact the excavation data so far available for this period suggest a substantially indigenous society, but one that was open to typically Etruscan

△▷ Above: *Aerial view of Pompeii: in the background, the amphitheatre; in the centre, the Stabian Baths, the theatre and the Temple of Isis; at the bottom, the Forum with the Temple of Venus and the Temple of Apollo.* Facing page: *Plan of the site: (1) House of Caecilius Jucundus; (2) House of the Moralist; (3) House of Julia Felix; (4) House of the Vettii; (5) House of the Silver Wedding; (6) House of the Faun; (7) House of Menander; (8) House of Octavius Quartus; (9) House of the Surgeon; (10) House of the Ancient Hunt; (11) House of Caius Secundus; (12) Villa of Cicero; (13) Villa of the Mysteries; (14) Temple of Apollo; (15) Temple of Jupiter; (16) Temple of Isis; (17) Temple of Fortuna;*

Pompeii:
The Time-machine

◁ *Location map:*
Lying at the mouth of
the river Sarno and
close to the sea,
Pompeii controlled
the region's
communications and
commerce.

cultural elements. Certainly, in the fifth century BC the settlement was occupied by the Samnites, a central-southern Italic group, who rebuilt the town wall with limestone blocks. Samnite domination, under which the town retained its administrative autonomy, lasted from the fifth century to the start of the first century, when the Samnite aristocracy was annihilated during the Social War (91–89 BC), and the Roman history of Pompeii began. In 80 BC it is recorded as the *colonia* Cornelia Veneria Pompeianorum administered by Publius Cornelius Sulla, nephew of the dictator Sulla.

Pompeii's flourishing agricultural production and its busy port made it prosperous. Its urban development was rather long and spasmodic. In the course of the second century BC new residential areas were built, with large villas and mosaic pavements. One of the most famous of these is the House of the Faun (so called because of a bronze statuette discovered there), which is a building complex of about 3,000 sq m (¾ acre) – larger than the royal palace of Pergamum. The ancient quarter, the south-eastern area of the town, centred upon the Forum, the main municipal buildings and the temples of Apollo and Jupiter. Most of the more important

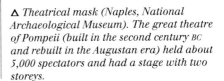

buildings were erected at this period: the Stabian Baths, the theatre, the Basilica and the Temple of Jupiter. The other quarters were developed successively in a sequence that, broadly speaking, went from west to east. In the centre of the town, on the slope to the east of the Stabian Gate, rose the open theatre, designed for dramatic shows and pantomimes, and the odeon, which was a covered auditorium

△ *Theatrical mask (Naples, National Archaeological Museum). The great theatre of Pompeii (built in the second century BC and rebuilt in the Augustan era) held about 5,000 spectators and had a stage with two storeys.*

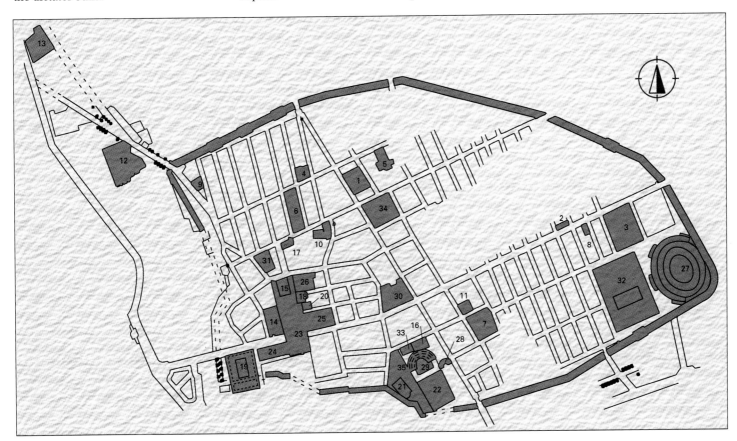

(18) sanctuary of the public Lares; (19) Temple of Venus; (20) Temple of Vespasian; (21) Doric temple; (22) Gladiators' barracks; (23) Forum; (24) Basilica; (25) Eumachia building; (26) market; (27) amphitheatre; (28) small theatre; (29) large theatre; (30) Stabian Baths; (31) Forum Baths; (32) large palaestra; (33) small palaestra; (34) central baths; (35) triangular Forum.

that mainly housed musical perform-ances and concerts.

In the first half of the first century BC (well before Rome) Pompeii acquired a permanent amphitheatre – still the oldest completely preserved building of this type – and in the Augustan era the large *palaestra* was built alongside it. Bath-houses, too, must have been included among the public buildings of particular importance, for two of them were built in the Republican era, and a third after the earthquake of AD 62. The process of development was completed by the construction of roads paved with blocks of basalt and pedestrian crossings made of raised ovoid blocks, like stepping-stones, that let those on foot pass dry-shod from one pavement to another, while at the same time allowing uninterrupted passage for carts and vehicles. The ruts made by the carts are still visible today as long, deep grooves in the road surfaces.

The rest of the urban complex was made up of residential quarters, shops and small craft and industrial work-shops. Some buildings have been given modern names derived from their

architecture or decoration or, in some cases, from the name or characteristics of their ancient owners: examples are the House of the Faun, the House of the Vettii, the House of the Centenary, the House of Menander and the suburban Villa of the Mysteries. In AD 62 Pompeii was damaged by an earthquake so severe that the Temple of Venus (the town's protective divinity) was still partly ruined at the time of the catastrophic eruption of 79.

Our knowledge of Pompeii, which to the general public might perhaps appear firm and established, is in reality being

△ *Virtual reconstruction of the Basilica. This public building was used for commercial transactions and the administration of justice.*

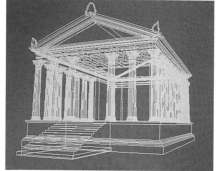

continually augmented by excavation and research. Outstanding discoveries are rare, but what is emerging from archaeological research allows partial reconstruction of the most obscure aspects of the daily life of the period. For example, excavation in region I, *insula* 16, has uncovered a kitchen with a dramatically complete assemblage of all the objects and materials used to prepare a hot meal. A terracotta pot had been placed carefully on the ashes of the hearth, along with other dishes in which the food must have been heated; leaning against the wall close by were amphorae for water, while other amphorae stood upside-down to dry before being filled with wine that had yet to arrive from the countryside.

▷▽ *Virtual reconstructions of the Temple of Apollo (right) as a 'wire-frame' model, and (below) in the completed version including the building materials. The temple was built in the first half of the sixth century BC and was rebuilt during the second century BC.*

Pompeii:
The Time-machine

The Forum

In the fourth century BC Pompeii's main square was a small open area, which was paved with stone and surrounded by numerous small shops. In the second century great transformations took place. The Forum was expanded in a north–south direction to 142 m (465 ft) in length and 38 m (125 ft) in width, and it became the fulcrum of the urban complex – with monumental gateways and sacred and public buildings on three sides and brick arches on the north.

The northern area of the Forum was expanded, around 150 BC, to create space for the Temple of Jupiter. This was a Corinthian hexastyle building on a high podium; it had a deep pronaos and a cella. After the establishment of Sulla's colony it was transformed into a

capitolium, and its nave and two aisles housed cult statues. On the western side of the Forum stood the Temple of Apollo, originally built in the first half of the sixth century BC and rebuilt in the second century BC. In its final version it became a peripteral temple, oriented towards the south, with an access stairway, a cella with a high podium, and a four-sided portico surrounding it.

The south-west corner of the square was occupied by the Basilica where

◁ *Computer-reconstructed details of the scene below, shown in 'wire-frame' form.*

judicial and commercial activities were conducted. Dating to the end of the second century BC, it is one of the oldest examples with a longitudinal plan comprising a nave and two aisles. It was preceded by a monumental covered entrance (*chalcidicum*), and at the back there was the tribunal (a dais for the magistrates) on two floors with a

△ *Virtual reconstruction of a section of the Via dell'Abbondanza (final version), which crosses the town from east to west. The streets of Pompeii were paved with blocks of basalt and had frequent pedestrian crossings made of three raised blocks that acted as stepping stones between the pavements.*

The Great Eruption

Pliny the Younger was eye-witness and chronicler of the eruption of Vesuvius which took place on 24 August AD 79. At that time he was stationed at Misenum under his uncle Pliny the Elder – commander of Rome's Tyrrhenian fleet, who was killed by volcanic gas while trying to bring help to the city with his ships.

Pliny the Younger's story has come down to us through two letters that he sent to the historian Tacitus (Letters VI, 16 and 20). These describe in detail

the physical phenomena of the eruption. With regard to the cloud of material ejected by the volcano, Pliny speaks of an 'umbrella pine', then of a mushroom explosion, an incandescent cloud of ashes and lapilli (lava fragments 4–32 mm in size, thrown up from the volcano in liquid form but solidifying in the air) that threw the territory into confusion. The cloud moved south-eastwards, affecting both Pompeii and Stabiae and – on the first day of the eruption – predominantly

depositing lapilli, which piled up to a depth of almost 3 m (10 ft) in open urban spaces, parks and gardens without claiming victims.

In the second phase of the eruption, a slow blizzard of ash was accompanied by fast-moving emissions of hot, poisonous gas that asphyxiated all the inhabitants who had not reached safety; others perished from the collapse of buildings and the unbearable heat. Some bodies, buried and encased in the cooled and solidified ashes, left their imprint in the form of cavities left after the decomposition of their bodies. This has enabled excavators to pour liquid plaster or special resins into the cavities to obtain solid casts of the buried human bodies.

After violent earthquakes, the eruption ceased on the third day, leaving the town covered in a blanket of ashes and lapilli over 4 m (13 ft) deep, which subsequent eruptions increased to 6–10 m (20–33 ft). The depth of this solidified blanket has

preserved the archaeological features both from the processes of natural erosion and, above all, from the theft and looting.

The whole dynamic of the volcanic eruption of Vesuvius has recently been studied by the National Vulcanology Group of Italy's National Research Council and by the IBM Research Centre at Pisa, which have developed mathematical simulation models. In this way it has been possible to recreate in the laboratory the eruption of AD 79, by studying the pressure of the magma chamber, the form of the volcanic channel, the ejecta and subsequent deposition of particles, the direction and intensity of the gases and winds, and so on. Such studies and research are not only useful for archaeological reconstruction, they also have a predictive potential, in the sense that the analysis of eruptions assists the monitoring of volcanic activity, perhaps in future allowing the ensuing devastation to be minimized.

◁ Casts of bodies in the positions in which they were found.

double order of superimposed columns. The four sides of its large rectangular hall were decorated with paintings in the First Pompeian Style and lined with 12 × 4 Ionic columns and semi-columns of stuccoed brickwork (the room was no doubt roofed over and provided a gallery serving as an ambulatory, emulating a Hellenistic porticoed square). The south side of the Forum was occupied by the public adminis-

tration buildings, where the most important men of the town worked: duumvirs, decurions and aediles. The central one had a series of niches in its walls, suggesting that it was probably a *tabularium* (municipal archive).

The east side was composed mainly of buildings of the Imperial period. One was the *comitium*, a building designed for popular assemblies and the election of magistrates, with the magistrates'

tribunal along the south side. A little to the north of it, beside the Via dell'Abbondanza, was the Eumachia Building – erected in the Imperial period by the patron of the fullers' guild, Eumachia, whose name appears on the architrave of the portico and in an inscription by the side entrance to the Via dell'Abbondanza. Inside the building – which is slightly out of alignment with the axis of the Forum –

The House of the Faun. Excavated in 1830–32, it was named after the bronze statue of a dancing faun (third-second century BC) that decorated the impluvium. *The building is important for its refined architecture and its wall-decorations. The skeleton of a woman was found in the* tablinum.

was a quadruple portico with two orders of columns and an apse containing a statue of the Concordia Augustus on its eastern wall. Also inside was a terracotta receptacle placed in the wall for the collection of urine, which was used as a degreasing agent in the preparation of woollen cloth.

Further north still was the Temple of Vespasian, a tetrastyle building on a high podium approached via a colonnaded entrance and a courtyard, at the centre of which was a marble altar used for sacrifices in honour of the Emperor. Beside this stood the sanctuary of the public Lares (protective gods of the town), which was built under Nero, partly in the space intended for the portico of the Forum. It comprised a covered atrium with niches in the walls and a large apse at the end surmounted by a tympanum. The last building on the eastern side of the Forum was the covered market (*macellum*), consisting of a rectangular courtyard surrounded by shops. At the back, in the south-east corner, there was a little shrine, dedicated to the cult of the Imperial family, which housed the statues of the re-founders of the *macellum*. Beside it were two rooms with an altar for sacrificial feasts and counters for commercial activities.

▷ *Computer reconstruction of the House of the Faun. On the threshold the inscription* Have *('Greetings') appears. Opening off the atrium, with its* impluvium, *are the* cubiculae *(bedrooms), the* tablinum, *the* triclinium, *a portico with Ionic columns and various service rooms. Beside the portico was an* exedra *with a mosaic pavement.*

The geometric centre of the Forum was paved with particular care, so as to leave space for an inscription in bronze letters commemorating the work. In the same place were the bases of statues honouring dignitaries from Pompeii and Rome. The development of the Forum was therefore completed in the first century BC, and it remained unchanged up to the time of the earthquake of AD 62. Its architecture followed formal canons then traditional in the Roman and Hellenistic world, both in the capitals (Imperial Fora) and in the western provinces, in emphasizing the south–north axis – which, in Pompeii, terminated in the majestic Temple of Jupiter.

Houses and gardens

The work of laboratories dedicated to palaeo-environmental and palaeo-botanical research and pollen analysis has opened up new prospects for reconstructing the gardens (*horti*) and, in general, the open spaces of Pompeii. The identification and classification of ancient organic materials, including the roots, seeds and pollens of various plant species, have recently enabled the *palaestra* near the amphitheatre to have the rows of plane-trees that once surrounded it restored.

The studies and analyses concentrated in particular on the green spaces of the Pompeian villas – which were significant examples of garden architecture, and indeed of architecture

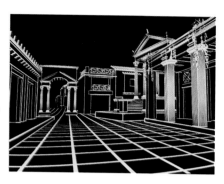

Reconstructions of the temple of Fortuna Augustus in a 'wire-frame' model (right) and in the final version (below). The temple, built to the north of the Forum, was identified thanks to the inscription originally placed on the architrave and later reused in the cella.

tout court. The harmony and the rational distribution and the alternation of structural elements, open spaces and luxurious mural decorations express the typical aesthetic tastes of the period and show off the characteristic features of that typical Pompeian residence, the atrium house.

From the fourth to the third centuries BC, the oldest houses in Pompeii were built to the characteristic Italic type of atrium plan, with an *impluvium* (a pool for collecting rain-water) in the centre.

The atrium communicated directly with the living room (*tabulinum*), beyond which was the *hortus*, the cultivated space, bounded and concealed by high walls. During the second century BC the Italic atrium was transformed into a Hellenistic peristyle, comprising a spacious columned portico with, at its centre, the *viridarium* (the garden proper), which became a true architectural element in luxury houses. This space was integrated into its architectural context just as perfectly as the wall-paintings inside the buildings – which reproduced or evoked its appearance in *trompe l'oeil*, brightening and enriching the rooms that opened to the garden with flowering shrubs, viburnum, laurel, palms, and gaily coloured wreaths and garlands;

there are more than fifty paintings of gardens in the houses of Pompeii. The *viridaria* had multiple functions: they were used to grow flowers and plants used as offerings to the gods and for medicinal herbs, and they also contained symbolic abodes associated with the divinities of the seasons.

The 'Pompeii Third Millennium Project': The time-machine

From May 1994 ancient Pompeii was spectacularly resurrected in a new and completely virtual space. The monumental temples of Apollo and Fortuna Augustus, the Classical architecture of the basilica, the picturesque Via dell'Abbondanza and Via della Concordia and the small shops, businesses and workshops beside them could now all be visited entirely through images generated by computers and stereoscopic devices.

Pompeii:
The Time-machine

△ *Oven at No. 17 from the triple crossroads of the Via Consolare. The most noted bakery of Pompeii is that of N. Popidius Priscus, with four lava querns, a conical-domed oven and a storeroom.*

elements, and shadow effects and reflective properties of the materials used in antiquity.

The most complex parts of the processing were those involving the positioning of the virtual viewpoints and lighting – including relationships between viewpoint and subject, depth of field, direct and reflected light and atmospheric density – so as to reproduce as faithfully as possible a stereoscopic vision of the original buildings. The final generation of realistic images (in 16.8 million colours) was achieved by means of complex algorithms designed to emulate the effects of light reflecting on many different types of materials and surfaces.

The stereo G system was developed by studying the reduction in mobility of the eyeball in relation to variations in the curvature of the crystalline lens and by calculating every 5 m (16.4 ft) the hyperfocal distance of the optical system of the eye. By varying the angle of ocular convergence, the perception of images on the retina, via the optic nerve, remains perfectly three-dimensional.

Virtual Pompeii, in part restored by the ancient annals, is accessible to the public in a large multimedia room which measures 1,200 sq m (12,900 sq ft) and situated, appropriately, in front of the excavation area.

At least forty-eight slide projectors and twelve video projectors synchronously transmit images and

△ *A drinking bowl in the shape of an ithyphallic mask. Of uncertain provenance, made in the first century BC. (Naples, National Archaeological Museum)*

The original appearance of Pompeii was thus revived and made accessible in the form of a virtual museum that offered a choice of 'walks' that ranged from close inspection of a single building to panoramic views of the whole excavated area. This was made possible by specific three-dimensional reconstruction techniques integrating computer-generated graphics with a new stereoscopic technology called 'stereo G system'.

Geometric modelling techniques, applied to digitized data from high-resolution scanning of stereoscopic photographs, produced complete three-dimensional reconstructions of ancient buildings that did not ignore even the most complex details. In order to complete these vector images, the different materials used in the buildings' construction were sampled: marble, stucco, brick, mortar, terracotta, etc. Via texture mapping (sampling and digitized reconstitution of materials), this gave the buildings a very realistic appearance, restoring the original colours, surface textures, relief

△ *Computer reconstruction of a Pompeian oven. Baking was introduced into Roman society during the second century BC. Initially the bread was unleavened, but leavened bread began to be made from the first century BC. The bread eaten by the rich was made of flour and was white; that of the poor was made of bran and was black.*

187

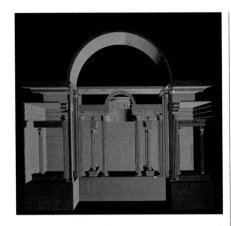

three-dimensional animations of Pompeii on a polarized screen 60 m (197 ft) long and 3 m (10 ft) high. Projection of the three-dimensional images (which are viewed through special stereoscopic spectacles) alternates sequences of slides about the excavations of Pompeii with others about the virtual procedures; the fixed images are integrated with film sequences that reconstruct, again in stereoscopic form, the catastrophic events of AD 79.

The animations have been created by taking some sequences from the film *The Last Days of Pompeii* and superimposing them on high-definition computer reconstructions. The visual images are integrated with evocative sound effects obtained with the 'Surround Sound' system, which is used to produce the most effective impact on the listener.

The Neapolis Project: Hypertext and archaeological systems

The Neapolis project was developed between 1987 and 1989 under the supervision of the Archaeological Superintendency of Pompeii. It set out to create a complex data-bank of scientific information on the excavations at Pompeii: maps, images, finds, texts, and architectural and urban data. This large and varied mass of information was put on computers and made accessible via hypertext systems

△ *Three-dimensional computer rendering of a fresco of an architectural subject from the Villa of the Mysteries.*

▽▷ *Computer model of the Stabian Baths, the oldest public baths of Pompeii, which were built in phases from the fourth to second centuries BC.*

well-known to the general public from the exhibition *Rediscovering Pompeii*, which was mounted in Rome, London and New York in 1993.

Besides seeing the finds, users could question the computer about the artistic, cultural, architectural and town-planning aspects of Pompeii. By simply touching the computer screen, they could roam freely over films, finds, reconstructions, texts, images and sound commentaries thematically illustrating the daily life of the Roman town. The hypertext applications developed were: *Introducing Pompeii*, *Artifacts in Action*, *Digging in Progress*, *Images on Walls*, and *Walking on Video*. *Introducing Pompeii* presents the general historical context of a Roman

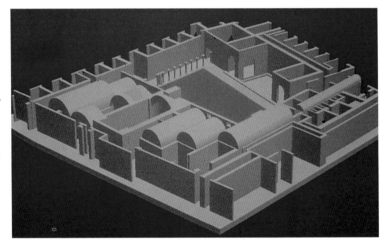

provincial town of the first century AD. *Artifacts in Action* analyses instead the different categories of objects recovered, explaining their functions, who used them and why, how they were made, and so on. *Digging in Progress* synthesizes the long history of the excavations carried out at the site, guiding the user through the principal discoveries, documentation techniques and methods of investigation. *Images on Walls* is intended to give the user an understanding of the elements that make up the wall-paintings, illustrating the techniques, themes, symbolism, meaning and formal structure. Finally, *Walking on Video* ends the hypermedia lesson by offering a virtual visit inside

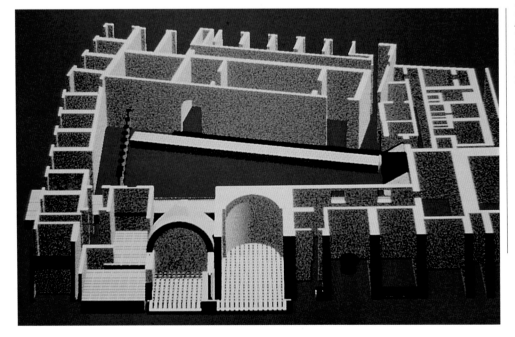

△ *Bronze food-warmer found in the House of the Four Styluses. The top is decorated with the figure of a Triton, and the front with a Medusa head.*

▷ *Digitally processed plan of the Forum of Pompeii. The colours distinguish the different buildings.*

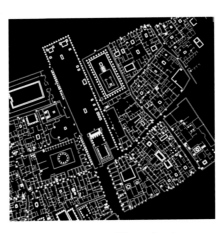

▽ *This wall-painting of Venus floating on a seashell has given its name (Venus marina) to the building in which it was found; the structure had evidently been damaged in the earthquake of AD 62.*

two famous villas, the House of Menander and the House of the Vettii, with the user, after being shown a complete plan of the buildings, being able to make his own choice of the route to be followed.

Other applications of information technology to the archaeology of Pompeii have included virtual restorations of the painted decorations and of the Herculaneum papyrus texts by means of digital images and specific information systems. In the first case, electronic techniques were developed to restore the missing parts of wall-paintings by sampling the colours of the remaining parts. In the second case, a graphic recognition program was devised in order to sample the identifiable letters of a chosen papyrus, so as to be able to insert in the lacunae the characters most closely related in form to those lost, and which were semantically most correct. If, for example, a word lacked an ending, the computer could suggest a list of complete words containing the same sequence of letters, or analogous sequences. In the same way, residual traces of ink were enhanced on the computer so as to reconstruct the lost writing.

▷ *False-colour digital image of the Herculaneum papyri. Digital techniques can enhance the writing of the characters and enable gaps in the text to be filled in.*

Bibliography

S. De Caro, 'Lo sviluppo urbanistico di Pompei', in *Atti e Memorie della Società Magna Grecia*, 3.1 (1992), pp. 67–90.

R. Etienne, *Pompeii: The Day a City Died* (London and New York, 1992).

M. Grant, *Cities of Vesuvius* (London, 1971).

Rediscovering Pompeii, exhibition catalogue (Rome, 1993).

L. Richardson, jr, *Pompeii: An Architectural History* (Baltimore, 1988).

R. Trevelyan, *The Shadow of Vesuvius* (London, 1976).

J. Ward-Perkins and A. Claridge, *Pompeii AD 79*, exhibition catalogue (London, 1976; Boston, 1978).

189

Urban Archaeology of the Indus Valley

Indus Valley

A frontier of urban life in the third millennium BC – and a frontier and a hard proving ground for archaeologists' ideas and methods. These two definitions sum up important aspects of the archaeology of the Indus Valley. We are dealing, to a great extent, with an urban archaeology, since it is the urban settlements of this area in the third millennium BC that have received more attention than the small suburban and rural centres, which still remain to be excavated. Some of the keys to deciphering the Proto-Indian phenomenon have still to be found, lying hidden in the ruins of cities yet to be discovered.

△ *Steatite seal with a mythical animal: the unicorn. Thousands of similar seals were found in the major cities of the Indus Valley.*

Urban life in the Old World around the middle of the third millennium BC spread along a vast, discontinuous and disparate arc of fluvial plains, deserts and sea coasts that extended from Egypt to the western Ganges plain. Some of the great proto-historic cities of the Near East covered hundreds of acres and housed hundreds of thousands of inhabitants, and the size of many Mesopotamian cities (such as Uruk or Ur) has long been known from the circuits of their great defensive walls. But it is less well-known, at least to the general public, that further east people were living in centres just as large and politically important: in the heart of the Iranian plateau and along the banks of the Indus.

Over the last sixty years archaeology has shown that, although the cities of the Near East and southern Asia were inhabited by different peoples and cultures, some of their basic technologies were quite similar. In their houses they used the same long, slender flint blades as well as fine knives and tools of copper and bronze; jewellers used similar types of drill to perforate hard-stone beads; and everywhere, from Crete to India, bureaucrats in the palaces controlled the movement of goods and access to the stores by means of seals, *bullae* and complicated administration that many of today's officials would still recognize.

However, alongside this relative uniformity, there were substantial differences. In the first place, there were different basic concepts of the city and how to organize, represent and run it. The Mesopotamian city (and the Near Eastern city in general) formed on a concentrated nucleus – craftworking areas on the periphery or in their own suburbs, residential areas packed with private houses and traversed by irregular street patterns, and, in the centre, large enclosures surrounding the sacred areas over which towered the large platform pyramids of the temples, the 'mountain-houses' in which the gods lived. The temples and the worldly seats of power were decorated with precious stones, bronze statues and mosaic panels inlaid with stone and wood. The luxury, magnificence, scale and power of these structures impressed themselves upon the individual, and the iconography of the divinity mediated between the inhabitants of the city, the earthly authorities and the Absolute. A citizen of medieval Europe would have had a similar perception of a Gothic cathedral

▽ *Aerial view of the ruins of the citadel of Mohenjo-Daro (Sind, Pakistan), including the remains of the so-called 'Great Bath' and 'Great Granary'.*

○ HARAPPA
◦ MOHENJO-DARO
○ LOTHAL

◁ *Location map:
Some important sites
of the Indus
civilization, which
developed in the
territory of the
modern states of
Pakistan and India.*

△ *An excavated street in an urban
residential quarter, in zone DK, at Mohenjo-
Daro (c. 2500–2000 BC).*

towering over clusters of small wooden houses. Mesopotamia was, basically, not so different!

The cities of the Indus Valley, on the other hand – at least from the start of the third millennium BC – seem to have had a totally different logic, and one that remains for the most part incomprehensible. For all the extensive excavations carried out at different sites

of large and medium size, no temple or palace has ever been identified with certainty (though they may well have existed), nor is any art known that is comparable with the great and uninterrupted Near Eastern tradition. The thread of public iconography, which in Mesopotamia linked the devout and the citizen to the idea of the divine through a social hierarchy, may perhaps never have been present in the Indus Valley. To put it simply (if speculatively), we could say that the inhabitants of the Indus cities lived on two levels of individual and collective representation, opposed but complementary. One was the public social structure and the 'urban universe', the

△ *A pit and a circular brick platform of
unknown function (c. 2500–2000 BC)
situated to the north of the citadel of
Harappa (Punjab, Pakistan).*

other the world of personal ornament and status symbols – one could almost speak of 'super-public' and 'super-private' worlds.

The enclosure walls of the monumental centres of the Indus Valley reveal a social logic that was quite different from those of every other contemporary civilization. Besides protecting the city from flood and external attack, they seem to have been planned and maintained to reflect complex rules of internal social behaviour. From the time of their foundation, some urban centres seem possibly to have been subdivided into a citadel – raised upon and protected by colossal mud-brick platforms – a middle city and a lower city. Access between these different sectors or quarters was through large gates with narrow entrances that often lacked any monumental elements, such as flights of steps or columns – which gives the impression that moving from one quarter to another was a critical event in urban life. The urban layout developed along grids of streets that tended to intersect at right angles. Close attention was also paid to the flow of water within the city and its discharge – leading proto-historic engineers to develop advanced hydraulic systems made of terracotta, plaster, bitumen and stone.

▷ *The brick-built drain of a private
dwelling at Mohenjo-Daro, dating to the
second half of the third millennium BC.*

On another level, the Indus artists and craftspeople of the third millennium BC expressed themselves on a very high level through a large range of 'minor' technologies, such as those involving shell, hardstones, high-fired ceramics (including faience, made with silica or

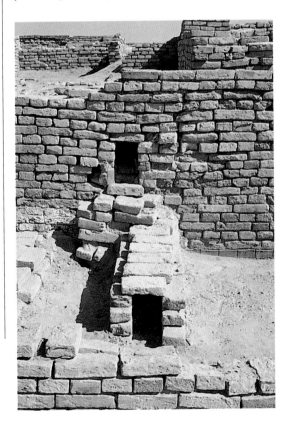

steatite), and jewellery. From at least the sixth millennium BC the artisans of the Indus developed the ability to transform common raw materials into artificial products – to the point where the original materials are often almost unrecognizable to the naked eye. The techniques which wrought these complex transformations are still, for the most part, unknown today.

The men who lived and worked on the platforms of the cities could show off, both in their daily lives and on ceremonial occasions, a series of luxury ornaments and status symbols made of a great range of materials; the artificiality of the urban world was mirrored in the artificial materials used for jewels, seals and headdresses. This was probably a way of expressing and legitimating social diversity among the groups of privileged people who, from political and ritual centres, governed parts of Indian proto-historic society of the third millennium BC – and of ensuring that the existing social divisions commanded a sufficiently widespread social consensus.

In the varied context of the formation of the first proto-historic states, the Indian world clearly seems to present an anomaly. From a historical point of view, this is an area of study of fundamental importance for understanding the development, in the second millennium BC, of the definition of castes and the institutionalization of social boundaries. Did the Bronze Age society play a role in the process, or was it the end of this society that made it possible? And, if it did play a role, which social or economic sectors of society benefited? We do not need to embrace the radical theses of some Indian scholars, who see the cities as already tripartite and peopled by the three upper castes of later Vedic India, to acknowledge that the social diversity of the Indus Valley cities has still not been studied systematically as an archaeological problem.

In making headway here, the archaeology of the Indus cities is constrained by a paradox: it must

◁ *Small terracotta head (c. 2500–2000 BC) from Mohenjo-Daro. (Karachi, National Museum)*

combine a general and holistic overall approach with the specificity and detailed research of 'dirt' archaeology. In terms of the urban context, we cannot comprehend the structure of a city if we do not increase the size of excavation areas so as to expose the city as a large-scale 'artifact'; yet, if we ignore the minutiae of accurate stratigraphic methods (that is, if we abandon the use of the trowel), we will not be able to understand how individual houses, platforms or working areas were built, maintained, used or came to be abandoned.

In this civilization there are no tablets and vanishingly few iconographic images that speak of gods, kings, soldiers and artisans. In traditional Near Eastern archaeology, even a palace excavated with the pick could yield an archive of tablets that released a real 'cascade' of history. For the archaeology of the Indus Valley, however, there are only the brief and still undeciphered Proto-Indian inscriptions. Only the most sophisticated of excavation techniques and the most carefully planned research can enable us to understand, for example, what activities were carried out on a baked clay floor that was continually swept and relaid every year. Without a basis of this sort of detail, it will not be possible to understand

◁ *Female terracotta statuette with an elaborate hair-style and jewellery (c. 2500–2000 BC) from Mohenjo-Daro. (Delhi, National Museum)*

whether the large buildings of Mohenjo-Daro were the houses of the rich or of the priests, whether they were ritual, workshop or commercial sites, and if their inhabitants and the activities carried out there changed over time.

Turning to the production of luxury ornaments, some types of worker – gem-cutters, shell-cutters, potters and metalworkers – operated in and around the large cities. The study of craft-working is made possible by the fact that many residues from production processes survive and can be identified on the surface and in excavations. A stratum containing work-shop waste looks – if it contains stone waste – like the remains of a

*Small perforated terracotta
[ves]sel, Indus civilization, second half
[of t]he third millennium BC.*

camp of Palaeolithic hunters; only an accurate assessment of how it was formed (often an exasperatingly laborious process) can help to establish whether a potter worked seasonally or was a full-time specialist, or if the same family occupied the same place for generations (a possible indication of

hereditary occupation, which, in traditional India, accompanies the caste system).

Laboratory research into artifacts includes archaeometric analysis to determine the raw materials from which they were made and hence their areas of provenance (one of archaeometry's most useful functions) and to reconstruct ancient manu-facturing processes. The variability of techniques is actually an important parameter of social differentiation: each technique has its particular ergonomic costs and its own 'style' and requires specific organizational conditions. This aspect of research into the ancient cities of the Indus seems particularly complex. Assessing the role of the large cities in controlling craft pro-duction involves extens-ive sampling of similar materials and manufactured products from contemporary sites, as well as using all available know-ledge of the rocks, minerals and animal and plant species exploited by the industries of the third millennium BC – a process that may have to be carried out in areas that today are both geographic-ally and politically difficult of access.

△ *Excavation of paved floor levels (the floors are surrounded by robber trenches) of a house at Harappa of the second half of the third millennium BC.*

Another problem is the complexity of Indian firing techniques in the third millennium BC. As already pointed out, their practitioners delighted in creating diverse artificial materials from steatite, clay, quartz, metal oxides and organic materials by recourse to high temp-eratures. It is a general rule of palaeo-technology that the further a technique is elaborated, the more difficult and costly it will be to reconstruct it: in which case the scientist inevitably has to dedicate himself – or herself – to long phases of archaeometric analysis in the laboratory.

At the start of the 1980s a mission of the Italian Institute for the Middle and Far East (IsMEO) attempted to investigate some of these issues. It began work at Mohenjo-Daro, in the Pakistani Sind, in conjunction with the German Mission of Aachen University, which for many years had been carrying out the exhaustive task of documenting the buildings (some 350) excavated in the 1930s and since partly restored several times, often without the work being recorded. This new phase of work was directed by Michael Jansen, a dedicated archaeologist-architect specializing in the Indus civilization, and Maurizio Tosi, who had previously carried out the surface investigation of Bronze Age sites in eastern Iran.

The part of the archaeological zone of Mohenjo-Daro that emerges from the recent alluvial plain of the Indus – the

△ *Stratigraphic excavation of a small kiln for firing ceramics at Harappa. It dates to the first half of the third millennium BC.*

△ *Sectional excavation of a kiln for the production of luxury ceramics at Harappa.*

▷ *Flint bladelets and micro-drills, flakes of agate, cornelian, jasper, lapis lazuli, garnet, limestone and quartzite recovered by wet-sieving a surface sample from the site of Moneer. They date to about the second half of the third millennium BC.*

lower city and the citadel – extends over about 80 ha (200 acres), although contemporary ruins and archaeological remains appear over an area at least five times greater. The excavations of the 1930s, despite using semi-stratigraphic methods, were not able to define a clear sequence of strata, ceramics and architecture to shed light upon the historical development of the city. So how was the question of the genesis of the *forma urbis* to be tackled? The most important constraint upon the new research was that excavation was not permitted (something originally perceived as a limitation, but, with hindsight, it was perhaps a great help).

While the German team was finishing its campaign of surveying the monuments with the aid of a balloon carrying stereo-photogrammetric equipment, the Italian team developed a geophysical survey programme that covered significant parts of the unexcavated mounds of the city. The surveys – carried out by the Lerici Foundation using electrical and geo-magnetic methods – were supplemented by dozens of deep cores aligned along 'sections' that cut into the major anomalies encountered. In this way it was possible to identify, along the southern side of sector HR, one of the major blocks or citadels of the urban establishment. It comprised a sequence of exceptional importance that included the remains of an ancient settlement (perhaps dating to the first half of the third millennium BC) that had been overwhelmed by an alluvial deposit about 10 m (33 ft) deep, as well as a colossal river embankment and fortification, comprising a mud-brick platform more than 200 m (650 ft) long, 5 m (16 ft) high and 6 m (20 ft) thick. The sequence also included a deposit consisting of a hill of sandy mud and rejects of vitrified pottery, plus an enormous mass of vitrified clayey nodules (probably deliberately manufactured 'stones'), whose function was to strengthen the protection of the southern side of the city; a succeeding alluvial phase, accompanied by continuous degradation and restoration of the mud-brick platform; strata of abandonment of the citadel of HR containing the remains of craft activities in secondary deposits; and a third, large, alluvial phase responsible for the existing plain and for the late soils developed on it. Successive excavations – limited to the surface strata, and usually interrupted after 20–30 cm (8–12 in.) at the point at which they met the eroding surfaces of the *in situ* buildings – confirmed this sequence and revealed the nature of the processes of degradation and the techniques involved in the maintenance of this impressive communal work. It was discovered that in a late phase the edge of the platform was rebuilt with a low embankment of fired bricks, which almost symbolically confirmed the value of the boundary, because by then the platform was completely buried. Evidently, the site of the city was strategically and ideologically important but very prone to flooding, and the risk posed (at least to the south side) by the river's violence was appreciated (later in the project, over a kilometre away to the south and in the actual bed of the Indus, the remains of a lower quarter that was probably not similarly protected were excavated).

An accurate survey of the surfaces of the mounds that had been eroded was

▽ *Surveying and sampling an area used for the production of semi-precious stones and microlithic flint tools on the southern slopes of the site of Moneer at Mohenjo-Daro.*

Surface sample of layers, rich in remains from semi-precious stone working, created by saline erosion at Mohenjo-Daro.

state organizations. The major effort was not in fact devoted to simply procuring exotic and prestigious raw materials by means of long-distance trade, as was frequently the case among societies organized as chiefdoms. Rather, it consisted in the use of elaborate techniques involving high temperatures to transform relatively low-cost local materials into more sophisticated new materials, such as stoneware, silicaceous faience with a glassy finish and steatite-based ceramics. The logic of some Indus production is very similar to, for example, that of the prized Arretine ware of the Roman world, produced with local clays but with exceptionally complex systems of firing.

The surface excavation method allowed something to be learned about the context in which this production took place. It seems that, for reasons still unknown, in the final phases of the city's life different activities were concentrated in the urban centre, the first of which was ceramic production

also carried out. This research immediately took the archaeologists into the heart of the artisans' area of the third millennium BC. More than fifty locations were identified where the surfaces were studded with the remains of various types of work, including furnaces and discards from furnaces, fragments of ceramic refractory containers (used for firing other ceramics), trimmings of sea shells, flakes of semi-precious stones, thousands of fragments of steatite and the flint blades from drills made and used in different ways.

The resumption of scientific sampling led to the identification and partial reconstruction of previously unknown technologies, and, fifteen years after the start of the project, the materials are still the subject of research and doctoral theses in Italy and the United States. Little by little, as the total reconstruction forms into a more coherent picture, it seems clear that luxury ornaments and objects were made in the cities of the Indus according to a system typical of evolved

building and its use for production purposes simply reflects fluctuations in political or economic conditions and the constant pressure to make the most of every possible resource, including space. It is nevertheless clear that the few furnaces installed in cities must have been a relatively sporadic phenomenon; a city the size of Mohenjo-Daro must have been served by an extra-urban network of villages specializing in the production of pottery and bricks.

In one area with traces of particularly complex working it was possible – by surface excavation and studying the nature of the erosion and the consequent movement of the objects – to locate and map 7,300 different objects and to establish a relative chronology of the different craft activities. The earliest production was the making of beads, ornaments and seals of steatite – in all likelihood in workshops inside the dwellings. There followed the installation of a large workshop, which had storerooms and furnaces, making sophisticated

(fifty production sites can probably be attributed to this phenomenon). According to both the old excavations and the new data, the areas occupied by potters, with furnaces and their refuse, seem to show houses and streets in a state of partial abandonment. In contrast to what was thought in the past, this does not necessarily imply some urban crisis: in contemporary India, the temporary abandonment of a

stoneware bracelets. The workshop occupied a block that was no longer inhabited, and used fired and mud bricks taken from the ruins. Later there were deposits of thousands of flakes of agate, jasper, garnet and quartzite, as well flint bladelets and hundreds of micro-drills used to perforate the beads made from them. The remains of the working of the sea shells were concentrated in several locations, and

195

△ *Jewels made by artisans of the Indus Valley civilization. Making refined ornaments in precious metals and hardstones and the manufacture of sophisticated ceramics were some of the most advanced industries of this proto-historic civilization. Important caches of jewellery were found in all the most populous centres.*

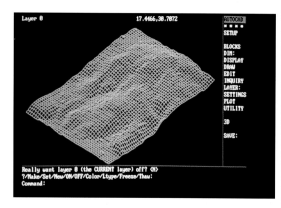

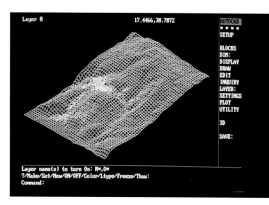

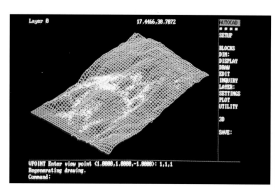

△ Top: *Computerized plan of a slope at Mohenjo-Daro with industrial deposits dating to the second half of the third millennium* BC. Centre: *Surface distribution of the remains of kilns used in ceramic production (yellow dots).* Bottom: *Distribution of flint bladelets, drills and flakes of hardstone (white dots), produced by a later workshop making personal ornaments.*

one 'activity area' was identified by a group of flint endscrapers, probably used for processing some organic material. The last occupation seems to be represented by some small kilns. It is possible that this relative sequence indirectly reflects an order of rank of the different activities: first the makers of steatite seals, then those of stoneware bracelets, followed, in turn, by the makers of organic materials, and, finally, by potters. It is a significant fact that the first two activities involved firing processes using appropriate refractory ceramics, and were more sophisticated and complex than the other processes.

Today, many of the hypotheses developed at Mohenjo-Daro have been expanded and integrated with the extensive excavations carried out at Harappa by American expeditions from the universities of Harvard and Madison (Wisconsin). The excavation at Harappa is distinguished by a high level of stratigraphic control, and by strict computerized counting and recording of the tens of thousands of finds and small objects coming to light each season. For the first time, this has allowed significant comparisons to be carried out between the various contexts excavated in the city. The archaeological paradox described at the beginning of this article has been tackled by means of a thorough and flexible excavation strategy.

Extensive enclosure-platforms of mud brick were revealed over large areas by excavations limited to depths of 30–40 cm (12–16 in.), which progressively built up the plan of a single massive structure. In contrast to those observed at Mohenjo-Daro, the imposing mud-brick enclosures that surrounded mound E (topographically similar to the citadel of HR at Mohenjo-Daro) seem to have had a curved outline and to have been built over more phases. They were probably adapted, over the course of time and different building campaigns, to the slopes of an archaeological mound dating to the third millennium BC. Limited deep trenches at key points of the street grid allowed the oldest strata to be sampled and the urban layout to be checked (traces of wagon-ruts were found that already followed the north–south axis of later periods).

Despite heavy disturbance to the upper layers of the site's stratigraphy (it was used as a source of bricks for ballast by the English builders of the Multan–Lahore railway in 1857), surface investigation has led to the discovery of a notable quantity of tools, production refuse, and half-finished artifacts. In the only place left undisturbed (it was protected by a police station) ancient seals were identified, along with traces of the working of steatite, agate and precious metals.

The erosion of a slope on the eastern side of mound E led to the discovery, inside the area protected by the walled enclosures, of a sector used for pottery production. A large kiln, of circular plan with a central pilaster, was surrounded by firing waste, tools for scraping the vessels, the remains of raw clay and the

◁ *Part of the site of Harappa. The brick structures are the much-restored remai* of the so-called 'workers' quarter' excavated in earlier campaigns at the foot of the citadel. The complex dates to the second half of the thir millennium BC.*

◁ *One of the dwellings at the prehistoric
site of Mehrgarh (Pakistan). The
structure is of mud brick, but the
roof was formed by a trellis
of poles and branches.
The earliest artisans
of the Indus
civilization lived in
huts like this.*

Bibliography

D.P. Agrawal, *The Archaeology of India*
(London and Malmö, 1982).
B. and F.R. Allchin, *The Rise of
Civilization in India and Pakistan*
(Cambridge, 1982).
R.H. Meadow (ed.), *Harappa
Excavations 1986–1990* (Madison,
1991).
G.L. Possehl (ed.), *Harappan
Civilization* (New Delhi, 1993).
M. Wheeler, *The Indus Civilization*
(Cambridge, 1953).
M. Wheeler, *Early India and Pakistan*
(London, 1959).

stains of ashes.
This kiln dates to
around 2500 BC, but
exploration of the lower
strata has revealed the presence
of two older kilns and a long series of
strata with traces of burning and firing
waste going back to earlier centuries
(testimony to a craft activity practised
for centuries in the same place in the
city, which perhaps implies hereditary
occupation).

Mohenjo-Daro and Harappa have
provided information of different types,
which show both how similar and how
contradictory the processes of urbanization in two city-states of the same
size and culture could have been. If the
archaeology of Near Eastern cities is
substantially an archaeology of power,
that of the Indus Valley cities almost
looks like an archaeology of consensus
based on ancient ideologies and social
structures which are still largely
unknown but seem to have been
influential and persuasive. It is by
perfecting methods of analysis, in the
field and in the laboratory, that we are
able to guess at the subtlety, complexity
and discontinuity of the web of social
conflicts that lay behind that façade of
consensus.

▽ *The so-called 'Great Granary' of
Harappa. The real function of the building
– a large structure of fired brick with a
complex plan subdivided into several long,
narrow, parallel compartments – is still a
mystery. It dates to the second half of the
third millennium BC.*

Bronze Age Cities in South-central Asia

South-central Asia

*S*outh-central Asia was the cradle of a highly complex urban civilization that, by the end of the fourth millennium BC, was already in direct contact with the Mesopotamian world to the west and with the area in which the Indus Valley civilization would emerge to the east. Real cities arose here, comparable in size and richness to the contemporary centres of Mesopotamia. Here artifacts of ceramic, bronze and precious stones were produced and exported, and a world with common forms and ideas was developing that in many ways would help to shape the development of the great civilizations of the East.

In South-central Asia urban civilization developed more or less homogeneously, with a cultural unity that arose out of a close-knit network of trade in raw materials and finished products. The term 'South-central Asia' here means the territory bordered by the Persian Gulf to the south and by the Asian steppes to the north, and extending from the Zagros mountains in the west, eastwards across the Iranian plateau to the mountains of the Hindu Kush. The high mountains acted as vast reserves of water, feeding innumerable rivers and allowing the formation of fertile alluvial lands. Human settlement lay not only in the foothill zone, along parts of the rivers, but also in the areas of flood plain where the water courses spread out in deltas.

Today it is difficult to comprehend the historical context of the urban societies of the fourth and third millennia BC; the data available are still too sparse and disparate. Apparently easier to understand, on the other hand, are the processes of development and adaptation that led to the formation of proto-urban societies from common roots – different from the Neolithic-Chalcolithic roots of Near Eastern civilizations – that date back to at least 6000 BC. The material basis of the Neolithic economy was consolidated, through the selection of the main domesticated species of wheat and barley, in the milieu of a dense and sedentary population living in villages that were linked socially by the control and exploitation of their territories.

This is evident from the copper mines discovered in central and southern Iran and by the complex water-control schemes that augmented the potential of fertile areas (Tepe Yahya, Geoksjur). In the second half of the fourth millennium BC radical changes took place that accelerated the processes of production, exchange and storage. A mosaic of regional units began to form around settlements that had food surpluses – the result of having well-watered, fertile territories and a high degree of labour specialization. After a period of quite stable

◁ *The region of Seistan with the inland delta of the Helmand. A Bronze Age urban civilization developed here with its principal centre at Shahr-i Sokhta.*

*Bronze Age Cities in
South-central Asia*

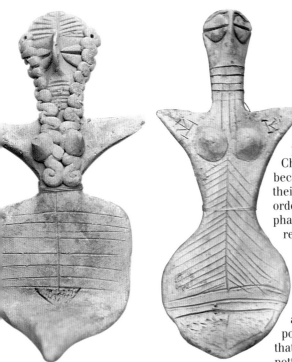

*Female terracotta idols from Altyn Tepe
(2300–2200 BC). Anthropomorphic and zoomorphic
terracotta figurines are common in all Bronze Age
cultures and provide clues about their ideology.*

economic growth that reached a plateau after 3200 BC, archaeological evidence suggests that the South-central Asian world underwent a radical social transformation. This came to a climax towards 2500 BC, when the ruling centres of each territory had reached their maximum physical expansion and began to show all the hallmarks of societies with growing hierarchical complexity.

The first state entities emerged in Mesopotamia towards 3200 BC, but South-central Asia underwent a different and slower development. The means for administering and regulating trade seem to have been present from the outset. Clay tablets with Proto-Elamite writing, abacus counters and cylinder seals and their imprints on clay *bullae*, indicating a centralized form of organization, were found at Shahr-i Sokhta, Tepe Sialk, Tepe Yahya, Tepe Tal-i Iblis and Tepe Hissar. Urban expansion appears to have taken place in two phases. In the oldest (3200–2600 BC), existing trends towards the reorganization of some of the craft industries led to the removal of some specialist types of work outside the

▷ *The great centres of urban civilization of
South-central Asia in the Bronze Age. Links
with Mesopotamia and the Indus Valley
made this area a crossroads for trade.*

domestic sphere. Craft workshops contributed to the enlargement of some centres, where growth in the volume and quality of fine products had already begun in the Chalcolithic, and each of these towns became a regional centre. The effects of their accumulation and new social order seem to emerge in the following phase (2600–2400 BC), which corresponds to period III at Shahr-i Sokhta, phase IV at Mundigak and phase V at Namazga.

Common to all these proto-historic centres in South-central Asia are stamp seals (of both stone and bronze) and certain forms of pottery and other objects – it seems that there were at least three different pottery traditions. This cultural unity between territories scattered over the region could be explained in terms of a network of trade in raw materials and finished goods: the most notable of which are such prestige items as ornaments of precious stones (turquoise, lapis lazuli and shell).

In the Early Bronze Age, the territorial organization of urban society in South-central Asia showed a tendency towards the concentration of population; some small centres grew enormously in size – and these can be identified as centres of control – whereas others remained simple rural villages. However, growth in the size of urban centres must be seen not only in relation to the concentration of population but also in relation to a growing number of specialized activities. Ceremonial infrastructures, administrative organizations, the storage of agricultural produce and craft activities are only some of the identifiable factors underlying this development.

With the advent of urbanization, craft activities, in particular – which had previously been scattered between residential areas or in small rural villages – became concentrated in certain quarters of the cities. Innovations occurred in technology and in the organization of production, which became separate from domestic activities. A division of labour according to sex and age seems to have evolved as a result of groups of workers specializing in the processing of particular raw materials.

The first half of the third millennium BC saw the completion of the urbanization process, the building of monumental architectural complexes (such as Shahr-i Sokhta, Mundigak and

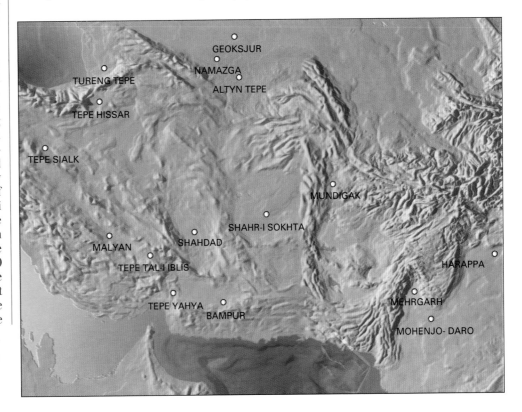

199

Tureng Tepe), and the division of towns into specific craft sectors: examples of which have been noted at Tepe Hissar, Shahr-i Sokhta, Altyn Tepe and Shahdad. Then, from 2200 BC, the urban system began to deteriorate, and the principal centres of South-central Asia fell into rapid decline. Archaeology has still not explained this phenomenon – although, rather than implying a complete dissolution of the social structures, it is now seen as a profound change in the organization of socio-economic structures.

Shahr-i Sokhta

Shahr-i Sokhta ('the burnt city') – which lies in present-day Iran, in the plain of Seistan near the border with Afghanistan – was the most important of the proto-historic centres of Seistan. The name given to the site by the inhabitants of the region can be easily understood by looking at its surface. A blanket of potsherds indicates that this was the site of a large settlement, and the burnt ground and the presence of charcoal are proof of the fire that destroyed part of the city.

In 1916 the archaeologist and explorer Sir Aurel Stein carried out a first investigation at Shahr-i Sokhta and was impressed by the expanse of sherds. He explained this phenomenon as the effect of wind and alluvial erosion which had completely destroyed the buildings. In fact, erosion activity was minor, as was demonstrated in 1961 by a first Italian Archaeological Mission directed by G. Tucci, in which the formation of a thick salt crust was seen to have protected a good part of the structures. Initial excavations in 1967, continued up to 1978 and carried out by an expedition from the Italian Institute for the Middle and Far East (IsMEO) directed by Maurizio Tosi, demonstrated the existence of a cultural sequence lasting almost 1,400 years.

In 2400–2300 BC (the period of its maximum splendour) the site extended over an area of around 80–100 hectares (200–250 acres), to which can be added

△ *Aerial view of the eastern edge of Shahr-i Sokhta, the capital of Iranian Seistan. Beginning as a small village at the end of the fourth millennium BC, this city turned into one of the main urban centres of South-central Asia and, at the height of its development (2400 BC), spread over 80–100 hectares (200–250 acres).*

the 21 hectares (52 acres) of the necropolis. The plain on which it lies is triangular, with an irregular outline that is indented along the northern and eastern edges. The area is now arid, but in the third millennium BC it was irrigated by the large inland delta of the river Helmand, and the people who first inhabited Shahr-i Sokhta found the river terrace an ideal setting in which to establish their first residential settlements. The layer of ceramics that extends over about 75 hectares (185 acres) of the eastern half of the site, above a height of 12 m (40 ft) above the plain, indicates that this was the real settlement zone, whereas the south-eastern half, covered by neither buildings nor ceramics, was reserved for the necropolis and for mainly ephemeral structures in the latest phases of the site.

Over the 1,400-year life of the complex, the settlement areas at Shahr-i Sokhta extended over between 110 and 120 hectares (270–300 acres), comprising 75 per cent of the entire archaeological area. The size of this vast area affected the planning of archaeological research and made it necessary to use ever more specialized techniques of sampling and ground analysis. Excavation data and surface investigations enabled both

chronological and functional differentiations to be traced inside the area and enabled the site to be subdivided into three areas.

The first area – the 'east residential zone', covering 16–20 hectares (40–50 acres) – was excavated between 1967 and 1970 and comprised the whole east side of the settlement and the highest areas on the plain, including the area of the so-called 'burnt palace'. The main mound was created by deposits of period I (3200–2700 BC), which were present only in this zone. The second area – the 'central quarters', covering some 20–25 hectares (50–60 acres) and bounded on the east, west and south by the three largest depressions found on the plain – was explored between 1975 and 1976. The oldest features were built at the end of period I (2800 BC) and were residential in character, but around 2500 BC large complexes were erected here. The third area – the so-called 'north-east monumental zone', extending over 20 hectares (50 acres) – comprised all the mounds and level areas on the northern and eastern edges of the plain. The materials collected and the excavation soundings enabled the first occupation of this area to be dated to 2600 BC. Thereafter, in period III (2500 BC), a large ruling complex was installed, as well as craft

quarters with lapis-lazuli, ceramic and metal workshops. It was from one of these quarters that one of the most interesting objects of the ancient culture came: a bronze statuette of a woman carrying a jar on her head in the traditional pose of the *canephorus*.

The settlement at Shahr-i Sokhta was therefore founded around 3200 BC, on the eastern edge of the terrace in the 'east residential zone'. It then expanded in period III (2500–2200 BC), which was a time of maximum population and was characterized by an abundance of raw materials (lapis-lazuli, turquoise, sea shells, and so on) imported from places outside the regional exchange network and worked on the site. These finds testify to the site's prosperity and to improvements in the organization of intra-regional and extra-regional trade at this time.

A little later, having reached its maximum development, Shahr-i Sokhta entered a period of crisis so profound that, over the course of a century, it came to be practically abandoned (2300–2100 BC). Little is known about this phase of decline, when large sections of the northern quarters seem to have been in a state of neglect.

▽ *Aerial view of the 'east residential zone' of Shahr-i Sokhta. The so-called 'burnt palace' is visible at the bottom.*

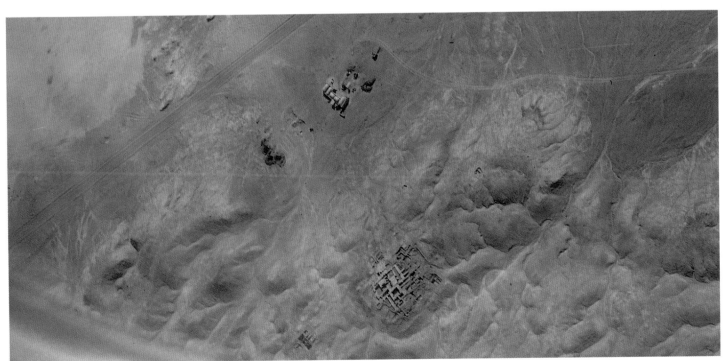

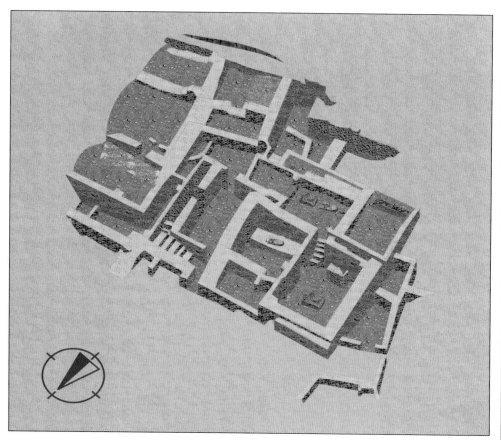

◁ *Perspective view of the House of the Small Well at Shahr-i Sokhta. Its fine state of preservation allows its separate rooms to be discerned – in particular a room with hearths and ovens for cooking.*

excavation – both in the proto-historic settlement and in the tombs (around 300 of which were excavated in the necropolis) – have helped greatly to elucidate the cultural development of Shahr-i Sokhta.

Life in southern Seistan continued after the abandonment of the site, thanks to the favourable geographic and environmental conditions. This is indicated by the remains of villages with pottery dating to the start of the third millennium BC which were scattered over the desiccated clayey plains. The decline of Shahr-i Sokhta does not seem to have been connected with depopulation and social introversion, nor with any hypothetical invasion of Indo-Aryan peoples from the north. It seems, rather, to have

Various causes, both natural and social, probably contributed to the decay, as part of a series of phenomena that were repeated in the Asian interior.

Despite the many questions about the cultural sequence of Shahr-i Sokhta that remain unanswered, there is a correlation between the stratigraphy of the site and its material culture. Its extraordinary state of preservation and the vast quantity of objects (ceramics, seals, anthropomorphic and zoomorphic figurines, stonework and metalwork) found in each part of the

△▷ Above: *Excavation in progress in the necropolis of Shahr-i Sokhta with details of some tombs of period III (around 2500–2200 BC). Right: A tomb of period I (around 3000 BC) with painted pottery vessels. The IsMEO expedition identified a necropolis extending over almost 21 hectares (52 acres) in which about 300 tombs were excavated.*

△ *The 'east residential zone' of Shahr-i
Sokhta, comprising the whole of the east
side of the settlement and the highest areas
on the plain. The excavations have
revealed only a small portion of the city,
organized into a tight network of streets
and passages flanked by houses.*

stemmed from a crisis in a hierarchical city that concentrated within itself the administration of all primary production and the most sophisticated forms of manufacturing. Whatever the explanation, from 2000 BC onwards (period IV), the new settlement structure was no longer the city but the oasis: an agglomeration of small, well-irrigated villages trading with the nomadic herders, whose lifestyle became the dominant economic model in the northern steppes of South-central Asia from the third millennium BC.

Bibliography

R. Biscione, 'Dynamics of an Early South-Asian Urbanization: The First Period of Shahr-i-Sokhta and its Connections with Southern Turkmenia', in N. Hammond (ed.), *South Asian Archaeology* (London, 1973).

R. Biscione, 'Archaeological Discoveries and Methodological Problems in the Excavations of Shahr-i-Sokhta', in J.E. Van Lohuizen-De Leeuw, *South Asian Archaeology*, edited by J.M.M. Ubags (Leiden, 1973).

'Le Plateau Iranien et l'Asie Central des origines à la Conquête Islamique', in J. Deshayes (ed.), *Colloques Internationaux*, 567 (Paris, 1977).

R.H. Dyson, jr, 'Tappeh Hesar: Reports of the Restudy Project', in S.M. Howard (ed.), *Monografie di Mesopotamia*, 2 (Florence, 1989).

P. Hinge, *New Fusions: Archaeological Information in the Relational Database* (1994).

C.C. Lamberg-Karlovsky and M. Tosi, 'Shahr-i Sokhta and Tepe Yahya: Tracks on the Earliest History of the Iranian Plateau', in *East and West*, 23 (1973), pp. 21–57.

C.C. Lamberg-Karlovsky, 'Third Millennium Modes of Exchange and Modes of Production', in J.A. Sabloff and C.C. Lamberg-Karlovsky (eds) *Ancient Civilization and Trade* (Albuquerque, 1975).

V.M. Masson, 'The Urban Revolution in South Turkmenia', in *Antiquity*, XLII (1968), pp. 178–187.

M. Tosi, *Prehistoric Sistan I*, IsMEO Rep. Mem. (Rome, 1983).

M. Tosi, S.M. Shahmirzadi and M.A. Joyenda, 'The Bronze Age in Iran and Afghanistan', in V.M. Masson and A.H. Dani, *History of Civilization of Central Asia* (Paris, 1992), pp. 191–225.

Bactria and Margiana in the Bronze Age

Central Asia

*O*ver the last ten years research by Russian archaeologists in *Afghanistan and in the Asian Republics of the former USSR has identified a new urban civilization of the Bronze Age. Now we can add, alongside the cultures of the Near East and South-central Asia, that of the communities of Bactria and Margiana, which developed in the third and second millennia BC. Teams from Western and Far Eastern countries are now involved with archaeological expeditions in Turkmenistan, making new contributions to the understanding of the evolution of the sedentary and nomadic communities that were associated with Central Asia from the Neolithic to the Islamic period. The Italian Institute for the Middle and Far East (IsMEO) has been participating by analysing the evolution of the population during the Bronze and Iron Ages in the Murgab delta.*

The geographical location and the environmental context are important to understanding the development of the Bronze Age communities in Bactria and Margiana. These regions are bounded to the east and to the south by the mountain chains of the Pamirs, the Hindu Kush and Kopet Dag, and reserves of water accumulate there that

periodically fill the river valleys, forming alluvial plains. In Bactria, it is the river Amu-Darya (Oxus) and its tributaries the Zeravshan, the Surkhandarya, the Balkhab and the Sherabad that have created the landscape, while in Margiana the Murgab and the Tedzhen (Harirud) have created basins that are smaller but have equally fertile sediments. It is in the alluvial plains, where continuous deposition of silt has formed soils that are suitable for growing cereals, that conditions were best for the birth of agricultural and pastoral communities.

However, the socio-economic development of a region cannot only be explained by the presence of water resources: in the case of Bactria and Margiana scarcity of other resources increased the speed with which more sophisticated aspects of social organization were adopted. In both Margiana and Bactria there is a paucity of data about the population during the Chalcolithic and Early Bronze Age up to 2500 BC. In Margiana only the complex of Chalcolithic settlements of Geoksjur in the Tedzhen delta are known, and such sites seem to be scarce or absent in the Murgab delta. Further east, only

the site of Sarazm, in Zeravshan valley, is known. In the Middle Bronze Age (2500–1800 BC) traces began to appear of a population that shared a common settlement system, similar forms of architectural complexes, and a series of affinities in material culture. This homogeneity has led Victor Sarianidi to define a single 'Bactria-Margiana Archaeological Complex'.

Bactria and Margiana are characterized by areas of settlement

➤ *A chlorite seal in the typical Margiana style (third millennium BC). A winged lion is incised on the side shown; the reverse has four birds with their wings spread.*

concentration that are very often defined as 'oases'. While this may describe the present-day geography well enough, it does not seem at all applicable to the ancient situation. Palaeo-ecological and geo-morphological data suggest more complex interpretations, with a mainly dispersed population spread extensively over the fertile terrain of the alluvial plains. Its distribution seems to have followed the ancient water courses, but it extended over wide areas where cultivation and settlement were made possible by the building of canals and other hydraulic works. In both Margiana and southern Bactria (north-eastern Afghanistan) the evidence shows a dispersed population in the Middle and Late Bronze Age (2300–1500 BC), occupying quite extensive sites at fairly low altitudes. Some sites have been seriously scoured by wind erosion and show no evidence of massive architectural structures, but at others there are fortifications surrounded by large residential areas. The principal recorded areas in which sites are concentrated include: Kelleli, Gonur, Togolok, Auchin and Tahirbaj in Margiana (Turkmenistan); Sapalli Tepe, Djarkutan, Bustan and Molali in

△ *Bronze axes. The production of metalwork is one of the most significant aspects of the Bronze Age culture of Margiana and Bactria.*

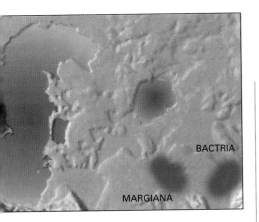

△ *The alluvial area between the Caspian Sea and the Hindu Kush, which was home to the Bronze Age culture of Bactria and Margiana.*

northern Bactria (southern Uzbekistan); and Dashly, Daulatabad and Farukhabad in southern Bactria (northern Afghanistan).

The best examples of sites among the 'oases' of Bactria are those of Dashly–1 and Dashly–3. Dashly–1 comprises a settlement measuring 110 × 90 m (360 × 295 ft), with a preserved elevation of 4 m (13 ft) and a poorly delimited extension of archaeological remains towards the north. Part of a fortress at the site was excavated; it measured 90 × 85 m (295 × 280 ft), was surrounded by a wall 3–4 m (10–13 ft) thick and had towers of circular and oval plan at the corners and on the sides.

Dashly–3 comprised a rectangular artificial mound measuring 125 × 100 m (410 × 328 ft) and up to 3.5 m (11 ft) high. Excavations by Victor Sarianidi of the Academy of Sciences in Moscow have brought to light a palace-fortress and another large complex of circular form surrounded by smaller habitations. The fortress, a rectangular area of 88 × 84 m (289 × 276 ft), was enclosed by walls that had square-section internal walkways, and from which *T*- and *P*-shaped structures projected outwards, and by a ditch 10 m (33 ft) wide and 3 m (10 ft) deep. Its external façade had small pilasters with a decoration that recalled similar buildings at Mundigak and Altyn Tepe.

▷ *Silver cover of a small cosmetic container with a relief of a bull's head, possibly of Mesopotamian inspiration (third to second millennium BC).*

The other architectural complex of Dashly–3 was a circular building about 40 m (130 ft) in diameter with a double curtain of walls, separated by a walkway, with a series of rectangular towers on the outside. This building, it has been suggested, can be identified as a cult complex. It appears to be surrounded by residential areas and is situated within a large fortification – 130 × 150 m (426 × 492 ft) – comprising a very thick wall surrounded by a ditch.

The architecture of the palace-fortress is repeated in the complex of Sapalli Tepe, excavated by A. Askarov between 1969 and 1973, which dates to between 2200 and 2000 BC. This is a small settlement of around 4 hectares (10 acres) with a central fortified area 82 m (270 ft) square. The very complex plan is based on a square central core with two *T*-shaped structures (with internal walkways)

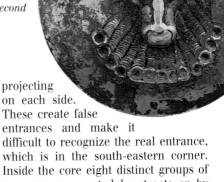

projecting on each side. These create false entrances and make it difficult to recognize the real entrance, which is in the south-eastern corner. Inside the core eight distinct groups of rooms are separated by streets or by narrow spaces. In the spaces hearths and kilns for the production of pottery have been found, as well as ovens for food and craft-working areas for the production of bone or bronze tools.

Towards the final period, the fortress of Sapalli Tepe was used as a necropolis, with the earlier buildings being used in part for burials. Excavations have identified 138 inhumation tombs with rich grave goods that allow a reconstruction of the social structure of Bactria in the Middle Bronze Age. Anthropological studies have identified a predominance of adults and a majority of females. The quantity of grave goods and the distribution of metals and precious stones is much the same in all the burials, which indicates that only the members of a specific section of Sapalli Tepe's population were buried inside the palace. The evidence of a major

△ *Small chlorite vessels used as cosmetic containers (third to second millennium BC). The incised decoration consists of geometric and stylized motifs.*

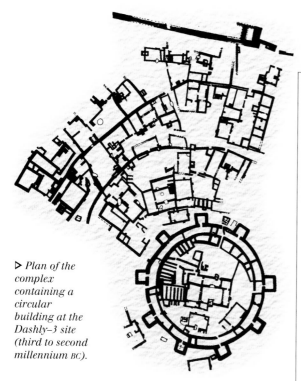

▷ *Plan of the complex containing a circular building at the Dashly–3 site (third to second millennium BC).*

The Digitized Archaeological Map

A project involving a systematic and intensive survey of the Murgab delta and the preparation of an archaeological map was begun in 1989. It was carried out under a joint programme run by the Academy of Sciences of Moscow and the Italian Institute for the Middle and Far East (IsMEO), with the local national university joining in after Turkmenistan gained its independence.

The Murgab delta, with its abundance of water and fertile silt, lies in the heart of the Kara-kum desert of Central Asia and extends over an area of about 7,000 sq km (2,700 sq miles). It was one of the main areas in which the process of populating Central Asia originated. Also, at least from the end of the third millennium BC, it was one of the most important centres for the formation of Iranian culture and ethnicity. The oasis of Merv (named after its main urban centre), along with the easternmost regions of Sogdiana and Chorasmia, was the area from which Iranian civilization diffused towards the world of the steppes and more easterly areas of Asia.

The research programme followed on from aerial reconnaissance of the alluvial plain carried out in 1968 by Soviet archaeologists. Although this area is today almost completely covered by desert, numerous habitation sites of the Bronze and Iron Ages had been identified, apparently clustered in systems of distinct 'oases' along the northern sections of the major ancient river-beds of the Murgab delta.

The archaeological remains of the ancient settlements are frequently reduced to surface concentrations of artifacts uncovered by wind erosion. Other sites, however, appear as artificial mounds which comprise buildings, some of them monumental. Field research has applied new methods to the identification and analysis of the archaeological data: palaeo-environmental reconstruction studies turned to the processing and interpretation of satellite and aerial photographs in conjunction with controls established on the ground; the intensive survey made use of such technical means as GPS (Global Positioning System) and the total station theodolite, which yielded precise topography on digitized cartographic base of 1:100,000 scale; the ground survey used systematic methods to collect surface material (quadrants, transects, removal of the surface and sample sieving in areas of particular interest), which provided an excellent foundation for typological and chronological attribution of the sites. The project has also enabled a computerized geographic information system (GIS) to be built up, in which data on the ancient population can be evaluated in spatial, geographical and chronological terms, including all the historic and economic variables.

concentration of wealth inside the female tombs – which also contained prestige objects of administrative significance, such as seals – is rather interesting. Of the male tombs, only two stand out for their burials in wooden coffins and for the presence of considerable numbers of metal objects.

The absence of deeply stratified sites with high tells has meant that archaeological research in Bactria and Margiana has favoured extensive excavations intended to explore architectural structures. Although this has pushed stratigraphic problems and the chronological division of building phases into second place, it does mean that extensive plans are available of some of the most important sites, such as Togolok and Gonur.

The Togolok settlement group consists of some tens of sites, distributed almost contiguously. Of these, Togolok 21 has been most completely investigated and published. It extends over an area of about a hectare (2½ acres), and consists of a perimeter wall with semicircular towers with a central building set within it on the same axis. The wall of the central building is notable for its thickness (5 m, or 16½ ft) and its massive towers,

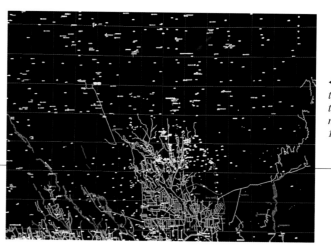

◁ *Digitized computer map of the Murgab delta. The project to create an archaeological map of this zone was begun in 1989.*

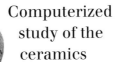

which are circular at the corners and semicircular on the east and west sides.

Gonur consists of numerous sites. These include Gonur 1, which is made up of two low but extensive mounds: south Gonur and north Gonur. In the southern mound excavations directed by V. Sarianidi (which are still continuing) have uncovered a palace with circular and semicircular walls surrounded by residential zones. In the northern area they have revealed a large fortified complex set in the middle of a wide elevated area with residential and production sectors. On the west side, excavations by the expedition of the Centro Studi Richerche Ligabue are exploring the necropoleis of the Middle Bronze Age.

Computerized study of the ceramics

The study of excavation material from Tahirbaj has provided much evidence for reconstructing the evolution of pottery between the Late Bronze Age in the first half of the second millennium BC and the Achaemenid era of the seventh to third centuries BC. Over this period there was a broad continuity in vessel forms. However, new pottery with painted decoration and not made on a wheel also appeared. This was typical of the Early Iron Age and was related to the Yaz culture, from the eponymous site in the centre of the Murgab delta. (The people of the Yaz culture have been widely identified as the earliest followers of Zoroaster.)

◁▽ *Composite female statuettes of chlorite and limestone, sculpted in the round. The quality of the execution and attention to detail are particularly notable.*

New techniques have allowed data on pottery production to be recorded on computer, which has not only assisted the work of drawing but has also helped to build up a typological sequence. The drawing of the potsherds was carried out with a special instrument that enables the profile of the sherd to be digitized and recorded and then completes the drawing process by calculating the diameter and shape characteristics.

Although this system is intended for use with small potsherds, the computerized data can be used to reconstruct vessel shapes in three dimensions. This makes it easier to evaluate the vessels' dimensions and calculate their capacity, not to mention devising hypotheses about their use.

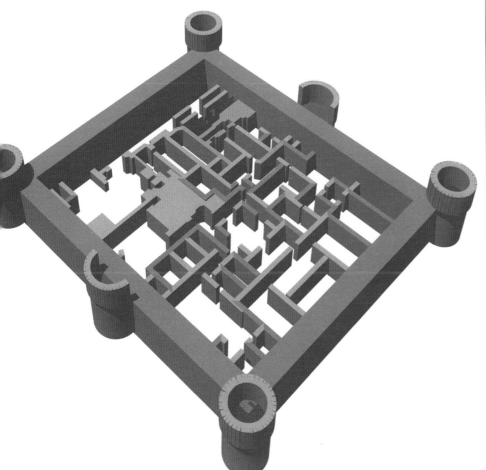

◁ *Three-dimensional reconstruction of the central palace at Togolok 21, showing its circuit wall with towers on the corners and in the middle of two of its sides (begun second millennium BC).*

The Excavation of Tahirbaj

The excavation at Tahirbaj Tepe developed out of the project of creating an archaeological map of the Murgab delta. A point of reference – in the form of a settlement investigated by stratigraphic sounding – was needed as a benchmark for comparing the stylistic and chronological sequences of materials collected from surface-excavated sites. The site best suited to such detailed analysis was identified in the tepe of Tahirbaj – which had a long life-span (from the end of the Bronze Age to the peak of the Achaemenid period, that is to say from the fifteenth to the fifth centuries BC).

Tahirbaj Tepe is a small artificial hill 9 km (6 miles) north of the modern village of Karakul. Its height of about 6 m (20 ft) above the surrounding plain makes it visible from long distances and marks it as one of the major sites for at least 20 km (12 miles) around. The site was discovered in the early 1950s by V.M. Masson, who proposed an Iron Age dating.

A preliminary season of research was carried out in 1991. The surface was mapped in detail, using a level with measurements spaced at every 30 cm (12 in.), which allowed the dimensions and shape of the tepe to be analysed and hypotheses to be formed about its original configuration. For example, the plan revealed a square shape with rounded corners that could be taken to indicate the presence of a fortification.

The surface was explored systematically. Initially, major types of finds were collected and their location recorded: for example certain classes of pottery, metal objects, pieces of precious stone (turquoise and lapis lazuli) and other indications of craft activity (slag from kilns, grindstones, etc.). Then an exhaustive collection was made over an area of 170 × 5 m (560 × 16 ft) divided into 5-metre squares. The pottery was sorted into classes and elements (rims, walls, carinations and bases), and was then weighed and counted; certain other materials were also mapped. This type of collection allowed comparisons with different sites and enabled a more detailed analysis to be made of the pottery's preservation and characteristics. Finally, an area identified from the previous surface collection as relatively rich in partly worked pieces of precious stone ornaments was scraped; the distribution of the finds enabled the craft-working zone to be located more precisely.

Although the main aim was to obtain a chronological sequence for the materials themselves, tracing the chronology of the settlement's structural organization was not neglected. As a consequence, two trenches were excavated. The one on the northern side, 80 × 5 m (260 × 16 ft), ran from the top of the tepe down to the surrounding plain where other archaeological remains had been identified by surface research. The other investigated the southern slope. From the two trenches it was possible to reconstruct a stratigraphic sequence that covered the period from the Late Bronze Age to the Achaemenid period.

△ Detail of the excavations at Tahirbaj Tepe carried out by the IsMEO expedition from Rome.

At the lowest level a Late Bronze Age citadel was identified. It was built on a platform and had a large circuit wall surrounded by a ditch. Above this, strata relating to successive periods were noted, showing several rebuildings of the structures and internal areas. The whole occupation sequence was thus identified, along with a good sample of related pottery, which gives us a better understanding of the chronological sequence.

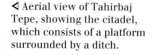

◁ Aerial view of Tahirbaj Tepe, showing the citadel, which consists of a platform surrounded by a ditch.

The attribution of texture (colour and surface appearance) to the same ceramic fragments, by means of sampling with a video camera, makes it possible to obtain virtual images of the vessels' original appearance. Finally, assembling the profiles and the other information in a database allows a much more precise and statistically based evaluation to be made of the entire pottery sequence.

Bibliography

P.L.Kohl, *The Bronze Age Civilization of Central Asia: Recent Soviet Discoveries* (New York, 1981).

C.C. Lamberg-Karlovsky, 'Central Asian Bronze Age - Special Section', in *Antiquity*, 68 (1994), pp. 353–427.

P.L. Kohl, *Central Asia: Palaeolithic Beginnings to the Iron Age* (Paris, 1984).

F.T. Hiebert, 'Origins of the Bronze Age Oasis Civilization in Central Asia', in *American School of Prehistoric Research Bulletin*, 42 (Cambridge, Mass, 1994).

G. Ligabue and S. Salvatori, *Bactria: An Ancient Oasis Civilization from the Sands of Afghanistan* (Venice, 1990).

V.M. Masson and V.I. Sarianidi, *Central Asia: Turkmenia Before the Achaemenids* (London, 1972).

M. Tosi, 'The Northeastern Frontier of the Ancient Near East', in *Mesopotamia*, 8–9 (1974), pp. 21–76.

▽ *Aerial view of south Gonur, excavated under the direction of V. Sarianidi of the Academy of Sciences, Moscow. The complex consists of a palace, with a massive towered circuit wall, surrounded by a tightly-packed residential area, which in turn is contained within a second wall with corner towers (late third or second millennium BC).*

The Scythians: Peoples of the Steppes

Eurasia

*C*lassical Greek sources describe the Scythians as the people who, from the seventh to the third centuries BC, inhabited the area between the river Don and the Black Sea. Herodotus defines them as nomads, emphasizing that they lived without houses and cities. Other nomadic peoples inhabiting the Eurasian steppes are described as Sauromatians or Massageti by the Greeks; as Sakas in Iranian sources; as the Sai by the Chinese; and as Sarmatians by the Romans. All these peoples have at one time or another been lumped together under the broad heading of 'Scythian' – even though they each had distinct ethnic identities.

Archaeological investigations document a quite complex situation, in which some common elements developed over a vast geographical area extending from eastern Siberia and Mongolia to Hungary. However, there were different historical and cultural features within this area, and political and economic structures remain particularly difficult to interpret. More specifically, the social and economic system of the nomadic pastoralists did not remain constant, and a variety of forms of stable settlement were established in different places and at different times by the peoples of the Eurasian steppes, including the Scythians. This dynamism and complexity originated in prehistory and evolved from the Neolithic and Chalcolithic cultures of central Asia (Botai) and Europe (Yamnaya and Sredni Stog), with increasingly marked diversification from the Chalcolithic onwards.

The grass or semi-desert steppe environment and the importance of communication and mobility in the search for new lands increasingly affected the evolution of nomadic peoples. Socio-economic mechanisms were directly related to the control of means of transport, including horses and wagon technology. The horse, in particular – used first as a draught animal and then as a mount – became an integral part of the socio-economic fabric and strongly influenced symbolic and ritual beliefs, being sacrificed and buried in tombs.

The domestication of the horse occurred in southern Russia around 3000 BC and seems to be linked to the dispersion, from west to east, of peoples with European characteristics. It was adopted by the central Asian peoples – above all by the Andronovo culture – and then spread to Mongolia and China. This culture provides one of the first examples of the decisive effect on the central Asian steppes of the diffusion of bronze metallurgy, the use of horse-drawn war chariots and the establishment of an economy that combined stock-rearing and agriculture. By the start of the second millennium BC wagons had evolved from using solid wheels to using spoked wheels – a technical development that was to cause profound ethnic and political changes throughout the Near East.

One peculiarity of the nomadic communities of the steppes was the construction of funerary tumuli known as *kurgans*. The custom of burying the dead in graves dug into the ground and building an earthen tumulus over them spread during the Chalcolithic of central and eastern Europe and became one of the distinctive features of the nomadic societies in Asia. The first of the waves of invaders from the steppe penetrated Europe around 4500–4300 BC and, because of their characteristic tumulus burials, are known as the 'kurgan peoples'. The *kurgans* are often imposing structures, 30–60 m (100–200 ft) in diameter and 2–10 m (6–33 ft) high. Their building would have required a significant communal effort and presupposes a community with social differentiation.

The *kurgans* came to assume important functions for the groups that helped to build them. They became symbols of affiliation and social aggregation at family and tribal level. Through their connection with genealogy, they also symbolized control

△ *Detail of an ornamental gold comb with a scene showing Scythian warriors in combat (fourth century BC), from the* kurgan *of Solocha.*

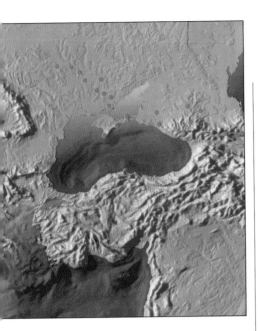

out in groups measuring 60 × 95 or 70 × 120 m (197 × 312 or 230 × 395 ft). Ditches were also documented at Novonikolkoye I and Petrovka II. The material found shows many influences of western origin.

Towards the middle of the second millennium BC the whole of Kazakhstan – from southern Siberia to the southernmost regions along the Syr-Darya (Iaxartes) and the Amu-Darya (Oxus) rivers – was inhabited by populations of a largely uniform level of cultural development. These have been called the 'Bronze Age peoples of the steppes' and are also known by the generic term 'Andronovo culture'. The economy of these populations included agriculture and stock-rearing (with a predominance of cattle and a high percentage of horses and sheep) and exploited some of the river valleys but, above all, the semi-desert or steppe zones. The production of bronzes and pottery with incised decoration (that is, geometric motifs such as triangles,

▽ *Ceramic fragment, 12.5 cm (4¾ in.) high, with incised decoration depicting a female face. Eastern Siberian culture of the third millennium BC. (Novosibirsk, Academy of Sciences)*

and domination of territory. The content and ritual of the *kurgan* burials changed over the centuries, and it is because of this that we can follow their evolution into the funerary tumuli of the Scythians, as described by Herodotus in the fifth century BC.

The most significant discoveries relating to the initial stages of these developments have been found in Asia – in the regions east of the Urals, around settlements dating to *c.* 2000–1900 BC. The excavations of Sintashta provide an example. Here, the tombs comprise large tumuli that cover relatively wide subterranean graves sealed with wooden covers. Inside the burial pits, some of the oldest wagons with spoked wheels were found; the wheels were 1 m (39 in.) in diameter and had ten spokes. Close to and on top of the covers horse skeletons were found, as well as numerous traces of ritual deposits of food and the remains of horse, cattle and sheep skulls. The grave goods included ceramic vessels, weapons and ornamental objects of bronze (axes, bracelets and rings). The residential settlement of Sintashta consisted of defensive works surrounding partly buried houses laid

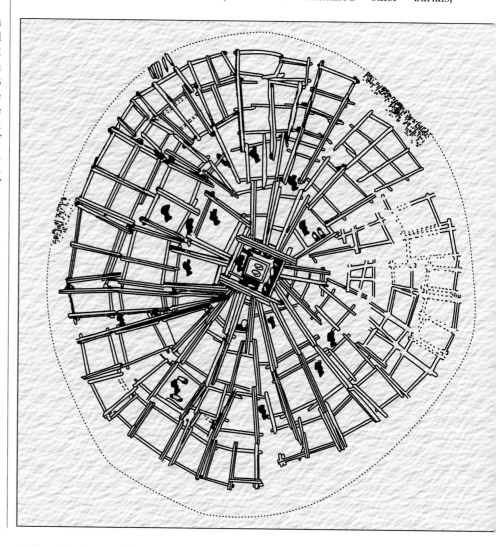

◁ *Bronze wagon finial with the figure of a stag. Such finials, which often acted as bells, were a characteristic form of ornament widespread throughout the world of the steppes.*

meanders and zigzags) was characteristic of the steppe peoples, and in particular of the Andronovo culture. Metal artifacts included axes, spearheads, daggers, arrowheads, hairpins, ear-rings and other ornamental pieces.

The archaeological evidence shows a continuous evolution of forms and materials up to the Iron Age (first millennium BC), when equestrian nomadism established itself. The links between the Bronze Age peoples of the steppes and the Iron Age nomadic community are seen in their metal artifacts and in the many examples of rock art – which, for the most part, depict animals. Today it is thought that the so-called 'animal' style, typical of Scythian decorative work, could have had its origins in these same representations; an example of the scarce evidence of this transition can be found in the Karasuk culture, which existed in southern Siberia between the thirteenth and eighth centuries BC.

Affinities in burial techniques, types of weapons and horse trappings, and in particular the rapid diffusion of a distinctive animal style of decoration, have led to the inclusion of the cultures of the Eurasian steppes under the term 'Scythian'. However, despite these similarities, each area seems to have distinctive traits that can be isolated and attributed to named cultures: the Tasmoli culture in central Kazakhstan, the Pazyryk culture in the Altai mountains and the Tagar culture around the plain of Minusinsk – not to mention the nomad cultures of northern Mongolia or northern China (Ordos).

Some insights into the level of cultural development achieved by equestrian nomadism are offered by the *kurgan* of Arzan. Located in the oasis of Tuva (southern Siberia), it dates to the eighth or seventh centuries BC. The tumulus is 120 m (395 ft) in diameter and is composed of a wooden structure divided by larch trunks into some 70 compartments that are superimposed and arranged radially. The main funerary chamber, in the centre of the tumulus, measured 8 m (26 ft) along one side, but its grave goods had already been plundered in antiquity. An adult man and a young woman were buried here in two wooden coffins; above the main chamber was a second chamber, with walls made of tree trunks, containing eight men, all in wooden coffins, and six horses.

The finds that have survived include numerous gold fragments (part of harness decorations or clothes), pieces of turquoise, the remains of skins, leather, wool and precious textiles, and, finally, metal objects: a bronze knife with a handle in the shape of a wild boar and a bronze collar. Such an assemblage indicates that the burials must have been richly provided with grave goods. In addition to those in the main chamber, the compartments of the tumulus contained other burials,

△ *Plan of the* kurgan *of Arzan with internal partitions formed by tree trunks. The main funerary chamber in the centre was surrounded by compartments, in some of which horses were buried (indicated by symbols). This gigantic* kurgan *was originally 105 m (345 ft) in diameter and probably 5 m (16 ft) high.*

including the remains of 15 adults and 160 horses.

One of the compartments – which had presumably not been plundered – contained eleven horses in full harness decorated with bronze plaques and other ornaments made of boar's tusks. This compartment also contained bronze horse-bits and three decorated bronze finials (together with arrow-heads, such finials were widespread among the peoples of the steppes, from Mongolia to Hungary). Another compartment contained a bronze plaque depicting a panther: the ultimate symbol of a wild animal.

The splendour of the burial and the complexity of the burial ritual reveal a society organized around a central person (probably a military leader), and one in which the possession of horses and their use in war played a significant role. It is here that we can speak with confidence of the process of equestrian nomadism reaching its apogee.

The figurative language of the animal style must have been the expression of a very complex society. This style concentrates not only on the almost exclusive representation of wild animals with a naturalistic appearance, it also, above all, seeks to express the dynamic of these animals. This led to compositions of great originality. These include motifs of zoomorphic combinations (assemblages of parts of different animals), contorted poses (as in the case of the panther of Arzan), and galloping poses (deer often have their hooves folded under their bellies or elongated to the maximum extent). The representation of profiles is distinctive, including bold efforts to synthesize different views of the animal in a single figure (including combining both profile and frontal views).

△ *Fragment of a felt saddle-covering from Pazyryk in the Altai mountains, where numerous items made of perishable materials survived intact in the frozen kurgan.*

Such characteristics of the art of these nomads appear to be almost identical throughout the Eurasian steppes. Almost contemporary with the *kurgan* of Arzan, or a little later, are the finds from southern Russia and Ukraine and from the Kuban river. The gold deer now in the Hermitage (a large plaque that presumably adorned the centre of an iron shield) was found at Kostromskaya stanitsa, and at Kelermes finds included a Scythian short sword with a gold sheath and a gold parade axe, both decorated in the animal style. Further west, beyond the Dnepr, in a *kurgan* discovered at Melgunov Litoj (Kirovograd), the imagery on the grave goods shows eastern influences that can be related to Urartian art. In the fertile 'black earth' area of Ukraine (along the Dnepr valley and along the coasts of the Black Sea) – which is well-suited both to cereal cultivation and to herding on the vast grasslands – the large number of *kurgans* identified and the many large settlements imply that the nomad population must have been very dense.

In the last decades of the sixth century BC a change can be discerned in Scythian society – by now characterized by a more regular nomadism and by a warrior aristocracy – through its relations with the nearby sedentary peoples of the northern steppes and the Greek cities of the Black Sea. In a first phase, marked by reciprocal trade, links with the Greeks did not lead to any clear cultural fusion. Later, however – during the course of the fourth century BC – the contacts intensified, augmented by a constant demand for goods, and led to a real symbiosis. It is especially in

◁ *Bronze plaque of a curled-up panther, found in the* kurgan *of Arzan. Probably the central part of a harness, this is one of the most significant examples of the animal art of the steppes (eighth to sixth centuries* BC*).*

213

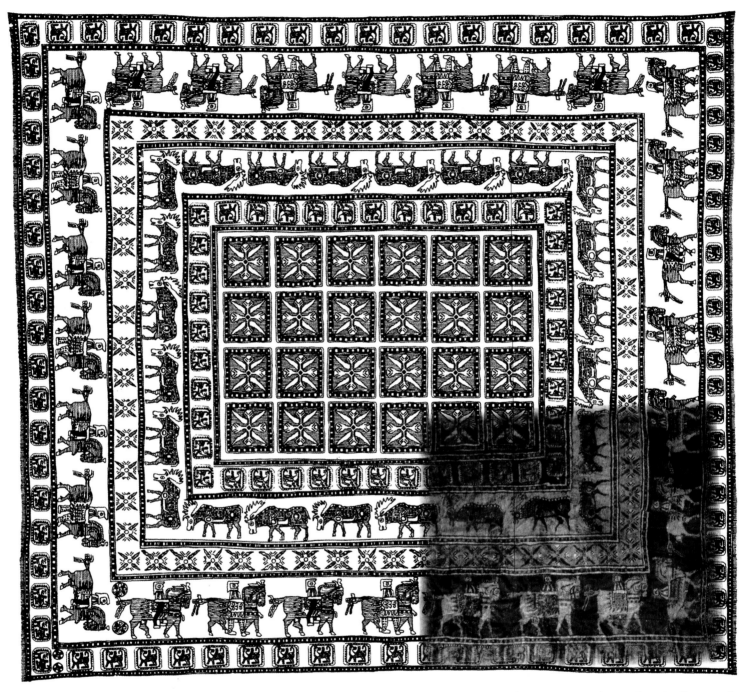

Scythian art that one can see the expression of hierarchical power, based upon military superiority, which assumed a hereditary character, but the fusion with the Greek world is expressed particularly in work (depicting the Scythian pastoral world) that was made by Greek artisans for Scythian patrons. The testimony of Herodotus helps us to understand the Scythian society north of the Black Sea, and, despite certain possible exegetical contradictions, much of what he says is confirmed by the archaeological record. Further east, frozen burials discovered at Pazyryk and elsewhere in the high mountains of the Altai have produced numerous, almost intact, items made of perishable materials. The burials from which many of the grave goods have survived date to the fourth to third

△ *Fragment of a woollen carpet with a frieze of elk and horses, with a hypothetical reconstruction of the complete original that must have measured 183 × 200 cm (72 × 79 in.). The find, from* kurgan *5 at Pazyryk, dates to the third century* BC. *(St Petersburg, Hermitage)*

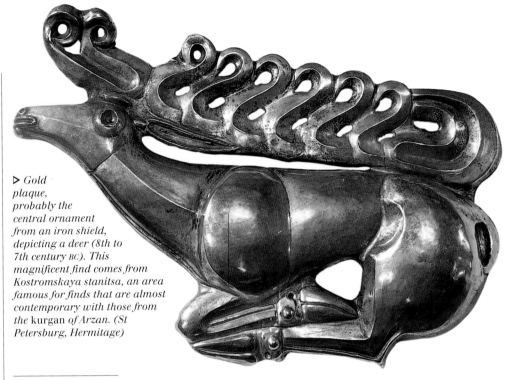

▷ *Gold
plaque,
probably the
central ornament
from an iron shield,
depicting a deer (8th to
7th century BC). This
magnificent find comes from
Kostromskaya stanitsa, an area
famous for finds that are almost
contemporary with those from
the* kurgan *of Arzan. (St
Petersburg, Hermitage)*

centuries BC. They follow the funerary custom of the *kurgan*, with the inhumation of the deceased and of richly equipped horses in graves dug into the ground and lined with tree trunks. The bodies of the men carry traces of tattoos with animal-style motifs. Best preserved are tattoos on the arms, depicting felines, ibex or deer. Although the burials were plundered soon after the original burials, some items have remained intact, such as textiles (rugs and carpets), skins, wooden furnishings with depictions of griffins, and horse-bits and trappings made of wood and leather.

Towards the middle of the first millennium BC the nomadic peoples of the steppes developed a new decorative vocabulary, often referred to as 'geometric ornamentation with shoots'. This seems to have arisen out of cultural exchanges with the workshops of sedentary peoples, and often motifs are simply imports from areas of Byzantine or Sogdian influence. Clan and personal symbols now assumed almost abstract forms and are interpreted as brands for animals. However, it is probably by chance that the most noble of these symbols (linked to the clan that established the powerful kingdom of the Kok Turks) merely depicted an ibex – more simply rendered here than in the period of the animal style, but still possessing dynamism and elegance.

▷ *Bronze bell finial in the shape of the head of a bird of prey, from Ul'skij (6th to 5th century BC). (St Petersburg, Hermitage)*

Bibliography

A. Askarov, V. Volkov and N. Ser-Odjav, 'Pastoral and Nomadic Tribes at the Beginning of the First Millennium B.C.', in V.M. Masson and A.H. Dani, *History of Civilization of Central Asia* (Paris, 1992), pp. 459–472.

V. Basilov, *Nomads of Eurasia* (Washington, 1989).

From the Lands of the Scythians: Ancient Treasures from the Museums of the USSR, exhibition catalogue, Metropolitan Museum of Art (New York, 1975).

V.F. Gening, G.B. Zdanovich and V.V. Gening, *Sintashta* (Chelyabinsk, 1992).

M.P. Griaznov, *La Sibérie du sud* (Geneva, 1975).

E. Jacobsen, *The Art of the Scythians* (Leiden, 1995).

J. Mallory, *In Search of the Indo-Europeans* (London and New York, 1989).

V.M. Masson, 'The Decline of the Bronze Age Civilization and Movements of the Tribes', in V.M. Masson and A.H. Dani, *History of Civilization of Central Asia* (Paris, 1992), pp. 337–356.

E.D. Philips, *The Royal Hordes: Nomad People of the Steppes* (London, 1965).

N. Polosmak, 'A Mummy Unearthed from the Pastures of Heaven', *National Geographic*, CLXXXVI, 4 (1994), pp.80–103.

S.I. Rudenko, *Frozen Tombs from Siberia: The Pazyryk Burials of Iron Age Horsemen* (London, 1970).

T. Talbot Rice, *The Scythians* (London, 1957).

R. Rolle, *The World of the Scythians* (London and Los Angeles, 1989).

The Age of Jade

China **T**he archaeology of the Asian giant, China, has progressed significantly over the course of the present century, producing a mass of new data to aid understanding of the crucial phases in the formation of the Chinese civilization. In the last ten to fifteen years particularly important discoveries have been made at sites belonging to Late Neolithic cultures. They have produced a large number of objects made of various types of jade; these had a range of functions, including personal ornaments, weapons, ritual symbols and objects connected with cult and religious practices.

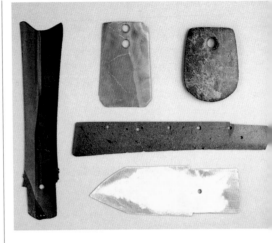

△ *Examples of Neolithic and Shang stone and jade weapons and ritual weapons. (London, British Museum)*

The Late Neolithic cultures with which these jade objects are associated developed during the fourth to third millennia BC in the north-east, east and south of China. Some of them had already been identified by preliminary excavations in the 1930s, but it is only as a result of the most recent discoveries that it has been possible to establish the framework for their development and characteristics.

One of the most unsuspected and spectacular aspects of these cultures is the production of jade artifacts – thousands of which have now been found. This has led many Chinese scholars to revise the subdivision into Stone, Bronze and Iron Ages – first proposed by C.J. Thomsen (1788–1865)

△ *One of the largest jade* cong *found in burial No. 12 at Fanshan (Liangzhu culture, c. 2500 BC). (Hangzhou, Zhejiang Institute of Archaeology)*

▷ *Group of ritual jade objects,* cong *and* bi *(disks in the foreground), from the late Neolithic Liangzhu culture (c. 2500 BC). (London, British Museum)*

– that had hitherto been used in China, as in Europe, to describe the stages in the development of ancient civilizations. To describe a cultural phenomenon typical of China, but which currently has no known counterpart in any other civilization, the concept of a 'Jade Age' is increasingly being accepted to denote a final phase of the Neolithic period immediately preceding the Bronze Age.

The introduction of this new classification is not intended, however, simply to emphasize the role that 'jade' played during a crucial period in the formation of ancient Chinese civilization, but to draw together a number of cultural implications exemplified by the production of jade objects. These objects – which took a very long time to make and required complex working techniques (and therefore imply the existence of highly specialized craftworkers) – were intended for members of the elite in cultures that seem socially more complex than preceding (or indeed many contemporary) cultures. This complexity is reflected by those jade items regarded as 'ritual' objects, many of which were decorated with images that probably had a religious meaning. These characteristics, and others, anticipate the important aspects of cultures of the succeeding Bronze Age (*c.* 2000–500 BC).

All this is clearly evident in the Liangzhu culture (*c.* 3000–2000 BC), which developed in eastern China, in

the area of the Blue River delta and near Lake Tai (the main expanse of water in the region). The working of jade had occurred in the same area under the preceding Majiabang and Songze cultures, but it reached levels of extreme sophistication in the Liangzhu culture. It is evident from analyses of grave goods that jade objects were a clear indicator of both social and religious status. Burials of common people of this culture have been identified, lying not far from settlements containing modest grave goods, such as stone and ceramic tools showing signs of use. Elite burials, on the other hand, were found much further from habitation centres, frequently in artificial tumuli or on the summits of hills, and the grave goods (amongst which jades were abundant) showed no signs of use and can therefore be

(1 acre) in area, which was interpreted either as an altar or else as a cere-monial platform (similar structures have also been found at other Liangzhu

△ *The site of Yaoshan (c. 2500 BC), which belongs to the late Neolithic Liangzhu culture. The photo illustrates the position of the burials close to the ceremonial platform.*

Burial No. 12 at Fanshan (c. 2500 BC, Liangzhu [cult]ure) at the time of its discovery.

interpreted as both symbols of authority and ritual objects used in religious ceremonies.

A cemetery area of the Liangzhu elite was discovered not far from Hangzhou, in the province of Zhejiang, at the Yaoshan site (a curious place-name that literally means 'plateau of precious stones'). Excavations on the summit of a small hill 35 m (115 ft) high between 5 May and 4 June 1987 revealed twelve trench graves, some of which contained fragments of lacquered wooden coffins. They were arranged in two more or less parallel east–west lines and lay near a raised structure of reddish earth, 400 sq m

Archaeology in the Far East

The three main countries of the Far Eastern area (China, Japan and Korea) all have long traditions of respect for and study of the past. However, archaeology – systematic investigation of the past based upon field research – is a relatively young discipline, having been adopted in each country in different ways at different times from the end of the nineteenth century to the beginning of the twentieth.

Despite some ups and downs, Far Eastern archae-ology has progressed enormously, with excava-tions increasing notably over recent decades. The almost 'mythical' past in which the roots of the Far Eastern civilization were laid down is emerging from the mists of legend and, in all three countries, is now one of the most promising fields of archaeological research. A multiplicity of historical periods are also being studied.

This rapid development, and the consequent massive accumulation of data from excavations has, however, been accompanied by a series of major difficulties: a vast number of salvage excava-tions, preparation that is not always uniform, and a still insufficient application of modern excavation tech-niques and advanced tech-nologies. Nevertheless, eco-nomic development in countries such as China and ever-closer scientific collab-oration among international experts point to a positive future for Far Eastern archaeology, as it makes more extensive use of the scientific knowledge of the present to reach a better understanding of the past.

◁ Bronze male head from the late Shang site of Sanxingdui (Sichuan).

Jade

From a strictly mineralogical point of view, the term 'jade' (yu in Chinese) covers two different minerals: nephrite and jadeite. Nephrite belongs to the actinolite-tremolite series of calcareous amphiboles, whereas jadeite is a sodic pyroxene. In China, the mineral that was always preferred for the production of jade objects was nephrite (the use of jadeite dates only from the eighteenth century, when this stone began to be imported from Burma).

Nephrite was also called zhen yu ('real jade'): an honorary term that emphasized its difference – now confirmed by mineralogical studies – from all related minerals by virtue of its intrinsic properties of quality and colour. One of its charac- *teristics – its density – makes nephrite one of the hardest of all stones to work, it is still not entirely clear what techniques and tools were used to manufacture the highly refined objects produced by the late Neolithic cultures.*

No other civilization in the world has ascribed such importance to jade as the Chinese. Used for the manufacture of ritual objects in the Late Neolithic and the Bronze Age, it was prized also in successive historical periods, not only for its aesthetic qualities but also for the intrinsic properties it was believed to possess. The alchemists of the Han era (206 BC–AD 220), for example, believed that jade had the power to preserve the body from decay, which explains the wide use of funerary jade in burials of the period. Even today, jade objects are some of the personal talismans most valued by Chinese people.

◁ Detail of the funerary clothing of the prince Liu Sheng (Han dynasty, 2nd century BC), composed of 2,498 jade plaques joined together by gold threads. It was discovered in 1968 at Mancheng, in Hebei province. (Beijing, Historical Museum)

graphic variants and stylizations on many jade objects from sites of this culture.

A new and promising line of research into ancient Chinese jades is mineralogical analysis of objects from the sites of different Late Neolithic cultures. The analysis is carried out on minute samples (of the order of two milligrams). A scanning electron microscope is used to examine the microstructure of the mineral, and spectrometry to establish the type of mineral, or minerals, that the object is made of. The results have so far shown that artifacts described generically as 'jade' in the excavation reports in fact belong to three mineralogically distinct categories: 'true jade', 'semi-jade' and 'pseudo-jade'. The first group consists of nephrite; the second, nephrite in combination with other minerals (such as calcite and steatite); and the third comprises materials that, although similar to jade, are actually another mineral.

The results of the laboratory analyses were extremely interesting. First of all, they showed that the oldest nephrite objects in the world so far discovered are a small group of ornaments found at the site of Chahai (Fuxin district, Liaoning province, north-east China), which date to the sixth millennium BC. These were precursors of the jade industry that developed in the Hongshan culture (c. 3500–2500 BC). On the other hand, analysis of 'jade' found in the area of Lake Tai have revealed that here the use of nephrite does not

sites, for example at Fuquanshan and Huiguanshan).

The burials yielded a total of 635 jade objects, as well as others of stone and pottery. The burials near the altar contained richer and more varied grave goods than those further away from it; this may have related to hierarchical differences between the deceased. No bone remains were found, so typological comparisons between the objects from these graves and those from other sites were made to determine the sex of the individuals buried at Yaoshan. These established that females were buried in the tombs of the upper line, and males in those of the lower line. The majority of the jades – similar to those found at Fanshan, another Liangzhu elite cemetery 5 km (3 miles) to the south-west – have complex decorations of an anthropomorphic figure with wide plumed headgear placed above a creature with zoomorphic characteristics. This decorative motif is thought to represent the principal divinity of the Liangzhu people and recurs in a number of

▷ *Recurrent decorative motif on Liangzhu jades found at Yaoshan and Fanshan: it depicts an anthropomorphic being with a plumed headdress, positioned above an animal.*

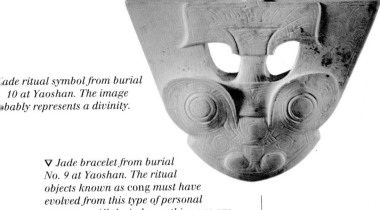

Jade ritual symbol from burial 10 at Yaoshan. The image probably represents a divinity.

▽ *Jade bracelet from burial No. 9 at Yaoshan. The ritual objects known as* cong *must have evolved from this type of personal ornament. All the jades on this page are from the Neolithic Liangzhu culture.*

Bibliography

Guang Wen, 'Chinese Neolithic Jade: a Preliminary Geoarchaeological Study', in *Geoarchaeology*, VII, 3 (1992), pp. 251–275.

Huang Tsui-mei, 'Liangzhu: A Late Neolithic Jade-yielding Culture in Southeastern Coastal China', *Antiquity*, 66 (1992), pp. 75–83.

predate the Liangzhu culture. More-over, it has been discovered that high-quality nephrite was used only for the production of 'ritual' jades – which were more refined in their decoration – and not for other objects such as ornaments. This reveals a sophisticated level of knowledge of the raw materials. The various types of nephrite also served to distinguish the different social ranks of the owners of the jade objects.

Finally, the analyses have pinpointed differences in the mineralogical struc-ture of jade objects found at the sites of different cultures. This indicates that the mineral deposits used by the differ-ent cultures were not identical, and also that they were not the Central Asian sources (for example, the Khotan area) from which jade was extracted in the historical era, from the Shang dynasty (sixteenth to ninth centuries BC).

▷ *Circular ritual emblem decorated with the triple motif of an undefined animal. From burial No. 2 at Yaoshan.*

△ *Jade* cong *decorated with stylized faces carved on its surface, from burial No. 10 at Yaoshan.*

R. Keverne (ed.), *Jade* (London 1991).

J. Rawson (ed.), *Chinese Jade from the Neolithic to the Qing* (London, 1995).

F. Salviati, 'Il materiale in giada della cultura Liangzhu allo stato attuale delle conoscenze: osservazioni', in *Rivista degli Studi Orientali*, LXI, 1–2 (1992), pp. 145–169.

The Shang Dynasty: New Discoveries

China **O**ne of the first important achievements of nascent Chinese archaeology at the beginning of this century was to establish the historical existence of the Shang dynasty (c. 1600–1050 BC) as a result of the discoveries made at Anyang, the site of the last Shang capital. Since then, it has continued to augment our knowledge of this dynasty, identifying further urban centres and numerous other sites and enabling the area of diffusion of the Shang culture to be traced – although the map is subject to constant updating.

In the last few years archaeological knowledge of the Shang dynasty has been advanced by two discoveries that are exceptional because of the types of object found. The first occurred at Sanxingdui, a site near Guanghan, about 40 km (25 miles) north of Chengdu, the capital of the south-eastern province of Sichuan. In a location where chance finds had been made in July 1986, archaeologists uncovered two large sacrificial trenches, measuring 4.6 × 3.5 m (15 × 13½ ft) and 5.3 × 2.3 m (17 × 7½ ft) respectively. They contained more than 700 artifacts, mostly of jade and bronze, which can be dated to the final Shang phase, between the thirteenth and eleventh centuries BC. A number of factors – including the fact that many of the finds show signs of deliberate breakage and the presence of remains of sacrificed animals – suggests that they were buried after some ritual ceremony.

Among the bronze objects that have aroused the most interest – because they are unique among Shang finds currently known – are some large masks, more than a metre (39 in.) wide,

△ *Bronze finial in the shape of a male head. From the late Shang (thirteenth to eleventh century BC) site of Sanxingdui, Guanghan.*

which depict faces that have humanoid characteristics but such marked peculiarities as large, protruding eyes and ears. The attachment points identifiable on the front and sides suggest that they were originally mounted on wooden supports like totemic emblems – as must have been the case for other bronze sculptures of human heads, which had cavities for supports in the neck. Even more unexpected was the discovery of a large bronze sculpture of a man standing on an elaborate pedestal: perhaps the image of an ancient priest. Not only are these finds unique, they also indicate the existence of advanced metallurgical knowledge in an area until recently regarded as marginal to the technological progress seen in central China, where the classical Chinese civilization developed. The later discovery of a circuit wall – which serves to identify

Sanxingdui as a notable urban centre in the Chinese Bronze Age – has aroused interest in the possibility of future discoveries at a site that will force some traditional views about the centres of development of the ancient Chinese civilization to be revised.

The second, equally interesting, discovery came to light in 1990 at Dayangzhou (in Xin'gan district in the southern province of Jiangxi). It was an enormous burial, dated (on the basis of typological parallels of the artifacts) to the final Shang phase. The finds from

△ *The site of Sanxingdui – near Guanghan, some 40 km (25 miles) from Chengdu, capital of the south-eastern province of Sichuan – where traces of a walled circuit were found, suggesting the existence of an urban settlement.*

▽ *Bronze mask, 60 cm (24 in.) high and over 1 m (39 in.) wide, with protruding eyes and ears.*

◁ *Restored bronze figure of a standing man (perhaps a priest) from Sanxingdui. It is almost 2 m (79 in.) high and shows the standard of metalworking reached in ancient China.*

this site show affinities with products from the foundries of Shang metropolitan centres (such as Zhengzhou and Anyang) but also have marked local characteristics, evident above all in the decorative motifs, among which the tiger predominates. The numerous jade items are also of great interest. The minerals used to make the more than 1,000 objects discovered seem to come from a number of provinces – for example Xinjiang, Liaoning, Shanxi and Zhejiang. Xin'gan therefore appears, despite its distance from the Shang metropolitan centres, to have lain at the centre of a wide network of contacts.

Ancient Chinese bronzes have stimulated the interest of scholars and collectors since the Song dynasty (AD 960–1127), when the emperors of the time began to collect and carefully catalogue the finds accidentally brought to light by peasants in the various regions of the empire. If the Song must be credited with establishing the stylistic approach to the study of the ancient ritual bronzes, which modern archaeological methods and discoveries evolved and enriched, then we must thank advanced technologies for expanding our knowledge of their manufacturing techniques.

Radiography allows even the most hidden parts of the objects to be studied without any physical damage being done to the object. With data thus obtained, the bronzes can be reconstructed as three-dimensional computer models, and identification can be made of residues of the clay originally used to form the moulds (the typical casting process used in ancient China was based on multiple moulds). Finally, samples of these residues can be subjected to thermoluminescence tests in order to verify the dating of the pieces and to prove that they are not fakes.

Bibliography

R.W. Bagley, 'Sacrificial pits of the Shang Period at Sanxingdui in Guanghan County, Sichuan Province', in *Arts Asiatiques*, 63, 1988, pp. 78-86.

K.C. Chang, *Shang Civilization* (New Haven and London, 1980).

K.C. Chang (ed.), *Studies of Shang Archaeology* (New Haven and London, 1986).

Li Chi, *Anyang* (Washington, 1977).

J. Rawson (ed.), *Mysteries of Ancient China*, exhibition catalogue (London, 1996).

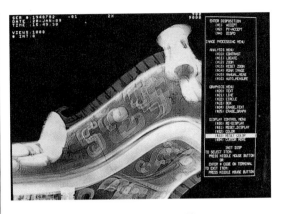

△▽ *Three computer images showing X-ray photographs of late Shang period bronze receptacles. Modern techniques are increasingly being applied to the analysis of finds; radiography and thermoluminescence tests are helpful in verifying authenticity. In the case of the Shang ritual bronzes, laboratory tests allowed a detailed examination of the composition of the metal alloys and of the sophisticated casting techniques, which involved the use of multiple ceramic moulds.*

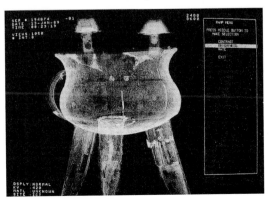

Qin Shi Huangdi's Terracotta Army

China The terracotta army set to guard the tomb of China's First Emperor has been considered the find of the century, a modern archaeological classic and 'the eighth wonder of the world'. It was found by chance in 1976, by some peasants digging a pit, and is now visited every year by millions of tourists, who admire the thousands of terracotta statues of warriors – restored and set up again in the positions in which they were originally found.

The army actually represents just one part, albeit the most spectacular, of the impressive funerary complex which Qin

Δ Detail of the head of one of the high officers of the terracotta army, found near the funerary tumulus of the First Emperor of China.

Shi Huangdi ('First August Emperor'; 246–210 BC) caused to be erected, so that his descendants would remember him and his works. The funerary mausoleum lies to the east of Xi'an in the furrowed plain of the River Wei, which flows to the north of the complex, and is flanked on the south by hills. One of the hills, Mt Li, gives its name to the whole of the archaeological complex, which is known as the 'necropolis of Mt

Li'. Begun in 246 BC, the year that Prince Zheng, the future First Emperor, acceded to the throne of the state of Qin, the mausoleum had still not been finished at the time of his death in 210 BC.

This enormous complex, which extended over an area of more than 56 sq km (21½ sq miles), centred upon the tomb of Qin Shi Huangdi: a tumulus that today is 50.5 m (165 ft) high, as opposed to its original 150 m (490 ft). The tumulus lies off-centre inside two rectangular circuit walls of beaten earth. Inside and outside these, sacrificial pits were identified, which contained the remains of human and animal victims sacrificed on the death of the First Emperor, as well as objects of his funerary assemblage, including terracotta statues of kneeling males and females. In the northern part of the area within the outer circuit wall, underground drainage channels and the foundations of various types of buildings were found. These – as we know from historical sources – are the remains of palaces, guard towers and temples used for the ancestral cult that once formed a complex associated with

the tumulus: they were built by the hundreds of thousands of conscripts and craftsmen who also made the clay statues that comprise the terracotta army.

The terracotta army was found 1.5 km (1 mi.) east of the tumulus in three large pits; a fourth, empty, pit was presumably never completed. Pit No. 1 is the widest: it measures around 210 m (609 ft) from east to west and 60 m (200 ft) from north to south. It consists of a series of eleven parallel bays – 2–3 m (6½–10 ft) wide by 200 m (655 ft) long –

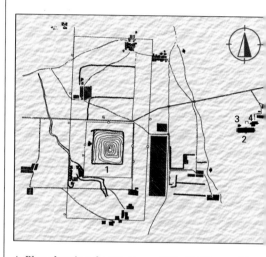

Δ Plan showing the structure of Qin Shi Huangdi's funerary complex. The tumulus (1) lies off-centre with two rectangular enclosures, and the pits (2, 3, 4) containing terracotta soldiers lie to the east of the complex.

▽ Reconstruction of pit No. 1, containing the statues of warriors in battle formation.

Tilled soil
Undisturbed
Earth fill
Plaster
Matting
Timbers
Brick

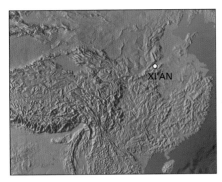

△ *Location map: The city of Xi'an lies in Shanxi province in east-central China.*

separated by walls of beaten earth and paved with bricks, which originally had wooden covers. The soldiers found in this trench comprise the infantry units and are arranged in battle order. The first ranks consist of around 200 archers and crossbowmen (unarmoured to give them maximum mobility on the battlefield), whose duty it was to fire their arrows over ranges of up to almost 200 m (220 yd). Behind them are six chariots and three squadrons of light infantry. The chariots (originally of wood, so they have now vanished, apart from traces left in the earth) were pulled by four horses and would have had space for a charioteer and one or two soldiers with flexible spears – up to

▽ *Panoramic view of pit No. 1, showing the terracotta statues of the warriors placed to guard the eternal rest of the First Emperor.*

The First Emperor of China

The title Qin Shi Huangdi, usually translated as 'First Emperor', actually incorporates complex meanings that shed light on the historical events of a crucial period of Chinese history and on a political project designed to leave its mark on successive centuries. From the eighth century BC – as the Western Zhou dynasty lost its authority through falling victim to its own land-allocation system and the creation of principalities to administer its territory – China broke up into many small kingdoms; 'Qin' was the name of one of these. From the fifth century BC, in the Warring States period, the former vassals became the rulers of autonomous states, struggling among

△ Presumed portrait of Qin Shi Huangdi, the 'First August Emperor'.

themselves for supremacy until the state of Qin finally conquered the other kingdoms in 221 BC. Prince Zheng, who achieved this, bestowed upon himself the title 'Huangdi', previously applied to the mythical sovereigns of antiquity who were considered to be the founders of Chinese civilization. The term 'Shi' – which can be translated as 'First' – alludes to the new emperor's desire to found a dynasty that would last for 10,000 generations (or all eternity).

For all his grandiloquent title, Qin Shi Huangdi was indeed the founder of the first centralized Chinese empire, which in essence was to last until the revolution of 1911. This self-proclaimed universal sovereign was obsessive in his search for immortality; famous for the burning of books, but also for unifying the China of his time, he succeeded in leaving his ineradicable mark on the pages of history.

6 m (20 ft) long and probably with bamboo shafts – to keep the enemy at a distance. It seems, though, that two of the chariots had a signalling role, co-ordinating the various phases of the battle by means of the bronze bells and drums they carried. The three squadrons of light infantry, who were armed with spears 2 m (6½ ft) long, would have assisted the archers and chariots. Behind them marched soldiers in armour composed of plaques of toughened leather stitched together to protect their chests and shoulders.

A similar formation, composed of a cavalry unit, chariots and armoured infantry, came to light in pit No. 2, which is still under excavation. Recent tests are revealing the great extent of

The Great Wall

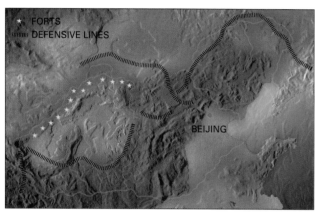

FORTS
DEFENSIVE LINES

BEIJING

◁ Plan and fortifications (indicated by asterisks) of the Great Wall in the Qin era (third century BC).

The building of the Great Wall has traditionally been ascribed to the First Emperor, who is said to have ordered its building to protect China's northern borders – largely unprotected by natural barriers – from the incursions of the nomadic peoples of the North. However, cross-checking the textual sources against the archaeological records leads today's scholars to believe that Qin Shi Huangdi in fact ordered the restoration, consolidation and connecting together of sections of defensive wall originally erected much earlier, under the Qi, Wei, Yan and Zhao kingdoms, which were later conquered by Qin.

The fortifications built at the explicit order of the First Emperor are found in the much more restricted area of the Ordos region, the *territory circumscribed by the bend of the Yellow River. A passage from the Shiji, compiled by the historian Sima Qian (c. 145–86 BC) under the Han dynasty, tells us that Qin Shi Huangdi ordered General Meng Tian to expel the nomads groups and drive them beyond the* *Yellow River, after which a series of fortifications (fortified citadels, according to other interpretations) were built to prevent further incursions. However, the history (and even the exact extent) of the Great Wall – continually restored, widened, partly rebuilt, and even moved, by the emperors of successive Chinese dynasties – is still in part obscure. It is to be hoped that the attention scholars and archaeologists are now devoting to it will lead to a fuller understanding of this important monument.*

▽ A stretch of the Wall at Badaling, 80 km (50 miles) from Beijing.

△ *One of the central bays of pit No. 1 at an advanced phase of excavation, with the terracotta horses that drew the chariots and an infantry unit, the backbone of the army of Qin.*

this pit, which, when completely excavated, could provide further information about the organization and nature of the First Emperor's army.

None of the soldiers carried shields, not even those placed on the sides and facing outwards who had the task of securing the flanks of the formation. The soldiers of the State of Qin – whose courage and ferocity, according to the texts, were enough to armour their spirits – were trained to attack. Strong discipline was maintained by merciless officials, who did not hesitate to kill soldiers who failed to carry out orders, or who showed cowardice or fear when launching their attack.

The clay generals who commanded the army of the First Emperor were found in pit No. 3, excavated between March and December of 1977. In this irregularly shaped pit were found a chariot and 68 statues – many representing officers – with an average height of 1.9 m (6 ft). Of the accompanying soldiers, probably a bodyguard, some wore light and others heavy uniforms. As with each of the thousands of other terracotta figures, the fearsome appearance and physical features of the officers were vividly represented in truly specific portraits, each modelled individually.

It is thought that this stress on individuality of feature could have been a deliberate effort to represent the ethnic variety of the China of the period – unified for the first time under the command of a single man. However, by representing each soldier individually, it was probably intended to make more 'alive' the army that had the task of

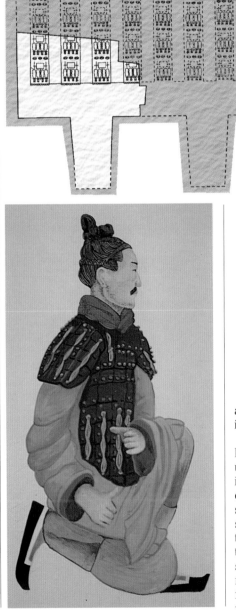

▷ *Plan of pit No. 2. The light-coloured squares represent the sections excavated so far; the grey areas indicate the probable arrangement of the soldiers and four-horse chariots in the various bays.*

◁△ Left: *One of the kneeling archers found in pit No. 2.* Above: *The original appearance of the statue, painted with bright colours.*

accompanying and protecting its ruler in the world of the dead.

Behind this startling and famous uniqueness of the terracotta army, there is a degree of standardization – essential in a project of such a vast scale. The lower part of each figure is solid but the torso is hollow, and so is the head, which was set on a long neck that fitted into a hole between the shoulders. The heads were shaped in a mould, but such details as the facial features, ears, moustaches and hair were then finished individually. The

forearms and hands were modelled separately, with the hands shaped to hold the weapons with which the figures were originally equipped (but which were later removed by rebels, who also fired and destroyed the pits).

One of the measures taken by Qin Shi Huangdi immediately after the unification of China was the confiscation of all the weapons in the country, so that the only armed force was the imperial army. History shows, however, that this measure to discourage possible insurrection did not prevent the popular revolution that caused the fall of the Qin dynasty (221–206 BC) and brought to the imperial throne Liu Bang, the founder of the succeeding Han dynasty (206 BC–AD 220).

Today the statues have the grey colour of the high-fired terracotta from which they were made, but originally they were painted with bright colours, as surviving traces of polychrome pigments show. One group of soldiers wears black armour with gold buttons, dark blue trousers and black boots with red laces; and a second group has brown armour with orange buttons. The clay used to produce the thousands of statues was extracted from nearby Mount Li and fired in kilns that have been identified close to the pits in which they were buried.

Although most of this immense project was carried out by thousands of anonymous artisans, Chinese archaeologists have identified signatures on some statues, which have been interpreted as those of the overseers who supervised the work. The terracotta army, and the further excavation and patient restoration work that it needs, will go on fascinating visitors and will continue to occupy an important place in the chronicles of archaeology – thus assuring Qin Shi Huangdi of the immortality he sought.

△ *Some of the statues of the terracotta warriors, still partly buried, seen during the complex excavation procedure. The work of the archaeologists goes hand-in-hand with that of the conservators, who have the delicate task of reassembling the terracotta figures, which were found in a badly damaged state.*

The Secrets of the Funerary Tumulus

The world-wide interest generated by the discovery of the terracotta army was also fed by the rumours surrounding the contents of the (still unexcavated) tumulus in which Qin Shi Huangdi was buried. Judging from the descriptions reported in historical texts, the vast funerary chamber inside the tumulus must have been conceived as a sort of microcosm centred around the body of the emperor, who was thus portrayed almost as a universal sovereign. The roof of the burial chamber, studded with precious stones representing stars and constellations, is said to have symbolized the sky. The burial was also said to have contained a miniature model of the territories and cities conquered by Qin Shi Huangdi – with the principal lakes and rivers of China represented not by water but by mercury, kept in continual motion by complex mechanisms. Vast quantities of treasure were reputed to have formed part of the funerary assemblage of the First Emperor, protected by defence systems worthy of an Indiana Jones film: booby-traps, false passages, and crossbows ready to fire arrows at anyone daring to desecrate the burial.

For the moment such descriptions of the inside of the tumulus are all we have. The tomb of the First Emperor has still not been opened by modern Chinese archaeologists who, lacking access to sophisticated techniques, are fearful of damaging the contents of the gigantic tomb. According to the textual sources, though, it was actually violated and sacked by the rebel forces that put an end to the brief flowering of the Qin dynasty. Uncertainty over what lies within the tumulus will be finally resolved only when it is opened.

◁ *The funerary tumulus containing the remains of the First Emperor, at Lintong. According to contemporary accounts, the tumulus (not yet excavated by modern archaeologists) is said to contain fabulous treasures and be protected by sophisticated booby-traps.*

Bibliography

G.L. Barnes, *China, Korea and Japan: The Rise of Civilization in East Asia* (London and New York, 1993).

Cina 220 BC. I guerrieri di Xi'an, exhibition catalogue (Milan, 1994).

A. Cotterell, *The First Emperor of China* (London, 1981).

M.K. Hearn, 'The Terracotta Army of the First Emperor of Qin (221–206 BC)', in Wen Fong (ed.), *The Great Bronze Age of China* (New York and London, 1980), pp. 353–68.

R.L. Thorp, 'An Archaeological Reconstruction of the Lishan Necropolis', in *The Great Bronze Age of China: A Symposium* (Los Angeles, 1983), pp. 72–83.

A. Waldron, *La Grande Muraglia. Dalla storia al mito* (Turin, 1993).

Museums and Restoration

China

*I*nevitable accompaniments to archaeological research are the problems of restoring and conserving the finds that are discovered. In these two areas China has been making notable progress, in part as a result of ever-closer collaboration between archaeologists, restorers and conservators from foreign countries.

The Chinese museum network is widespread, extending to every region of the country, and there are museums in all the major cities. At a national level there are two institutions housed in Beijing: the Historical Museum and the Palace Museum, or Gugong, housed in the Forbidden City. The Gugong is centred essentially upon the art collections assembled over the centuries by various emperors, but the Historical Museum has a more pronounced archaeological focus. By presenting the main finds from throughout the country in chronological order, it aims to illustrate the historical and cultural development of China, from the first traces of human settlement in the Palaeolithic right through to the cultural remains of the last dynasty.

Alongside these two institutions, there are museums in each provincial capital, where the finds from that region are kept. Major cities, such as Shanghai or Xi'an, boast museums that are first-class – indeed world-class – not only because of the importance of their collections, but also because of the way they are displayed and the sophisticated techniques that are being used to restore, conserve and study them.

The Shaanxi Provincial Museum, based in Xi'an, is equipped with information networks, telecommunication systems, an enormous library, an auditorium and vast stores where the finds not on display are protected by sophisticated security systems. One of its most important exhibits is the display of some of the frescoes from the many tombs of the Tang period (AD 618–907) found around Xi'an, the dynasty's capital (which was then called Chang'an).

△ *Group of headless stone statues found near the tomb of the emperor Gao Zu (AD 566–635) of the Tang dynasty located near Xi'an.*

In order to foster the establishment of professional archaeology and restoration, Italy recently signed an agreement with China to create a permanent school of restoration at Xi'an in conjunction with the Shaanxi Provincial Bureau for Museum and Archaeological Data. The initiative has been promoted by the National Museum of Oriental Art in Rome and Italy's Central Institute for Restoration and directed by the Italian Institute for the Middle and Far East (IsMEO) and a former Italian Ambassador to China. By the end of the first year it is estimated that the School will have trained between twenty and twenty-five new restorers.

For some years now, there have been numerous investigations and projects aimed at safeguarding important Buddhist sites and monuments established at the time that Buddhism spread to China. These are monastic complexes found in caves, mainly in the northern provinces of the country, and are known collectively as 'Caves of the Thousand Buddhas', on account of the

▽ *Detail of a fresco found in the tomb of Li Shou (AD 577–630) and conserved, like many similar finds, by a special section of the Shaanxi Provincial Museum at Xi'an.*

△ *Votive monument in the shape of a stupa (Buddhist monument containing a holy relic) erected opposite the site at Dunhuang, known popularly as the 'Cave of the Thousand Buddhas' (Mogao, Gansu province).*

many paintings, reliefs and sculptures on Buddhist themes that they contained.

Some of these cave complexes were included by UNESCO in its list of monuments that form part of the World Cultural Heritage – among them the caves of Mogao, near Dunhuang, in the north-western province of Gansu. This complex, which was active from the fourth to the fourteenth centuries AD, consists of thousands of monks' cells, niches for sacred images and vast halls hollowed out of the side of a long hill. The frescoes and sculptures that decorate most of the caves were made from rather delicate materials, including wood, plaster and straw mixed with mud. In order to avert their ever more rapid deterioration (confirmed by measurements taken with sophisticated instruments), drastic steps were taken, including the closure of the caves to the public.

Another Buddhist cave complex to be placed under strict surveillance is that of Yungang (Datong, Shanxi province). Here, a series of measures were taken to prevent rainwater infiltration that was threatening the caves, particularly those long exposed to the atmospheric

△ *A large statue of the Buddha, 14 m (46 ft) high. Amongst the first to be produced at Datong (Yungang, Shanxi province), it dates to the second half of the fifth century AD, the time of the Northern Wei dynasty (AD 386–535).*

action as a result of the collapse of the original roofs. Safeguarding this important monument also involves a three- to four-year project to change the main economic activity of the area – charcoal-burning – which has for a long time been having a damaging effect on the preservation of the complex and its artistic heritage. A series of archaeological investigations was also set up to establish the type and original arrangement of the structures that had been erected to protect the caves at various periods, with the intention of eventually reconstructing them.

△ *View of the outside of the caves at Datong and of the excavations being carried out by Chinese archaeologists. These excavations have uncovered the foundations of wooden buildings that protected the site in past centuries. Today, all the major Buddhist monuments and complexes in China are protected.*

The Archaeology of Mongolia

China

Excavations in provinces on China's periphery, such as Inner Mongolia, have produced new data about the peoples with whom the Chinese civilization maintained contacts over the course of the centuries. Work in regions well away from the Yellow River valley and central China – the area long regarded as the cradle of Chinese civilization – will certainly form a very important part of Chinese archaeological research in future years.

Although the major power centres of the various ruling dynasties were traditionally concentrated in the central Yellow River (Huang He) valley, China and its civilization have always benefited from continuous influences and stimuli coming from the peripheral regions. These were inhabited by populations that were not ethnically Chinese, and which the historical sources quite frequently refer to as 'barbarians'.

Mongolia, and all the vast territories to the north of China, was one of the most important of these areas. Mongolia is now subdivided into two separate political entities, of which Inner Mongolia is an Autonomous Region of the Peoples' Republic of China. It derives its name from a people that has left its mark on the history not only of China but also of central Asia, India and eastern Europe. But the people in question, the Mongols, were just one of the many ethnic groups from this vast region that we know of from Chinese historical sources.

Archaeological discoveries made in this century, and in particular in recent decades, have now allowed us to learn something of the material culture of the peoples that, over the centuries, converged on the territory of Inner Mongolia. Fossils of *Homo sapiens*, dating to around 35,000 years ago and found at the beginning of this century at sites near the River Sjara-osso-gol (Ordos region), indicate that Inner Mongolia was already inhabited during the late Pleistocene. Around 10,000 BC climatic changes occurred that created conditions favourable to the development of agriculture, and around 6000 BC there appeared Neolithic groups partly dependent on agriculture, which are collectively known as the Xinglongwa culture.

As a result of excavations mainly carried out during the 1970s, the cultural sequence is quite well established in the district of Aohan, around Chifeng, in eastern Inner Mongolia. Here the Xinglongwa culture was followed by the Zhaobaogou phase, a predecessor of the Hongshan culture (around 4500–4000 BC) that succeeded it. The last is noted, in particular, for the numerous jade objects of a symbolic nature discovered in burials associated with the remains of ceremonial structures (such as those found at Niuheliang, in eastern Liaoning); all these elements indicate an advanced cultural level and growing social complexity. The summit of this evolutionary sequence is exemplified by finds from a series of proto-urban settlements dating to the third

△ *Painting of the Ming dynasty (AD 1368–1644) depicting a Mongol archer on horseback. The horse was traditionally associated with the semi-nomadic life of the Mongols.*

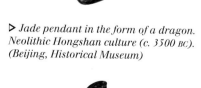

▷ *Jade pendant in the form of a dragon. Neolithic Hongshan culture (c. 3500 BC). (Beijing, Historical Museum)*

▷ *Gilded bronze funerary mask dating to the Liao dynasty (AD 916–1125). Such masks often occur in the grave goods of high-ranking people under this dynasty and are indicative of funerary practices different from traditional Chinese ones. (Paris, Musée Guimet)*

with those found in central China, and are associated with the emergence of a proto-urban civilization that came to maturity in the Bronze Age with the Erlitou culture (*c.* 2000–1600 BC) and with the Shang dynasty (*c.* 1600–1050 BC).

Apart from this developmental sequence, contacts, trade and exchange between the Chinese metropolitan centres and the cultures of

The mobility of the ancient peoples of Inner Mongolia lies at the root of the difficulty that historians and archaeologists face in trying to establish links between the names of the various ethnic groups as reported in the Chinese sources and the finds made in areas they are traditionally said to have occupied. One example is that of the Xiongnu, an outline of whose history is provided by Sima Qian (*c.* 145–86 BC), the historian of the Han era (206 BC–AD 220). Here archaeological work has succeeded in adding a good deal of flesh to this skeleton of historical information in recent years, so that the main

millennium BC. That of Laohushan (2800–2300 BC) covers some 130,000 sq m (32 acres) and is surrounded by a circuit wall of earth covered by stones. Within the wall lay the houses, predominantly square in plan and semi-sunken, while outside it pottery kilns were found. Laohushan and the other fortified sites are contemporary

Inner Mongolia are also well documented. After later climatic changes, which occurred around 1500 BC, the economy of the populations of Mongolia changed from an agricultural to a predominantly pastoral one – and this was a determining factor in the origin of the nomadic *modus vivendi* of the following cultures.

features of the material culture of the Xiongnu are quite well known.

The Xiongnu were the first ethnic group of the steppes to create a political structure of importance in the Eurasian region. Based upon a confederation of tribes led by a chief, this became the prototype for the successive social and military organizations of all those

△ *Computer reconstruction of the appearance of a Mongol encampment. It has a uniform plan in which the* yurts, *the typical Mongol tents, are ranged in straight lines on either side of that of the leader (in the centre).*

Beijing

It is no exaggeration to call Beijing, the present-day capital of the People's Republic of China, an inheritance from the Mongols. The city (whose Chinese name, Beijing, means 'Northern capital') lies on the northern edge of the Yellow River valley – a region where most of the Chinese capitals were built over the centuries: Erlitou, Xi'an, Luoyang and Kaifeng.

Beijing's history is linked to its geographical position, at the northern side of the large central plain and near the mountain passes that lead towards the Mongolian plateau. This was one of the main reasons that led first the Khitan and the Nüzhen, and then the Mongol founders of the Yuan dynasty (AD 1271–1368), to choose the area of present-day Beijing as the site of their imperial capital. Of Kambaluc (the city's name under the Mongols), which was described by Marco Polo, there remain only sad vestiges today, such as a part of the original circuit wall discovered by archaeologists and now protected from the advances of the modern city.

Nevertheless, the dynasties that succeeded the Yuan – first the Ming (1368–1644) and then the Qing (1644–1911) – inherited from them the urban grid plan and the tradition of spectacular monuments.

Foremost among such monuments was the Forbidden City,

which comprised the residence of the emperor, the centre of his activities, and an architectural display of the power of the 'Son of the Sky' (as he was also called). It was not a coincidence that the walls of the city where he lived were purple – a colour traditionally attributed to the Pole Star – thus associating the queen of the stars with the emperor of men.

△ Digitized image which graphically reconstructs the probable original appearance of the Forbidden City in the Mongol era. The buildings immediately beyond the bridge formed the main entrance to the palace complex.

◁ Computerized 'bird's-eye' view of the whole of the Forbidden City. In the centre, on a marble platform, are the buildings in which the emperor carried out his official duties (the central pavilion is known as the 'Throne Room'). His private quarters are in the background.

▷ A digitized image of Beijing as it appeared in the Mongol era, with its grid of streets running north–south and east–west. The square shape close to the near wall is the Forbidden City, with the 'lake of Bohai', a private park of the emperor to the left of it. The canal that flows from the lake leads to the Summer Palace, some kilometres outside the urban enclosure.

peoples that took advantage of moments of weakness in the Chinese empire – even managing to occupy the throne and found their own dynasties.

This was achieved in northern China by the Tuoba Xianbei, founders of the Northern Wei (AD 386–535), and by the Qidan (or Khitan) who established the Liao dynasty (AD 907–1125), which in turn was followed by that of the Jin (AD 1115–1234), founded by the Nüzhen (or Juchen). Finally, the Mongols, under Genghis Khan during the thirteenth century, carried the power of the pastoralist confederations to a level never reached before.

The Mongols were one of the various tribes that, in 1206, were unified under the command of a single man: Temüjin, better known by his honorary title of Genghis Khan ('Powerful Universal Sovereign'). After his election as head of the tribal confederation, Genghis Khan undertook a series of military campaigns southwards against China and westwards as far as the Black Sea, conquering in succession the cities of central Asia, Samarkand and the Caucasus zone. He returned to the Mongolian steppes in 1226, his health damaged in a fall from his horse, and died the following year, after dividing the subjugated territories among his three sons. The conquest of China was launched in 1211 and completed in 1279 with the overthrow of the Song dynasty by Kublai Khan, Genghis Khan's grandson.

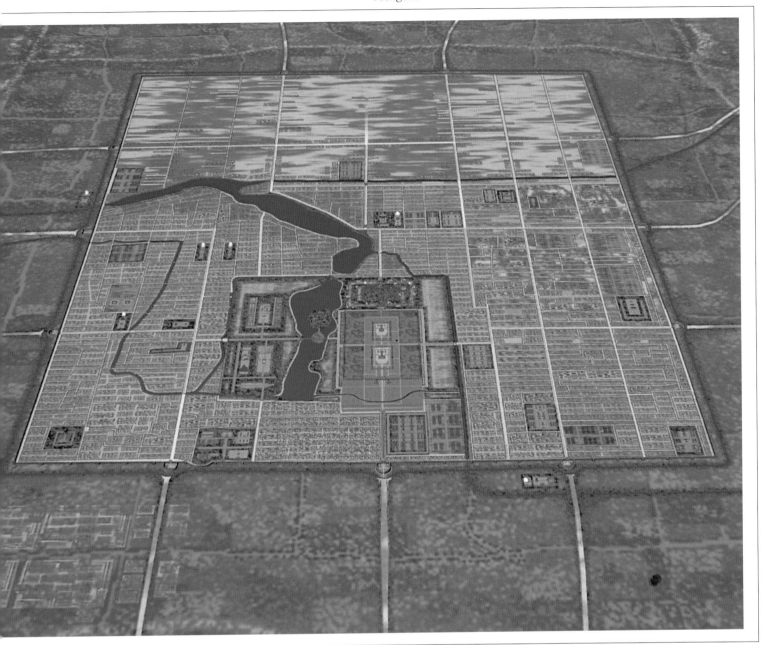

However, Kublai's death in 1294 heralded the rapid disintegration of the Mongol empire, one of the largest and shortest-lived in history. Rebellions in China began around the middle of the fourteenth century, culminating in the expulsion of the Mongols, the return to the throne of a Chinese emperor and the foundation of the Ming dynasty (AD 1368–1644).

Bibliography

T. Tse Bartholomew and others, *Mongolia: The Legacy of Chinggis Khan* (London, 1995).

A.T. Kessler, *Empires Beyond the Great Wall: The Heritage of Genghis Khan* (Los Angeles, 1993).

S. Milledge Nelson (ed.), *The Archaeology of Northeast China: Beyond the Great Wall* (London and New York, 1995).

E.D. Phillips, *L'impero dei Mongoli* (Rome, 1985).

J.F. So and E.C. Bunker, *Traders and Raiders on China's Northern Frontier* (Seattle and London, 1995).

Weng Wan-Go and Yang Boda (eds), *The Palace Museum, Peking: Treasures of the Forbidden City* (London, 1982).

Ancient Japan

Japan

Discoveries made at Yoshinogari have increased our knowledge of the Yayoi period (third century BC to third century AD) in ancient Japan, which marks the introduction of rice cultivation to the country. The Yayoi phase was followed by the Kofun period (fourth to seventh centuries AD), which is remarkable for the large tumulus burials that were carried out for members of the emergent elite.

The site of Yoshinogari lies in the Saga prefecture of the island of Kyushu in southern Japan. Its location is important because the island of Kyushu is crucial to understanding the archaeology of the cultural links between Japanese civilization during the period of its formation and continental Asia. The Korean peninsula lies only 140 km (87 miles) from Kyushu across the Korean Strait.

It was during the Yayoi period (300 BC–AD 300), which followed the very

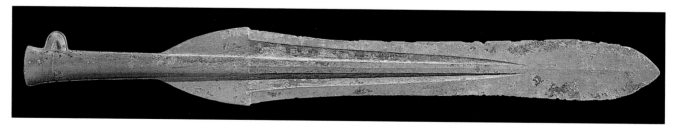

▷ *Terracotta anthropomorphic figurine found at Kamikurogoma (Misaka-cho, Yamamashi district). This is one the most typical finds from the Jomon period and dates to 3000–2000 BC. (Tokyo, National Museum)*

long Jomon phase (*c.* 10,000–300 BC), that rice cultivation and knowledge of metalworking were introduced into Japan: elements that helped to accelerate its cultural and technological development. Numerous traces of both have been identified at sites on Kyushu, the north-eastern part of which was one of the centres of the first Yayoi diffusion.

Rice, a fundamental part of the diet of Asian peoples today, was first domesticated in China around 5000 BC – as finds at the site of Hemudu, a little way south of the Blue River delta, have shown. Cereal cultivation must have diffused from here, via Korea (where its presence is indirectly attested around 2000 BC), to Kyushu, and thence to the rest of Japan.

Sites on Kyushu have also produced the earliest bronze artifacts yet found in Japan – among them weapons (swords, spearheads and halberds), bells and mirrors, all of which are derived from prototypes from outside Japan. The swords are of the Liaoning type – the name is derived from that of the north-eastern province of China where the oldest examples were made – which came to Japan by way of Korea. The Japanese bronze bells (known as *dotaku*) of the Yayoi period are, however, of distinctly Korean inspiration, but the mirrors are of Chinese manufacture. The imported objects indicate the extent of Japan's cultural contacts with other Far Eastern countries; it was during this era that the first reports appear in the Chinese sources of the people that inhabited the Japanese archipelago. Because of their association in the archaeological record with the burials of members of an emergent elite, the imports also provide evidence of the growing complexity of the Japanese society of the middle and late Yayoi. This would culminate in the appearance of the first proto-state entities during the following Kofun period (AD 300–700).

The discoveries made at Yoshinogari – a site that was continuously settled throughout the whole Yayoi period – have contributed enormously to a better understanding of the period and provided a firm foundation on which to base new interpretative hypotheses. Before the discovery of Yoshinogari, knowledge of this period was based largely on finds made at Toro, in the Shizuoka prefecture. While the perfect state of preservation of the Toro site has provided valuable data on rice cultivation – not only in Japan but also in the

▽ *Bronze spearhead of the Yayoi period, 80.6 cm (31.7 in.) long and thought to come from the site of Okamoto-cho (Kasuga, Fukuoka prefecture). Such weapons, with their characteristic 'violin' profile, derive from prototypes found in the north-eastern Chinese province of Liaoning. (London, British Museum)*

whole of eastern Asia – is was none-theless a small agricultural village, whereas Yoshinogari was the centre of a late Yayoi elite.

Yoshinogari lies on a low ridge, some 600 m (650 yd) wide, which extends for 3 km (2 miles) from the foot of Mt Sefuri down to the Saga plain. The part of the site that can be assigned to the middle and late Yayoi covers an area of 25 hectares (62 acres), within which traces of habitation structures and the cemetery were identified. The whole area is bounded by a ditch, partial excavation of which has recovered various materials: shells, bone arrow-heads, worked deer antler and other artifacts assignable to the Early and Middle Yayoi. A second ditch, inside the

△ *Digitized image showing the original appearance of the funerary tumulus of the Emperor Ojin (Osaka prefecture).*

first, delimits and protects the habita-tion area on the summit of the ridge. In the north-eastern part of this area, post-holes for supporting raised structures are coming to light; this can perhaps be thought of as an area reserved for the elite. Outside the ditch, on the other hand, traces are emerging of buildings that, given their strategic position, are possibly identifiable as the guard towers mentioned in descriptions of Late Yayoi sites in contemporary Chinese texts. At Yoshinogari subsistence was based upon rice (shown by the various iron tools usually associated with its cultiva-tion) and upon hunting and fishing. Animal bones found in the ditch surrounding the settlement included those of pigs: animals hitherto thought to have been introduced from Korea only during later periods.

Some of the most significant finds from Yoshinogari come from a group of

◁ *Yayoi-period bronze bell of the* dotaku *type, found at Sumiyoshi-cho (Higashinada, Kobe) and dating to the second or third century AD. (Tokyo, National Museum)*

burials some of which were in a tumulus within the ditch at the northern end of the site. This – the largest Middle Yayoi tumulus so far discovered – was oval in form and about 40 m (130 ft) long by 30 m (98 ft) wide; it is now 2.5 m (8 ft) high, but must originally have risen to around 4–5 m (13–16 ft). There were traces of a track leading to the tumulus from the south, along which ceramic receptacles, probably used for ceremonial purposes, were found. At the end of the track steps were identified, which perhaps led to the entrance to the tomb.

In the construction of the tumulus (which has been dated to the first century BC) the 'packed-earth' tech-nique was used. This had been widely used in China since the Neolithic period, but in Japan had hitherto only been documented from the seventh and eighth centuries AD. The eight inhumations identified in the tumulus were jar burials of a type fairly widespread in Yayoi tombs in Kyushu, in which the deceased was placed inside two large pottery jars with the rims abutting. Given the location of these burials (on high ground and inside the tumulus) and the type of objects that made up the grave goods, these could be the burials of high-ranking individuals of different generations, perhaps members of the same clan.

The oldest burial (No. 1006), found near the centre of the tumulus, contained the skeleton of an individual aged about thirty. The seven other burials were placed around this one in a star pattern. One of the most important is No. 1002, which contained a bronze sword of Liaoning type, similar to Korean models but probably made in Japan. Alongside the sword (other examples came to light in Nos 1005, 1007 and 1009) seventy-five small, light-blue glass cylinders were found, perhaps originally elements of a head-dress.

Besides the burials in this tumulus at Yoshinogari, at least twelve cemeteries were documented. These were predominantly jar burials (around two thousand of them), but there were also examples of burials in cist tombs (13), trench graves (380) and wooden coffins (6). Evidence of violent deaths seems to support the hypothesis that the Yayoi period was one of military conflict, but it must have been one of widespread trade, because some of the bracelets found were made from a specific type of shell imported from distant regions.

One of the burials also produced fragments of silk, to add to those found at other sites – all of them on Kyushu. Finally, fragments of

◁ *Funerary terracotta (haniwa) in the form of an armoured warrior dating to the sixth century AD and found at Kami-chujo (Kumagaya). These objects are among the most typical of the Kofun period, and are found near funerary tumuli. (Tokyo, National Museum)*

Yoshinogari and the Mythical Kingdom of Yamatai

To understand the great impact that the discovery of the Yoshinogari site has had in Japan, one must recall a semi-legendary figure from Japanese history: Queen Himiko. At some time in the third century AD she is said to have governed the kingdom of Yamatai, which is referred to in Chinese texts of the Wei period (AD 220–264). For centuries, a large part of Japanese historiography, including the archaeological research of more recent times, has sought to find out where this kingdom was. One of the favoured locations is the island of Kyushu.

According to the Chinese sources, Queen Himiko was an old woman with magical powers, who lived in a fortified home protected by guard towers. In AD 238 Himiko sent gifts and tribute to the Chinese court, receiving in return the honorary title of 'Queen Friend of Wei'. After her death, some years later, she was buried in a large tumulus.

The discovery of the site of Yoshinogari has therefore revived interest in this in some ways still mysterious page in Japanese history. Yoshinogari has produced a series of remains that could fit the descriptions in the Chinese texts: buildings with raised foundations (perhaps housing the elite) and a tumulus burial that could perhaps be that in which the Queen lies.

However, popular imagination will have to wait for some time yet before the enigma of Queen Himiko can be finally clarified.

moulds used to cast metal objects came to light in another burial, indicating that Yoshinogari was an important centre for early Japanese metalworking.

The gradual evolution towards complex forms of social organization, already visible in the Late Yayoi phase, intensified in the following Kofun period (fourth to seventh centuries AD). This term, which means 'ancient tombs', emphasizes one of the most important characteristics of the period: the monumental tumulus burials in which the members of the elite of the time were buried.

Typically, these are keyhole tombs, so called from the shape of their plan. This results from adding a trapezoidal raised structure to the circular tumulus containing the funerary chamber. This led to a staircase that gave access to the top of the tumulus, where a circular platform was ringed by funerary terracottas (haniwa) that proclaimed the social status of the deceased. It must

be said, though, that this description is based on possible reconstructions proposed by archaeologists – the original appearance of a large number of these tombs (more than 3,000 have been identified throughout Japan) having been modified over time by natural causes or the hand of man. Moreover, the keyhole tomb is only one possible form: the *kofun* could, in fact, be circular, square or a combination of both (for example, it might perhaps have a square base and rounded end).

Although tumulus burials are typical of the Kofun period, they were first built during the Late Yayoi phase (at Yoshinogari, for example). The main difference lies in the scale, which in the Kofun era assumed large proportions, connected to the greater importance of members of the elite at this time. Tumuli were not, however, an isolated phenomenon in eastern Asia between the fourth and seventh centuries: rulers of contemporary Korean states of the Three Kings period (AD 300–668) were buried in tombs of similar appearance and dimensions, and other examples of the keyhole form have also been found in Korea. Such similarities in the form of tombs – and in grave goods – reveal direct connections between the various Japanese political entities of the Kofun period and those of Korea. *Sue* ware, swords with annular guards and personal ornaments made of precious materials found in Japanese *kofun* are frequently so similar to analogous Korean finds that they may actually have been either imported or made by Korean craftsmen who had emigrated to Japan.

Despite such exchanges, the burial cults associated with the *kofun* are largely original and typical of Japan, as the presence of bronze mirrors and the use of ceramic funerary figures (*haniwa*) – to mention just two of the most

◁ Sue *ware funerary terracotta (sixth century AD) of the Kofun period.* (London, British Museum)

important elements – shows. The bronze mirrors were either imported from China or made in Japan after Chinese prototypes (the distinction is often unresolved, as in the case of thirty-three examples found in the *kofun* of Tsubai Otsukayama in the Kyoto prefecture). They played an important role in Japanese funerary rituals – perhaps as a consequence of the talismanic qualities attributed to them in China – as their decoration of divinities, constellations or mythological animals shows. Their importance is also demonstrated by their position in the burials: in the *kofun* of Otsukayama they were found along the sides of the funerary chamber, and in that of Koganezuka a Chinese mirror,

dated to AD 239, was placed on the sarcophagus of the main burial. After the fourth century the number of imported mirrors diminished considerably, and grave goods show an increase in objects such as armour, swords, helmets and spearheads, all of which are associated with military activities and the emergence of an elite class of warriors.

Less well known than the famous burials are the habitation settlements of the Kofun period, with exceptions such as the site of Mitsudera, in the prefecture of Gumma, dating to between the end of the fifth and the start of the sixth centuries. The area where the elite lived is separated from that of the common people by a ditch, within which were the elite living quarters and a series of buildings probably used for ritual purposes. That the leading individuals in the Japanese society of the Kofun period exercised both religious and command functions is suggested by the expression *matsurigoto*, which from this time came to acquire the double meaning of both 'governing duties' and 'ritual activities'.

△ *A large group of* sue *ware funerary terracottas. These objects, which vary in height from 6.6 to 52.6 cm (2.6 to 20.7 in.) and differ also in form and function, are grouped here to show the variety of form and decoration of* sue *ware. They come from sites on Honshu and Shikoku. (London, British Museum)*

Computers and Archaeology

Modern techniques – especially computer graphics – offer the possibility of visually reconstructing the original appearance of sites from archaeological data. This is a technique that, in the case of Japan, could be applied to the villages of the Yayoi period or to the tumulus burials of the Kofun period.

Broadly speaking, the computer reconstruction of a kofun involves as its first stage the choice of the type of tumulus – selected from types already identified and stored in a database that contains standard parameters. To this are added data specific to the burial to be reconstructed: the measurements of the tomb, the type of soil on which it is built, and the natural environment of the surrounding landscape. This atten-

tion to the topography is particularly important in computer reconstructions of Yayoi villages such as Yoshinogari.

The main difficulty stems from the fact that the original wooden buildings have disappeared and have left only a few traces. However, such traces as the post-

holes do at least provide approximate indications of a building's dimensions and type. Using these archaeological remains, as well as the depictions of buildings that are found on various artifacts, it is possible to reconstruct the probable appearance of the houses on computer.

The military role was an important part of the activities of the Kofun elite, and it is possible to detect in this the germ of elements characteristic of samurai times. Numerous funerary terracottas take the form of warriors wearing armour made up of plaques (probably of leather) stitched together. They were armed with quite elaborate swords, the hilts of which were worked into the shapes of mythical birds and other animals, and another of their attributes was the horse, which – as the funerary *haniwa* show – was decked out with harness of gilded bronze and fine saddles.

◁▽ Facing page: *Two computer images of a reconstruction of the Yayoi village found at Yoshinogari, showing various houses and the raised buildings that were perhaps used for storing foodstuffs. In some parts of Asia such buildings have not changed substantially over time, as can be seen from the photo (below) of a present-day village in southern China.*

Bibliography

G.L. Barnes, *Protohistoric Yamato: Archaeology of the First Japanese State* (Ann Arbor, 1988).

G.L. Barnes, *China, Korea and Japan:The Rise of Civilization in East Asia* (London and New York, 1993).

M. Hudson, 'From Toro to Yoshinogari: Changing Perspectives on Yayoi Archaeology', in G.L. Barnes (ed.), *Hoabinhian, Jomon, Yayoi, Early Korean States: Bibliographic Reviews of Far Eastern Archaeology* (Oxford, 1990), pp. 63–111.

M. Hudson and G.L. Barnes, 'Yoshinogari: a Yayoi Settlement in Northern Kyushu', in *Monumenta Nipponica*, XLVI, 2 (1991), pp. 211–235.

O. Mitsuzane, 'Mounded Tombs in East Asia from the 3rd to the 7th Centuries AD', in R. Pearson (ed.), *Windows on the Japanese Past: Studies in Archaeology and Prehistory* (Ann Arbor, 1986).

Pueblo Bonito and the Anasazi

North America

Pueblo Bonito, in Chaco Canyon in the American *Southwest, was one of the most remarkable towns in pre-Columbian North America. It was built by the Anasazi in the period AD 950–1150, on a D-shaped plan. The complex at one time consisted of five semicircular platforms around a vast central square dotted with numerous pits that led to underground ritual areas (kivas). The town had both commercial and religious roles and was one of a group of sites in the San Juan basin connected by a unique road network.*

▷ *Location map: Chaco Canyon lies in the north-western corner of New Mexico, in the American Southwest. It was one of the most important centres in this region.*

The Anasazi culture developed in the so-called region of the 'Four Corners', where the states of Utah, Colorado, Arizona and New Mexico converge. This culture did not know writing, so it

is through archaeological remains that we can retrace the stages of its development (because of the dry climate the remains are well preserved). Its apogee dates to between AD 950 and 1150 when its political, social, economic and religious structures were at their peak. This was a period of material prosperity, as is illustrated by many finds at several sites, including Pueblo Bonito.

The town was built in successive phases and today covers an area of one hectare (2½ acres). Built of *adobe* and wood, the flat-roofed buildings were superimposed upon each other to form a crescent-shaped 'block' that faced south; the general shape of the site and its orientation suggest that this plan was

linked to the movement of the sun and to natural phenomena. The rubble-filled *adobe* external walls protected the town from the north winds and captured the heat emitted by the sun's rays. Likewise the roof-terraces, which were regularly heated by the sun, were well suited to the drying of maize, which was both a staple of the diet and an important commodity to be exchanged throughout the region; the rooms, on the other hand, were always cool, and therefore well suited to maize storage. The rooms also served as dwellings for the population of Pueblo Bonito, which must have numbered around 1,200 people. The central square is divided into two almost equal parts, and its surface is peppered with circular structures of various sizes: semi-subterranean ritual areas that also served as storerooms. Their number suggests that, between AD 950 and 1150, the religious activities performed at the centre of Pueblo Bonito were particularly intense.

The building of the town required enormous quantities of sand, clay, water and wood, which were brought

to the site by means of the road network that linked the towns of Chaco Canyon. The towns also used this network to import agricultural produce, turquoise, certain minerals and other products from the Pacific coast and also from central Mexico. It would seem that the Anasazi chose to settle in Chaco Canyon because of its central location. As a consequence, Pueblo Bonito served not only as a religious centre but also as a place of storage, exchange and redistribution of goods.

Either round or square in shape, the *kiva* was an underground space with multiple functions. Its form recalls the underground dwellings of earlier peoples in the Southwest. Despite the subsequent evolution of local architecture and the appearance of the first 'unitary-block' villages, or *pueblos*, the *kiva* continued to be built in all the large sites of the American Southwest. According to Frank Waters, the term *kiva* signifies 'the underworld' and symbolizes the maternal matrix of the earth from which men were formed, and from which life also spread to the plants upon which the humans subsisted.

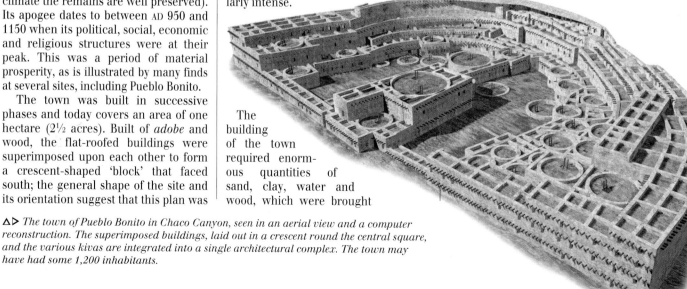

△▷ *The town of Pueblo Bonito in Chaco Canyon, seen in an aerial view and a computer reconstruction. The superimposed buildings, laid out in a crescent round the central square, and the various kivas are integrated into a single architectural complex. The town may have had some 1,200 inhabitants.*

The Historical Sources

The principal sources of information on the Anasazi are the chronicles compiled by the Spanish who, arriving from Mexico around 1530, discovered the populations of the northern region of Mexico. From 1540 to 1542 an expedition under Francisco Vasquez de Coronado was sent by the Spanish Viceroy to explore the Anasazi region. The chronicles produced as a result of this mission are the oldest documents that relate to the Anasazi culture. During the following half-century the Anasazi were in contact with many other Spanish groups, who also wrote about them in letters, texts and chronicles. In 1598, Juan de Oñate led an expedition into the valley of the Rio Grande that marked the start of the European presence in Anasazi territory.

The Indians that lived in the adobe villages were called the Pueblos by the Spanish, to distinguish them from other groups in the region bordering Mexico. This term was retained and continues to designate the groups in the American Southwest that have maintained an architectural tradition similar to that of the Anasazi.

◁ Painted ceramic jug. It is one of the rare examples of the use of the human form in Anasazi art.

Today the *kivas* in the central squares of Native American villages are generally rectangular and oriented east–west, like the course of the sun across the sky. They are entered by a ladder through a roof opening, generally made of plant material. The interior essentially comprises two spaces: 'the East' for non-initiates, and 'the West', which is reserved for the clansmen who organize the ceremonies. The *kiva* symbolizes the world, the myth of the emergence of humans and their passage through four successive worlds. Human life is regulated by a series of seasonal ceremonies, such as that of the New Fire at the spring solstice, or the Ceremony of the Masks (*kachinas*), which is connected with the return of mythical ancestors.

Pueblo Bonito has numerous *kivas*, which indicates that they must have been used by a large population throughout the year. The *kiva* served as a meeting place, a public room, and as a sacred space in which the history of the creation of the world could be regularly represented.

Bibliography

L. Cordell, *Prehistory of the Southwest* (New York, 1984).

B. Fagan, *Ancient North America*, 2nd ed. (London and New York, 1995).

W.M. Ferguson and A.H. Rohn, *Anasazi Ruins of the Southwest in Color* (Albuquerque, 1987).

S. Plog, *Ancient Peoples of the American Southwest* (London and New York, 1997).

F. Waters, *Book of the Hopi* (New York, 1982).

Traditional Chronology for the Anasazi	
Basketmaker II	AD 200–400
Basketmaker III	400–700
Pueblo I	700–900
Pueblo II	900–1100
Pueblo III	1100–1300
Pueblo IV	1300–1600
Pueblo V (modern)	1600–1900

△ *Virtual reconstruction showing part of Pueblo Bonito's central square and kivas, which were entered via wooden ladders. Circular in form and of various dimensions, these underground sacred spaces recalled the myth of the creation of the universe, when the animals appeared from the earth to help humans to populate the world.*

Cahokia: An Ancient North American City

North America

The site of Cahokia, consisting of over 100 mounds, lies across the Mississippi from the present-day city of St Louis. In its heyday, around AD 1200, it reached a population of 10,000–15,000 and was the largest settlement in pre-Columbian North America. Grouped within a defensive palisade stood great platform mounds of varying size, the largest and most famous of which is called Monk's Mound. Cahokia is frequently likened to the somewhat later and smaller town of Moundville in Alabama, which has a similar layout and group of mounds.

The site of Cahokia in the modern state of Missouri stretches over an area of 13 sq km (5 sq miles) in the fertile Mississippi basin. The cultivation of maize in the rich alluvial soil, and the exploitation of fish in the marginal swampland, made it possible for groups to settle permanently and

◁ This Mississippian effigy-head vessel, 15 cm (6 in.) high, depicts a mother suckling her baby. It comes from the Cahokia area.

prosper. The so-called 'Mississippian' culture, of which Cahokia was a part, flourished in a vast geographical zone that stretched from the present-day state of Oklahoma in the west to Georgia in the south-east, and from Wisconsin in the north to the Gulf of Mexico in the south.

The site developed from AD 800 to 1250, after the decline of the preceding Hopewell culture, and its monumental dimensions indicate the scale of the work required to build it. Thousands of Mississippians must have been involved in planning, organizing and building

the immense and numerous temple-platforms. The town is articulated around a main temple-platform, called Monk's Mound after the French Trappist monks who at one time occupied the site. This mound, which is estimated to contain 60,000 cu m (2.1 million cu ft) of earth, reaches over 30 m (100 ft) in height and is 316 m (345 yd) by 241 m (263 yd) wide. It was built in fourteen successive stages between AD 950 and 1150 and dominated a central plaza. It lies at the centre of an area containing sixteen smaller earthworks, the whole of which

△ Virtual reconstruction of houses at Cahokia. Covered by thatched roofs, they were grouped near the city's cult places.

was bounded by a palisade on three sides. About a hundred other tumuli are dispersed throughout the Cahokia archaeological zone.

At Cahokia, some mounds were surmounted by thatched structures that served as residences for the elite, while others were also used as burial places. In the most spectacular tombs, the funerary goods – which are extremely rich – consisted of objects made of bone, carved shell, pottery, stone, copper and mica. The size of the site and the abundance and quality of the offerings demonstrate the prosperity of this North American metropolis, with its focus on grandiose architecture, a funerary cult and large-scale commerce.

Some scholars have perceived Mexican cultural influences in the Mississippian culture. Certain types of ceramics and sculpture were decorated with motifs of seemingly Mexican origin, such as the plumed serpent, known as Quetzalcoatl in Mexico. A hierarchical social structure and the veneration of the sun are also features that developed in both great cultural areas.

Mississippian art is characterized by the presence of numerous painted or incised symbols. The most frequent symbols are those of the cross, the solar disk, the arrow, an eye in the centre of an open hand, the death's head and the bone: all elements that seem to be directly connected with death. The same theme is also illustrated by various scenes painted or carved on artifacts of this culture, such as incised shells, stone axes, masks, pectorals, ceramics and sheets of copper incised or worked in relief. These carry, in different forms, representations of war,

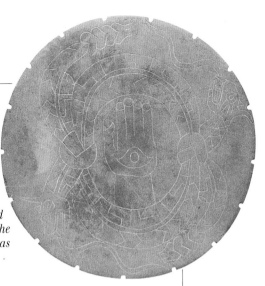

The Temple-platforms of Moundville

Cahokia declined around 1250, but the Mississippian culture continued at Moundville and elsewhere until the fifteenth century. Moundville, which flourished in the fourteenth and fifteenth centuries AD, is situated in present-day Alabama and covers an area of 120 hectares (370 acres). Arranged around a vast central plaza are 20 rectangular or square platform mounds whose heights vary from 7 to 17 m (23 to 56 ft); the largest is estimated to contain 112,000 cu m (3.9 million cu ft) of earth. Some tumuli were used as burial places, but others must have been surmounted by houses intended for the elite. At its peak, the site of Moundville was inhabited by 3,000 people.

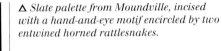

△ *Slate palette from Moundville, incised with a hand-and-eye motif encircled by two entwined horned rattlesnakes.*

trophy-heads and human sacrifices involving decapitation.

At the beginning of the eighteenth century, Europeans discovered the ruins of Cahokia, which had by then been abandoned. The people they found living in the area were the Natchez, who occupied the lands around the modern town that carries their name. Also followers of the solar cult, the Natchez group were the last Native Americans to carry on some of the great traditions of the Mississippian culture that had gone before them.

Bibliography

B. Fagan, *Ancient North America*, 2nd ed. (London and New York, 1995).
M. Coe, D. Snow and E. Benson, *Atlas of Ancient America* (New York, 1986).
R. Silverberg, *Mound Builders of Ancient America* (Greenwich, 1968).

◁ *Virtual reconstruction of the interior of a Mississippian house. It shows the opening in the roof through which the smoke rose from the fire on the centrally positioned hearth.*

Teotihuacan: The City of the Gods

Mexico

*I*n a side valley in the north-east of the Valley of Mexico lies Teotihuacan – the most important site in Mexico and the greatest surviving example of a planned Mesoamerican city. The site (which is still being explored) covers an area of more than 20 sq km (8 sq miles) centred on the Avenue of the Dead. The grid layout of this metropolis, its striking monumental buildings and its wall-paintings, give us an insight into the political and economic lives and religious beliefs of the perhaps 200,000 inhabitants of what, in its heyday around AD 600, must have been the sixth-largest city in the world.

The urban centre of Teotihuacan lies at an altitude of 2,300 m (7,500 ft), some 40 km (25 miles) north-east of the later Aztec capital of Tenochtitlan and of present-day Mexico City. Sitting in the middle of a river plain, its stone architecture is integrated with the surrounding landscape, and the pyramids of the Moon and the Sun echo the shape of the mountains behind.

Teotihuacan had emerged as a major force by about AD 100 and, after the collapse of the rival city of Cuicuilco, dominated the Valley of Mexico until about 750. During this period, Mesoamerican cultural traits and the evolution that had taken place during the pre-Classic era led on to the florescence of a great, formally planned urban centre. Mountains within easy reach of the site provided building materials but the nearby San Juan river and Lake Texcoco played an equally important role in the choice of the site, since the availability of water enabled agriculture to be developed; the Teotihuacanos may have canalized the San Juan river for irrigation purposes. This assured limited but satisfactory resources to feed a population that, between the fourth and seventh centuries, reached about 200,000 people.

As well as being a notable example of a densely populated urban environment, it is also an early example in Mesoamerica of trade and manufacturing ultimately taking precedence over agriculture. Strategically, Teotihuacan's location allowed its trade and influence to be extended from the

◄ *Alabaster funerary mask, 20 cm (8 in.) tall, from Teotihuacan. It dates to the fifth or sixth centuries AD. (Mexico City, National Museum of Anthropology)*

Central Plateau as far as the Gulf Coast and Yucatán and for fruitful commerce to be established between the different groups of the whole Mesoamerican area. Analysis of archaeological material and elements that appear in the wall-paintings show that certain exotic imports (such as *copal*, a resin used for the manufacture of incense, and parrot and *quetzal* feathers) were traded for products made at Teotihuacan, which

◁ *Location map:
Teotihuacan lies about
40 km (25 miles) north-
east of Mexico City in
the Valley of Mexico.*

have been discovered at many other Mesoamerican archaeological sites.

In the settlement complexes of the city – which extended over an area of almost 20 sq km (7¾ sq miles) – nearly 400 workshops have been identified. The objects made here included shell-work, pottery and lapidary work, some of it made of obsidian mined at Otumba and Pachuca. The most famous artifacts are the funerary masks, which are sometimes encrusted with mosaic. The pottery – monochrome, bichrome or trichrome – is characterized by negative-painted curvilinear motifs and small anthropomorphic statuettes with flexible limbs connected to the body by wires. Finds of pottery and lapidary work at other sites indicate that, at its peak (fifth to seventh centuries AD), Teotihuacan was exercising considerable influence over much of Meso-america. Between the seventh and eighth centuries, however, the city's power declined, and it was supplanted culturally by Xochicalco to the south, Cacaxtla and Cholula to the east and Tula to the north. However, the much later centre of Atzcapotzalco, situated in the Valley of Mexico, preserved the traditions of Teotihuacan.

Cultural influences were not limited to the trade in ornaments and utilitarian objects. Pottery inspired by the Teotihuacan style has been found at the sites of Monte Albán and Tajin, but it is in the Maya zone – almost 1,000 km (600 miles) away – that the strongest traces of its cultural influence are found. Although made of local *adobe*, structures A7 and B4 of the site of Kaminaljuyú in Guatemala show the same proportions, the same architectural elements and the same style as those of Teotihuacan. The architecture that was conceived and elaborated in the building of Teotihuacan could be considered as one of the most powerful elements of the city's influence.

Through its forms and proportions – indeed through its very historical origin – it implies the presence of a powerful political system.

The creation of such an original building style and its diffusion over a large part of Mesoamerica presupposes a strong central power endowed with a solid economic base and with builders capable of organizing and executing

in many different buildings at Teotihuacan and became the site's architectural *leitmotif* (and, elsewhere, an indicator of the Teotihuacan state and its emulators during the Classic era). It is a rhythmic component *par excellence*, and the surrounds of open spaces and the platforms of the step-pyramids and temples are all built up from this basic module.

projects on a vast scale. The skill of the builders of Teotihuacan lay in their ability to construct a city of closed buildings in an open urban space that had no natural topographical limits. The key to their success is strikingly expressed in the layout of the site, with its systematic organization and strictly orthogonal and symmetrical grid plan, which seems to have been able to support the growth of the city without upsetting its day-to-day rhythm.

The builders' basic architectural element was the *talud-tablero*, an alternation on vertical surfaces of a panel with a sloping batter (*talud*) and a vertical panel (*tablero*) set between projecting cornices. Being both repetitive and variable, the *talud-tablero* was used

△▽ Below: *Temple decoration at Teotihuacan depicting the head of the plumed serpent.* Above: *Reconstruction of the same decoration in its original colours.*

◁ *Virtual reconstruction of the centre of Teotihuacan in its heyday, between the fifth and seventh centuries AD: (1) Pyramid of Quetzalcoatl; (2) Ciudadela (citadel); (3) Avenue of the Dead; (4) Palace of the Four Temples; (5) Pyramid of the Sun; (6) Pyramid of the Moon; (7) Palace of Quetzalpapalotl; (8) Palace of the Jaguars.*

Chronological Phases of the Site of
Teotihuacan

Patlachique period (proto- Classic Cuicuilco V)	100 BC–AD 0
Tzacualli period:	AD 0–150
Miccaotli period:	150–250
Tlamimilolpa period:	250–450
Xolalpan period:	450–650
Metepec period:	650–750

▽ *Aerial view of the Pyramid of the Moon, the palace of
Quetzalpapalotl (foreground) and other small
pyramids. Located at one end of the Avenue of the
Dead, which crosses the whole of the site, the Pyramid
of the Moon is lower than the Pyramid of the Sun and is
composed of four main levels; its summit is reached via
a central stairway.*

Always built in the same way, the *talud-tablero* was used to face the sloping mass of stone and lava rubble that formed the core of the building. On this slope, which was angled at 45–50° (which corresponds to the incline of a natural talus or scree slope), horizontal panels of local volcanic material were set on top of miniature vertical walls that projected at regular intervals. Superimposed bands of *talud* and *tablero* were infinitely repeated to create stepped buildings with two, three and four, or more, stages. The resultant alternation of sloping, vertical and horizontal surfaces – receding in upward echelon – created a play of light and shade over the surface of the building that accentuated its contours and enhanced its aesthetic effect. The structures, which today blend in closely with the surrounding grey volcanic landscape, were then completed by decorating them with sculptures covered with a thin layer of stucco and painted in various colours, among which red and green predominated.

The monumental proportions of Teotihuacan's cult installations suggest that religion must have played a large part in the city's life. The principal religious buildings were the Pyramid of the Sun and the Pyramid of the Moon –

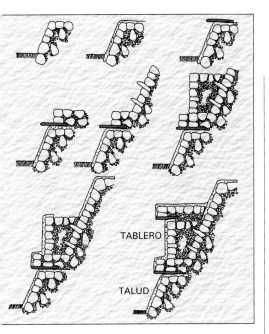

△ *Successive stages in the building of a section of a* talud-tablero *pyramid. This technique, which appears on numerous Classic-period buildings at Teotihuacan, Chichén Itzá and elsewhere, can serve as a chronological marker. The* talud *is the oblique surface that sits below the vertical* tablero, *which has horizontal cornices above and below. The vertical alternation of these two elements helps to determine the characteristic stepped profile of the pyramid.*

the former measuring 225 × 222 m (738 × 728 ft) at its base and 65 m (213 ft) in height. In ancient times these pyramids were surmounted by temples, of which no traces remain. They flank part of the city's main axis – the Avenue of the Dead, 40 m (130 ft) wide and 2 km (1¼ miles) long – which led from the Pyramid of the Moon; past the Pyramid of the Sun to the vast plaza of the *Ciudadela* (citadel) and beyond.

The restored Palace of Quetzalpapalotl, next to the Pyramid of the Moon, has columns around the courtyard that feature painted bas-reliefs of owls and *quetzals*. Many palaces and temples at Teotihuacan were decorated with frescoes made with lime and natural pigments, a great number of which have been discovered and repaired in recent years. Through their clear pictorial language, these frescoes reveal

the gods of Teotihuacan and the ordered world they governed.

Particularly prevalent are images of the War Serpent, Tlaloc (the rain god), Quetzalcoatl (the plumed serpent), a netted jaguar and, above all, the Great Goddess, a female deity of fertility, war and divination (the largest single sculpture yet discovered at Teotihuacan honours her cult). Another important cult focused on Quetzalcoatl and the War Serpent, to whom the great *Ciudadela* structures were dedicated. Undulating over the exterior of the Temple of Quetzalcoatl plumed serpents (*quetzal coatl*) bearing the War Serpent headdress on their tails proclaim war, sacrifice and victory as the building's purpose.

In Aztec thought of later centuries Teotihuacan, the 'city of the gods', was known as the place where the sun and the moon were created. These were regarded as complementary energies and vital to the sedentary agricultural peoples of Mexico. The myth tells that two divinities were elected: one, Tecuciztecatl, had to be transformed into the sun to shine upon the world; and the second, Nanahuatzin, who was crippled and disfigured with running sores, was more modest and was to become the moon. However, before the brazier into which he had to throw himself, Tecuciztecatl lost his courage. Nanahuatzin, who then showed himself the more valiant by throwing himself first into the flames, was therefore transformed into the sun, whereas Tecuciztecatl became the moon.

Everything in Teotihuacan indicates the importance of maintaining and reinforcing the memory of traditions and history. The monumentality of the site, its architectural grandeur and its geometry confirm that coherence and equilibrium were important for this culture – one which had the capacity to think in terms of the past, present and future dimensions of the world, and to express this in an architecture that was, at the same time, both rational and religious.

▷ *Fragment of a wall painting from Teotihuacan, dating to the fifth to seventh centuries* AD. *Rich adornment indicates the social prestige of the warrior depicted.*

Bibliography

K. Berrin and E. Pasztory (eds), *Teotihuacan: Art from the City of the Gods* (London and New York, 1993).

M. Coe, *Mexico: From the Olmecs to the Aztecs*, 4th ed. (London and New York, 1994).

M. Coe, D. Snow and E. Benson, *Atlas of Ancient America* (New York, 1986).

E. Matos Moctezuma, *Teotihuacan: The City of the Gods* (New York, 1990).

A.G. Miller, *The Mural Painting of Teotihuacan* (Washington, 1973).

M. Miller, *The Art of Mesoamerica*, 2nd ed. (London and New York, 1996).

M. Miller and K. Taube, *The Gods and Symbols of Ancient Mexico and the Maya: An Illustrated Dictionary* (London and New York, 1993).

R. Miller, *Urbanization at Teotihuacan*, vol I, *The Teotihuacan Map* (Austin, 1973).

Tikal: A Jungle Metropolis

Guatemala

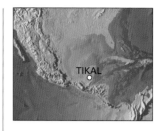

◁ *Location map: Tikal lies in the Petén lowlands of norther Guatemala, which extend northwards into Mexico's Yucatán peninsula.*

*T*he great Maya city of Tikal, in the Petén region of northern Guatemala, flourished during the Classic period (AD 250–900). Like Teotihuacan in the Valley of Mexico, this city of the tropical lowlands had a dense urban population, perhaps reaching 50,000–90,000 at its height. A true city-state, it is distinctive for its major building complexes, linked by causeways, and six massive temple-pyramids that dominate the urban landscape. Its buildings, which extend over an area of 16 sq km (6 sq miles), make it the grandest of all Maya cities and one of the largest in the whole of pre-Columbian America.

Although it was first discovered in the eighteenth century, Tikal did not become well known to the outside world until the late nineteenth century, when Gustave Bernoulli took the carved wooden lintels of Temple IV to Basel. Even though its scope became clearer in the early twentieth century, and many of its unusual monuments were brought to light, Tikal escaped careful exploration until the middle of the century, when William Coe and the University of Pennsylvania carried out a decade-long excavation. What has long been clear to investigators, however, is that Tikal was one of the earliest of the Classic Maya cities and one of the last to go into decline – making it one of the longest-lived, as well as the most massive.

Tikal may have derived an early benefit from its location. Natural resources were abundant and the site's surroundings were well suited to intensive agriculture. The cultivators exploited the topography and water resources of the area by establishing a system of terraces on the slopes and by exploiting the swampy *bajos* – low-lying areas regularly flooded by the seasonal rains. Eventually Tikal farmers were cultivating crops of both maize and *ramon* (an edible soft nut), some of which they may have stored in *chultunes*: masonry-lined cavities that were dug out of the bedrock. Later on, the city may have benefited from the suitability of its location for developing long-distance trade routes.

Whatever the causes of its early success, Tikal was certainly effective in manipulating the political environment in the Petén. For centuries it dominated less powerful city states of the region. Ultimately, though, others sought to curb the power of Tikal, and the city was weakened. Eventually it shared in the collapse of civilization in the central and southern Maya areas and by the tenth century AD had probably been largely abandoned.

The chronology of the site extends from AD 292 to 869, according to dates revealed on numerous stone stelae, and the peak of the metropolis dates to

◁△ *Plan and virtual reconstruction of Tikal: (1) Great Plaza; (2) North Acropolis; (3) Central Acropolis; (4) Temple I; (5) Temple II; (6) Temple III; (7) Temple IV; (8) Temple V; (9) South Acropolis; (10) Square of the Seven Temples; (11) group G; (12) group II; (13) Temple of the Inscriptions.*

between the seventh and eighth centuries. Different inscriptions on the stelae designate the kings by such names as 'Jaguar's Paw', 'Curl Nose' or 'Stormy Sky'.

In the fourth and fifth centuries, influences from central Mexico – particularly from the Valley of Mexico – are evident. Certain central Mexican gods, such as the rain god Tlaloc, feature on Tikal stelae, and a black incised vessel depicts both central Mexican and Maya lords, as well as temples characteristic of the two different locations.

◁ Jade pectoral from Tikal. The main figure, wearing a complex headdress, sits on a throne and seems to be turning towards the small figure on the left. Jade was the most precious type of stone in Maya civilization and was a symbol of abundance and fertility.

its quadrants, linking together what would otherwise have been separated settlements.

The architectural horizontality and verticality of Tikal are perfectly proportioned, since the extensive surfaces translates the shape of the walls or pillars right up to the roof ridge. Both functional and symbolic, it is based on and symbolically represents the form of the traditional Maya hut, made of perishable materials, which is frequently depicted in carvings. Tech-

△ *The archaeological remains of the site are now scattered through the tropical rainforest. Many buildings had to be freed from the encroaching vegetation before investigations could begin.*

correspond to the dizzy heights of the pyramids of the Great Plaza, which rise in some cases to 70 m (230 ft) in height. A key element in these buildings is the corbelled vault, which extends and

nically, the corbelled vault involves building out over a corridor or gallery with slightly projecting courses of squared stone, each course projecting more than the one below, until a single

The archaeological zone of Tikal today comprises thousands of buildings and nearly fifty carved stone stelae. The buildings are mainly concentrated towards the centre of the city and follow no orthogonal grid plan; instead they cluster together in groups, their density diminishing as their distance from the Great Plaza increases. The urban web of Tikal was therefore much more dispersed than that of Teotihuacan. Nonetheless, the size of the city necessitated some means of movement and communication throughout the zone, and of ensuring the cohesion of the city and its inhabitants, and huge stone causeways (or *sacbeob*) connected

▷ *Virtual reconstruction of Tikal, showing the city without its present-day rainforest surroundings. Rainwater from the forest was at one time collected in reservoirs.*

course of capstones can link the two sides. The external profile of the roof often follows the interior shape of the corbel, giving the hipped or mansard profile that reproduced in stone the shape of the thatched roof of the Maya hut. The corbelled roof, often reinforced by cross-ties, serves to identify and

△ *Detail of a Maya pot depicting a figure wearing an elaborate headdress, seen in profile. The Maya used pottery in daily life and in cult practices, and deposited it as offerings in burials. Painted and incised, the pottery is frequently adorned with anthropomorphic, zoomorphic and mythical figures.*

unify the architecture of the Maya area, being found in the cities of the Usumacinta valley (e.g. Bonampak, Yaxchilán, Palenque), and those to the north (e.g. Uxmal, Chichén Itzá, Kabah, Sayil) and south (e.g. Copán).

Maya temples – which were often exercises in mass (the great elevations of the pyramids, rising through up to nine levels) and space (the small temples at the top) – were often crowned with roof-combs, perhaps to proclaim the particular cult or family to which the temple was dedicated. As an extension of an already tall pyramid, this gave a powerful 'skyscraper' profile to Maya buildings. At Tikal the roof-combs seem to express an almost obsessive aspiration for height, and they project above the forest canopy – making them both orientation points

over considerable distances and possibly even sites for long-distance signalling.

Many Maya pyramids cover earlier buildings, and almost all include rubble from previous structures, but the tall free-standing pyramids at Tikal were almost all built directly on to bedrock, and some – like the famous Temple I – protected rich tombs built in their bases.

In contrast to the monumental buildings, the palaces were only built on one, two or three levels, and so were lower. Grouped in complexes, they were composed of long and narrow rooms arranged in groups that received only a weak light through a few small openings. Thick masonry walls supported the corbelling. The royal family lived in the Central Acropolis, and, as time went on, lesser nobles built smaller palaces away from the heart of the city.

At the North Acropolis the Early Classic-period kings found their final resting places. Consisting of more than a hundred buildings from the second century BC, the North Acropolis was also the final repository of many carved monuments, set in front of the ancient tombs. Inside one temple archaeologists found Burial 48, a tomb unusual for its elaborate paintings of the fifth century AD. Underneath Structure 34, Burial 10

probably housed the remains of 'Curl Nose', an early fifth-century king of Tikal.

Stelae lined the Plaza side of the North Acropolis, and some plain ones may once have been stuccoed or painted. Set up from AD 292 to 869, they show a remarkably homogeneous imagery that testifies to the powerful role of tradition at Tikal. The central scene features a standing lord – usually a Tikal king – and texts alongside relate his names and deeds. Elaborate head-dresses, sophisticated clothes and rich paraphernalia indicate status, lineage and divine associations. Some stelae included caches at their bases, often including the so-called eccentric flints, as well as other materials precious to the Maya.

The Maya at Tikal must have lived well, observing and attending to celestial phenomena, observing ritual practices and visiting sweat baths. The political structure included lesser lords, or governors, who kept the social order and who supported the king in times of stress. As the first millennium wore on,

▽ *The impressive Temple II at Tikal is basically composed of three elements: the pyramidal base, the temple and the roof-comb. Three setbacks form the base. The temple appears to have been dedicated to the wife of Ruler A; she is featured on a wooden lintel once in place on the monument.*

however, such times of stress became increasingly frequent throughout the Maya area, and by the tenth century most of Tikal had probably been abandoned. A variety of ideas as to the cause of the decline have been suggested – including overpopulation, earthquake, climatic change, epidemic and revolution – but most archaeologists suspect that there was no single reason for Tikal's tragic end, and a combination of several causes seems the most likely explanation.

Bibliography

C. Baudez and S. Picasso, *Lost Cities of the Maya* (London and New York, 1992).

M. Coe, *The Maya*, 5th ed. (London and New York, 1993).

M. Coe, D. Snow and E. Benson, *Atlas of Ancient America* (New York, 1986).

M. Miller, *The Art of Mesoamerica: From Olmec to Aztec*, 2nd ed. (London and New York, 1996).

L. Schele and D.A. Freidel, *A Forest of Kings: The Untold Story of the Ancient Maya* (New York, 1990).

△▷ Above: *The North Acropolis complex, where many Early Classic kings of Tikal were buried, with carved stelae ranged in front of it.* Right: *Temple I rises on a nine-level pyramid, perhaps reflecting the nine levels of the Maya underworld.*

Palenque and the Mysterious Pyramid

Mexico

At Palenque in the dense forest of the Sierra de Chiapas, the furthest west of all major Maya sites, an intact burial chamber was found in 1952 in the foundations of the famous 'Temple of the Inscriptions'. Here Pakal, the city's greatest ruler, was buried with a rich assemblage of grave goods in a stone sarcophagus that was covered by a great slab carved with an image of the king falling into the open jaws of the underworld. At Palenque, too, Maya architecture was adapted to local conditions and achieved a lightness and space that is seldom to be found elsewhere.

Dense, humid rainforest surrounds the site, and the high rainfall supports its lush, tropical canopy. The ancient architects made use of the rainfall and the topography of the site by channelling the Otulum river into an aqueduct that divided the city, and they used the natural elevations of hills and mounds to raise the buildings. Today, 250 years after the site was rediscovered, archaeologists and art historians have managed to piece together some of the history of the kings who ruled the city, and for whom those architects worked.

△ *Aerial view of the Temple of the Inscriptions and the Royal Palace at Palenque, showing the tropical vegetation that surrounds the site.*

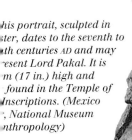

...his portrait, sculpted in ...ster, dates to the seventh to ...th centuries AD and may ...resent Lord Pakal. It is ...m (17 in.) high and ... found in the Temple of ...nscriptions. (Mexico ..., National Museum ...nthropology)

magnificent 'Egyptian statues'. However, the development of photography and its use in recording archaeological sites in the later nineteenth century began to make more objective images available.

The role and function of Palenque, which dominates the countryside as far as the sea, are still difficult to determine. Its general layout is similar to that of other Maya metropolises, however, and its architecture recalls numerous elements from other sites. One unusual feature is

▷ *Location map: Palenque lies in the rainforest of the Sierra de Chiapas in south-eastern Mexico.*

PALENQUE

the Royal Palace. Built on a mound 10 m (33 ft) high, it is 100 m (330 ft) long and 80 m (260 ft) wide and has internal courtyards and open galleries on all four sides. Its external façades are decorated with figural scenes modelled in stucco. Dominating this complex is

Kinich Hanab Pakal ('Sun-faced Shield') came to the throne in AD 615 and died in 692. His son Kan-Balam II succeeded him, to be followed in turn by Kan Hok Chitam II, his younger brother. After him, there were three more rulers, and the last recorded accession dates relate to Kuk Balam II and 6-Kimi Hanab Pakal in 764 and 799 respectively. The chronology of the site therefore extends from the seventh to the ninth centuries AD.

After Palenque was first discovered by the Spanish priest Antonio de Solís in 1746, a number of soldiers, scholars and adventurers were associated with its history, among them Guillermo Dupaix, Juan Galindo, Lord Kingsborough, John L. Stephens, Abbé Brasseur, Désiré Charnay and Alfred Maudslay. Count Waldeck arrived in 1832 and lived among the ruins for over a year, straightening the stelae and cleaning the temples and reliefs. His drawings show that it was difficult for him to be totally objective about the origins of the city, and in 1838 he published a drawing of a building that he called the 'Pyramid of the Fortune-teller' flanked by four

▷ *General plan of the site: (1) Temple of the Inscriptions; (2) Royal Palace; (3) Temple of the Sun; (4) Temple of the Cross; (5) Temple of the Foliated Cross; (6) Temple of the Beau Relief; (7) Ball-court; (8) Temple of the Count; (9) north group. Other structures are indicated by Roman numerals.*

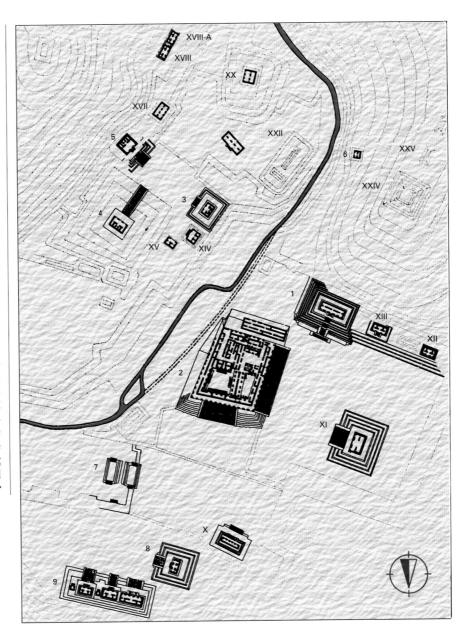

one of the last elements to be built, the four-storey tower (an unusual feature in Maya architecture) from which stargazers may have observed the heavens, or guards surveyed the almost

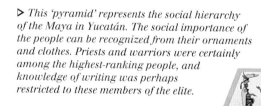

▷ *This 'pyramid' represents the social hierarchy of the Maya in Yucatán. The social importance of the people can be recognized from their ornaments and clothes. Priests and warriors were certainly among the highest-ranking people, and knowledge of writing was perhaps restricted to these members of the elite.*

flat land stretching away to the Gulf of Mexico.

The dimensions of Palenque's architecture have always appealed to modern observers. The temples are grand but the scale remains human and approachable, and smaller interspersed temples seem to form a unity with the landscape. Architecture at Palenque seems to be dedicated to interior space – rather than external mass, as at other sites. This space was achieved partly through innovative vaulting techniques and also by lightening the roof-

△ Left: *The crypt of the Pyramid of the Inscriptions.* Right: *Rubbing (made by Merle Green Robertson in the 1970s) of the relief on the huge stone slab that covered Pakal's sarcophagus.*

combs; ponderous elsewhere, at Palenque they become light webs that support the images of kings and gods. Equally striking is the integration of bas-relief sculpture and writing. (Only one free-standing stela has survived from the site, and stucco ornament was apparently the rule.) Soft, wet stucco was applied to a stone armature, shaped and then painted in a bright palette of red, blue, green and yellow. Set under cornices, or inside buildings, the stuccoes have survived surprisingly well.

The Maya Calendar

Two of the 800 known signs Maya hieroglyphic writing. The Maya combined three different cycles: the 'solar cycle' of 365 days, the divinatory cycle' of 260 days, and a 'great cycle' of 52 years.

The dates on the inscriptions at Palenque refer to the divinatory, or ritual, year of 260 days (tzolkin), *made up of 13 months* (uinal), *each of 20 days* (kin).

Days	
1	imix
2	ik
3	akbal
4	kan
5	chicchan
6	cimi
7	manik
8	lamat
9	muluc
10	oc
11	chuen
12	eb
13	ben
14	ix
15	men
16	cib
17	caban
18	etznab
19	cauac
20	ahau

The courtly sculpture of Palenque has often made students of the Maya suspect that this was a city dedicated to the arts, to astronomy and writing. Just like any Maya city, though, Palenque engaged in warfare with its neighbours. All the same, it does have a compelling and individual style that lasted for almost two centuries. Distinct from that of Tikal, it is perhaps the most lyrical of Maya architectural styles.

At the end of the seventh century King Kan Balam built three unusual temples: those of the Cross, the Foliated Cross and the Sun. Decorated inside and out with elaborate stuccoes, they derive their names from the huge limestone reliefs in their internal

△ *The Maya corbelled vault is formed by two walls that are gradually extended inwards until they meet; horizontal slabs of stone then seal over the join.*

shrines: a Maya World Tree in the Temple of the Cross; the Night Sun, the jaguar god of the underworld, in the Temple of the Sun; and a great stylized maize plant in the Temple of the Foliated Cross. The Cross group of temples was lightened and unified by the use of stylized, openwork roof-combs and a cross-corbelled construction that stabilized the buildings.

The Temple of the Inscriptions, which is 21 m (70 ft) high, dominates the heart of Palenque. The building takes its name from the extraordinary texts

△ *Maya glyphs carved on limestone steps at Palenque. Maya writing used a mixed logographic and syllabic system in the form of glyphs arranged in registers or columns. Great progress has been made in deciphering these glyphs over the last two decades.*

Maya Dress

The reliefs and sculptures at Palenque tell us about the different Maya costumes and ornaments. Cotton was widely used to make clothes. Once harvested, it was spun with weighted terracotta spindles, then woven on wooden looms, and finally dyed with vegetable extracts. The goddess Ixchel governed the work of the weavers and protected them, and there is a depiction in the Madrid Codex (Codex Tro-Cortesianus) that shows her weaving on a loom of the type still used today by the Indians in the Maya area.

In Maya pictorial art, the men generally wear a cotton loin-cloth (called ex by the Maya) with the ends decorated with feathers of various colours; this garment had been used as far back as the pre-Classic period by the Olmecs and was to remain in favour until the arrival of the Spanish in the sixteenth century. Men also wear tunics and jerkins, with the more elaborate costumes reserved for the elite. Over a long skirt women mainly wear a dress or blouse, frequently with fancy woven designs – many of them akin to those worn by Maya women today and known as the huipil. Noblemen often wear a short hip-cloth or kilt. Long capes are worn by visiting nobles and short ones are worn in battle. Necklaces and pectorals are also worn.

Headdresses of simple form appear both in paintings and on Maya ceramics, often worn by musicians or servants. They include tiaras and diadems, or simply stiff, straight hair. Some headdresses, however, were particularly elaborate and would have reflected the degree of power, the function and the rank of the individuals wearing them. Many headdresses consisted of masks supported on frameworks of rushes or wood and decorated with textiles, layers of jade, and so on. They were generally surmounted by long feathers from the quetzal, a small bird that was highly prized in Mesoamerica. Innumerable forms of sceptre or 'ceremonial baton' are depicted, and these, like the headdresses, must have indicated the rank of the individual.

The most elaborate headdresses are inseparable from the very particular Maya skull shape, with its receding forehead. This was a deliberate deformation, induced from a very young age by wearing two pieces of wood strapped to the head, so as to impart the desired shape to the child's growing cranium. Body painting was also practised in the Maya world, and Jacques Soustelle claims that the priests of Yucatán painted their bodies blue.

The Maya wore many different varieties of sandals; Sylvanus Morley detected at least twelve types. The sandal was generally attached to the foot by means of straps that passed between the toes and were decorated with a knot. The heel was held and protected by means of a decorated heel-piece that rose up to the ankle.

Jewels, which appear in abundance, both in pictorial representations and in Pakal's crypt at Palenque, were general. composed of beads and sheets jade. This stone, collected Mexico, was a symbol of fertili which the Maya associated wit water. Jade, tun in the Maya language, was used for the man facture of beads, 'ear ornaments rings, pendants and mosaic Materials such as jadeite, serpen ine, diorite, amazonite, onya calcite, turquoise and shell wer also used.

△▷ *Top:* Detail of a wall-painting in Room 2, Structure 1, at the Maya city of Bonampak, dated to AD 792. Ruler Chaan-muan presides over captives. *Right:* Maya lords in Room 2.

inscribed on three limestone tablets set into the wall of an interior chamber. Today, however, it is best known for the secret it kept hidden until 1952: the burial chamber and stone sarcophagus of King Pakal. Reached from a rear chamber of the temple by an internal staircase that leads down through the core of the pyramid, the crypt lies 25 m (82 ft) from the top, or 4 m (13 ft) below the level of the plaza in front of the pyramid.

Covered in cinnabar and weighted down with jade (including a jade mosaic mask), King Pakal had the most sumptuous assemblage of grave goods to accompany him into the underworld that has yet been discovered in a Maya burial. His sarcophagus had an elaborate image carved on the upper surface of its lid, showing Pakal's descent into the jaws of the underworld, and all four of its sides carried depictions of ancestors. One anomalous feature of the crypt is the so-called 'psychoduct', or soul tube, connecting it to the outside air at the pyramid's summit.

△ *Images from a virtual reconstruction of the Throne Room of the Royal Palace at Palenque. The medallion shows two figures, with a twin-headed jaguar below the main figure. This was located above the throne, which was decorated with sculpted figures. The drawing* (bottom left) *was made by Merle Green Robertson.*

Bibliography

C. Baudez and S. Picasso, *Lost Cities of the Maya* (London and New York, 1992).

M. Coe, *The Maya*, 5th ed. (London and New York, 1993).

M. Coe, D. Snow and E. Benson, *Atlas of Ancient America* (New York, 1986).

M. Miller, *The Art of Mesoamerica: From Olmec to Aztec*, 2nd ed. (London and New York, 1996).

L. Schele and D.A. Freidel, *A Forest of Kings: The Untold Story of the Ancient Maya* (New York, 1990).

257

Copán: City of Art

Honduras

*T*he city of Copán lies at the south-eastern edge of the Maya zone, in Honduras. It is famous for its ballcourt, decorated with stone macaw heads and used for the ritual ball game, for its Hieroglyphic Stairway, with sixty-three steps and 2,500 glyphs, and for its relief sculptures. The last are perfectly blended into the architecture of the city. Here, as at other Maya cities, an individual style was developed that was original and yet at the same time retained or adapted models that were widespread in Mesoamerica.

△ *Maya civilization is famous for the splendour of it sculptures. This fleshless stone head represents the Maya god of the underworld.*

Like Teotihuacan and Palenque, Copán rose to prominence in the Classic period, flourishing from the fifth to the ninth centuries AD. Built on the banks of the River Copán, a tributary of the Motagua, it lies about 30 m (100 ft) above the meandering river on a vast artificial terrace made up of almost 1 million cu m (35 million cu ft) of earth. It was the largest city in the south-east of the Maya area and covers 40 hectares (100 acres), with the Central Acropolis, Ballcourt and Hieroglyphic Stairway at its heart. As time went on, some of the nobles built smaller, rival complexes on sites that lay further away from the site's core.

At Copán, almost all architecture was sculptural, and sculptors and builders worked together, using a volcanic tuff that was soft when quarried but later hardened to resist weather and time. Every important building was decorated with sculpture in both low and high relief, and the Great Plaza included many free-standing stelae and monolithic altars. Some of the altars took the form of enormous mythological animals, many of which featured in the Maya calendar or in the underworld.

These include snakes, saurians and excarnated (defleshed) figures: symbolic elements that related to the underworld. These sculptures show a very neat contrast in style, which veers between overstatement and understatement, particularly in representing figures, which are remarkable for the purity and serenity of their features.

Like all the Maya aristocracy, the lords of Copán kept an eye trained on the stars – though scholars now know that Copán was no more specifically an observatory than Palenque was. Starwatching was an important business, nevertheless, and the Maya often timed important political or economic events to coincide with auspicious movements in the heavens.

▽ *Virtual reconstruction of the centre of the city of Copán: (1) Eastern Plaza; (2) Temple 16;*
(3) Acropolis, comprising the Temple of the Inscriptions and Temples 16 and 11; (4) Western Plaza;
(5) Temple 11; (6) Hieroglyphic Stairway; (7) Courtyard of the Hieroglyphic Stairway; (8) stele;
(9) Northern Plaza; (10) Great Plaza; (11) Ballcourt; (12) Temple of the Inscriptions.

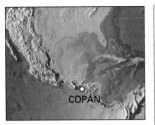

*Location map:
Copán lies in western
Honduras, in the
Cordillera del
Merendon, a few
kilometres from the
Guatemalan frontier.*

Maya religion and mythology

According to Mesoamerican thought in general, the universe had been annihilated and restored several times. Each time, humanity returned to the surface of the earth – which was generally perceived as a rounded, uneven surface, probably the back of a turtle.

No single and unified set of beliefs prevailed among the Maya, but in at least one version the sun and the moon were understood to be a married couple, vulnerable to human emotions, including jealousy and envy. The unfaithful (female) moon was caught *in flagrante delicto* by the sun, who hid under a deer-skin to sneak up on her, and thereafter the moon was forever dimmed. According to the *Popol Vuh* – the most authoritative surviving text of Maya beliefs, discovered among the Quiché Maya in the nineteenth century – the sun and moon (or perhaps the sun and Venus) were embodied by a pair of hero twins, Hunahpu and Xbalanqué, who conquered the world of death, Xibalba. Unlike the Venus of the Old World, who presided over erotic love, the Maya Venus guided the Maya to war. Many gods dwelt in the underworld and those that did were the source of decay and disease. Representations of them often feature visible rot and skeletonized features.

In Maya religion, as in almost all Mesoamerican religions, maize plays an important role, as the staff of life. According to the *Popol Vuh*, the old creator gods fashioned humankind from maize dough, in the same way that tortillas are made today.

▽ *One side of the Ballcourt, which was used for the ball game, is situated among the religious buildings. The ball game was more a ritual act than a sport.*

Bibliography

C. Baudez and S. Picasso, *Lost Cities of the Maya* (London and New York, 1992).

M. Coe, *The Maya*, 5th ed. (London and New York, 1993).

M. Coe, D. Snow and E. Benson, *Atlas of Ancient America* (New York, 1986).

W.L. Fash, *Scribes, Warriors and Kings: The City of Copán and the Ancient Maya* (London and New York, 1991).

M. Miller, *The Art of Mesoamerica: From Olmec to Aztec*, 2nd ed. (London and New York, 1996).

L. Schele and D.A. Freidel, *A Forest of Kings: The Untold Story of the Ancient Maya* (New York, 1990).

◀ *The most common iconographic themes in the monumental sculpture of Copán are anthropomorphic and zoomorphic. This picture shows a stela, one of thirty-eight found at the site.*

The Discovery of Tenochtitlan's Great Temple

Mexico

*D*uring a five-year excavation campaign in modern Mexico City, archaeologists have revealed the centrepiece of the Aztec capital Tenochtitlan: the Templo Mayor, or Great Temple. Its twin shrines to Huitzilopochtli and Tlaloc, the gods of the sun and of rain – were uncovered for the first time since the sixteenth century, when the Spanish conquerors destroyed it and built over the site in an effort to stamp out the Aztecs' pantheistic religion.

In 1521 the Spanish razed the buildings and temples of Tenochtitlan to the ground, re-using the materials to erect the first buildings of the colonial era. This destruction was loaded with significance: not only did it bring about the disappearance of one of the greatest pre-Hispanic civilizations, it also marked the start of a campaign of religious destruction and oppression designed to eradicate the memory of the old religion and impose Christianity in its place.

On 13 August 1790 the sculpture of the earth goddess Coatlicue (mother of

▽▷ Below: *Map of Tenochtitlan and the Gulf of Mexico – a hand-coloured woodcut from* Praeclara de Nova maris oceani Hyspania narratio *(Nuremberg, 1524).* Right: *A detail of the central square with a depiction of the Templo Mayor and the* Tzompantli, *with a legend stressing the human sacrifice and decapitation that took place there.*

Huitzilopochtli and Coyolxauhqui) was found under the patio of the old university, near the cathedral. It had been deliberately buried on the orders of the clergy, to prevent the indigenous people of Mexico seeing this symbol of their past culture. It was promptly reburied. A few months later a huge carved stone disc came to light, and this time the authorities decided to preserve the 'calendar stone' in the atrium of the cathedral of Mexico. These initial finds revived a collective memory, and from then on an awareness of the pre-Hispanic past became one strand in the growth of Mexican nationalism that would ultimately lead to the country reclaiming its independence from Spain.

In 1898 more archaeological traces of the Aztec capital emerged when engin-

eers were laying a sewer near the Cathedral, and in the twentieth century the building of a subway system throughout Mexico City led to the discovery of objects, temples and domestic dwellings. Subsequently, on 21 February 1978, the huge sculpture of the goddess Coyolxauhqui was uncovered during the laying of electric cables, right on the edge of what we now know to be the site of the Templo Mayor, or Great Temple, of Tenochtitlan.

The 1978 find, in particular, confirmed the importance of the site and the need for it to be excavated. There were, however, two limitations. The first was the marshy nature of the subsoil in the excavation area, which did not permit particularly deep

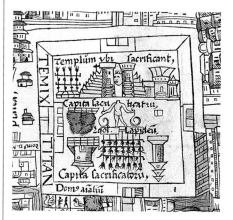

soundings because of the high water-table – the ancient city had been an island – and the consequent threat of flooding. The second was the fact that the site was already built over; Spanish religious buildings and the central car park constituted the major impediments. Nonetheless, the archaeologist Eduardo Matos Moctezuma succeeded in persuading the authorities to clear the excavation area.

The site was to prove rich, but what made the project so stimulating was the opportunity to use and validate ethnohistoric data in archaeological research. There were accounts by contemporary Spanish clerics and *conquistadores* (including Bernardino de Sahagún, Hernán Cortés, Bernal Díaz del Castillo, Toribio de

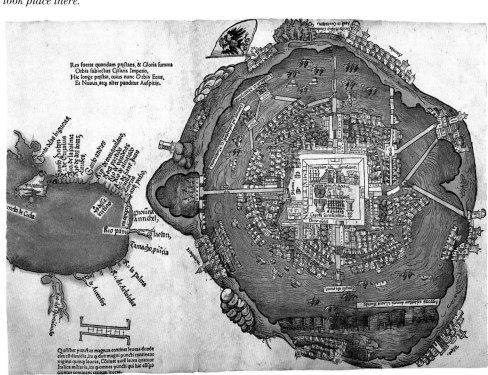

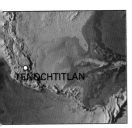

◁ *Location map: Now buried under Mexico City, the Aztec capital of Tenochtitlan lay on an island in Lake Texcoco in the Valley of Mexico.*

zone into three main sectors, installing a restoration workshop, and profiting from multi-disciplinary collaboration between chemists, biologists, designers, photographers and geologists, this programme was successfully completed.

The present-day appearance of the site of the Templo Mayor is created by superimposed stairways belonging to the temple's different building phases. The main façade faced west, and the complex stood on a vast platform on top of a pyramid of four steps. Two stairways led to the upper level, where there were two sanctuaries: that of Huitzilopochtli, the Aztec tutelary deity and warrior, on the south; and that of Tlaloc, the rain god, on the north.

The temple had been enlarged six times, each phase corresponding to a historical period. The first phase is represented by the remains of material that have deteriorated too much to be reconstituted. The dating becomes precise from phase II, which includes

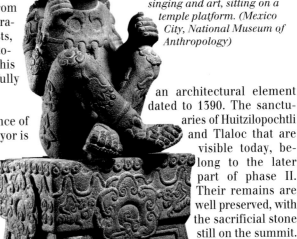

◁ *Basalt sculpture representing Xochipilli, the god of love, dancing, singing and art, sitting on a temple platform. (Mexico City, National Museum of Anthropology)*

Torquemada and Diego Durán) who had seen the principal temples or recorded elaborate details of Aztec life. In addition, the indigenous chroniclers Tezozómoc, Ixtilxochitl and Chimalpahín also provide precious data about the old Aztec city. Here was a chance to test the connections that could be established between archaeology and ethnohistory, and – in the case of the Spanish documents – to check the usefulness of the European chroniclers' observations and analysis of Aztec history. To the delight of the researchers, this comparison has produced excellent results.

Eduardo Matos Moctezuma was able to set up a research programme divided into three phases: assembling all the documentation and conducting stratigraphic excavations, begun in March 1978 and ended in November 1982; studying and interpreting the resulting material; and displaying the results, the objects and the site to the public. By means of dividing the archaeological

an architectural element dated to 1390. The sanctuaries of Huitzilopochtli and Tlaloc that are visible today, belong to the later part of phase II. Their remains are well preserved, with the sacrificial stone still on the summit. Eight anthropomorphic stone sculptures of standard-bearers and the glyph '4 rush', which corresponds to the year 1431, were found on the stairs of the part of the temple that belongs to phase III.

Phase IV produced a number of braziers and several very well-preserved stone serpent heads. Phase IVB corresponds to the enlargement of the west face of the large platform on which the Templo Mayor stands. It is decorated with undulating serpents and also includes a small altar flanked by two frogs sitting on cubes of stone. Eduardo Matos Moctezuma thinks that phase IV corresponds to the reign of Moctezuma I (1440–69). The glyph '1 rabbit', found on a structure at the rear, is equivalent to the year 1454, and the glyph '3 house', incised on the south side of the platform, corresponds to 1469, the year of his death.

From phase V a stucco-covered platform and an area of paving survive. Phase VI walls carry the heads of serpents, and phase VII yielded a masonry-faced platform.

A variety of archaeological finds, both in portable offering-boxes and in pits, were discovered in the filling material of the various construction phases. Many items of organic material were found, together with pottery and

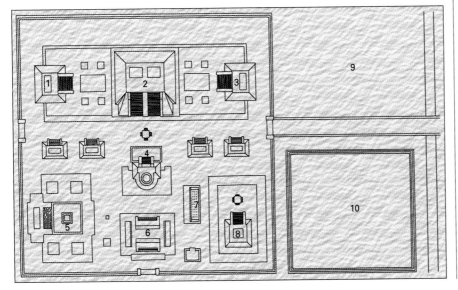

△ *Plan of the ceremonial centre of Tenochtitlan: (1) Temple; (2) Templo Mayor; (3) Temple of Tezcatlipoca; (4) Temple of Quetzalcoatl; (5) priests' quarters; (6) Ballcourt; (7) Tzompantli (skull rack); (8) Temple of the Sun; (9) site of Moctezuma II's palace; (10) Zócalo or Great Square.*

stone objects: snakes, eagles, tortoises, jaguars, molluscs and crocodiles. (During the five-year excavations almost 7,000 finds were uncovered.) Offerings were always oriented according to symbolic axes (north–south, east–west, or in the middle of the stairs) related to the temple's plan – including, for example, those found in the temples of Tlaloc and Huitzilopochtli. The tribute offerings found demonstrated the extent of Aztec influence in Mesoamerica: they came from Guerrero, Teotihuacan, the Mixtec country, Tabasco, Veracruz, Puebla and Cempoala.

In the course of the research, it was found that the general theme of the temple complex related to life and death, which were very important concepts in Aztec thought. The Aztec religion was not concerned with the moral opposites of heaven and hell. It revolved around the concept of duality, in which life and death were the two complementary extremes of human existence and of creation in general. People who died by drowning reached Tlalocan, the world of abundance presided over by Tlaloc. Those who died of natural causes went to Mictlan, the underworld ruled by Mictlantecuhtli (which the Spanish compared to hell). And the victims of sacrifice, warriors killed in combat and women dying in childbirth followed the course of the sun – to be reincarnated as humming-birds or butterflies.

△ *Human sacrifice was a principal element of the Aztecs' world view. Because they believed that the wor̄ was always threatened by destruction, they practised human sacrifice in imitation of the sacrifice made by the gods to generate a new race of humanity. In a world that was constantly losing energy, ritual death was the only means of regenerating life – by harnessir̄ the* tonalli, *or individual energy of human sacrificial victims.*

The Aztec pantheon was extremely rich, although Templo Mayor offerings focused on Tlaloc (particularly in the collections of marine material) and Huitzilopochtli ('Humming-bird on the Left'), the Aztec tribal deity and war god who had guided their early wanderings and led them to settle at Tenochtitlan. Offerings to Huitzilopochtli included not only the tools of sacrifice and its product but also vessels that may have held the cremated ashes of the ruling family.

Other gods took their place on the Templo Mayor, particularly to demonstrate their relationship to Huitzilopochtli. The great Coyolxauhqui stone features the god's dismembered and defeated warrior half-sister. Tezcatlipoca, an old Toltec deity, is represented, associating his cult to that of Huitzilopochtli. Other deities featured in the Temple include Mayahuel, god of *pulpe* (an alcoholic beverage); Xiutecuhtli, god of fire; Chalchiutlicue, the wife of Tlaloc; Painal, who was one of the 'lieutenants' of Huitzilopochtli according to Sahagún; Coatlicue, a goddess associated with the earth and fertility; and Mictlantecuhtli, god of the underworld, where the spirits of those who died of natural causes resided.

The presence of these divinities indicates the fundamental role played by the economy and by war in the social organization of the Aztec people. In the

▽ *Virtual reconstruction of the outline of the Templo Mayor, or Great Temple, superimposed on a present-day aerial view of its site. Built in seven phases, between 1428 and 1520, it had not long been completed at the time of the Spanish conquest.*

◁ *Virtual view of the island city of Tenochtitlan, 'Venice of the Americas', greatly admired by the conquistadores but largely destroyed by them after the conquest. The island was connected to the mainland by three causeways. The choice of this site is described in the legend of the Aztec wanderings that were guided by the tribal deity Huitzilopochtli ('Humming-bird on the Left').*

Bibliography

M. Coe, *Mexico: From the Olmecs to the Aztecs*, 4th ed. (London and New York, 1994).

H. Cortés, *Letters from Mexico*, trans. and ed. A. Pagden (New Haven and London, 1986).

N. Davies, *The Aztecs: A History* (New York, 1973).

B. Díaz del Castillo, *The True History of the Conquest of New Spain*, trans. A.A. Maudslay (London 1908–16; New York 1986).

D. Duran, *The Aztecs*, trans. F. Horcasitas and D. Heyden (New York, 1964).

E. Matos Moctezuma, *The Great Temple of the Aztecs* (London and New York, 1988).

B. de Sahagún, *General History of the Things of New Spain*, trans. A.J.O. Anderson and C.F. Dibble (Santa Fe, 1950–69).

R.F. Townsend, *The Aztecs* (London and New York, 1992).

Aztec religion, war and politics, economics and religion all worked together to serve the cult of Huitzilopochtli. History and philosophy, too, can be understood in terms of a unified social and political organization.

The Museum of the Templo Mayor in Mexico City today offers an overview of the development of Aztec culture before the Spanish conquest. If the description of Díaz del Castillo is to be believed, Tenochtitlan fell in flames, combat and horror, and all or part of Moctezuma's treasure of golden objects disappeared with it. As the Franciscan friar Bernardino de Sahagún wrote: 'when they arrived at the treasure house, called Teulalco, they removed all the objects interwoven with feathers, such as the cushions of *quetzal* feathers, the fine shields, the gold discs, the necklaces of idols, the nose pendants of gold, the leggings of gold, and the diadems of gold. All their gold shields and their insignia were removed immediately. Later, all were piled up and set on fire. As far as the gold is concerned, the Spanish reduced it to ingots.' One ingot survives from this meltdown; found in Tacuba Street, it is now on display in Mexico City. Today's

Museum of the Templo Mayor, erected on the site of the Great Temple itself, preserves a lost world of knowledge that it took a very long time to gather together.

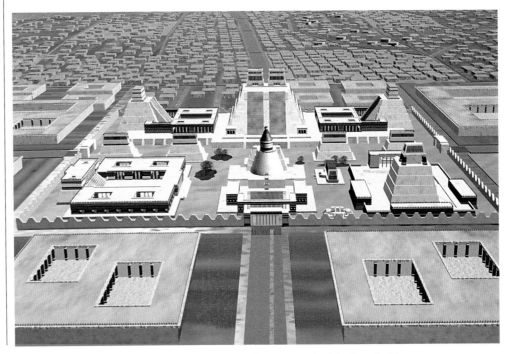

△ *Virtual reconstruction of the ceremonial centre. On the summit of the Templo Mayor (Great Temple) are the shrines dedicated to Tlaloc, the rain-god, and Huitzilopochtli, the warrior god of the sun and patron deity of the Aztecs.*

Deciphering the Aztec Script

Mexico

*T*he available archaeological data is not complete, but it is possible to reconstruct in outline the history and evolution of Mesoamerican writing systems. They formed a progression beginning with the Olmec 'iconographic' texts, and proceeding via the Aztec glyphs and the various Maya, Mixtec and Zapotec systems, to the 'hybrid' forms that developed after the Spanish conquest in the sixteenth century.

It is fairly probable that the basic idea of visual codification – fundamental to the evolution of writing throughout the New World – originated in the Olmec period (1500–100 BC) and was transmitted to other Mesoamerican civilizations, with innovations and changes in stylization occurring as a result of linguistic differences. Comparison of the different writing systems clearly shows the same basic principles persisting: for example, certain signs can be found to recur from the Olmec period, through the civilizations of Teotihuacan, Mitla, Tula and Tenochtitlan, right up to the sixteenth to eighteenth centuries AD.

The Aztecs never separated the written image from the sound it represented in their spoken tongue, Nahuatl. The basic elements of their writing have often been described as figurative representations directly connected to reality. However, closer analysis shows that the Aztec pictorial convention was anything but naturalistic: to become glyphs, the things or beings underwent a process of stylization and simplification

that conformed to traditional and indigenous conventions of artistic design. What is called a 'glyph' is in fact an assemblage of numerous basic elements; and, in turn, the complex images found in the pages of the codices are made up of assemblages of glyphs.

The graphic rules that the Aztec image followed were not based solely on the recognition of a standardized graphic 'type' – although this is

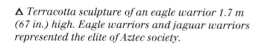

△ *Terracotta sculpture of an eagle warrior 1.7 m (67 in.) high. Eagle warriors and jaguar warriors represented the elite of Aztec society.*

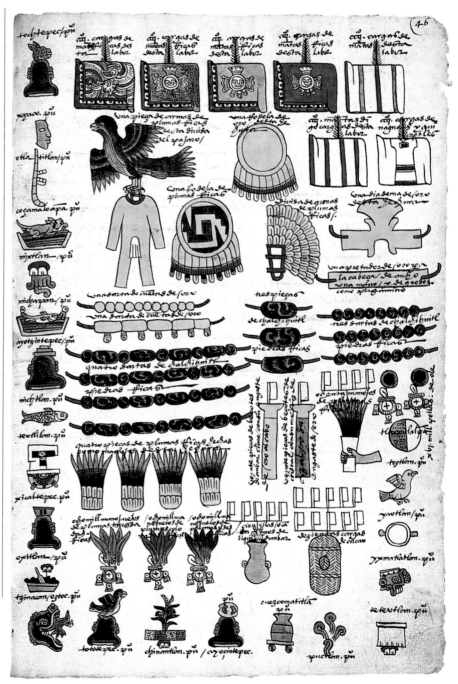

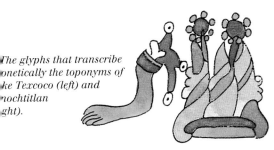

The glyphs that transcribe phonetically the toponyms of Lake Texcoco (left) and Tenochtitlan (right).

certainly a necessary precondition for a complete reading of the text. Meaning was conveyed not only by the different iconic shapes that provide the basic syllables, but also by colours and by the relative size of various groups of glyphs, as well as their positions and associations with one another on the page. An understanding of these factors, too, was essential to the correct interpretation of the content of the texts, which were mythical, historiographic, economic and ethnographic in nature.

The *tlacuilo* – the wise painter-writer who according to the Aztecs played the role of a scribe – was an artist whose creativity was governed by rules. He was subject to strict conventions governing the grammar and syntax of Nahuatl and also to the artistic and aesthetic conventions of Aztec culture. To treat the images in the codices as 'inventions' or 'discoveries' by individual scribes is therefore to overlook the long-established status of writing as 'pictures to be read'. In reading Aztec texts, the main problem for today's specialist is that of learning to throw off his own over-rigid and ethnocentric preconceptions. These are a hindrance because they reflect the reading conventions of Indo-European languages (and in particular of the Latin alphabet). Such conventions are founded on a view of the separateness of text and image (and of the primacy of text over image) that is foreign to the Mesoamerican system.

Our lack of understanding of Mesoamerican writing systems undoubtedly stems largely from a kind of contempt for images. Those belonging to the civilization that inherited the Greek alphabet and the Latin primer find it hard to understand the concept of writing that does not use letters. Alphabetic writing was erroneously considered as superior and as the only basis of comparison by which to judge every other possible way of fixing oral language, however refined or perfected it might be. From this point of view, the role of the image is limited to complementing the text – as a pure and simple 'illustration'.

Today, five hundred years after the discovery of the New World, fifteenth-century and Renaissance thinking still underlie the assessment of indigenous American forms of expression. Getting to know the indigenous image and its elements, laws and conventions is not a simple task, nor one that can be accomplished quickly; it means immersing oneself in a complex form of expression without ready-made basic tools for analysing it. One must learn to abandon preconceived criteria and simply look and see.

Over the centuries during which they evolved, the great American civilizations adopted painting and drawing as their way of transmitting ideas. Though they modified and adapted their systems of notation, the American peoples never abandoned the image. Thus it is that the Nahuatl language has a unique term that refers as much to painting as to writing: *tlacuiloa*, which means 'to write painting'.

The means at the disposal of the *tlacuilo* were richer than those available to the European scribe. They included not only the (stylized and conventionalized) forms of the objects of the Aztec world, but also the colours (truly 'phonetic' colours) and a rich and flexible use of space and shape. For example, *tepetl* (the glyph of a mountain, often used in place-names) was open to an infinite series of elaborations that modified its significance and reading. Thus, if the summit of the pictogram was curved and rolled up, the glyph meant 'in the place of the curved mountain'; whereas if the colour green was replaced by white, it was read as 'near the white mountain'. A glyph's syntactic function could also change according to its position on the page. Hence, *tepetl* could cease to be an adverb of place and become a noun, and it could incorporate verbs such as 'elongate' and 'split', and it could be combined with other glyphic elements to form a larger unit.

The lack of comprehension of this complex system that European scholars showed for so long can in part be explained by the evolution (or, more precisely, involution) of the codices

produced in the post-colonial period. The introduction of new themes – and, above all, the adoption of European volumes and perspectives that the *tlacuilos* encountered through Spanish paintings – were extraneous to the Aztec system, but they slowly

◁ *A page of the Codex Mendoza, listing the tribute paid to the emperor by subjugated cities (whose glyphs are shown at the left and bottom). The drawings represent a true form of codified writing of the Aztecs' spoken language, Nahuatl. The annotations in Latin script are a gloss added by a Spanish scribe.*

△ *The heart of the Aztec empire comprised the region of Lake Texcoco. Tenochtitlan, the empire's capital, was built on an island in the lake.*

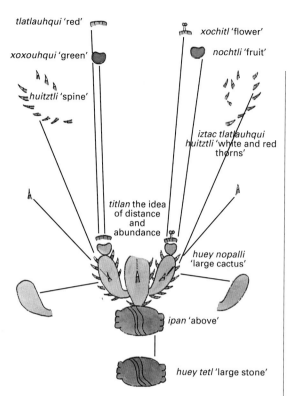

tlatlauhqui 'red'

xoxouhqui 'green'

huitztli 'spine'

xochitl 'flower'

nochtli 'fruit'

iztac tlatlauhqui huitztli 'white and red thorns'

titlan the idea of distance and abundance

huey nopalli 'large cactus'

ipan 'above'

huey tetl 'large stone'

△ *Composition of the glyph that expresses the name of Tenochtitlan: the cactus* (nopalli) *with numerous fruits* (nochtli) *rests on a stone* (tetl).

transformed the role of the image towards that of illustration. The first thing that Aztec writers adopted was decoration: the addition of elements that could not be read, but which made their products more precious and made them resemble those of the *conquistadores*.

The introduction of Christianity also removed an important number of the previous uses of writing – no longer could divinatory calendars be made up, and there were no more ceremonies involving the reading of the horoscope. These traditional functions of writing were replaced by new, post-Conquest uses, and so the mixed codices were born: manuscripts containing elements from the indigenous tradition but also showing some European influences – especially glosses and texts in Latin letters. These, for all the help that they have given to scholars and decipherers, have frequently generated misunderstandings and misinterpretations.

My own efforts to decipher Aztec writing are the result of long and patient research, undertaken since the 1950s. The first hypothesis upon which I based my work was to remember that the Mesoamerican image was a system of writing that transcribed all the features of the spoken language, as well as the thought and perception, of the indigenous world. The second hypothesis was that the elements of the Mesoamerican image must be the product of a series of artistic laws and rules generated by conventions rooted in the complex systems of thought that characterized the pre-Columbian cultures.

These rules, which followed those of the grammar of the spoken language, therefore needed to be rediscovered.

▽ *Virtual reconstruction of the ceremonial centre of Tenochtitlan, dominated by the massive structure of the Templo Mayor. This area was only brought to light by excavations in the 1980s.*

An Aztec scribe, tlacuilo, *with the ls of his trade. The word* tlacuilo *ans 'he who writes painting' and resses the fundamental and dissoluble link between sign and und in the Aztec script.*

For this, it was necessary to develop and use a method of systematic and scientific research, and to avoid blindly following the route taken by other scholars at the time, which had led to subjective and personal interpretations, changing according to the document under consideration. The first step was to compare and analyse as many pictographic manuscripts as possible – so as to establish a meaningful corpus and build up a typology – and thereafter, for each type identified, to analyse a specific document and study its constituent elements in detail.

The first document selected to form the basis of a corpus of glyphs in the Aztec system was the Codex Mendoza. This important document contains a large number of toponyms, as well as information of an economic nature, since it records the conquests of the Aztec emperors and the tributes that the subjugated populations had to pay regularly to Tenochtitlan.

Initially I considered those glyphic elements which could be used as a basis for extracting data on pre-Hispanic agriculture, so the first elements analysed were those representing the ground and cultivated plants, irrigation channels and agricultural tools. Comparing the pictographic place-names (the toponymic glyphs) with the glosses in Latin characters associated with them (often derived from the readings of the glyphs) led me to conclude that the latter were not always correct interpretations. They were very often partial, incomplete or erroneous, and some were transposed or jumbled. It was necessary to build up a card-index, glyph by glyph,

with a toponymic glyph on each card. It was thus possible to analyse each glyph, study its elements and note their possible readings, syllable by syllable. In this phase, the sound of the glyph was considered first of all.

In order to analyse each glyph individually – removing it from its context but still keeping in mind its relationships with all the elements associated with it and with the whole page – the method of classification used by J. Cooper Clark (1937) and by A. Nowotny (1962) was adopted; this consisted of a group of figures and letters. It was only much later that I perfected a personal codification that met the other needs of classifying all the drawings on the page (that is to say, both glyphs and icons, the small images and the large) and their basic

elements. A second stage of analysis – after the classification of shapes and colours – consisted of noting the thematic and symbolic content of each element. For this, it was necessary to create a special system for classifying the thematic content, using as a guide that elaborated by A. Leroi-Gourhan in *L'Homme et la matière* (1943–49) for techniques and source material.

It became necessary to record an increasing quantity of data on each card, which ultimately documented seventy-two

▷ *The famous Calendar Stone is a monolith 3.6 m (12 ft) across and weighing 24 tons. On it is represented not so much a real calendar as a record of calendrical cataclysm.*

different aspects derived from the analyses. At a time before the computer was used, it was possible to maintain complex record-cards by means of coloured indicators in different positions in the upper part of each card (six colours in twelve positions). The right half of each card contained a graphic representation of the glyph; on the left data were noted in Latin characters, including the personal or place name, the fragment or fragments of words

> *This glyph reproduces the word* tepetl *('mountain'). The glyph, the basic element of the Aztec script, is both a stylized drawing and a phonetic transcription.*

of the gloss and their translation. In the lower part of the card classification reference data were recorded: the number of the folio on which the glyph appeared, classification numbers provided by Cooper Clark, Peñafiel (1885) and Nowotny, and my own card-index number for the glyph. However, the most valuable information was concentrated in the upper border of the card, which was divided into twelve parts corresponding to the twelve positions selectable in the classification table copied from Leroi-Gourhan. These data in the upper border did not refer directly to the sign but to its referent. Nevertheless, they were fundamental to correct identification of the thematic content of the basic elements and to deciphering them.

Let us take an example. The toponym *Tlaollan* – from *tlaolli* ('hulled maize') and *tlan* (a locative suffix signifying 'abundance') – is classified thematically, by noting how its element 'maize' was recorded (in this case through agriculture, flagged by a green indicator in the first position), the appearance of the vegetable-fibre container in the glyph as a tool (green indicator in the second position), the primary material comprising the glyph, and so on.

Later, it became necessary to use at least one other card sequence to record the explanation and significance of the different elements that were produced as a result of the detailed and systematic analysis. In this case, it was possible to advance an interpretation on five different levels: sonic, thematic, symbolic, plastic and formal.

In addition to the card-indexes for the data and their interpretation, a third card-index, with words in Latin characters, was constructed and kept up-to-date as the research advanced. This was a 'sound index' that contained and indexed the sequence of the transcribed sounds (according to the mono-, bi- and tri-syllabic cases) via the basic graphic elements that comprised the toponymic glyphs. This card-index also noted abbreviations encountered in the course of the research, recording all cases in which certain syllables were read and pronounced but not written. In such cases the reading was implied by laws of 'graphic or plastic economy', since drawings corresponding to these sounds do not appear inside the glyphs. Such phenomena also allowed me to discover and take account of certain rules determined by the parameters of the drawing and by the graphic or symbolic methods developed by the scribe: positions, dimensions and spatial arrangement. The corpus of toponyms was progressively expanded by personal names, titles of civil and military duties, and some icons or large images. As the research advanced, I came to realize with increasing conviction that all the drawings of which each page was composed were intended to be read: both the large and the small images were the product of the same artistic and plastic convention – all were glyphs!

The reading of the large glyphs was done in exactly the same way as that of the small images, since the large images followed the same rules. I was convinced, therefore, that it was necessary to create a new index, following the same criteria but taking into account the icons or large images. Collectively, the individual cards for the

glyphs (since all the elements of the system could be so called) formed the sequence of an idealized 'Dictionary of glyphs of the Aztec/Nahuatl system of writing', arranged in the card-index on the basis of the chosen system of classification. A further stage consisted of creating tables in which the glyphs were arranged in alphabetical order of the first syllable of the translated word (including personal names, place names, titles or icons). Starting from this, I was able gradually to build up an acceptable series of comparative tables.

In what could be called the 'manual' period of the research, the drawings were copied one by one – with the consequent risk of errors and corruptions that could have grave consequences for the succeeding analysis. This was followed by the 'mechanical reproducibility' phase, when, using the first photocopiers, it became possible to reproduce the original faithfully and, at the same time, to carry out a series of useful research operations on it. Its elements could be disassembled and rearranged, and even those that did not transcribe the first syllable of a word, but the following syllables, could quite easily be separated from their context

> *A page of the Codex Telleriano-Remensis, a divinatory calendar produced in the sixteenth century. Here again, the Latin writing was added by a Spanish scribe to explain drawings that were otherwise incomprehensible to Europeans. This codex, composed of fifty sheets, is kept in the Bibliothèque Nationale, Paris.*

and regrouped together, even before they figured in the repertoire of existing toponyms.

These analyses, methodically developed on paper, showed visually and almost intuitively, *d'un seul coup d'oeil*, that the basic elements of Aztec script were recurrent and combinable, and that they transcribed the basic sound and/or semantic elements of Nahuatl.

The analytical work resulted in a *Dictionary of Aztec Place-name Glyphs* and a *Dictionary of Basic Elements of Nahuatl* (both unpublished), both based on the *Codex Mendoza*. This is only the start of a large dictionary, on the basis of which all the laws and rules of the Aztec imagery can be explained. Data obtained by applying the same method to other pictographic manuscripts have gradually been added to the elements from the Codex Mendoza.

It is thirty-five years since this process began. Today, this analytical system, which is the result of visual classification, can be stored in a computer's memory by means of a similarly constructed program that is currently being developed. Thanks to the computer it will be possible to examine a large quantity of data and analyse the combinations of graphic parameters already explored, and perhaps also to identify new and unpublished ones.

In future we can envisage paperless books of images that use the new mass-storage media, such as floppy disks, optical disks and CD ROM, that will allow the reader to print out parts of the data on paper, while preserving the research material intact and complete. In this way it will be possible to 'play' with texts and images, to carry out further research and to make different comparisons, since contemporary technology allows us reduce to a minimum the 'donkey work' that in the past took time and energy away from 'pure research'.

The Codex Mendoza

The Codex Mendoza is a Mexican pictographic manuscript produced by

the indigenous Nahuas for Don Antonio de Mendoza, Viceroy of New Spain in about 1525. Composed from three older manuscripts, it is made up of seventy-two sheets of European paper and consists of three parts: the first is historic and narrates, year by year, the wars of conquest undertaken by the Aztec leaders over a period of around two hundred years; the second part is a copy of a list of the tribute paid by almost 400 *pueblos* to Motecuhzoma II (1502–20), the last ruler of Tenochtitlan; the final part is ethnographic in

△ *Folio 2 recto of the Codex Mendoza, which describes the last 194 years of Aztec history from the foundation of Tenochtitlan. The blue outer border of the page represents a cyclical calendar with a duration of fifty-one years.*

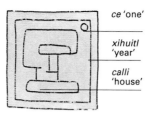

ce 'one'

xihuitl 'year'

calli 'house'

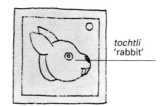

tochtli 'rabbit'

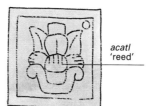

acatl 'reed'

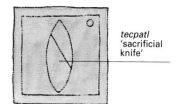

tecpatl 'sacrificial knife'

△ *Four basic glyphs were used to indicate years. Each was qualified by a number between one and thirteen (represented by a small circle), and the blue colour stood for the word* xihuitl *(year). This system produced a complete cycle of fifty-two (13 × 4) years.*

character and tells of Aztec daily life from birth to death.

To clarify the description of the system that I have already outlined, it seems useful to try to link to it the first page of this very important codex: folio *2 recto*. Looking at the reproduction of this folio on preceding page, one can see that it consists of three elements: a double frame, a landscape, and some scenes with figures. The outer frame, which defines the plastic space inside the page, is in reality a chronological framework that can be read anti-clockwise from the top left. The first year, '2 house', and the last year, '13 reed', indicate the period covering the foundation of Tenochtitlan and the government of Tenochtzin, the first emperor or *huey tlatoani* ('great orator') of the Aztec state.

The inner frame is closely linked to the landscape element, since it represents the lake that surrounded the island capital of Tenochtitlan and the channels that divided it into five sections: four of them (triangular) on the island and the fifth on terra firma. The landscape formed by the aquatic elements, the earth, the plants, the large stone in the centre of the page, the mountains, and by the five buildings could justly be called a 'phonetic landscape'. Using a system of super-imposed spatial planes, it transcribes a complex text that gives the geo-graphical and mythical co-ordinates within which the foundation of Tenochtitlan took place.

The elements of the landscape are located on various spatial planes, with their distance from the reader determining the order of reading. The eagle resting on the cactus (*nopalli*) and the stone (*tetl*) are the nearest to the reader, so reading these takes precedence over reading the remaining plant elements, the buildings and the water channels.

Figures, without doubt, constitute one of the most difficult aspects to comprehend in the Aztec system of writing. In fact, despite the identifying names 'floating' above their heads and connected to them by means of a 'graphic law' (a clearly recognizable device in drawing and writing), the human beings seem on first appear-ances none other than 'portraits'. Nevertheless, a closer look shows that, where a name is lacking, the depictions of people do not possess any indi-viduality and consist of a montage of glyphic elements that is consistent with the phoneticization of names, titles and traditional metaphors. For example, the great and venerated Tenochtzin, who sits on the ground in the left-hand section, has a succession of attributes – long hair tied with a white knot; ornaments, white on the ear and red on the face; the turquoise speech scroll; the white cloak with a double border and fringe; the nails of the bare feet; and the yellow seat of reed-matting on which he sits – which, read in sequence, are a clear metaphorical expression of power. Without his name ('the venerable man of the stone cactus, the venerable Tenoch') written in the small image behind his head, this figure is simply a great priest, a supreme commander, a great nobleman, a great lord and judge: a combination of offices that clearly could also be carried out by some other individual.

In the lower part of the page the figures are not shown seated and covered by a white cloak (an attribute of nobility) but are depicted as warriors in action, who are conquering the first enemy cities to be subjugated: Colhuacan and Tenayucan. The top-onyms that express the names of these two cities are located to the right of and on an inferior spatial plane to the two flaming temples that are the traditional signs for the defeat of a *pueblo*. The left-hand pair of symbols forms a noun-verb signifying Colhuacan. It could be read thus: 'Near the curved mountain the yellow rush roof of the large temple on the pyramid tilts and falls in flames' – in other words, 'The city of Colhuacan is destroyed'.

▷ *Wall-painting from Teotihuacan. Even though the Teotihuacan script seems to have been based on the same principles as the Aztec script, it remains undeciphered.*

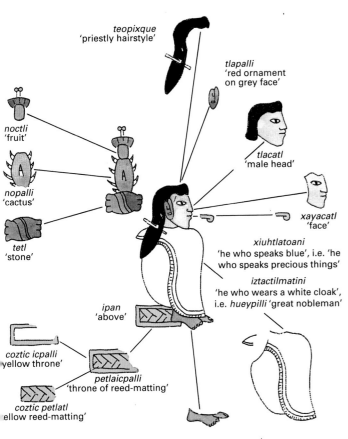

teopixque 'priestly hairstyle'

tlapalli 'red ornament on grey face'

noctli 'fruit'

tlacatl 'male head'

nopalli 'cactus'

xayacatl 'face'

tetl 'stone'

xiuhtlatoani 'he who speaks blue', i.e. 'he who speaks precious things'

iztactilmatini 'he who wears a white cloak', i.e. *hueypilli* 'great nobleman'

ipan 'above'

coztic icpalli 'yellow throne'

petlaicpalli 'throne of reed-matting'

coztic petlatl 'yellow reed-matting'

△ *Breakdown into basic elements of a figure from Folio 2 recto of the Codex Mendoza. Analysis of the glyphs shows that the figure represents a complex phrase and personal name.*

▽ *On folio 2 recto of the Codex Mendoza, the inner blue border indicates a terrestrial space bounded by watercourses in which rushes (tollin) and reeds (acatl) grow; the central glyph of a cactus (nopalli) on a stone (tetl), indicates that the place is Tenochtitlan, which had a complex system of canals.*

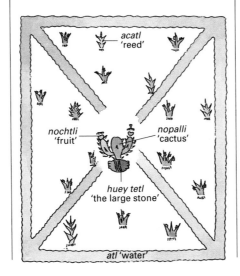

acatl 'reed'

nochtli 'fruit'

nopalli 'cactus'

huey tetl 'the large stone'

atl 'water'

▽ *In the lower part of folio 2 recto of the Codex Mendoza, the Aztecs' conquest of two cities is described. The glyphs that transcribe the toponyms indicate that the cities were Tenayucan and Colhuacan.*

Bibliography

F. Berdan and P. Anawalt, *The Codex Mendoza* (Berkeley, 1992).

C. Dibble, 'Writing in Central Mexico', in R. Wauchope (ed.) *Handbook of Middle American Indians*, vol. 10, pt 1 (Austin, 1971).

J. Galarza and A. Siliotti, *Tlacuilo, il segreto della scrittura azteca* (Florence, 1992).

J. Marcus, *Mesoamerican Writing Systems: Propaganda, Myth and History in Four Ancient Civilizations* (Princeton, 1992).

H. Nicholson, 'Phoneticism in Late Pre-Hispanic Mexican Writing Systems', in E. Benson (ed.), *Mesoamerican Writing Systems* (Washington, 1973), pp. 1–46.

H. Premm, 'Aztec Hieroglyphic Writing System: Possibilities and Limitations', in *Verhandlungen des XXXVIII. Internationalen Amerikanisten-kongresses*, vol. 2 (Munich, 1970), pp. 159–65.

The Great Inca Empire of the Andes

South America

*T*he Inca state was probably the only true empire in pre-Hispanic South America. It developed in the Andes from the thirteenth century AD, and from the beginning of the sixteenth century its power extended over an area of almost 900,000 sq km (350,000 sq mi). To control and govern this empire, a sophisticated political, economic and administrative organization was established. Two myths explain the appearance of the first Incas in the region of Cuzco. According to one version, their history begins with the emergence of four brothers from a cave and their journey to Cuzco. A second version tells that Manco Capac was born out of the waters of Lake Titicaca (on the present-day Peruvian–Bolivian border), and that his father, the sun, assigned him the task of civilizing humanity with the help of Mama Ocllo, his companion.

The Andean region was discovered by Europeans less than ten years after the conquest of Mexico. Vasco Núñez de Balboa had heard talk of other lands, and in 1513 he crossed the isthmus of Panama and on its Pacific coast founded the city of Panama, which became the base for exploring the new ocean. It was one of Balboa's officers, Francisco Pizarro, who headed south and launched the conquest of the Inca empire. In 1532, after many hardships, he reached Tumbes (in the north-west of present-day Peru) and set out southwards with a force of only 198 foot soldiers and 62 horsemen.

The conquerors encountered an empire that was already torn by civil war. The last great emperor Huayna Capac had died some time between 1525 and 1527, and his sons Huascar, based in Cuzco, and Atahualpa, based in Ecuador, had been fighting for the succession. The victor, Atahualpa, at the head of an army marching towards Cuzco to take possession of his newly-won realm, was encamped at Cajamarca when he accepted an invitation to meet Pizarro. There he was ambushed and taken prisoner by Pizarro in November 1532. To secure his liberty, Atahualpa gave the Spaniards an enormous ransom in gold and silver artifacts (these were subsequently melted down into ingots before being sent to Spain). Notwithstanding the payment of the ransom, Pizarro orchestrated a plot that led to his captive being accused of idolatry and incest and condemned to die at the stake. To preserve his body intact, as demanded by Inca beliefs, Atahualpa converted to Christianity and died by strangulation in July 1533. The Spanish then marched on Cuzco, which they took a few months later. Pizarro installed Manco Capac, Huascar's younger half-brother, on the throne and established a new capital at Lima on the central coast of Peru.

The Spanish colonization later extended along the length of the Andes. A large part of present-day Chile and Bolivia and part of Colombia were progressively subdued. However, the situation within the Spanish colony deteriorated. The obsession with gold generated domestic disputes, and Pizarro was assassinated by one of his men in 1541.

△ *Silver statuette of an alpaca. Herding of llamas and alpacas provided meat and wool and beasts of burden in the highland regions of the Inca empire.*

△ *The legendary founder of the Inca nation, Manco Capac, and his companion Mama Ocllo, from the* Primer Nueva Corónica y Buen Gobierno *by Felipe Guamán Poma de Ayala. This illustrated chronicle provides much information about Inca history and daily life at the time of the Spanish conquest.*

The Incas
...ed upon a
...work of over
...000 km (15,500
...es) of roads to
...minister and control their
...t empire. It was a major feat
...ngineering.

...acking writing, the Incas
...d a system of quipus *or*
...tted cords. It was possible to
...ord information by the use
...cords of different colours and
...angements, each with knots
...different number, type and
...sition.

Over the course of barely two hundred years, from the thirteenth to the fifteenth centuries AD, the Inca realm had developed from a small state in the Cuzco region into an empire. It expanded along the Andes and ultimately occupied an area that stretched from southern Colombia, via Ecuador and Peru, to central Chile.

The development of this empire occurred under successive generations of Incas (rulers). Viracocha, who annexed part of the Urubamba valley, was the first to pursue an expansionist political policy. But in 1438 the Chancas attacked the Inca capital of Cuzco. Viracocha's son Yupanqui organized the defence of the capital and defeated them. He then deposed his father and acceded to the throne, taking the name of Pachacutec ('earth-shaker'). He began great political reforms and started the reconstruction of Cuzco, which became a true capital. During his reign, Pachacutec and his son and military commander Topa Inca expanded the Inca empire southwards as far as Lake Titicaca and northwards as far as central Ecuador, in the process conquering and subduing the kingdom of Chimor, which had become established on the northern coast of

Artifacts of Everyday Life

Inca archaeological material essentially consists of pottery, stone objects, textiles and metalwork. The pottery largely used standardized shapes decorated with geometric motifs. Two of the most common shapes are a bowl with a zoomorphic handle and a jar with a conical base – the so-called aryballoid jar, known in Quechua as urpu *– large examples of which were carried on the back.*

The textiles represented a weaving tradition that goes

back at least three thousand years in the Andes. Under the Incas their patterns tended to become increasingly geometric, partly due to the influence of standardized weaving techniques.

Hard-stone receptacles served as mortars and generally had handles in the shape of animal heads. Many archaeological finds are of metalwork. These comprise weapons, bronze tools and jewellery and decorative objects made of gold, silver and silver-gilt. Sadly, a great

deal of the work in precious metals was melted down for bullion by the Spanish conquerors.

▽ The *urpu*, a large receptacle for transporting liquids. The vessel was held on the porter's back by a cord passed through the handles at the sides.

△ *The Spanish colonial church of Santo Domingo in Cuzco stands on an enormous wall – the remains of the ancient Temple of the Sun – almost as a symbol of two deeply contrasting cultures. The wall, built of dressed and fitted stone blocks during the reign of Pachacutec, has survived numerous earthquakes, but the colonial building has been rebuilt many times.*

Capac, who extended the borders of the empire still further north in Ecuador.

All the rulers of the empire had to face the problem of organizing and maintaining the coherence of a complex ethnic 'mosaic' of subject peoples. For this, they developed a sophisticated system operating at both regional and imperial levels to administer all the territory they controlled. This system was greatly helped by a communications network, based on two road systems, that allowed contact between the provinces and the capital to be maintained. The first route ran along the coast and linked Ecuador to central Chile, the second followed highland valleys and stretched from Quito in Ecuador to Santiago in Chile. It was along these two axes that Inca armies, officials, herders (of llamas and alpacas), artisans and agricultural produce moved. Suspended bridges across gorges and rivers allowed the network to reach otherwise inaccessible areas, and staging posts, called *tambos*, were dispersed along the roads.

Peru. When Pachacutec died in 1471, Topa Inca succeeded him and expanded the realm westwards, overcoming the states of the southern Peruvian coast, and southwards as far as the Maule river in south-central Chile. In 1493 Topa Inca was succeeded by Huayna

The strength of the empire was based upon the collective work of labour groups (*mitmaq*) who, along with the rest of the empire's record-keeping, were accounted for by means of *quipus*. Interpreted by the *quipucamayoc*, the *quipu* was an assemblage of cords with

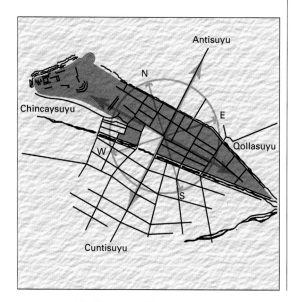

△▷ *Cuzco was likened to a puma, a symbol of strength and power. This plan shows the city's orientation in relation to the cardinal points of the compass and the four provinces, or quarters (*suyu*) of the empire.*

Textile Art

◁ As this very well-preserved war tunic shows, textiles were important to the Andean populations. (Paris, Musée de l'Homme)

Textiles occupied a very important place in the economic, political, religious and military systems of the Inca. They were highly prestigious goods whose production was regulated and overseen. Gifts of textiles were made during political negotiations, and they were used to thank and honour faithful subjects of the empire. On a social level, textiles were used to distinguish also an individual's social rank. The army was also a great user, and, being often in action, had to renew its equipment regularly.

Textiles had an important religious function and were made by men and women who had learned the techniques of weaving from infancy. Weavers were divided into three classes. The Hatun Runa *produced textiles used for state purposes; the* Cumbi Camayoc *made high-quality textiles, some of which were used by the military; and the most skilled women called* Mamacona *made the clothes of the Inca himself and the drapes that decorated the walls of the temples.*

knots on them that recorded accurate census data on population, goods and animals. The empire's laws were strict – one could not lie, steal or be idle – and transgressions were met with harsh punishment. Restive subject peoples were controlled by forcing them to emigrate to different parts of the empire. To maintain order and protect the empire there was a permanent army. In addition each man was obliged to serve for a time in the labour groups.

The populations that made up the empire – which were forced to speak Quechua, the Inca language – were however protected by laws, particularly those which concerned the land. Each village that contained families held together by ties of kinship (*ayllu*) was placed under the authority of a *curaca*. The *ayllu* was a real social entity, and each possessed a *marka* of cultivable land that was divided into plots and distributed to each family. The plots were situated at different altitudes, so that the cultivators could grow a variety

△ *The fortress of Sacsayhuaman ('royal eagle' in Quechua), which overlooked and protected Cuzco, was the largest fortification in the American continent. It is formed of three successive lines of walls, which are around 0.5 km (550 yd) long and rise about 20 m (65 ft) high. The walls are reinforced by oblique bastions, which project in a zigzag fashion.*

Agriculture

Characteristic of Inca agriculture was the use of terraced cultivation, which helped to enlarge the agricultural area and limit soil erosion. Potatoes (which are indigenous to the Andes) were cultivated, along with maize, beans, coca, peppers and different species of squash (gourds).

Llamas were reared mainly for use as pack animals, which allowed the products to be transported over the whole of the territory. They were also eaten or sacrificed during ceremonies, and their wool was used to weave cloth, and their skins to make bags. Other domestic animals of the period were alpaca, the guinea-pig and the dog.

The first traces of cultivated plants and some ears of maize (dating to the third millennium BC) were found in the cave of Guitarrero. Agriculture seems to have appeared later in the coastal regions. The cultivation of the bean, certain species of squash and cotton is dated to 3000 BC. From this period, the cultural centres of Kotosh, La Galgada and Chavín based their economies on the rearing of camelids and the cultivation of maize and potatoes. This tuber of Andean origin was cultivated in the coastal zone from 2000 BC, and more than 200 cultivable species of potato existed, both in the valleys and at high altitudes. They were eaten both fresh and in dried form (chuño), after they had been exposed alternately to sun and freezing temperatures. Other varieties of tubers were cultivated on the high plateaux: mashua, ulluco, oca, maca (roots) and quinoa, a grain rich in minerals.

▷ Andean ceramics were often shaped like fruits or vegetables; this bottle looks like a bunch of maize-cobs.

◁ Two stages in the cultivation of maize: tilling and sowing; and transporting the harvest to the store.

of crops, and the area of land assigned was regularly reviewed in line with the size of the family.

Andean farmers were able to make immense areas of the cordillera (mountains) productive. Around forty plant species were cultivated in the different ecological zones, ranging from the warm, humid eastern foothills up to the cold highlands. In contrast to the potato, maize was only grown at altitudes below 4,000 m (13,000 ft). Its cultivation required good irrigation and a supply of fertilizers, amongst which was *guano* (bird excrement), which the Incas carried from the coast on the backs of llamas. To work the land, the men used hoes, spades, picks, wooden shovels and digging-sticks called *taclla*.

◁ The Inca fortress of Ollantaytambo. Its dry-stone walls, made of large polygonal blocks fitted together, were built with great precision.

Large quantities of maize were consumed, and enormous reserve stocks were built up for use on important political and religious occasions. To meet these requirements, the Incas systematically terraced the slopes of the cordillera and made use of the mountain waters by means of extensive complexes of irrigation channels. Maize cultivation was accompanied by an elaborate ceremonial and by propitiatory rites intended to protect the crops and to ensure rain. Maize was

Architecture was one art at which the Incas excelled. Their stone-cutting was precise and accurate – as is shown by the 'twelve-angled stone' in the wall of a late pre-conquest building in Cuzco.

also regarded as a sacred plant, and was used in the manufacture of *chicha* – a fermented beer drunk during ceremonies and used in libations. For pouring out the libations, the Incas used the *pajcha*: a vessel made from a single piece of wood and shaped into a cup with a sculpted and perforated handle. Maize flour, mixed with llamas' blood, served in the preparation of the *sancu*, which was used in sacrificial rites or given as offerings. The Incas also asked the gods for permission to sow the maize, and sowers presided over this ceremony, which was accompanied by the sacrifice of animals. The local chiefs (*curacas*) had to organize similar ceremonies in their regions. Offerings of ears of maize made of stone were given to mummies as well as to the gods and the *huacas* (holy sites), that is, to all that possessed a sacred character. In

▷ *A view of the archaeological complex of Machu Picchu. In the background rises the peak of Huayna Picchu, with its characteristic sugar-loaf shape.*

spring villages organized large festivals in honour of *Zara mama* ('mother of the maize').

The capital of the empire was Cuzco, the ruler's seat of power. Four routes branched out from its central square and led to the four quarters (*suyu*) of the empire – each quarter administered by a provincial governor (*tocrioc apu*). Situated at an altitude of 3,326 m (10,900 ft), Cuzco is dominated by mountains almost 4,000 m (13,000 ft) high. It housed thousands of inhabitants and had religious, administrative and residential buildings built of large blocks of stone accurately cut and assembled without mortar. It was overlooked and protected by the zigzag triple-circuit walls of the fortress of Sacsayhuaman. The Spaniards were quick to note that the walls of the *Coricancha* (Temple of the Sun) were covered by large sheets of gold, and that the gardens were decorated with animalesque sculptures made of gold and silver. The city's layout was regular, with the streets crossing at right angles, and it was bounded on two sides by canalized rivers.

Bibliography

C. Bernard, *The Incas* (London and New York, 1994).
J. Hemming, *Conquest of the Incas*, rev. ed. (Harmondsworth, 1983).
J. Hemming and E. Ranney, *Monuments of the Incas* (Boston, 1982).
A. Kendall, *Everyday Life of the Incas* (London, 1973).
M.E. Moseley, *The Incas and Their Ancestors* (London and New York, 1992).
F.G. Poma de Ayala, *Nueva Corónica y Buen Gobierno* (1615), in *Travaux et Mémoires de l'Institut d'ethnologie*, 23 (Paris, 1936).
R. Stone-Miller, *Art of the Andes* (London and New York, 1995).

The Mysterious Nazca Lines

Peru *The Nazca culture developed on the desert coast of southern Peru between about 300 BC and AD 600. It is particularly known for its textiles and pottery and for the extraordinary geoglyphs at Nazca Pampa.*

△ *Stirrup-spout pottery jar with polychrome decoration depicting fertility demons and the heads of sacrificed enemies.*

Analysis of its polychrome pottery shows that the Nazca culture, which developed in the fertile Nazca and Ica valleys, moved through eight phases from the fourth century BC to the seventh century AD. Its farmers cultivated the lower-lying land, but on the higher, uncultivable ground of Nazca Pampa they inscribed on the stony desert landscape the so-called Nazca Lines: immense geoglyphs in geometric patterns and in the shapes of human figures, plants, animals, birds, insects and fish. The method they used to trace these gigantic motifs was simple: they just removed the top layer of weathered soil and stones to expose the lighter-coloured stratum below.

▷ *Aerial view of a geoglyph in the form of a gigantic humming-bird. Several of these mysterious signs depict animal motifs, others represent geometric figures.*

Given their dimensions, the geoglyphs of the Nazca Pampa can only be seen in their entirety from above. Nevertheless, they can also be read and followed on the ground. The geometrically shaped geoglyphs (the 'lines' proper) are thought to be astronomical configurations linked to the calendar. Maria Reiche, who has dedicated much of her life to studying the geoglyphs, is convinced of their calendrical function, possibly connected with the observation of solstices.

On the other hand, the presence of offerings of pottery at some sites shows that certain geoglyphs also served as cult places. The overall iconography follows the main themes found on the painted ceramics of the Nazca culture. Geometric figures flank quadrupeds, birds, fish, whales, spiders, and anthropomorphic figures. And in the region of the Paracas peninsula certain motifs, such as that of a gigantic cactus visible from far offshore, seem to have been topographic references for navigation.

The geoglyphs and alignments of the Nazca Pampa thus seem to have served a range of purposes, including astronomical observation points, calendrical devices and spaces associated with seasonal rituals.

During the third century AD, strong population growth led to the appearance of numerous villages in the Pisco, Ica and Nazca valleys. The pottery made in this period was intended for cult purposes and as funerary offerings. It is characterized by its polychrome decoration and by the appearance of a new technique that fixed the colours during the firing. The pots were modelled by hand and decorated in up to six different colours with patterns of geometric designs and mythical animals.

The less sophisticated ceramics are older. Their designs are sober and are generally drawn on a bright base of a

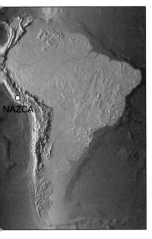

◁ *Location map:
Nazca Pampa lies
near the coast of
south-central
Peru. The dry
climate of the
coastal desert has
contributed to the
preservation of
the geoglyphs.*

NAZCA

△ *Amongst the best-known geoglyphs are
the stylized shapes of a spider, a monkey
and various birds.*

single white or brown colour. A second category of ceramics is characterized by ornamentation composed of volute and abstract motifs. Polychrome pottery of the late phases has a different style of decoration with dense and intricate designs made up of mythical figures and geometric forms.

Bibliography

A, Aveni (ed.), *The Lines of Nazca* (Philadelphia, 1990).
M. E. Moseley, *The Incas and Their Ancestors* (London and New York, 1992).

A. Morrison, *The Mystery of the Nasca Lines* (Woodbridge, 1987).
J. Reinhard, *The Nasca Lines: A New Perspective on Their Origin and Meaning* (Lima, 1987).

The Cult of the Dead

In the Nazca culture the dead were buried in shallow graves. The funerary chambers have roofs made of a wooden frame, covered and consolidated by a layer of clay with mud bricks on top. The deceased was generally accompanied by pottery vessels deposited as offerings. The sophistication of the funerary cults testifies to the importance that the dead held in the Peruvian tradition. The belief in a life after death, and in the preservation of human remains as the support of the spirit, was a constant preoccupation for the Peruvians.

Knowledge of Nazca beliefs and funerary cults is still very limited, because no independent texts exist, as is the case with the other pre-Columbian cultures. We only know, from Spanish chroniclers, that in the Inca period the dead were thought to go either to a celestial world or to an underworld – a place mistakenly compared to hell by the Spanish clergy of the conquest period.

However, archaeology can study the mummy bundles that are typical of the Nazca cultural area. These are made up of a mummy, in a foetal position, covered by several layers of textile and enclosed in a funerary 'envelope', which is generally decorated. In some cases, an artificial head (of textile or wood) was placed on the top of the bundle, and this was generally decorated with other materials to represent the eyes and the mouth. It was intended to give the mummy bundle anthropomorphic form.

The different textiles that protect the bodies of the Peruvian mummies – which are often highly decorated and coloured – have contributed significantly to their preservation, along with the dry burial conditions of the desert. Offerings were often placed between the layers of textiles, including masks and jewellery made of hammered gold sheet with relief patterns of stylized figures. These are some of the best examples of Peruvian goldwork.

△ Mask made of thin gold sheet.

▷ Wooden dummy head intended to be placed on top of a mummy bundle.

The Moche Civilization

| **Peru** |

*M*oche civilization flourished between 200 BC and AD 600 on the northern coast of Peru, but its cultural influence extended as far as the southern coast. Particularly renowned for its ceramics and jewellery, this culture also developed architecture and civil engineering projects. Archaeological remains show that the Moche were organized as a hierarchical society, dominated by a warrior class.

daily life – which was in part conditioned by proximity to the Pacific and its resources; these were abundant because the Humboldt Current normally made the water off this coast cool and rich in phosphates, providing a favourable environment for the plankton on which the fish fed. A wide range of marine life is depicted on Moche pottery. Fish and mammals include shark, anchovy, tuna, dab, boulter, skate,

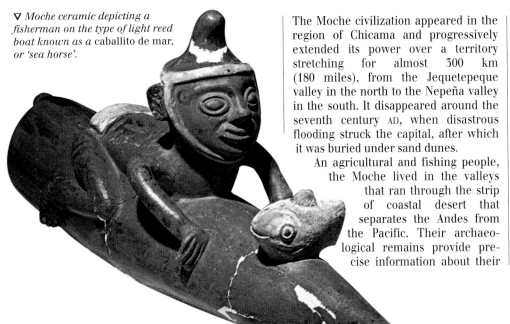

▽ *Moche ceramic depicting a fisherman on the type of light reed boat known as a* caballito de mar, *or 'sea horse'.*

The Moche civilization appeared in the region of Chicama and progressively extended its power over a territory stretching for almost 300 km (180 miles), from the Jequetepeque valley in the north to the Nepeña valley in the south. It disappeared around the seventh century AD, when disastrous flooding struck the capital, after which it was buried under sand dunes.

An agricultural and fishing people, the Moche lived in the valleys that ran through the strip of coastal desert that separates the Andes from the Pacific. Their archaeological remains provide precise information about their

sea-lion, dolphin, as well as all sorts of molluscs (mussel, king conch, oyster, etc.). The sea birds (cormorants, pelicans, gulls) provided *guano* (excrement) that sometimes piled up a couple of metres high and made an excellent fertilizer. Seaweed was also collected, eaten and used in traditional medicine for its soporific and calming properties.

Fishing seems to have been a primary activity in the Moche economy and a number of different techniques were used. Molluscs were collected on foot, and crustaceans were caught with throwing nets, woven baskets and dipnets. They also used larger nets made of plant fibres – fitted with weights and

△ *A reed boat of a type similar to the ones shown in Moche pottery and still in use today.*

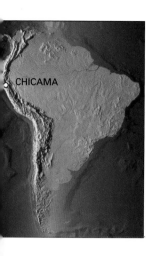

◁ *Location map:
The Chicama
region lies on the
north coast of Peru,
where short valleys
running from the
Andes to the Pacific
cut through the
coastal desert. It
was here, between
200 BC and AD 600,
that the Moche
developed their
remarkable
civilization.*

◁ *Stirrup-spouted pottery
libation jar depicting two
people, perhaps farmers,
grinding maize (third to
fifth century AD). Such
ceramics provide
valuable insights into the
daily life of the Moche
civilization.*

with floats made of gourds – and harpoons and fish-hooks carved from bone. The Moche used a well-known type of one-man boat called a *caballito de mar* ('sea horse'). Made of bundles of reeds tied together, this had a tapered bow and square-cut stern and could be manoeuvred from a lying or kneeling position.

Moche pottery provides what almost amounts to an illustrated handbook of Moche daily and social life. It was produced in large quantities, moulded or modelled by hand, and is notable for the perfection of its shapes and the systematic use of bichrome painting in brown on a cream ground. Besides the innumerable depictions of marine creatures, animals and plants, there are images of warriors, representations of people connected with religious life, scenes of ritual and sacrifice, and portraits of individuals. The style can be realistic (in the portraits), geometric or completely abstract. In many scenes anthropo-zoomorphic figures – perhaps members of the elite, and very likely people with religious power – are shown confronting or fighting half-human, half-animal figures from an

iconography that drew on a world of fantastic and mythological allegory. The pottery gives remarkable insights into the complex iconography of this civilization and, in particular, shows that the social organization of Moche society was strongly hierarchical and dominated by a warrior class. In both the sculptural and the painted pottery, warriors appear as victors and as prisoners – generally with sophisticated arms and clothing, wearing elaborate headdresses and feline masks and carrying maces.

Jewellery is also frequently found and is technically the equal of pottery. Gold, silver and copper were abundant in the Peruvian and Andean regions. The oldest traces of goldworking, found at Andahuaylas in southern Peru, date to around 1500 BC, but it was on the north coast – particularly in the Vicús, Moche

△ *Kneeling warrior, holding a shield. This
bichrome-painted ceramic exemplifies the
sculptural realism of Moche pottery.*

▷ *Fragment of a Moche polychrome fresco
from Pañamarca, depicting sacrificial and
ritual scenes.*

and Chimú cultural areas – that Peruvian metalworking and jewellery were most developed. The chroniclers of the sixteenth century record that gold and silver had a symbolic significance – as the 'sweat of the sun' and the 'tears of the moon' respectively.

Moche metalsmiths worked in gold, silver, copper and a variety of alloys. The basic techniques most frequently used seem to have been hammering and lost-wax casting. Making jewellery generally involved a combination of techniques, perhaps including making a basic model by the lost-wax method, soldering on to it other elements made by hammering over a wooden form, and decorating it with other pieces consisting of mosaic inlay (turquoise and gold). All the techniques sought to enhance the qualities of gold, 'brilliant as the sun' and well-suited to ornamental use because it was rare, precious, light, malleable and imposing in its sheen. Gold – collected as dust from gold-bearing sand – served essen-

tially to reinforce the prestige of the elite; gold ornaments were also used as funerary offerings, being deposited in burials such as that of the Lord of Sipán, discovered in 1987 by Walter Alva in the Lambayeque valley. Various gilding techniques were often used to endow objects made of other metals with the aesthetic qualities of pure gold.

The material found in the tomb of the Lord of Sipán consisted of hundreds

of pieces of jewellery, some of considerable size, which displayed the whole repertoire of Moche metalwork. Objects of gold, silver and copper covered the body of the Lord. Some of the most spectacular pieces were necklaces, some made from enormous gold nuggets, others from hundreds of gold and shell beads; pectorals in the form of *tumi* (crescent-shaped ceremonial knives); headdresses and ornaments for ears, arms, legs, nose and waist; as well as weapons and the coverings of ceremonial batons.

It is clear from the scenes on Moche pottery and jewellery that textiles were very important in ceremonial display, but, because of climatic conditions, they have not survived. A major example of Moche architecture, on the other hand, has survived in the form of the remains of the Huaca del Sol in the Moche valley. This was a vast ceremonial complex, 288 m (945 ft) long and 36 m (118 ft) wide, made of almost fifty million sun-dried mud bricks and arranged in three levels with a ramp. The façade is believed to have been faced with plaster and decorated with paintings; the ramp was at one time decorated in polychrome, though only a few traces of this remain today. (At Pañamarca, in the Nepeña valley, fragments of polychrome murals survive, depicting a mythological scene that probably deals with the theme of the post-sacrificial treatment of the body.)

There are other architectural remains in the neighbouring Virú, Chicama and Nepeña valleys. The Moche also organized and managed the irrigation of cultivable land by means of large-scale water-distribution networks involving aqueducts, canals and

---

The Tomb of the 'Lord of Sipán'

Walter Alva, Director of the Brüning Regional Museum at Lambayeque, and his team of archaeologists discovered the tomb of the 'Lord of Sipán' in 1987 in the Lambayeque valley. A reconstruction of the whole burial reveals that the man lay in a wooden sarcophagus, accompanied by numerous offerings and by various other people. Two young women, wives or favourites, lay one at his feet and one at his head. Two men were also found, one either side of the Lord's body. One of them, apparently a

warrior, had a woman and a dog lying on their sides at his feet. On three sides of the grave were niches filled with offerings and jars containing the remains of food. The fourth wall contained the remains of a ten-year-old youth, and above the funerary chamber there was the body of another warrior, who must have served as a 'guardian' of the tomb.

The archaeologists took ten months to record the finds from the tomb. Despite what was already known of the art of the population

groups of the Lambayeque valley, this was the first time in the history of Peruvian archaeology that researchers were able to conduct a scientific excavation to recover the material from an intact burial – one which revealed details of the funerary rite and the journey into the next world.

▽ The tomb of the Lord of Sipán. Two women and two servants accompanied the Lord on his journey into the afterlife.

Chronology of the Moche Valley	
Chavín influence	1200 BC–AD 400
Vicús and Frías	500 BC–AD 500
Moche	200 BC–AD 600
Huari influence	AD 700–1000
Lambayeque-Sicán	700–1100
Chimú	1000–1460
Inca influence	1460–1533

reservoirs. The most significant examples are the aqueduct – 1,500 m (1,600 yd) long and 15 m (50 ft) high – at Ascope in the Chicama valley; the La Cumbre canal, which was 110 km (68 miles) long; and the reservoir of San José, which could hold hundreds of thousands of cubic metres of water.

△ *The Huaca del Sol is an immense stepped pyramid, built of rectangular mud bricks. It is thought that its exterior was once covered by plaster and decorated with paintings.*

Bibliography

W. Alva and C.B. Donnan, *Royal Tombs of Sipán* (Los Angeles, 1993).

E.P. Benson, *The Mochica* (London and New York, 1972).

C.B. Donnan, *Moche Art* (Los Angeles, 1978).

F. Kauffmann Doig, *Manual de arqueología peruana* (Lima, 1978).

L.-G. Lumbreras, *The People and Cultures of Ancient Peru* (Washington, 1974)

M.E. Moseley, *The Incas and Their Ancestors* (London and New York, 1992).

C. Plazas, *Museo del oro* (Bogotá, 1991).

▷ *Erotic pottery is widespread along the northern coast of Peru, but was particularly common among the Moche. This container makes a clear allusion to the male and female sexual organs.*

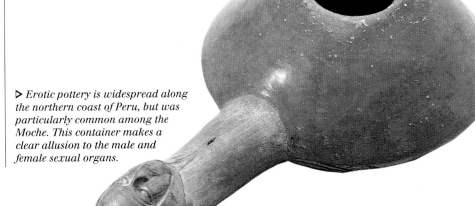

283

Glossary

(Words printed in SMALL CAPITALS can be looked up in their own glossary entries)

abacus: Slab which, with the ECHINUS, forms the DORIC capital; it sits between the echinus and the ARCHITRAVE.

acropolis: Elevated part of an ancient city, where the temples or SANCTUARIES were generally located.

acroterion: Plinth for a statue or other decorative element placed at the two ends and the apex of a PEDIMENT.

agora: Main public space of a Greek city, where the administrative buildings and cult places of the gods protecting public life were located.

amber: Fossil conifer resin. It may be light to dark yellow or brown and often contains plant remains or insects. It is mainly found in the Baltic.

ambulatory: Space between the COLONNADE and the main structure of a temple.

amphiprostyle: Used of a building with a PORTICO at each end, but no columns along the sides.

amphitheatre: Open-roofed building of oval or circular form, consisting of a central space (the ARENA) surrounded by tiers of seating for spectators; used for gladiatorial contests and large-scale public entertainments.

antefix: Decorative marble or polychrome terracotta ornament on the eaves and CORNICES of a Classical building, concealing the ends of the roof tiles.

antis, in: Used of a temple building in which the lateral walls of the CELLA extend to form part of the FAÇADE, enclosing the sides of the PRONAOS (cf. PROSTYLE).

Apadana: Great reception hall found in Persian royal palaces.

apse: Semicircular end of a Classical building or Christian church.

architrave: In a Classical building, the lowest part of the ENTABLATURE, positioned above the COLUMNS and CAPITALS, and beneath the FRIEZE.

arena: The open space surrounded by the tiered seating in an AMPHITHEATRE.

aryballos: Small vessel used as a container for unguents and perfumes.

atrium: Inner open court and central space of a Roman house, located near the entrance and flanked by various rooms. Rainwater coming through the open roof collected in a cistern (IMPLUVIUM) in the centre.

ayllu: Quechua term used in Peru and Bolivia for a social and administrative unit made up of related families and owners of land cultivated in common.

basilica: Public meeting hall – generally rectangular and divided into a nave and aisles – used by the Romans for the administration of justice and commercial transactions.

baths: Building used for public bathing, where people could also walk, converse and read (a library was also provided). The essential features were the FRIGIDARIUM (for cold baths), the CALDARIUM (for hot baths), the TEPIDARIUM (for warm baths), the laconicum (for steam baths), the apodyterium (dressing-room) and the latrines. Baths, which existed as early as the 4th century BC, reached their maximum development in the Roman period (1st century BC–4th century AD).

black-figure: Pottery-painting technique, invented in Corinth, consisting of painting solid black figures on the pot and rendering the internal detail by incision, revealing the colour of the terracotta beneath.

bluestone: A type of stone characteristic of the second phase of Stonehenge; its source has been traced to the Preseli Hills of south Wales.

caldarium: Hot room in BATH complex.

canopic jars: A name given in modern times to the vases used by the ancient Egyptians to contain the viscera of the deceased (removed to enable embalming to take place) and buried in the tomb with the mummy. Some Etruscan cinerary urns from northern Tuscany are called canopic urns, because of their similar shape.

capital: The element at the top of a COLUMN that sits between the column and the arch or ARCHITRAVE it supports. In Classical architecture the shapes of the column and its CAPITAL conform to the relevant architectural ORDERS.

cardo: Street running north–south in a Roman urban plan; the cardo maximus was the main north–south road.

caryatid: Sculpted female figure, used in place of a COLUMN to support an ENTABLATURE.

cella: The main section of a temple, particularly a Classical temple, where the image of the deity was kept.

chopper: Stone tool with a cutting edge produced by flaking on one side only.

cippus: A short stone pillar usually serving as a gravestone.

circus: In the Classical world an oblong, unroofed building with rounded ends containing tiered seating on three sides of an open central space; used for chariot races.

cist: Burial structure made out of stone slabs set on edge in a box shape and buried either below ground level or in a TUMULUS.

colonnade: A row of COLUMNS supporting an ENTABLATURE or arches.

colony: (1) In the Greek world, a city founded by a contingent of Greek citizens in a foreign territory for agricultural and/or commercial purposes.

(2) In the Roman world, a transfer of Roman citizens to a settlement in order to administer it in collaboration with the magistrates of the capital (colonia Romana); a city that kept its own laws, coinage and magistracy but, in exchange for a commitment to provide military aid, its citizens acquired the right to trade and contract marriages with Roman citizens.

column: A vertical architectural element of circular section wall and usually supporting an ENTABLATURE or other part of a building. In Classical architecture, columns conformed to one of the architectural ORDERS; standing on a STYLOBATE, they consisted of a base (except in the Greek Doric order), a tapering shaft made up of a number of drums and a CAPITAL at the top. (See also ENTASIS.)

copal: Incense used in Maya rituals, obtained from the resin of various tropical trees.

corbelling: A technique for building a 'false' arch or vault by building out from either side of the space to be covered, with each successive course of bricks or stone blocks projecting slightly beyond the one below, until the two sides of the arch or vault meet.

core: In Stone Age contexts, the piece of stone left after the KNAPPING off of flakes for use as tools; sometimes itself used as a tool.

Coricancha: The principal temple of the Inca empire, in Cuzco, where images of the sun, the creator god and the god of thunder were kept.

Corinthian: Architectural ORDER distinguished by closely-fluted COLUMNS with bases and acanthus-leaf CAPITALS, and a flat FRIEZE.

cornice: In Classical architecture, the topmost and projecting part of an ENTABLATURE, above the FRIEZE.

cromlech: See HENGE.

cuneiform: Ancient writing used in Mesopotamia but of Sumerian origin (4th millennium BC). Characters that had originally been PICTOGRAMS became IDEOGRAMS and then developed into stylized, wedge-shaped signs impressed on clay tablets with small sticks of cane or split reed.

curaca: A rank in the Inca empire. Different grades of *curaca* were the chiefs of provinces or villages, in charge of between 100 and 10,000 people.

decumanus: East–west street in Roman urban plans; the *decumanus maximus* was the main east–west street.

demotic: A word proposed by Herodotus (5th century BC) meaning 'of the people', to indicate an Egyptian cursive script that

developed after hieroglyphics and was much more comprehensible.

distyle: Of a Classical building, having two COLUMNS on the FAÇADE.

dolmen: European megalithic chambered tomb characteristic of the Neolithic period (see MEGALITH).

Doric: Architectural ORDER characterized by fluted COLUMNS (without a base in Greek architecture) and CAPITALS consisting of an ECHINUS and ABACUS, supporting a FRIEZE of METOPES and TRIGLYPHS.

dromos: Access corridor open to the sky; can also be used to mean a race-course.

echinus: Ovolo moulding at the top of a DORIC column that, together with the ABACUS, forms the CAPITAL.

entablature: The upper part of an architectural ORDER, sitting between the CAPITALS and the PEDIMENT and consisting of the ARCHITRAVE, FRIEZE and CORNICE.

entasis: Slight swelling of the middle of a COLUMN shaft introduced so as to correct the optical illusion of concavity and make the column appear straight. It is most accentuated in the Archaic period.

façade: The main (usually the entrance) front of a building.

fibula: Brooch (often elaborately decorated) made on the same principle as a safety-pin, consisting of a bow, spring coil, pin and catchplate (foot).

filigree: Metal-working technique which consists of forming fine metal wires – generally of gold or silver – into patterns and soldering them together.

forum: The main public space of a Roman city, with political, commercial and social functions.

frieze: Vertical architectural surface that is part of the ENTABLATURE, situated between the ARCHITRAVE and the PEDIMENT.

frigidarium: Unheated room in a BATH complex, used for cold baths.

geoglyph: A pattern or figure inscribed on the ground, possibly of very large scale – e.g., the Nazca Lines.

granulation: Metal-working technique which consists of

applying tiny globules of soldered gold or silver to the surface of jewellery.

gymnasium: Building used for physical exercise and education.

henge: Megalithic monument made of upright stones arranged in a circle or semicircle (see MEGALITH).

hexastyle: Of a Classical building, having six COLUMNS on the FAÇADE.

hieroglyphic writing: Writing system, used by the ancient Egyptians in documents and monuments (hieroglyph in Greek means 'sacred carving'). The term is also applied to a Cretan script and to the Maya script. (Cf. DEMOTIC.)

horreum: Warehouse used for the storage of wheat or other foodstuffs.

ideographic writing: A form of figurative writing, derived from PICTOGRAPHIC writing (which only refers to objects); its symbols (ideograms) can also express an abstract concept, an idea. (Cf. HIEROGLYPHIC WRITING.)

impluvium: Basin in the ATRIUM of a Roman house, used to collect rainwater.

insula: Literally meaning 'island', the term is also used to mean either a block of houses bounded on all sides by streets or a Roman apartment block.

Ionic: Architectural ORDER involving a flat or convex FRIEZE and closely fluted COLUMNS with bases and CAPITALS with volutes.

kiva: Circular underground or semi-subterranean chamber, typical of the North American PUEBLO cultures, used as a space for meetings and religious ceremonies.

knapping: The breaking of flakes off a piece of stone by percussion. This technique was used in the Stone Age to make and sharpen stone tools.

kurgan: Tomb covered with a TUMULUS, quite common in the Eurasian steppes and generally attributed to the Scythians.

mastaba: Arabic word meaning 'bench', used in archaeology to refer to an Egyptian funerary monument in the shape of a truncated pyramid.

mausoleum: Grandiose monumental tomb for illustrious persons: the name derives from Mausolus, King of Caria, whose enormous tomb (4th century BC) at Halicarnassus was one of the seven wonders of the ancient world.

megaliths: Monuments (often tombs) dating mainly to the European Neolithic or early Bronze Age, built of large blocks of unworked stone. Single stones are sometimes called menhirs (cf. STELE); stones arranged in a circle are called henges or, sometimes, cromlechs; those forming a chamber tomb may be called dolmens.

megaron: The internal hall of Cretan and Mycenaean palaces.

menhir: Large standing stone (see MEGALITH).

metope: Plain, carved or painted surface between the TRIGLYPHS in a FRIEZE of the DORIC order.

natatio: The swimming-pool in a Roman BATH complex.

necropolis: Literally meaning 'city of the dead' in Greek, the term is used in all cultural contexts to denote an area containing tombs of all types. In the Classical world, these were often found along the main roads leading into cities.

obelisk: Literally meaning 'skewer' in Greek, but used to denote a tall, free-standing pillar, with a square section and a pointed top, found in ancient Egypt. Originally, obelisks were erected at Heliopolis in honour of the sun-god: the first ray of the sun struck one of the faces of the point, which was shaped like a small pyramid.

odeon: Covered building, used for musical performances and concerts.

opus incertum: Roman masonry technique using stone faced on one side only.

opus mixtum: Roman masonry technique using courses of brick and faced stone

order, architectural: Group of two fundamental elements in Greek and Roman architecture – the COLUMN (or PILASTER) and ENTABLATURE, which make up a compositional, stylistic and structural unit.

Vitruvius (1st century AD) distinguished five orders: DORIC, IONIC, CORINTHIAN, Tuscan and Composite.

palaestra: A wrestling-ground, often part of a GYMNASIUM or BATH complex.

papyrus: Reed of the *Cyperaceae* family, native to Egypt, used by the ancient Egyptians to make light boats and a type of very long-lasting paper. The word is also used to mean a document written on such paper.

Parian: A particularly prized variety of white marble with large crystals which, absorbing the light, glows in the sun (from Paros, an Aegean island).

pediment: A low-pitched gable forming the top section of the FAÇADE of a building. It is generally formed by continuing the cornice at the top of the ENTABLATURE along the ends of the roof slope to form a triangular shape.

peristyle: Open square or rectangular space surrounded by COLUMNS.

petroglyph: Signs incised or painted on a natural rock face.

photogrammetry: A technique for making maps or plans from photographs (usually aerial photographs).

pictographic writing: Primitive form of writing in which the signs (pictograms) are more or less stylized pictures of the objects they represent. (Cf. IDEOGRAPHIC WRITING.)

pilaster: Column of rectangular section, both load-bearing and decorative, projecting from and attached to a wall. In Classical architecture it conforms to one of the architectural ORDERS.

plaza: In Latin American contexts, a square or open courtyard.

podium: The raised base on which a building is constructed; a raised platform inside a building.

Pompeian styles of wall-painting: First style (2nd century BC): used stucco or paint to imitate a wall decorated with marble veneer on a high plinth. Second style (1st century BC): *trompe l'oeil* architectural perspectives inspired by Hellenistic-Roman stage sets,

often with a picture at the centre, gave depth to walls. Third style (20 BC–AD 45): walls were framed and subdivided into large monochrome fields on which were painted slender classical structures and miniature landscapes, often surrounding a large central picture. Fourth style (AD 45–79): pictures painted over the whole wall, bounded by cornices and frames often in relief.

portico: A roofed space, open or partly enclosed at the sides and commonly supported on COLUMNS; frequently used as the porch or entrance structure of a larger building.

pronaos: The vestibule in front of the CELLA of a temple.

propylaeum (plural 'propylaea'): Monumental entrance. There are various forms, generally involving a COLONNADE (of four columns) positioned in front of an entrance cut into a continuous enclosure wall. The propylaeum may have columns both outside and inside the enclosure wall.

prostyle: A FAÇADE composed solely of free-standing COLUMNS (cf. ANTIS, IN).

protome: Decorative motif in the form of a human or animal head used in ancient art.

pueblo: Type of village in the American Southwest (New Mexico and Arizona) consisting of many living and ceremonial rooms grouped on various levels or on artificial terraces. The term 'Pueblo' is used generically of the cultures that inhabited these structures.

pylon: In ancient Egypt a monumental temple entrance, consisting of two wide towers flanking a relatively small gateway.

pyramid: (1) In ancient Egypt a structure of square plan, in its developed form with sloping sides meeting at the apex. Originally a burial monument generally reserved for pharaohs.

(2) In the Americas, a high platform rising via several step levels to a flat summit, usually supporting a temple or sacred building and often with an elite burial encased within it. (Cf. ZIGGURAT.)

quetzal: Bird of the mountains of southern Mexico, Guatemala and Honduras, whose feathers were particularly prized by Mesoamerican cultures for their decorative and symbolic value.

quipu: Inca artifact made of knotted multi-coloured strings, used for keeping records and accounts.

red-figure: Vase-painting technique invented by Attic potters around 530 BC, which consisted of painting a black background, leaving the unpainted red clay of the pot to form the figures, of which only details were then painted in black.

repoussé: Metal-working technique for producing figures and patterns in relief on a sheet of metal by resting it on a bed of pitch and raising the design from the reverse side by striking it with a hammer or punch.

rhyton: Pottery or metal drinking vessel, often with no feet, in the form of a horn or a human or animal head. Originally characteristic of the Persian world, then adopted by the Greeks (6th to 5th centuries BC) and Etruscans.

sanctuary: The innermost and most sacred part of a temple (also known as the adytum); an area or complex dedicated to a deity.

peripteral: Surrounded by a single row of COLUMNS.

sarsen: A sandstone found in north Wiltshire (southern England) and used in building MEGALITHS, particularly the stone circles of Stonehenge and Avebury.

scraper: Stone tool, used for working wood or scraping skins, made by knapping and retouching a blade or a CORE.

serapeum: A temple of Serapis, a Greco-Egyptian god whose cult began in Egypt at the start of the Ptolemaic period and lasted throughout the Roman period.

situla: Bucket-shaped container, made from sheet or cast metal,

terracotta or wood and covered with sheets of silver, bronze or ivory. It may be conical, cylindrical or ovoid, with one or two handles and a lid. The decoration is plastic or incised.

stadium: Rectangular unroofed structure with one semicircular end and tiered seating, used for athletic competitions.

stele (alternative spelling, especially in the Americas, 'stela', plural 'stelae'): Inscribed or decorated stone or marble slab erected in many cultures as a funerary or commemorative monument. May also have a votive significance; sometimes used as a boundary marker. (Cf. MEGALITH.)

stoa: A free-standing covered COLONNADE or hall, often open on one side.

stratigraphy: In geology and archaeology, study of successive layers of natural or artificial material, which will (broadly speaking) be older as depth below the present-day surface increases.

stylobate: The substructure on which the COLUMNS of a temple or other building stand.

syllabic writing: Writing in which the signs reproduce phonemes or groups of phonemes (consonants plus vowels, or *vice versa*).

taberna: Roman term for a room opening on to a street or on to a PORTICO or *STOA*, used as a workshop or shop.

tablinum: A central room opening off the ATRIUM of a Roman house.

tell: Arabic term used in archaeology to denote a large mound formed by superimposed habitation layers, particularly in the Middle East. 'Tepe' (Persian) has the same meaning.

temenos: A sacred area bounded by a wall.

tepidarium: Room in a BATH complex that was heated to a medium temperature.

tetrastyle: Having four COLUMNS on the FAÇADE.

theatre: In the Classical world, an unroofed semicircular building used for public spectacles. Consists essentially of tiered seating for the spectators around a ground-level *orchestra* for the chorus, with a raised stage and scene buildings behind it.

tholos: A circular Classical building, or a circular chamber or tomb with a CORBELLED roof.

treasury: Building used to contain precious objects – annexes of sanctuaries, for storing the offerings and goods of the sanctuaries and of the donor cities to which they belonged.

triclinium: The dining-room of a Roman house.

triglyph: The square or rectangular projecting element, with three vertical grooves, that alternated with METOPES in a DORIC frieze; it originally had a load-bearing role.

trilithon: Two upright stones, or MEGALITHS, supporting a third (horizontal) one; found especially at Stonehenge.

tumulus: Mound of earth and stones covering a burial.

tympanum: The triangular space within a PEDIMENT, or the space between the top of a door and its surrounding arch.

tzompantli: The skull rack on which, in the Aztec and some other Mesoamerican cultures, the skulls of sacrificial victims were displayed.

urn: Container used to contain human remains after cremation. Made in various forms, first in terracotta and later in bronze, the urn often had REPOUSSÉ decoration.

writing: See CUNEIFORM, HIEROGLYPHIC, IDEOGRAPHIC, SYLLABIC.

ziggurat: Temple typical of Mesopotamian religious architecture from the Sumerian period (4th–2nd millennia BC), in the form of a high stepped pyramid generally built of sun-dried bricks and faced with fired bricks. At the summit was a shrine dedicated to a deity.

Sources of illustrations

Agenzia Stradella/Archivio 2P 245 centre, 251 below, 255 below, 280 above; Agenzia Stradella/Lamberto Caenazzo 249 centre left, 276 below, 277 centre left, 277 below right; Agenzia Stradella/Erminio Papetti 224 below; Agenzia Stradella/Amedeo Vergani 117 centre right, 122 above right, 126 above left, 127 right, 128 below, 150 below, 153 below, 154 below. – Arts of Asia, March-April 1993 221 above right, 221 centre right, 221 below right. – BEIJING-HONG KONG: Giade della cultura Liangzhu (Liangzu wenhua yuqi), 1989 217 above, 219 above, 219 centre left, 219 centre right, 219 below. – BOLOGNA: Cineca, Laboratorio di Visualizzazione Scientifica e Supercalcolo, Maurizio Forte 148 above, 148 below, 167 above right, 167 centre left, 174 centre left, 207 below; Ministero per i Beni Culturali 3, 133 above, 133 below right, 136 centre, 136 below right, 137 centre, 137 below, 138 below, 139 above, 139 below, 139 right, 140 above left, 140 centre right, 140 below, 141 below right; Gianluca Rossi/Sasso Marconi 265 above, 266 above, 267 above, 268 centre, 270 above, 271 above left, 271 right, 271 below; TE.M.P.LA., Tecnologie Multimediali per l'Archeologia 1, 27 below, 28 above, 28 below, 29 above left, 29 above right, 29 below left, 29 below right. – CINCINNATI: Benjamin Britton, University of Cincinnati 10 above, 10 below; Sam Sherrill, University of Cincinnati 12 below, 248 below right, 249 centre right, 249 below right. – Alan Kalvin, IBM 9. – FERRARA: Carlo Peretto 102 below left, 103 right, 105 above left. – FLORENCE: Scala 112 centre right, 176 above, 185 above. – HANGZHOU: Wang Mingda 216 centre left, 217 centre left, 218 below right. – Journal of Hellenic Studies, 1984 169 above. – KARLSRUHE: ZKM (Eine Computer-animation von Heinrich Klotz und Monique Mulder, 1995) 73 below. – LONDON: Victoria and Albert Museum 230 centre. – MAINZ: Egg M., Spindler K., Die Gletschermumie vom Ende der Steinzeit aus der Ötztaler Alpen, 1993 114, 115 left, 116, 117 above, 117 below, 118, 119. – MILAN: Agenzia Luisa Ricciarini 18 below, 25 above, 59 centre right, 64 above, 65 above, 72 above, 72 below left, 73 centre left, 86 above, 86 below, 88 centre left, 91 centre right, 92 below, 97 right, 100 below, 112 below, 131 below right, 173 below, 178 above, 184, 187 above left, 210, 212 above left, 213 above, 215 above, 215 below, 267 below; Lorenzo De Cola 16 left, 16 centre; Archivio Mondadori 6, 22 below left, 24 below, 25 below, 29 centre right, 30 left, 45 below left, 63 below, 64 below right, 70 centre right, 73 above right, 84 left, 87 below right, 90 above, 91 above left, 91 below right, 93 above, 95 below right, 106 below right, 122 above left, 123 below, 124 above left, 124 below, 129 above left, 129 centre right, 129 below left, 130 above left, 135 above, 141 above, 143 centre right, 143 above right, 144 above right, 150 above right, 152 below, 153 above, 154 above, 156, 157 above left, 160 centre left, 162 centre left, 166 below left, 169 centre right, 170 above right, 171

below, 174 above left, 174 below right, 175 below, 181 centre right, 187 centre right, 189 above left, 190 centre left, 192 above right, 193 centre left, 195 centre, 211 below, 213 below, 216 above right, 216 below, 217 below, 220 left, 221 left, 222 centre left, 223 centre right, 224 above right, 225 below left, 226, 227, 234 centre, 254 below, 235 below left, 236, 237 above, 237 below, 240 centre left, 241 above, 242 left, 243 above right, 244 centre, 246, 247 below, 249 above, 252, 253 above left, 254 above right, 257 below left, 260 centre right, 260 below, 261 above right, 262 above, 264 left, 264 right, 267 centre right, 268 below, 269, 272 left, 272 below, 273 above centre, 273 below right, 274 below right, 276 above right, 276 centre, 280 below, 281 above left, 281 centre, 281 below right, 283 below; Futura Film 110; IBM SEMEA 188 above, 188 right, 188 below, 189 above right, 189 below. – NAPLES: Roberto De Nicola/Sabatino Laurenza 202 above. – National Geographic Society 24 above; National Geographic Society/Victor R. Boswell 21 above; National Geographic Society/David Hiser 262 below; National Geographic Society/Claude E. Petrone 21 above right. – National Geographic/Georg Gerster 84 below. – OSAKA: Kazumasa Ozawa, Electro-Communication University 235 above, 238 above, 238 below. – PARIS: Serge Cleuziou 74, 75 centre, 75 below; Explorer 43 below; French Archaeological Mission 99 above right; Audran Labrousse 32 above, 32 centre, 32 below left, 32 below right; Daniel Lévine 282 below, 283 above; Musée de l'Homme 273 below centre, 275 above, 279 centre right; Musée de l'Homme/J. Oster 278 above left; Musée de l'Homme/Photo Kido 279 below; Bruno Picard-I. Willerval 101 below; J. Suire 96 below; Isabelle Tisserand-Gadan 258 above right, 259 centre, 259 below. – PARMA: Maurizio Cattani 198, 206 below, 207 above, 207 above left, 207 above right, 208 above right, 208 below left, 209. – PISA: Maria Carmela Betrò, University of Pisa 36 above left, 36 above right, 36 below, 36-37, 37 above, 38 left, 38 below, 39 above left, 39 above right, 39 below, 40 below, 41 above, 41 right; Edda Bresciani, University of Pisa 33 above, 33 below, 34 above, 34 below left, 34 below right, 40 above left, 40 above right, 42 centre, 42 below, 44 below left, 44 right, 45 above, 45 below right, 46 centre, 46 below right, 47 above, 47 centre,

48 above, 48 below left, 49 above left, 49 below, 50 centre, 50 below, 51 below; Laboratorio di Topografia Storico-Archeologica del Mondo Antico, Scuola Normale di Pisa 146 left, 146 below right, 149 above, 149 below. – REGGIO EMILIA: Mauro Cremaschi 14 above, 14 below, 15 left, 15 below, 17 below; Maurizio Forte 130 below, 131 above right, 131 centre, 132 above, 152 centre, 132 below, 134 below right, 135 below, 142 centre, 143 below, 144 above left, 144 centre left, 144 below, 145 centre, 145 left, 145 below left, 147 above right, 147 below. – Luisa Ricciarini/Archivio 2P 251 above; Luisa Ricciarini/Andrea Baguzzi 158 below, 159 above left; Luisa Ricciarini/Foto W.P.S. 60 below, 69 above, 191 above right, 191 centre left, 274 above, 275 above, 278 below; Luisa Ricciarini/ Giorgio Nimatallah 122 below, 133 centre, 133 centre left, 134 above, 134 below left, 152 above, 173 above, 192 left; Luisa Ricciarini/Publiaerfoto 160 below, 180; Luisa Ricciarini/Giovanni Ricci 161 above right, 162 above right, 163 above, 163 centre; Luisa Ricciarini/Roberto Schezen 172 right; Luisa Ricciarini/Emilio Simion 94 below left, 98, 99 below, 123 above, 125 left, 170 below, 179 above, 189 centre right; Luisa Ricciarini/Work in Progress 223 below. – ROME: Louis Godart 120 left, 121 above, 121 below, 124 above right, 125 above right; Hochfeiler 78 below, 81 above, 81 centre left, 81 below; Infobyte 62 above right, 62 centre right; Mario Necci (by kind permission of Missione Archeologica Italiana in Siria dell'Università di Roma "La Sapienza") 76, 77 above right, 77 below, 78 above, 79 above, 79 below right, 80 above, 80 below, 82 above left, 82 above right, 82 below, 83 above; Daniele Pellegrini 102 centre right; Filippo Salviati 109 centre, 109 below left, 218 left, 220 centre right, 220 below, 225 below centre, 228 above, 228 below, 229 above left, 229 above right, 229 below, 230 below left, 231 above, 239; Andreas M. Steiner 112 above left, 113 centre right; Studio Altair 4 182 above, 182 centre right, 182 below, 183 centre, 183 below, 186 above, 186 below; Massimo Vidale 190 below, 191 below right, 193 above right, 193 below left, 194 above left, 194 centre, 194 below right, 195 above left, 195 centre right, 196 left, 196 below, 197 below; Village H.T.C. 54 above, 55 above, 56 above, 66, 129 below right, 155 below,

159 right, 162 below right, 163 below right, 172 below left, 185 below, 187 below. – SANTA BARBARA: Studios and Pathways Production 8 242 below, 243 below, 257 above left, 257 above right, 257 centre. – THESSALONIKI: Archaeological Museum 164 right, 165 below left, 165 below right, 166 above, 167 below, 168 above, 168 below, 169 below left. – TOKYO: Taisei Corporation 2 12 above, 13, 68 above, 68 below left, 88 below, 89 above, 89 below, 90 centre left, 90 below right, 93 below, 152 centre, 175 above, 176 below, 177 above, 179 below, 231 centre, 232 left, 232 above, 233, 241 centre, 263 above, 263 below, 266 below. – VENICE: Archivio Centro Studi Ricerche Ligabue 199 above, 200, 201, 202 below left, 202 below right, 203, 204 below, 204 right, 205 right, 205 below. – VERONA: Alberto Silotti 11 above, 11 below, 18 right, 19 above right, 20 right, 22 above, 23, 26 right, 30 above right, 31 above, 35 below, 44 above, 51 above, 52, 53 above right, 54 below left, 54 centre right, 55 below, 56 centre left, 56 below, 57 above, 57 below, 58, 60 above, 61 above, 61 below left, 61 below right, 62 below left, 63 above, 64 below left, 67 above right, 67 centre right, 67 below right, 68 centre right, 69 below, 70 below, 71 above left, 72 centre right, 85 below, 87 above, 87 centre left, 92 above, 94 below right, 95 above right, 96 above, 97 above left, 101 above, 106 left, 107 below right, 108, 109 above left, 111 above right, 111 below, 155 above, 245 below, 250 left, 250 below, 254 above left, 254 below, 255 above left, 255 above right, 256 above left, 256 below right, 270 below. – VICENZA: Studio Pagus Media 15 above, 17 above, 19 above left, 19 below, 20 below left, 26 left, 27 above, 31 below, 43 above left, 43 above right, 53 above left, 53 below, 59 above left, 59 below, 65 above, 67 below left, 71 above right, 71 below, 75 above left, 77 above left, 84 above, 85 above, 85 centre right, 88 above, 95 above left, 95 below left, 99 above left, 103 above left, 104, 105 below right, 107 above left, 113 above, 115 above right, 120 below right, 126 below, 127 above left, 128 above, 136 below left, 137 above, 138 above, 138 centre, 142 below left, 143 above left, 147 above left, 151 above, 151 below, 157 above right, 157 below, 158 above, 161 above left, 161 below, 164 below left, 165 above left, 171 above right, 177 below, 178 below left, 181 above left, 181 below, 191 above right, 197 above, 199 below, 205 above, 206 above, 211 above left, 212 below, 214, 222 centre right, 222 below, 223 above left, 224 centre left, 225 above right, 240 above right, 240 below, 242 above right, 244 below, 245 above left, 247 above, 248 above, 248 below left, 253 above right, 253 below, 258 below, 259 above left, 261 above left, 261 below, 265 right, 273 above left, 274 below left, 279 above left, 279 above right, 281 above left.

The publishers apologize for any inadvertent errors or omissions in the sources of illustrations.

The publishers would like to express sincere thanks to the following organizations for their invaluable help in producing this book:
• Taisei Corporation, Tokyo
• Cineca, Laboratorio di Visualizzazione Scientifica e Supercalcolo, Bologna
• Hochfeiler, Rome
• IBM SEMEA, Milan
• Infobyte, Rome
• Santa Barbara Studios and Pathways Production
• Studio Altair 4, Rome
• Studio Pagus Media, Vicenza
• TE.M.P.LA., Tecnologie Multimediali per l'Archeologia, Bologna
• Village H.T.C., Rome
• SO.BE.CA., Informatica e Servizi per il Restauro e l'Ambiente, Rome

Index

Page numbers in *italic* refer to captions